Keep this book. You will need it and use it throughout your career.

TRAINING
for the
HOSPITALITY
INDUSTRY

Educational Institute Books

UNIFORM SYSTEM OF ACCOUNTS AND EXPENSE
DICTIONARY FOR SMALL HOTELS, MOTELS, AND
MOTOR HOTELS
Fourth Edition

RESORT DEVELOPMENT AND MANAGEMENT
Second Edition
Chuck Y. Gee

PLANNING AND CONTROL FOR FOOD AND
BEVERAGE OPERATIONS
Third Edition
Jack D. Ninemeier

STRATEGIC MARKETING PLANNING IN THE
HOSPITALITY INDUSTRY: A BOOK OF READINGS
Edited by Robert L. Blomstrom

TRAINING FOR THE HOSPITALITY INDUSTRY
Second Edition
Lewis C. Forrest, Jr.

UNDERSTANDING HOSPITALITY LAW
Second Edition
Jack P. Jefferies

SUPERVISION IN THE HOSPITALITY INDUSTRY
Second Edition
Raphael R. Kavanaugh/Jack D. Ninemeier

ENERGY AND WATER RESOURCE MANAGEMENT
Second Edition
Robert E. Aulbach

MANAGEMENT OF FOOD AND BEVERAGE
OPERATIONS
Second Edition
Jack D. Ninemeier

MANAGING FRONT OFFICE OPERATIONS
Third Edition
Michael L. Kasavana/Richard M. Brooks

STRATEGIC HOTEL/MOTEL MARKETING
Revised Edition
Christopher W. L. Hart/David A. Troy

MANAGING SERVICE IN FOOD AND BEVERAGE
OPERATIONS
Anthony M. Rey/Ferdinand Wieland

THE LODGING AND FOOD SERVICE INDUSTRY
Third Edition
Gerald W. Lattin

SECURITY AND LOSS PREVENTION
MANAGEMENT
Raymond C. Ellis, Jr., & the Security Committee of AH&MA

HOSPITALITY INDUSTRY MANAGERIAL
ACCOUNTING
Second Edition
Raymond S. Schmidgall

PURCHASING FOR HOSPITALITY OPERATIONS
William B. Virts

THE ART AND SCIENCE OF HOSPITALITY
MANAGEMENT
Jerome J. Vallen/James R. Abbey

MANAGING COMPUTERS IN THE HOSPITALITY
INDUSTRY
Second Edition
Michael L. Kasavana/John J. Cahill

MANAGING HOSPITALITY ENGINEERING
SYSTEMS
Michael H. Redlin/David M. Stipanuk

UNDERSTANDING HOSPITALITY ACCOUNTING I
Second Edition
Raymond Cote

UNDERSTANDING HOSPITALITY ACCOUNTING II
Second Edition
Raymond Cote

MANAGING QUALITY SERVICES
Stephen J. Shriver

MANAGING CONVENTIONS AND GROUP
BUSINESS
Leonard H. Hoyle/David C. Dorf/Thomas J. A. Jones

HOSPITALITY SALES AND ADVERTISING
Second Edition
James R. Abbey

MANAGING HUMAN RESOURCES IN THE
HOSPITALITY INDUSTRY
David Wheelhouse

MANAGING HOUSEKEEPING OPERATIONS
Margaret M. Kappa/Aleta Nitschke/Patricia B. Schappert

CONVENTION SALES: A BOOK OF READINGS
Margaret Shaw

DIMENSIONS OF TOURISM
Joseph D. Fridgen

HOSPITALITY TODAY: AN INTRODUCTION
Second Edition
Rocco M. Angelo/Andrew N. Vladimir

MANAGING BAR AND BEVERAGE OPERATIONS
Lendal H. Kotschevar/Mary L. Tanke

POWERHOUSE CONFERENCES: ELIMINATING
AUDIENCE BOREDOM
Coleman Lee Finkel

ETHICS IN HOSPITALITY MANAGEMENT: A BOOK
OF READINGS
Edited by Stephen S.J. Hall

HOSPITALITY FACILITIES MANAGEMENT AND
DESIGN
David M. Stipanuk/Harold Roffmann

MANAGING HOSPITALITY HUMAN RESOURCES
Robert H. Woods

FINANCIAL MANAGEMENT FOR THE
HOSPITALITY INDUSTRY
William P. Andrew/Raymond S. Schmidgall

HOSPITALITY INDUSTRY FINANCIAL
ACCOUNTING
Raymond S. Schmidgall/James W. Damitio

INTERNATIONAL HOTELS: DEVELOPMENT AND
MANAGEMENT
Chuck Y. Gee

QUALITY SANITATION MANAGEMENT
Ronald F. Cichy

TRAINING for the HOSPITALITY INDUSTRY

Second Edition

Lewis C. Forrest, Jr., Ed.D.

EDUCATIONAL INSTITUTE
of the American Hotel & Motel Association

Disclaimer

This publication is designed to provide accurate and authoritative information in regard to the subject matter covered. It is sold with the understanding that the publisher is not engaged in rendering legal, accounting, or other professional service. If legal advice or other expert assistance is required, the services of a competent professional person should be sought.

—From the Declaration of Principles jointly adopted by the American Bar Association and a Committee of Publishers and Associations

The author, Lewis C. Forrest, is solely responsible for the contents of this publication. All views expressed herein are solely those of the author and do not necessarily reflect the views of the Educational Institute of the American Hotel & Motel Association (the Institute) or the American Hotel & Motel Association (AH&MA).

Nothing contained in this publication shall constitute a standard, an endorsement, or a recommendation of the Institute or AH&MA. The Institute and AH&MA disclaim any liability with respect to the use of any information, procedure, or product, or reliance thereon by any member of the hospitality industry.

© Copyright 1990
By the EDUCATIONAL INSTITUTE of the
AMERICAN HOTEL & MOTEL ASSOCIATION
1407 South Harrison Road
P.O. Box 1240
East Lansing, Michigan 48826

The Educational Institute of the American
Hotel & Motel Association is a nonprofit
educational foundation.

Printed in the United States of America
9 10 94

Library of Congress Cataloging-in-Publication Data

Forrest, Lewis C.
   Training for the hospitality industry.

   Includes bibliographical references
   1. Hospitality industry—Employees—Training of.
I. American Hotel & Motel Association.   Educational
Institute.   II. Title.
TX911.3.T73F67   1989   647.94′0683   89-23747

ISBN 0-86612-044-0

Editor: Ann M. Halm

Contents

Preface

The need for trained personnel has never been greater in the history of the hospitality industry. The industry continues to grow at a rapid pace, adding new jobs and increasing its use of technology. Guest demands, employee turnover, dependence on part-time personnel, and the economic realities of a highly competitive business environment all cry out for a full-time commitment to developing and maintaining a competent work force through training. For training to receive the support it needs, managers themselves must become competent trainers. My commitment to this objective has been my constant motivation in writing and revising this book.

The second edition of *Training for the Hospitality Industry* attempts to cover every facet of training for the new or established hospitality operation. It is aimed at managers—the individuals who are responsible for developing competent employees. The book can be used in hospitality management curricula and as an authoritative reference for anyone interested in the training and development of people.

This edition includes three new chapters that address ongoing training, management training and development, and pre-opening training. This edition also includes case scenarios which demonstrate key principles. While some of these cases seem far-fetched, they are based on actual situations. The names have been omitted to protect the parties involved and some details have been highlighted to emphasize the point being illustrated.

The new chapters—as well as other revisions—are the result of reader suggestions. Since the first edition, I have served as a consultant to a number of hospitality companies in implementing systems for management and non-management training. I am especially grateful for the willingness of those organizations to apply the techniques presented in this book. This continued application has helped me refine the concepts and to see where difficulties lie. In the second edition I have tried to provide ways of overcoming the obstacles that cause training plans to break down.

I also wish to thank the following reviewers for their contributions to this text: Debbie Barosko, CHRE, Human Resource Director, Clarion Hotel & Conference Center, Lansing, Michigan; Cindy Bowen, Assistant General Manager, Sheraton Inn, Lansing, Michigan; Nick Horney, Ph.D., Corporate Director of Training, Stouffer Hotel Company, Solon, Ohio; Jill Lord, Director of Human Resources, Colony Resorts, Minneapolis, Minnesota; Colleen Maloney, CHA, CFBE, General Manager, Cabot Lodge Jackson North, Ridgeland, Mississippi; John McClenahan, Manager of Training, Las Vegas Hilton, Las Vegas, Nevada; Judy Nelson, Vice President, Membership and Staff Administration, Best Western International, Phoenix, Arizona; Mickey Warner, Associate Professor,

Florida International University, Miami, Florida; Peter Watson, Director of Training, Canadian Pacific Hotels & Resorts, Toronto, Ontario, Canada; and George Wooten, Director of Human Resources, Alexander Hotel, Miami Beach, Florida.

And finally, I appreciate the constant support and assistance provided by my wife, Linda, in the preparation of the second edition. Without her help in every phase, the revision process would have been much more difficult. Likewise, I appreciate the support and encouragement of my sons, Bryan and David.

Lewis C. Forrest, Jr., Ed.D.

Part I

Introduction

1 A Framework for Training and Coaching

The hospitality industry is diverse, extends around the world, and has two specific segments. One segment—lodging properties—evolved from quaint wayside inns into operations such as modern hotels, motor lodges, motels, and cruise ships. In addition to rooms, lodging establishments often provide a full range of guest services, including food, beverages, retail shops, meeting rooms, convention services, and recreational facilities.

The other segment of the industry—food service operations—ranges from hot dog vendors on major city streets to restaurants, cafeterias, snack bars, industrial and institutional feeding operations, fast-food stores, airline catering, and similar operations that prepare and serve food and beverage products.

All indications are that the lodging and food service needs of the world will continue to grow; the hospitality industry must be prepared to meet these needs. Each type of operation—as well as each individual enterprise—has goals it strives to attain. These goals can only be met through the efforts of competent employees.

Training provides a means by which an operation can develop a competent staff. It is not enough to hire experienced personnel; someone has to train personnel to ensure consistency in service and standards. New employees must be taught what is expected of them, experienced employees must be taught the standards of the organization, and everyone must be updated as changes occur in the operation. The selection, training, and development of personnel should be viewed as ongoing processes in every hospitality operation.

The effective management of people in any business is measured by the productivity of its employees. Productivity is achieved through the careful balance of employee effectiveness and employee efficiency.[1] Training should always be approached with an understanding that it is designed to increase effectiveness and efficiency. As one authority says:

> Those who are involved in training, whether they are from the training department or are the immediate supervisor of the trainee, should view training as a means of improving a person's ability to produce. The philosophy should be that people are trained because they either can't do something, can't do it well enough, or are now

Exhibit 1.1   Dimensions of Employee Competence

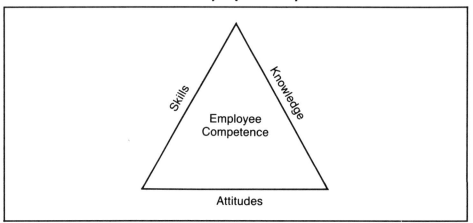

doing it incorrectly. Training should never be viewed as a chore or an insignificant part of the job, something to do when there is spare time. It is a corrective measure, designed to maximize the utilization of an employee's potential. It's a way of getting more and/or better performance for the same or less money . . . we are wasting money when we don't use a person's potential. Training is a way to make use of that potential.[2]

The importance of managing people to their full potential cannot be overemphasized—especially in the hospitality industry. By its very nature, hospitality is a people industry—and thereby labor-intensive. To control labor costs, productivity must be achieved without sacrificing hospitality and personal service. This is why training is an essential activity in a successful hospitality operation.

Training, Coaching, and the Training Process

In order to develop competence, training must integrate *knowledge, skills,* and *attitudes.* Competence—the goal of training—can be visualized with these three dimensions as shown in Exhibit 1.1.

Training

Training can be defined as the process by which a learner acquires and develops knowledge, skills, and attitudes that lead to changes in behavior in line with established performance goals. Training is usually limited to acquiring and developing competencies that meet a specific defined need while **education** is learning that contributes to total life growth.[3] Two authorities define training as follows:

> Training is a learning process that involves the acquisition of skills, concepts, rules, or attitudes to increase the performance of employees.[4]

Training can be viewed as any activity that results in learning, but is directed toward basic job competence and improved job performance. If the learning experience increases or strengthens knowledge, improves

Exhibit 1.2   Basic Steps in the Training Process

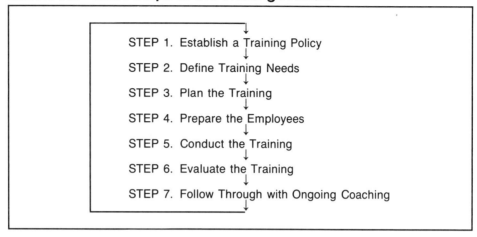

STEP 1. Establish a Training Policy

STEP 2. Define Training Needs

STEP 3. Plan the Training

STEP 4. Prepare the Employees

STEP 5. Conduct the Training

STEP 6. Evaluate the Training

STEP 7. Follow Through with Ongoing Coaching

skills, and develops desirable attitudes which are observable in the behavior of the trainee, then the training will be considered effective.

Coaching

Coaching can be defined as the constant reinforcement of learning that was acquired through training.[5] Training focuses on *acquisition* of knowledge, skills, and attitudes. Coaching focuses on the actual on-the-job *application* of what was learned in the training sessions. Through a training system, an employee learns how and why to perform in a specified manner. Through a coaching system, the same employee is challenged, encouraged, corrected, motivated, and positively reinforced to apply what was learned.

Coaching may be informal or formal. Informal coaching is usually done at the work station and often deals with the refinement of a single skill, the application of a single piece of knowledge, or the adjustment of a behavior that demonstrates an inappropriate attitude. Formal coaching is usually done in a private place away from the work station and focuses on knowledge, skills, or attitudes that are affecting a sizable segment of the employee's job performance.

Training and coaching are the direct responsibility of operational management. These activities should be carried out by the managers who actually supervise the employees involved on a day-to-day basis. When training is taken over by staff specialists who are not accountable for the ultimate performance of the staff, managers lose their influence and become ineffective in leading their employees. The focus in this book is always on the operational manager as the trainer and coach.

The Training Process

Exhibit 1.2 shows the related steps in the training process. Each step will be briefly introduced in this chapter and discussed in more depth in later chapters.

In many ways the training process is cyclical and repetitive. For example, training goals must be established as an integral part of the planning process. Training is later evaluated to determine the extent to which these goals were met. In turn, the evaluation process can lead to the identification of new goals which should be addressed in the design of future training activities.

Step 1: Establish a Training Policy

Training must be planned and carried out as an organized activity of the business enterprise. The cost-effectiveness of training is directly related to the commitment that is made to training by the organization. To support this commitment, it is important that the organization state its training policy in writing.

> Training policies should be developed that will provide guidelines on the detailed planning of training by defining the scope and aims of the training, the basis of training plans, the procedures for developing formal training programs, and methods of evaluating and controlling training.[6]

A **policy** may be viewed as a general guideline for decision-making or as a statement of specific action that must or must not be taken in a given situation. The degree of commitment to the desired action is indicated by the strength of the wording and the specifics addressed in the policy. As one authority comments:

> Many organizations fail to develop full-scale policies on matters like training. It's not enough that the policy is that "we believe in training." It's not sufficient to just say supervisors are responsible for seeing that the people under them are trained. There has to be a firmer statement of objectives, specific actions and consequences for violation of the policy.[7]

Corporate-Level Training Policy

If the hospitality operation is part of a larger organization which operates a number of similar enterprises, it is important for a training policy to be established at the corporate level. This unifies the commitment of the organization to a common standard of excellence through training and development. A sample corporate training policy appears in Exhibit 1.3.

Operating-Level Training Policy

Chain organizations should have an operating-level policy that goes beyond the corporate policy in specifying how training will be carried out at that level. The operating-level policy should be within the requirements of the corporate policy but should also consider the local situation. If the hospitality operation is an independent entity, the elements of the corporate training policy should be combined into a single working policy. Among the important items to address in an operating-level training policy are:

- Whether training must be conducted on a daily, weekly, monthly, or "as needed" basis
- Whether training for employees who speak English as a second language must be conducted in the employee's native language

Exhibit 1.3   Sample Corporate Training Policy

Corporate Training Policy

Regardless of position, all newly hired personnel in our company will receive training for their specific assignments. The training will be planned, implemented, and evaluated in such a manner as to ensure that every employee is provided the opportunity to develop their potential to perform at a level of excellence which is commensurate with the performance standards established in every operational area. The general manager of each operation is responsible for ensuring that this policy is carried out.

For each job position in each department, there will be a list of specific skills, job tasks, or duties that are required by the staff member who holds that position. Schedules will be prepared to cover the training in each skill area. "Experienced" personnel hired by any operation must also be trained to ensure consistency of standards and methods of performance. All personnel must be able to perform the established basic duties of their positions before they are assigned to a work station without the direct supervision of a designated trainer.

Under no circumstances will an employee be placed at a job station with no training nor will training be limited to a "follow-system" with no organized structure for the instruction. Based on assessed needs for improvement, training and retraining will be scheduled on a regular basis to ensure that staff members beyond the entry-level are always performing in accordance with the company's high standards and optimum efficiency.

- Whether training must be conducted personally by department heads, or whether it may be delegated (and to whom)
- What records must be submitted by department heads to document training
- How departmental training costs are to be approved and monitored
- Who is responsible for the development of training materials
- What systems will be used to evaluate knowledge, skills, and attitudes as the basis for verifying competence within the operation
- What cross-training is expected within the operation, and how the responsibilities and costs of such training will be handled when the cross-training involves more than one department
- How training and development of the management staff will be handled at the operational level
- How corporate policies and standard operating procedure manuals will be made available to the staff to support training activities
- Whether smoking will be permitted during classroom training if smoking is otherwise restricted for employees on duty

Standard Operating Procedures for Training

It is quite common for management personnel within the hospitality industry to be frequently transferred or rapidly promoted. To maintain consistency and continuity, it is very important that training standards not change every time the manager changes. Procedures and standards should be established and followed by each department manager. If it is necessary to change a procedure or standard, this should be a management team activity with the final approval of the general manager or corporate office.

In multi-operation situations, the corporate office usually produces policy and procedural manuals that establish operating guidelines. The guidelines are sometimes very general and give minimum levels of acceptable performance. In other cases, the procedures are very specific and do not allow for much deviation.

Step 2: Define Training Needs

By defining training needs, an organization determines what specific knowledge, skills, and attitudes to develop or improve to bring employees' performance up to the organization's standards.[8] Training needs define specific training activities and justify the investment in training that is made by the hospitality operation.[9]

Needs of New Operations

When a new hospitality operation opens, everyone needs training. For new operations, training needs are largely determined by the corporate staff, the owners, and the management team. Pre-opening training is often the easiest type of training for several reasons:

1. Management is highly motivated to support and participate in the training process to get started on the right foot.

2. Employees learn fast because they have not formed any negative attitudes toward their job or the operation.

3. The entire staff wants to know what the performance standards will be in the new operation.

The difficulty of pre-opening training lies in the magnitude of the task. Training activities are often arranged around last minute construction details. However, a great deal can be taught and mastered in a relatively short amount of time if activities are properly planned and efficiently executed.

Needs of Established Operations

Determining training needs for established operations is more difficult. In these operations, training needs are more specific to smaller segments of the staff, based on their need to improve performance in defined areas.

Sometimes, everyone in an established operation should participate in a training program, such as when some new procedure, system, or equipment is placed into operation. Also, an entire staff may need retraining when a manager takes over a department and finds that the quality of performance needs upgrading.

When Is Training Necessary?

Training is not the solution to every operational or performance problem nor the cure-all for all human-resource-related problems. It is a step in the process of preparing employees to achieve organizational goals and standards. However, there are some indicators or signals of inadequate employee performance that may suggest a need for training.

Guest Dissatisfaction. Training may be in order when guests complain about the way they are treated by employees, or about the quality of the product as it relates to the work performed by the staff. By analyzing the cause of a negative guest comment, managers can determine whether the problem is the result of inadequate training.

Disorganization and Confusion. When employees have difficulty working together, it may be because they have not been taught how to work as a team. The group may also be disrupted when certain employees do not know how to perform their required job duties or tasks.

Low Morale. When employees are unhappy with their jobs, it usually shows in poor performance. Inadequate training can be a cause of low morale because it may cause employees to feel unprofessional.

Low Sales. Managers often calculate sales per employee hours worked. By doing so, they can quickly spot slippage in productivity. When a drop occurs in sales per employee hours worked, inadequate training may be the cause.

High Waste. Employees should be aware of the cost of waste in *all* areas. When they understand how these losses affect profitability—and hence, the funds available for wage and benefit increases—they will work to reduce waste. Where appropriate, departmental training should always include emphasis on ways to curtail costs.

Low Productivity. Productivity can be measured in several ways. Whatever measure is used, the measure should relate employee output to benefits gained by the operation. When possible, training programs should be designed to increase revenues or reduce controllable expenses without increasing labor costs.

When employees spend long periods in unproductive activity, there is something wrong with the training and scheduling of the staff. While there are legitimate slack periods, effective managers try to plan backup duties for employees and have them cross-trained to perform other duties or job tasks.

Sanitation Problems. Unsanitary facilities are an indication of unproductive employees who have not been taught to use time wisely. Employees must be taught to clean constantly when they are not busy attending to the needs of guests or other assigned duties. An unsanitary operation almost always indicates that employees—and management—need training.

Miscellaneous Indicators. Other indicators which suggest the need for training include:

- Excessive employee turnover, absenteeism, overtime, or negative information collected in exit interviews

- Employee grievances, discrimination charges, and unfair employment practice suits

- A high frequency of work-related injuries, accidents, or illnesses

- Substandard quality products or services

- Excessive labor cost per occupied room, number of guests, or restaurant cover

- Low number of repeat guests

- Low business volumes when compared to the market

- High level of employee theft

- Problems of drug and alcohol abuse among the staff

- Compromise of internal control systems

- Excessive energy and water consumption

- Excessive damage to the furniture, fixtures, and equipment through improper cleaning or maintenance

Techniques for Determining Training Needs

Once managers observe signals that training may be needed, it is a good practice to take additional time to carefully identify the specific problems. Plunging into training based on signals alone may result in treating the symptoms rather than the real problem. There are several techniques that can be used to conduct a thorough needs analysis.

Training Needs Surveys. Surveys may be conducted to objectively focus on specific areas of performance deficiency. These surveys may be conducted by management or experienced research professionals outside the operation. The surveys may consist of written questionnaires or personal interviews with the management and staff. Personal interviews provide more opportunity for probing into the real causes of performance problems and reduce the likelihood of treating symptoms rather than the real problems.

Management Observation. A very effective way to determine specific training needs is by observing the staff at work in the areas where the deficiencies exist. In the routine performance of his/her job, the manager can observe the work being performed and judge whether it meets established standards.

Employee Surveys. Employees should always be involved in the needs analysis process. They are expected to meet the established standards, and they are the closest to the problems and deficiencies that management may observe. Furthermore, most employees will be objectively critical of the performance of their work group, and even themselves.

The best way to survey needs from employees is to ask them how they feel the operation is measuring up to the established standards. Exhibit 1.4 shows a sample questionnaire for the banquet service

Exhibit 1.4 Sample Questionnaire for Employees

Needs Survey
Banquet Service Questionnaire

To Banquet Food and Beverage Servers:

Please rate how well we, as a team, are achieving the following standards within our department. For each standard, give us a score from zero to one hundred percent, based on your most objective opinion.

Standard	Performance Level (0–100% Rating)
1. Banquet food service is provided only by trained servers.	_____
2. Banquet servers are dressed in the approved uniform when they serve functions.	_____
3. All side tables, open-end tables, coffee break tables, head tables, and registration tables for functions are skirted.	_____
4. For all sit-down banquet meals, food is brought from the kitchen on 27-inch oval cork-lined trays and placed on tray stands in the function room before the food is served to the guests.	_____
5. Serviceware cleared from guest tables is placed on 27-inch oval cork-lined trays and carried to the soiled dish area on these trays.	_____
6. An appropriate centerpiece of flowers, fruit, or candles is used on all banquet tables, whether purchased by the guest or provided by the banquet department.	_____
7. Whenever possible, plated food courses are served from each guest's left side with the server's left hand.	_____
8. Whenever possible, beverages are served from each guest's right side with the server's right hand.	_____
9. Whenever possible, the guest's food and beverage dishes and serviceware are cleared from the guest's right side with the server's right hand.	_____
10. Beverages that are poured at the guest's table are poured to the glass or cup without the guest or server having to touch or pick up the container.	_____
11. If a guest declines the offer of wine service, the wine glass from that cover is removed so that the guest will not be asked again about wine service.	_____
12. Cleaning is a continuous process throughout the function meal service; as guests complete a course, the serviceware for that course is removed.	_____
13. Servers who serve functions work pleasantly but quietly, with the absolute minimum conversation with guests or with fellow employees.	_____
14. As soon as the program for a function begins, servers begin working their way out of the room until the program is completed—except when the host requests that desserts and coffee be served during the program.	_____
15. The banquet check is presented privately following the conclusion of the banquet function.	_____

List what you consider to be the top three immediate training needs for banquet food and beverage servers:

1. _____

2. _____

3. _____

department. The standards are part of the questionnaire. Of course, if the standards are never written or communicated until they are made part of a survey form, then it is highly unlikely that the operation will score very high on actual performance.

Guest Comments. Informal, unsolicited guest complaints serve as a signal that something is wrong and that the needs of these guests are not being met. Management may also wish to provide for continuous guest input. Forms can be prepared on which guests can comment on all aspects of the operation. Responses can be compiled to determine whether a complaint is an isolated incident, or whether it occurs enough to indicate a need for training or other action.

Formal interviews of guests can be conducted to focus directly on specific areas where there may be some indication for an in-depth needs analysis (Exhibit 1.5). Each question asked in these interviews should be directed toward an established standard of service or product quality. When there are no defined and agreed-upon standards, a needs analysis only confuses the issue. However, if standards are clearly in place, the interview determines how far the operation is off the mark in actual performance.

Marketing Surveys. An extension of the guest comment procedure is the formal marketing survey. Managers may use this technique when they wish to obtain information from others besides current guests. The survey may include former, present, and potential guests; other businesses in the marketplace; and competitive operations. The survey may be much broader in scope than the guest interview, and may solicit information about the general reputation of the operation. In order to improve the image of the operation through training, advertising, and public relations, management must first know how the general public perceives the business establishment.

Repeat Business. A high percentage of repeat guests is a good indication that the operation is doing a lot of things right. Repeat guests return for definite reasons and, if asked, they will usually share these reasons with an interested manager. Managers should get to know their repeat guests and should ask them from time to time to suggest ways that employee performance could be changed to better meet these guests' needs.

Employee Meetings. When employees are involved in setting standards of performance, the standards will often be much easier to achieve. When signals indicate that performance is below standards, an employee meeting can be held in which employees informally discuss the job tasks they feel they do well—as well as those they feel need improvement. Employees can be asked to suggest goals aimed at improving performance; they can also be encouraged to suggest ways that goals might be met.

By probing, the manager coordinating the meeting can try to determine the specific areas where employees feel more training is needed. If employees already know how to perform their duties, they will say so and identify reasons why they are not performing according

Exhibit 1.5 Sample Guide for Interviewing Guests

Needs Survey—Interview Guide
Room Service/Food and Beverage

Guest Name _____ Room # _____

Date of Service _____

Introduction: "The hotel is taking a survey of guests who have experienced our food service in their rooms during their stay. Our records show that you were served a room service (breakfast) (lunch) (dinner) in your room yesterday. May I have a few minutes of your time to ask you some specific questions?"

1. When you travel, do you usually have room service meals, or was your decision to do so yesterday somewhat unusual?

2. Did you use the room service menu that is in your room to decide what you wanted to order?

3. How would you describe the individual who answered the room service phone and took your order? (Courteous? Helpful? Friendly?)

4. How many times would you say the phone rang before it was answered by the room service department?

5. Did you order exactly what you planned to before placing the call, or did the room service receptionist influence you to change your mind about your selections or to order anything extra?

6. How well was the room service receptionist able to answer your questions about how various items would be served?

7. After taking your order, did the room service receptionist repeat your order back to you to be certain that everything was as you wished?

8. What was the time estimate given to you by the room service receptionist as to how long it would take to serve your order?

9. How close was the estimate to the actual time it took for your order to arrive?

10. How would you describe the service provided by the server who delivered your order?

11. When your order was brought into your room, was it placed where you requested or in an otherwise convenient location for you?

12. Did the server offer to check your order to be sure that everything you requested was there? Was anything missing?

13. Was there anything among your food and beverage selections which required special service in your room, such as opening a bottle of wine or boning your fish? If so, how was this service handled?

14. How would you describe the quality and acceptability of the items which were served to you on your room service order?

15. How was the guest check presented to you by the server?

16. What instructions were provided by your server concerning what you should do with the tray, dishes, etc. when you finished your meal?

17. Was the server prompt in returning to pick up your serviceware without rushing you?

18. What was the most pleasing thing about your room service experience?

to the standards. At the least, managers will hear about the employees' perspective, which can be helpful as decisions about training are made.

Inspections. In most states, inspections are made by government agencies in such areas as health, energy, and safety. These inspections may reveal deficiencies that can be corrected by better training.

Internal inspections performed by managers are useful tools for assessing performance. An operational audit checklist can be prepared for each department that lists the key areas of performance and the standards for each. The inspection is an audit of actual performance in comparison with the stated standards. This is a formal approach to the routine management observation that goes on daily. By giving formal attention to the process, the finer points of performance are not missed and the specific areas of deficiency are isolated.

After any inspection, managers should review the results and determine whether there is a need for training, or whether the findings suggest some needed changes in the operation. It is also a good idea to share inspection findings with the employees. They can probably shed some light on the causes of the deficiencies, and help determine if the problems should be corrected with training or by some other means. If operational changes are made, training will probably be required to teach the revised procedures.

Priorities for Training

Once training needs are determined, management should establish priorities about where to begin. In setting priorities, it is important to emphasize that job skills are not the only subject of training. A considerable amount of knowledge concerning operating rules and procedures must also be covered during this time. In addition, attitudinal training must be integrated with skills training to achieve positive guest relations.

Essential Training. The first priority for a *new operation* should be those job tasks that must be mastered for the operation to survive opening day. For an *established operation,* first priority must be given to those job tasks that will give the employee enough basic knowledge, skills, and attitudes to be efficient when assigned to a limited job station. The first priority training topics can be referred to as priority "A" duties or job tasks. For a receptionist, a priority "A" duty might be "the ability to register guests into the hotel."

Desirable Training. Priority "B" duties are those job tasks that management would like to cover before opening day, or before assignment to a job station, but can be covered during the first one or two weeks on the job. An example of a priority "B" duty might be "the ability to process guaranteed no-show reservations."

Expendable Training. The third group of duties or job tasks, referred to as priority "C", are those that are nice to know but not essential. Priority "C" duties should be taught after all employees have mastered all of the priority "A" and "B" tasks. Under priority "C", the receptionist might develop "the ability to give directions to local restaurants outside of the hotel."

When Training Won't Work

Not all performance problems can be corrected through training and coaching.[10] Therefore, managers must analyze the causes of poor performance to determine whether training will be helpful.

Non-Training Causes of Poor Performance

Three common causes of poor performance by trained employees are:

1. Inadequate equipment to do the job the way they were taught

2. Lack of freedom to perform the job without supervisory harassment

3. Unrealistic performance expectations

If a job has unrealistic standards or procedures, the employee may avoid the task or find it physically impossible to perform the job according to standards. Managers must develop a balanced approach to setting standards and accept standards which they can live with, which employees can achieve, and which guests will accept. Take, for example, the following Case in Point.

A Case in Point: Unrealistic Expectations

In one 200-room hotel, receptionists at the front desk were expected to telephone every guest within 30 minutes following registration to confirm that the guest had found the room satisfactory. Normally only two receptionists were scheduled for the desk during the evening shift. Each receptionist was to maintain a record of the guests who were telephoned and their comments. The receptionists found it impossible to carry out this assignment on a consistent basis, especially on nights when there was a large number of arrivals. They knew exactly how to make the calls, but there was not enough time and too many interruptions during the early evening hours to achieve this standard. A study of the situation resulted in a revised procedure with the manager on duty making 10 calls to randomly selected guests who had checked in before 9:00 p.m.

Other factors—such as employee attitudes—can result in poor performance and unsuccessful training. When a performance problem is identified, managers need to carefully determine the real cause so that a solution can be implemented.

Step 3: Plan the Training

Planning the training consists of eight important procedures:

1. Analyze the job

2. Set broad training goals

3. Select the trainees

4. Set specific learning objectives

5. Design the training program

6. Select the training methods

7. Plan for evaluation

8. Prepare training budgets

Analyze the Job

For training to be effective, the trainer must first consider what level of performance should be observable after training is completed.

In job-related skills training, the planning process should include a complete job analysis to develop the basic tools or aids to be used by the trainer. These tools or aids include job lists, job breakdowns, and job performance standards. Chapter 2 covers the process of developing these aids in detail. For now, it is sufficient to note that the development and use of these aids is an important part of the planning process.

Set Broad Training Goals

Training must be practical and it must develop the abilities that are essential for successful job performance. The "ability to do" is the goal of effective employee training and constitutes the basis for more specific training objectives. Training should not be devoted just to the "ability to know." Managers should limit the knowledge aspect of training to that which will make "doing" easier or better. Knowledge for its own sake is not usually an efficient business training goal.

An example of a broad training goal for a front office training program might be: "The training will result in the reduction of guest complaints concerning the check-in and check-out processes." To be attained, a training goal must be supported by specific training objectives, topics, demonstrations, and other exercises. No matter how well it states the desired outcome, a training goal by itself does not communicate what it takes to achieve the desired performance level.

Select the Trainees

By analyzing jobs, managers can establish objective qualifications which can be helpful when employment decisions are made. Hiring the best employees available is an important first step in helping to ensure that, through training, staff members attain competence.

Set Specific Learning Objectives

Each duty or job task should have a performance objective which states what the employee will be expected to do following the training. Objectives should not be too general; they should address specific observable and measurable behaviors. For example, a performance objective could be: "Following the training, the food server will be able to sell a dessert order to more than 50% of his/her guests and serve desserts correctly, in accordance with prescribed service procedures for each dessert."

Where it is appropriate, reasonable criteria for measuring success should be included in the objective statement. For the dessert example, the measurable criterion is "more than 50% of his/her guests." The observable elements are the actual sale and the service in accordance with established procedures. Performance objectives are necessary to help managers plan predictable outcomes from training activities. Objectives also become the basis for assessing what employees know before training and what they know at the conclusion of training. Objectives are important because they force management to focus their thinking on the desired results of training during the planning process, as opposed to just focusing on the activities being planned.

Design the Training Program

At this point in the planning process, the manager must actually design the instructional program and the learning activities. The skills to be developed should be arranged in logical order. Materials should be prepared or assembled to support the learning activities. Designing a solution to performance problems through training methods and procedures is the goal.

A convenient way to organize learning is according to instructional units. An instructional unit is a group of duties or job tasks, along with policies and standard procedures, that are closely related and can logically be covered in a reasonable period as part of the total training. Within each instructional unit there may be several training sessions. For each session, it will be necessary to develop a session outline to plan how the actual training will be conducted.

Select the Training Methods

There are many training methods available to managers. Some are more expensive than others, but a costly approach may not be any better than an inexpensive method. Often, the least costly training method can achieve the best results. Before selecting a training method, managers should consider the capabilities of the employees, their own abilities as trainers, the job duties they will be teaching, the training budget, and the time available for training.

A general rule for selecting a training method is that the level of sophistication should not exceed the sophistication of the trainees or the training abilities of the trainer. Also, the method and materials used in the training should be no more complex than the duties or job tasks that are being taught. When the method is complicated or confusing, the objective of the learning process is lost.

Plan for Evaluation

In order to assess performance after training, the trainer must know the level of performance before training begins. Training is effective to the extent that performance of the job after training is closer to the ideal than before the training was undertaken. An effective evaluation plan includes pre-testing, post-testing, and ongoing evaluation. More will be said about the evaluation process under Step 6.

Prepare Training Budgets

Training costs are determined by considering the instructional units to be covered, duties or job tasks included in each instructional unit, necessary materials and training aids, the specific employees to be trained, the length of time necessary, and the total payroll costs. In calculating labor costs for training activities, it is important to include the cost of employee benefits and other payroll-related costs.

There are several potential costs associated with training. Often the trainer or evaluator will not have direct access to many of the costs (facility costs, equipment costs, etc.) but must obtain figures or reliable estimates from his or her organization's budget operation. Usually, all of these cost categories can be accounted for with little guess work.[11]

Costs of training must be considered just like any other costs; that is, the training expense must be justified and the results must be worth more than the cost of the training. At the times when annual, quarterly, and monthly budgets are developed, managers should assess their plans for training, along with all other anticipated expenses for the budget period. It is unlikely that the budget will permit all of the training activities which a management team desires. This is why it is necessary to establish priorities for training activities and the use of available training funds.

The training budget will influence what training methods may be used and what materials are affordable. In determining training priorities, managers must decide what training costs the budget can absorb as well as what costs will be incurred if training is not undertaken. Among the areas to carefully evaluate when budgeting for training are those areas where performance deficiencies visibly affect guest satisfaction, guest or employee safety, or employee morale.

Step 4: Prepare the Employees

To maximize the training effort, it is important to communicate openly with the staff concerning all training plans and the importance of maintaining standards at approved levels. Employees can be taught to perform their jobs more effectively, but first they must have a basic understanding of what their job involves. Training is a basic method for communicating the expectations of management to employees.

If the trainees have never performed the behaviors that are to be developed through the training process, it is hard for them to visualize what the correct performance will look like. The trainer should help them form this important mental picture of correct performance by demonstrating the desired standard, or by having an experienced employee demonstrate the behaviors. A great way to introduce any training activity is to start with the desired end result and then back up through the description to the starting point of the training. This will help the learner see how the steps in the training fit together and lead to a desirable outcome.

The smart manager will promote the training effort to the staff by focusing on the benefits and features of the training as they relate to each individual employee and to the work group as a team. When explaining the training program to the employees, it is always important to allow time for questions. Unanswered questions and confusing explanations can be barriers to learning. The more the employees know from the start, the less time they will require later.

Step 5: Conduct the Training

One of the manager's most important responsibilities is training. All managers have concerns about people, performance, production, safety, sanitation, internal controls, financial results, etc. A manager can prevent most of these concerns from becoming problems through effective training. Training will not solve every problem, but where effective training is implemented, many of the problems faced by managers can be minimized or eliminated.

Characteristics of a Trainer

Some managers personally conduct training for their staff while others delegate training responsibilities to a member of the work group. The latter can succeed if the individual is carefully selected, properly prepared, and if the manager is closely involved. Whether it is the manager or someone else who conducts the training, he/she should have the following characteristics:

Desire to Teach. A person who enjoys helping others learn will probably enjoy training. A person who does not like the training assignment will probably fail. When selecting a trainer, the past experiences of the candidate should be considered. Individuals who have had successful training experiences in other situations will probably be successful again.

Working Knowledge of the Job. Some experienced employees are outstanding trainers. Others may possess the knowledge, skills, and attitudes to perform a job with great efficiency and effectiveness, but may not have the personality or interest to be good trainers.

A trainer does not have to be an expert in the job to teach the steps in correct performance—especially if he/she uses good training aids such as job lists and job breakdowns. However, training will *not* result in improved performance unless the trainer is able to correctly explain and demonstrate the job tasks, and give sound reasons for mastering job knowledge and attitudes. The following Case in Point describes the criteria set by one chain operation for its trainers.

A Case in Point: The Designated Trainer

One chain operation delegates training in each segment of each department to a skilled, experienced trainer who is recognized as "The Designated Trainer." To become a designated trainer, the employee must:

1. Excel in all skills and knowledge of the job
2. Demonstrate a consistent positive attitude
3. Demonstrate loyalty toward company policies and procedures
4. Have an excellent attendance record
5. Demonstrate maturity in making decisions and solving routine job-related problems
6. Have good communications skills
7. Have a desire to be a trainer
8. Have a personal commitment to excellence in all areas of performance
9. Be effective in organizing work tasks and accomplishing duties on a timely basis

Each person selected as a designated trainer is given five days of training by the corporate training staff in how to plan, conduct, and evaluate training. All supervisors and managers are also required to complete this five-day training program so that the designated trainers and their managers are in agreement over how training will be conducted. The designated trainers and managers work together to analyze training needs and jobs, write training materials, and plan and evaluate the training. The designated trainers then present the training to the staff. The managers are ultimately responsible for the performance of the staff. This responsibility cannot be delegated to the designated trainers.

The designated trainers receive special recognition within their departments as follows:

1. They wear a special uniform.
2. They are treated as part of the department management team.
3. They are given special recognition when their department meets or exceeds performance goals.
4. They are paid a premium pay rate because they perform training in addition to their regular job duties.

Training sessions are held daily by the designated trainers for new employees and for experienced employees based on an ongoing evaluation of training needs. All training is documented with training records for each individual employee. A record is kept of the total hours devoted to formal training during each payroll period. This information is reflected in the financial statements by separating training labor hours from production labor hours. This makes it possible to constantly monitor training costs in comparison with performance results. The performance results in this company are outstanding, and everyone is in tune with the value of ongoing training.

Ability to Convey Understanding. Some people have difficulty communicating what they know. They may talk very slowly or too rapidly. They may have difficulty organizing their thoughts or may use complicated terminology, confusing the trainees in either case. These people are not effective trainers.

Patience. A person who gets angry easily, becomes tense when the work piles up, and can't understand why some people learn more slowly than others may be a poor risk as a trainer. Training requires an objective, patient personality. Employees must be able to feel that the trainer wants to help them, is interested in their growth, will be patient with their mistakes, and will be pleased by their success.

A Sense of Humor. Laughter projects warmth and acceptance. When people laugh together, artificial barriers between the trainer and employee are broken down. They become equals who are enjoying themselves and working toward shared goals.

A trainer does not have to be a good joke-teller to demonstrate that he/she has a sense of humor. Life is filled with its own humorous situations, and the person who possesses natural humor enjoys a good laugh. The wise trainer realizes that 45 minutes of instruction and 5 minutes of laughter may achieve much more than 50 minutes of straight instruction.

Time to Train. One of the biggest headaches for the trainer is finding time to carry out the responsibility. The best trainer is likely to do a poor job if his/her schedule is already overburdened.

No matter who does the actual training, it is up to the manager to see that this important function receives the proper amount of attention. That may mean shifting some of the regular workload away from the trainer.

Respect from Trainees. Trainees will gain minimal benefit from the training if they do not respect the trainer. Respect is earned; it cannot be demanded. Respect comes from the relationship that is developed prior to the training session or during the early stages of the training; it almost always has to do with the competence level of the trainer.

Enthusiasm for Training. When the trainer is genuinely enthusiastic, the enthusiasm will typically carry over to the trainees. This positive attitude usually comes naturally when the trainer has spent the necessary time preparing for the training activities, and is personally convinced that the training will achieve the desired results.

The Training Session

Planning is the hard work of training; executing the training activity is the fun part of the process. It is the trainer's time to be on center stage before an enthusiastic audience. It is one of the most rewarding experiences that a manager or designated trainer can undertake.

Control the Training Environment. Managers must provide the proper physical and emotional environment for training if employees are to benefit the most from training activities. Employees sometimes feel punished or threatened by training activities. They can immediately spot poorly planned training and may consider it a waste of their time and an insult to their intelligence. When some employees receive training and others do not, those receiving training may feel that the expectations held for them are higher than for others—and may consider it unfair. Likewise, employees who are not receiving training may resent management spending time with other employees instead of with them. For best results, management must create an environment where training is important to everyone, and is planned and carried out in a skillful manner. Training must be conducted when the manager can devote time to the activities without a lot of interruptions.

Explain What Is Going to Take Place. Little, if anything, will be gained in training by being secretive. It is much better to be completely open, telling the participants what is going to happen from the outset. This removes most of the anxiety which may interfere with the learning process, and makes it clear that the training has specific objectives.

If the training activity is going to require a series of sessions to achieve one specific objective, it is advisable to provide participants with an outline of the program. It is always a good idea to give the trainees a copy of the learning objectives and, when applicable, a copy of the job list, job breakdowns, and job performance standards. When materials are given out ahead of time, participants can review these materials on their own time and be better prepared to learn.

A good formula for training employees is to:

- Tell them what you are going to teach them.
- Demonstrate and explain every detail carefully.
- Remind them of the learning objectives.
- Test the mastery of the concepts and skills.

Present the Training. Regardless of the method selected to achieve the learning objectives, the trainer must make optimum use of the training time. Training sessions should begin and end at the scheduled time. All training aids, materials, and equipment should be prepared and assembled at the training site before the beginning of each session. Trainees should never be required or permitted to stand around waiting for the trainer.

Employees must be regarded as adult learners. Trainers must remember that learning occurs more rapidly and more effectively in an environment where trainees receive positive encouragement and feedback for their accomplishments. The secret of training success lies in the attitude that surrounds the program. If training is viewed as burdensome work or punishment for failure to achieve standards, it will fail. Consider, for example, how one trainer sets the tone for training activities.

A Case in Point: Give and Take

One trainer was concerned about the difficulty of getting trainees to open up and participate in discussions, to ask or answer questions, or just to relax and enjoy the learning process. To help this problem, the trainer took a sponge rubber football into each training session and began by tossing the football to first one trainee and then another. Each time a trainee tossed the ball back, they were in essence casting off some of their nervousness and inhibitions which could hinder the learning process. Soon everyone was laughing and ready to begin the exchange of information.

Learning must be give and take, especially when it involves adult trainees. Trainers should create the kind of environment that leads to a well-planned, productive learning experience.

Step 6: Evaluate the Training

Evaluation is the process of determining the extent to which the training has done what it was supposed to do. When evaluating training, at least two components should be appraised:

1. The *results* of the training system, program, and individual training activities.

2. The *training plan* and its *execution*. This is needed to determine whether the training function is well organized and whether managers have the expertise necessary to accomplish the goals of the training.

Together, these two evaluations provide a basis for determining whether the training was successful, and whether it should be continued or repeated. The ultimate goal of the evaluation process is the increased effectiveness of the employees, as measured by their job performance.

No training program is complete without evaluation. Evaluation should occur before training so that behavioral reference points can be established, and progress should be evaluated throughout the training program.

Step 7: Follow Through with Ongoing Coaching

The final step in the basic training process is the technique of coaching. Coaching is planned and directed supervisory communication. The purpose of this communication—which usually occurs on the job—is to emphasize expectations covered in training, and to re-establish the standards for performance. Also, while a manager is supervising the staff, and engaging in coaching communications, he/she can correct performance that has moved away from the steps covered through the formal training. Coaching is a fine-tuning procedure, designed to bring out the highest level of performance from each individual. It is most effective when it is part of a well-executed training process.

Notes

1. Peter F. Drucker, *Management: Tasks, Responsibilities, Practices* (New York: Harper & Row, 1974), pp. 45–46.
2. Martin M. Broadwell, "Training and Development of Employees," in *Supervisory Handbook: A Management Guide to Principles and Applications,* edited by Martin M. Broadwell (New York: Wiley, 1985), p. 21.11.
3. For definitions of training and education, see: Leonard Nadler and Zeace Nadler, *Developing Human Resources* (Houston: Gulf Publishing Co., 1970), pp. 40–41, 60; R. Glaser, ed., *Training Research and Education* (Pittsburgh: University of Pittsburgh Press, 1962); Malcolm Knowles, *The Adult Learner: A Neglected Species,* 2nd ed. (Houston: Gulf Publishing Co., 1978), pp. 104–107; and Dugan Laird, *Approaches to Training and Development* (Reading, Mass.: Addison-Wesley, 1978), pp. 9–10.
4. Lloyd L. Byars and Leslie W. Rue, *Human Resource Management,* 2nd ed. (Homewood, Ill.: Irwin, 1987), p. 198.
5. For definitions of coaching, see: Ferdinand F. Fournies, *Coaching for Improved Work Performance* (New York: Van Nostrand Reinhold Co., 1978); Richard P. Calhoon and Thomas H. Jerdee, *Coaching in Supervision* (Chapel Hill, N. C.: Institute of Government, University of North Carolina, 1976); and Arthur X. Deegan, *Coaching: A Managerial Skill for Improving Individual Performance* (Reading, Mass.: Addison-Wesley, 1979).

6. Michael Armstrong and John F. Lorentzen, *Handbook of Personnel Management Practice: Procedures, Guidelines, Checklists, and Model Forms* (Englewood Cliffs, N.J.: Prentice-Hall, 1982), p. 132.

7. Broadwell, "Training and Development of Employees," pp. 21.8-21.9.

8. Kay Tytler Abella, *Building Successful Training Programs: A Step-by-Step Guide* (Reading, Mass.: Addison-Wesley, 1986), p. 3.

9. Byars and Rue, p. 199.

10. Robert F. Mager and Peter Pipe, *Analyzing Performance Problems* (Belmont, Calif.: Fearon Publishers/Lear Siegler, Inc., 1970).

11. B. S. Deeming, *Evaluating Job-Related Training* (Englewood Cliffs, N. J.: ASTD/Prentice Hall, 1982), p. 96.

2 Job Analysis and Development

Guest satisfaction is the ultimate goal of training in the hospitality industry. It is virtually impossible for employees who have not mastered basic job skills to render service which will result in guest satisfaction, repeat business, and profitability. An effective program of skills training is the first step in guaranteeing that the staff can deliver the highest quality service that benefits both guests and the organization. In order to design effective employee training, trainers must first understand exactly what each employee's job involves.

Definition of a Job

The work that an individual does and gets paid for can be referred to as a **job.** The word job is used interchangeably in this book with the words **occupation** or **position.** An employee may be hired for such jobs as food server, chef, cashier, receptionist, room attendant, or bellperson. Each of these titles also represents an occupation or a position within the hospitality operation.

A job is made up of a group of related technical duties or job skills. When grouped into clusters of interrelated behaviors, these groups become competencies. A competent employee is one who can effectively perform the individual duties required in his/her position in accordance with the established standards for quality and productivity. Competence also means that the employee has mastered the interrelationships of his/her duties in order to effectively apply them in actual job situations.

Competence is much more than knowing a lot about a skill or mastering all the skills required in a position. It is also much more than being a robot that works with cold, calculated efficiency. Competence is a well-rounded concept that includes knowledge, skills, attitudes, timing, sensitivity to situations, and intangible feelings about excellence in individual and group performance. The competent employee uses the job skills he/she has mastered to ensure that every guest perceives a positive image of the hospitality operation.

The term job also refers to a piece of work, or a single duty, task, or skill that is part of the total responsibilities of the employee, such as "He did a good job of cleaning the windows" or "She did a good job of decorating the cake." These casual uses of the term should not be confused with the technical meaning used in **job-related training.** This term refers to the total technical training provided to an employee so that he/she might become competent in all responsibilities associated with his/her position—be it simple or complex, managerial or non-managerial.

Some jobs are judged more complex than others, and sometimes jobs are classified according to complexity. Differences in complexity may result in different wage scales, benefits, or the amount of time required for a person to completely master a position. However, the absence of complexity should not imply that it is unnecessary to design training for that job. Any job that is complicated enough to require instruction should be analyzed to identify each of its elements before attempting to train personnel to perform the required duties. The only exception for *not* designing training is the job that is so simple that it can be performed in accordance with the desired standards without any instruction.

The Job Analysis Process

The reason for conducting job-related training is to tell and show employees how their jobs should be done. There may be more than one way to do a job. The **job analysis process** will help the trainer teach the safest and most friendly, courteous, economical, expedient, and efficient way of doing the job, in accordance with quality and quantity standards. As a result of this process, the best training method will emerge as less effective or less efficient alternatives are ruled out.

The job analysis process is essential for the manager who is planning and developing effective training programs. It is the solid foundation upon which training should rest. Failure to perform a detailed job analysis before training will always result in reduced effectiveness of the performance improvement process.

Job analysis begins with identifying the duties that must be performed and developing a **job list.** It continues with a study of each identified duty, and the development of written **job breakdowns.** The concluding procedure considers quality and quantity requirements which specify the criteria for judging correct performance of the job duties. These criteria are expressed as **job performance standards.**

The three tools developed through the job analysis process—job lists, job breakdowns, and job performance standards—are essential training tools. Organizations that develop detailed job lists, job breakdowns, and job performance standards will find not only that these tools are essential for training, but that they are more effective training tools than **job descriptions.** Job descriptions are primarily useful in human resource selection, placement, promotions, and establishing compensation rates; they are of very limited value in training. If an organization still desires to develop job descriptions, the easiest way is to write them from the three job analysis tools. This not only speeds the writing process but also ensures consistency between training and other human resource functions.

Preparing Job Lists

The first step in the job analysis process is to prepare a job list for each category of employee to be trained. A job list is a list of all duties that must be performed by an employee in a given position. Duties included on the list should begin with a phrase such as "How to . . ." or "The ability to . . ." and end with a phrase that states an observable job duty. The job list should state all specific duties for which the employee will be held accountable when his/her performance is reviewed. When each duty is broken down and analyzed in the job breakdowns, both knowledge and attitudes will be included as an integral part of that activity.

Questions that should be addressed as elements in the job list are identified include:

- What specific duties must an employee perform?
- What units of work must be completed?
- What materials must be handled?
- What equipment must be operated?
- What administrative chores must be completed?
- What cleaning requirements are part of the job?

Job List Examples

Tools may be required to successfully complete a specific duty on the job list. However, it is advisable to identify a duty in terms of a skill rather than in terms of the use of a tool. "The ability to use a French knife" should be identified as "the ability to slice, dice, chop, and mince." This distinction is necessary since an employee could learn to do the duty using a food processor instead of a French knife. Exhibits 2.1 and 2.2 show sample job lists with duties that involve the use of more than one tool. Although interrelated, each duty can stand by itself and can be taught separately. The total list of all job duties should represent the total job responsibilities of an employee. Note that the job lists given as examples can serve as an index to job breakdowns (by number) for easy indexing and reference.

The development of job lists does not need to be unwieldy or overwhelming. The manager who is writing job lists will find it helpful to interview personnel in each position, observe them as they perform their jobs, note specific duties being accomplished, participate in the actual performance of the work, review the organization's standard operating procedures, and so on. The manager who is unable to define and list the duties that must be mastered by the employees he/she supervises will certainly be unsuccessful as a trainer or as a supervisor.

Failure to Prepare Job Lists

Managers might think of excuses for not preparing written job lists and subsequent job breakdowns. One excuse might be that such lists would be almost endless because of the complexity of the jobs. If the jobs are so complex that it is not possible to list the duties involved, how can employees ever master their jobs and become productive? Preparing job

Exhibit 2.1   Sample Job List #1: Food Server

Job List*	
Position: Food Server	**Date Prepared:** 00/00/00
Duties: Employee must be able to:	**J.B. Number****

1. Greet and seat restaurant guests	32
2. Serve water and light candles	33
3. Take beverage orders and serve drinks	34
4. Present the food menu and wine list	35
5. Assist guests in making food and beverage selections	36
6. Place orders in kitchen by using the call system	37
7. Serve food and clear table between courses	38
8. Serve wine and champagne	39
9. Serve desserts	40
10. Serve coffee and hot tea	41
11. Prepare the guest check and present to guest	15
12. Collect sales income; make change	16
13. Clear, clean, and reset tables for next party	26
14. Remove stains from dining room carpets	19
15. Provide booster seat or high chair for children	20
16. Clean side stations and service pantry	27
17. Resolve guest complaints	45

*This is a partial job list. The list developed for a specific operation should include all duties to be performed.
**Job Breakdown Number. This refers to the specific job breakdown that breaks down the duty into its identifiable, specific steps. A given duty—and the appropriate job breakdown—can be applicable to and used in the job list of more than one position. For example, the host may also "Greet and seat restaurant guests." If so, the job breakdown number (32) for the food server position would also be applicable to the host position.

lists will expose those positions which should be simplified or reduced in scope to provide a logical basis for training. Take, for example, the discovery made by one restaurant operation in the following Case in Point.

A Case in Point: Unreasonable Workload

When a specialty restaurant undertook the development of job lists and job breakdowns, the company discovered that most employee positions consisted of 15 to 30 duties. One position in the kitchen was found to have 87 separate specific duties. The company had been experiencing high turnover in that position, and it was always difficult to get employees trained to a level where they could handle all duties according to established standards. Following the job analysis, the position was divided in two. In addition, some of the duties were redistributed to other positions which left the job more realistic and manageable.

Some managers might claim they do not have time to prepare job lists and analyze jobs because they are busy running the operation. This attitude results in disorganized training that is inefficient, fails to cover

Exhibit 2.2   Sample Job List #2: Reservationist

Job List*

Position: Reservationist   **Date Prepared:** 00/00/00

Duties: Employee must be able to: J.B. Number**

1. Operate the reservations computer terminal for all reservations menus	63
2. Identify room availability from the computerized rooms inventory	64
3. Identify room rate structures for both individual and group bookings	65
4. Determine the current physical status of any given room from front office inventory controls	66
5. Operate the reservations telephone	67
6. Take and process telephone reservations	68
7. Take and process reservations through correspondence	69
8. Take and process reservations from the 800 reservations center	70
9. Take and process in-person reservations	71
10. Take and process individual reservations for a group booking	72
11. Score reservations to group blocks	73
12. Process reservations confirmation slips	74
13. Use the reservations filing system	75
14. Give directions to the hotel from all areas of the city	76

*This is a partial job list. The list developed for a specific operation should include all duties to be performed.
**Job Breakdown Number. This refers to the specific job breakdown that breaks down the duty into its identifiable, specific steps. A given duty—and the appropriate job breakdown—can be applicable to and used in the job list of more than one position. For example, the receptionist may also "Take and process in-person reservations." If so, the job breakdown number (71) for the reservationist position would also be applicable to the receptionist position.

important points, and lacks attention to detail. Disorganized training is often worse than no training. It demonstrates to employees that management does not have a commitment to performance standards. On the other hand, employees develop respect for organized managers who give priority to planned, high-quality training.

Another reason managers might cite for not developing job lists is the belief that employees will pick up the skills they need to know over time. Instead of teaching specific skills, managers often limit their training to a general job orientation and some specific discussion of "human relations skills." They encourage employees to be "nice" to people, to watch experienced workers, and to "catch on" to the job the best they can. One problem with this trial and error approach is that employees will often "practice" their new skills with guests. In such situations, any blunder an employee makes is likely to result in negative guest feedback. This can lead to negative employee attitudes toward the job and toward guests. Guests should not be expected to train employees, nor should they be served by untrained employees, no matter how "nice" employees try to be.

It is important to note that all aspects of employee training must be practical. The more time-consuming the training design project, the less likely the activity will be undertaken or completed. This point is made in order to stress that:

- The job list is important.

- It does not need to be extremely detailed.

- Its benefits far outweigh the time and effort required for its development.

Most hospitality operations require fewer than fifteen job lists; many require only three or four. Any confusion over what items should or should not be on job lists should be cleared up in the second step in planning for training—the development of job breakdowns for each duty included on the job list.

Developing Job Breakdowns

Job breakdowns are the *most valuable* tools available to a manager who is preparing to teach employees their job duties. The process of preparing job breakdowns is sometimes referred to as task analysis. One of the principal goals of this process is to analyze activities and categorize them into their underlying components of skills and knowledge.[1]

A complete set of job breakdowns for a position details how the technical duties of that job should be performed. One job breakdown is written for each duty on the job list to show:

1. What is to be performed

2. Materials needed to perform the duty

3. Steps for performing each job

4. Additional information about the job steps

The format for job breakdowns can be varied to suit the preferences of each trainer. The forms shown in this chapter are simple and effective. Job breakdowns use simple, step-by-step logic to specify how management expects each job to be performed and to document standard operating procedures.

A Process Approach to Training

The job analysis approach to on-the-job training is a *process* approach because it emphasizes job processes rather than job content. This approach to training produces employees who know how to do their jobs. The *content* approach produces employees who know about their jobs; application of skills is not necessarily emphasized. Few programs are totally process- or content-oriented. The primary emphasis in training based on job analysis is to teach the processes required to perform the job. The goal of effective employee training should be "how to" do something in an approved manner. For training to be practical and cost-effective, it must develop abilities that are required for job performance. The sample job breakdowns presented later in this chapter are all process-oriented.

Many hospitality organizations have manuals that specify how to perform all the duties in their operations. However, without significant modification, few of these manuals can be used as lesson plans for training. Small, independent hospitality operations frequently have no operations manuals at all. Job analysis will yield a complete set of detailed breakdowns of each job. These can become a very effective operations manual. And, of course, job breakdowns can serve a second practical purpose by functioning as lesson plans or training guides that direct instruction and learning in the training program.

Job Breakdown Examples

Standard operating procedures for any duty are determined by management with input from employees who normally perform the duties. When job breakdowns are written, those standard procedures are incorporated into them. A standard operating procedure, whether in job breakdown format or in some other format, should specify how job duties must be performed to be correct within the environment of the hospitality operation. If these manuals or materials contain optional approaches to performance, then they will not serve as standards against which employee behavior can be objectively evaluated.

The first example of a job breakdown shown in Exhibit 2.3 documents "the ability to assist guests in making food and beverage selections." The duty is taken from the job list of a food server for a full-service restaurant. The restaurant could be a freestanding restaurant or a hotel restaurant. Note that the job breakdown also identifies equipment needed to accomplish the specified duty and its various steps. This equipment list should be prepared when the job breakdown is written; it should include all tools or materials that the trainer will need to assemble before beginning a training session. By doing so, the trainer will expedite the actual training activity.

The amount of detail that is required depends, in part, upon the complexity of the duty being analyzed. For example, the operator of a coffee shop might look at Exhibit 2.3 and say that this approach does not apply since most coffee shops do not offer cocktail service. It is not possible to develop a set of job breakdowns that will apply in every situation in the hospitality industry because standard operating procedures differ. Job breakdowns are nothing more than standard operating procedures written in a format that can be used to conduct training.

In Exhibit 2.3, the additional information column stresses such aspects of the job as guest hospitality, safety, sanitation, courtesy, and follow-up on details. It includes information that the trainer will need to present but might forget if not noted in the job breakdowns. The additional information column is largely *content* information while the steps and procedures in the first two columns are primarily *process* elements. There is no clear division between content and process in this approach since there is also some content information in the second column describing each step. This, of course, is acceptable as long as it is meaningful and useful to the trainer and trainee.

Attitudinal training or guest relations training must not be omitted from the job analysis process. The additional information column is not intended to be optional information. Rather, it should be viewed as essential information that must be included in the training process—and

Exhibit 2.3 Sample Job Breakdown #1

Job Breakdown

Job Breakdown #36: The ability to assist guests in making food and beverage selections.
Equipment needed: Guest check, pen. (Guests will already have menus and wine list.)

What to Do	How to Do It	Additional Information
1. Approach the table.	1. Stand erect. Look at the guests, smile, and greet them pleasantly. Introduce yourself. If you know their names, use them when you greet them. Be courteous.	1. You win the table with your first contact when you are pleasant and personable.
2. Take cocktail order.	2. Ask if guests would like a cocktail or appetizer wine. Be sure to get the complete details of the order, such as on-the-rocks, straight up, or extra olives. Remember which guest ordered each cocktail.	2. Most guests know which drinks they prefer. Be prepared to make suggestions, if appropriate. Do not push your personal preferences. Do not act surprised when a guest orders some non-standard drink.
3. Serve cocktails.	3. Place a cocktail napkin in front of each guest. Serve all beverages from the right with the right hand, when possible. Place cocktail glasses on napkins. Do not ask who ordered each drink. (You must remember.) As each drink is served, state what it is, such as Scotch and water, double martini, or Scotch-on-the-rocks.	3. Knowing who ordered what shows that you care about the order. Guests feel special when you repeat their order as you serve their drinks.
4. Check back for a second cocktail order.	4. Be courteous and bring the second round, if ordered, following the same procedure as the first round. Remove all first round empty glasses and napkins. Put down new napkins and serve the drinks.	4. Check back when drinks are approximately two-thirds consumed.
5. Take the food order.	5. Ask the guests if they are ready to order. Explain the chef's specialty and answer any questions about the food. Take orders beginning with the women, when possible. Suggest appetizers, soup, or salads, as appropriate, to help them plan a complete meal. Proceed to the male guests. Be sure to inform the guests of the approximate cooking times of their selections. Communicate with the guest during this very important step. It is more than taking orders. It should be menu planning.	5. Guests expect you to know about the food. When you are asked a question and do not know the answer, do not bluff. Go to the kitchen or manager and find out the answer. Then go back and tell the guest. Suggesting menu items helps a hesitant guest make a decision he/she really wanted, especially if they may require some wait.

Exhibit 2.3 *(continued)*

What to Do	How to Do It	Additional Information
6. Take the wine order.	6. Ask, "Have you chosen a wine?" When you are asked to help, ask whether the guest prefers red or white, dry or semi-sweet, and other questions to get some idea of his/her preferences. Then point out two or three choices that fall within the characteristics described. The guest can choose according to price or other factors. Excuse yourself from the table and assure the guests that you will be right back with the first course.	6. Know the wine list. Always be careful to recognize the timid guest who is a novice at selecting wines. Be prepared to coach the guest through a selection process that will meet his/her needs. Experienced wine drinkers will usually know what they want to order and will not expect much assistance. This is not the time to feed your ego by demonstrating your technical wine knowledge and intimidating the guest. Be confident, but be courteous.

on job breakdowns—for the training to be complete. In many respects, column three contains information stressing *why* the performance steps and procedures are as they are. Beyond that, the information should define the human relations behaviors or intangible qualities required for correct skill execution.[2]

Training in "people skills" is not a matter of changing an employee's personality. Rather, it is a matter of changing an employee's behavior.[3] Every hospitality operator must be concerned with the guest relations aspect of each employee's performance. The appropriate behaviors that result in positive guest relations can be taught in one of two ways:

1. As part of the correct way to execute job-related skills as detailed in columns two and three of the job breakdowns for the position.

2. Separate and apart from technical skills training. This type of training has been labeled by trainers as "smile training."

Both approaches to training have their place, but efficiency is greater when the first approach is used. It makes no sense to train employees in their job skills without incorporating the intangible aspects of quality performance. On the other hand, to attempt smile training with employees who are technically incompetent is a waste of time. Such employees tend to quickly forget the goals of this type of training—especially when their job performance upsets either their supervisor or a guest. Human relations training, separate and apart from technical skills training, is only recommended for employees who have already mastered the technical skills of their jobs. Such training further reinforces and encourages employees to remember the guest relations skills that they know but may be failing to apply.

Exhibit 2.4 provides a sample job breakdown for "the ability to wash serviceware." A mechanical rack-conveyor dish machine is used in this

Exhibit 2.4   Sample Job Breakdown #2

Job Breakdown

Job Breakdown #84: The ability to wash serviceware.
Equipment needed: Dish, glass, and silver racks, dish machine, silverware soak tub, garbage can with liner.

What to Do	How to Do It	Additional Information
1. Scrape and sort.	1. a) Use a "decoy system" by setting up one piece of each type of serviceware as a lure for service personnel to help sort according to the "decoys."	1. a) Cooperation with service personnel will make your job and their job easier. Organizing the dishwashing function will speed the process and increase efficiency.
	b) Deposit all linen napkins and tablecloths in a linen bag.	b) Protect linens—they are expensive.
	c) Scrape all food into garbage cans using heel of hand.	c) A special rubber scraper may be used to scrape food if preferred.
	d) Place all silver into soak tub and soak before washing.	d) Soak tub should have one tablespoon of detarnish powder and be two-thirds full of water. Presoaking makes washing easier, and detarnish solution reduces spots.
2. Rack and prewash.	2. a) Rack each type of china separately to avoid breakage.	2. a) Heavy china will bump against delicate serviceware causing breakage if racked together.
	b) Rack glasses in glass racks.	b) There are special glass racks for each size of glass. Do not mix glasses.
	c) Miscellaneous items should be racked in open racks.	c) Do not overcrowd or overload the racks because the wash and rinse water must reach all surfaces to clean the items.
	d) Spray serviceware with warm water from the prewash spray. Push racks into the machine.	d) Prewashing removes some of the food particles that otherwise would enter the dish machine. It also reduces the number of times that wash water will need changing.
	e) Sort silverware from the soak tub. Place silverware in plastic cones with the handles down.	e) Presorting reduces handling of clean silverware.
3. Feed the machine and wash dishes.	3. a) Turn on conveyer and pump.	3. a) Push black buttons on control panel to start. Push red buttons to stop.
	b) Push the rack of soiled items into the machine far enough for the conveyor to engage the rack; the conveyor will move it through the machine.	b) The rack should engage at one-third to one-half of the way in. Check wash temperature to be sure it is at least 140°F. Rinse temperature should be at least 180°F. If temperatures are low, stop machine and contact your supervisor.

Exhibit 2.4 *(continued)*

What to Do	How to Do It	Additional Information
	c) Rack more items and feed into machine as fast as it will take them.	c) Do not allow soiled dishes to pile up and hinder the service personnel. Help them unload trays and bus tubs. Work to maintain good relationships with other employees.
4. Remove clean racks.	4. Machine will push racks out of rinse end. Pull them completely free. Shake rack to remove excess water. Allow items to air dry before removing.	4. If rinse water is 180°F, items will air dry quickly. Serviceware should never be wiped dry.
5. Stack and store serviceware.	5. Store glasses in the wash racks. Stack china and store in clean dish area.	5. Plates and bowls are placed on dish carts. Glassware is left in racks and placed on glass carts. Silverware is placed in flatware racks for transport to service stations.
6. Check for serviceware not properly cleaned.	6. Look for food, water spots, chips, cracks, or other problems which indicate items cannot be used.	6. You are the quality control inspector of clean serviceware. Check carefully and rewash all soiled items. Remove all chipped and cracked items and discard. Guests judge the cleanliness of the kitchen by the condition of the serviceware.

example. This duty is a very important one in the hospitality industry. Very complex equipment may be used, but the emphasis of the duty should not be on mastering equipment operation. Rather, the emphasis should be on the use of the equipment to accomplish the important job of washing serviceware to meet the sanitation standards of the guests, the operation, and of the local health authorities. The employee's performance will be evaluated based upon the cleanliness of the dishes, glassware, and flatware. This job breakdown is rather complex since it tells how to efficiently scrape, stack, rack, wash, and store all types of serviceware. Quality control of clean serviceware is also stressed. The ability to set up the machine for operation is a prerequisite that should be covered in a separate job breakdown.

The training of dishroom personnel must be effective since their work affects the dining room service staff as well as the kitchen staff. When dining room and dishroom personnel constantly quarrel over delivery of soiled dishes to the dish return area or over improperly cleaned serviceware, the guest will suffer because attitudes of service personnel toward each other will affect other areas of performance. When the guest complains about soiled dishes or spotted glassware, the service staff will be embarrassed and will blame the problem on the dishroom personnel. A cooperative working relationship between the dishroom and the dining room staff can be developed through good training and coaching. The dishroom staff should be able to work in harmony with the dining room staff and supply the servers and buspersons with spotlessly clean serviceware.

Hospitality managers often find dishroom training a problem because: (1) they fail to study and analyze the job of dishroom personnel, and (2) they do a less than adequate job of training the staff. Job breakdowns leave very little to chance. It is critical that employees perform their jobs according to specific procedures. Therefore, it is important to break down the duties and document those procedures. The training program becomes a means of teaching the employees to do the duties the exact way that management expects the duties to be done.

A final example of a job breakdown is shown in Exhibit 2.5, "the ability to register a guest." The receptionist establishes the tone for the guest's stay. If the registration and room assignment process are handled with courtesy and efficiency, the guest's first impression of the hotel will be good. First impressions influence all other impressions during the guest's stay in the hotel.

Cost-Effectiveness of Job Breakdowns

The use of job breakdowns is a logical approach to planning training activities. Without this preparation or a similar approach, the trainer will be training without adequate background. Any time saved by not developing written job breakdowns will be lost through inefficient training and, subsequently, poor job performance. The lost time can be readily appreciated by considering the number of trainees who were taught by inefficient methods. The time saved by using job breakdowns will result in a tremendous return on investment for the manager.

Writing Job Breakdowns

If one person in a hospitality operation is responsible for writing all the job breakdowns, he/she will probably never complete the job, unless the operation is very small with a limited number of duties. A fast-food operation may require 40 to 60 job breakdowns, each of which will be one to three pages in length. While that sounds like a lot of work, recall that the result is a *complete* operations manual that can be used as the training manual for every duty that is performed by the staff.

In a large operation, whether it is primarily food service or lodging, job breakdowns can be written by a team which includes management groups and experienced non-management employees. A good way to begin is to assemble a group of "writers" and, using a flip chart, have the group list the duties that are performed by a given category of employees (such as room attendants). To keep the process practical, the group must be experienced in either performing or supervising the duties being analyzed. The job list for room attendants includes cleaning the guestroom. This could be broken down further into such duties as making beds, vacuuming carpets, dusting and polishing furniture, cleaning blinds, cleaning windows, cleaning and sanitizing toilets, cleaning the tub and shower, cleaning tile floors and walls, etc.

Once the duties have been identified, different members of the group can volunteer or be assigned to write the job breakdowns for the duties that are most familiar to them. In a period of three hours, a group of six people can probably write most of the job breakdowns required to train room attendants. This includes the duties that the room attendant

Exhibit 2.5 Sample Job Breakdown #3

Job Breakdown

Job Breakdown #82: The ability to register a guest.
Equipment needed: Registration card/folio, credit card imprinter, pen, room rack, room key.

What to Do	How to Do It	Additional Information
1. Greet the guest.	1. Friendly, warm smile. "Good evening. May I help you?"	1. Guests are often tired when they check in. They may have been traveling and/or working all day. Unless the receptionist establishes helpful communication quickly, the guest may vent his/her tired feelings on the employee.
2. Identify the name of the reservation.	2. "Sir (Madam), what name was that under?"	2. Reservations may be under the guest's name, a company name, or the name of the person who made the reservation. Check each name in the above order until you locate the reservation.
3. Secure complete folio information.	3. "Here we are Mr. (Ms.) _____. Please complete the lower portion of the form."	3. Complete information is important for identifying the guest. This information may be used to locate the guest, mail the bill, return lost and found items, or forward mail and packages.
4. Secure credit information.	4. "Sir (Madam), will you be paying with a charge card?" If the answer is yes, ask the guest if you can imprint the card. If the guest plans to pay cash, positive identification is required and the first night's room rate must be collected. If the guest refuses to have the charge card imprinted, the card must be verified and the number recorded on the back of the registration card.	4. Company policy and state laws require positive guest identification. A charge card is sufficient. If a charge card is not available, a driver's license or passport is acceptable.
5. Assign room.	5. Follow procedures learned under Assigning Guestrooms—Job Breakdown #83. Complete the folio showing room assignment and rate. Tell the guest the room number you have assigned him/her. "Sir/Madam, that is room 1226, a double, and the rate is ____."	5. If possible, the room should be in accordance with the guest's request.
6. Page bell staff.	6. Say "Front, please." Tell the bellperson, "Mr. (Ms.) _____ will be in room 1226." Give the bellperson the rooming slip and the room key. Tell the guest, "Please have a good stay."	6. The receptionist who has established goodwill and has the guest in a good mood can pass that feeling on to the bellperson. He/she should introduce the guest and say something pleasant as the guest follows the bellperson to the room.

performs outside the guestroom, such as stocking the room attendant's cart, stocking hall closets, cleaning public restrooms, cleaning stairwells and elevators, and cleaning lobbies.

Several writing sessions can be planned to prepare job breakdowns for all departments in the operation. This concentrated effort can result in a complete set of training materials for a very complex hospitality operation in just a few weeks. In a smaller, less complicated operation, job breakdowns can be completed in a few days. The approach that one hotel company took toward developing training materials is illustrated in the following Case in Point.

A Case in Point: Detailing Excellence

One large hotel company decided to develop a skills training program for its restaurant outlets. Unlike many companies that begin by designing training for their *worst* operation first, the company decided to design the program starting with its *best* restaurant first. This restaurant was a fine dining operation serving lunch and dinner, and was known for its excellence in food and service. The restaurant used a captain-server-busperson service organization and the menu included considerable tableside preparation and service. The service staff of the restaurant consisted of six of these three-person teams plus a wine steward and a maitre d'.

A training design team was assembled that consisted of two captains, the restaurant manager, maitre d', wine steward, food and beverage director, and the corporate vice president of food and beverage. An outside training consultant facilitated the project.

The two captains were selected based on their past performance and their popularity among guests. One of the captains had worked as the server on the other captain's team for several years before being promoted to captain. Therefore, there was almost total agreement between the two as to procedures and service techniques.

The plan was to develop the job lists, job breakdowns, and job performance standards for the restaurant service staff. Then, the two captains would retrain all the other captains, servers, and buspersons who worked in the room. The overriding goal of the project was to further refine the consistency of service, and to have all teams execute service according to the standards exemplified by the two teams headed by the two captains.

A number of work sessions were required to fully document each step in the restaurant's complex service procedures. The job list for captains included opening duties and tableside preparation of Caesar Salad, Steak Diane, flaming desserts, and special coffees—plus skills such as how to decant fine wines, bone fish at tableside, and present after-dinner cigar service. Each of these duties was detailed in job breakdowns, along with the listed skills for servers and buspersons.

The final result was to establish a standard approach for training and excellence for the entire company. The initial decision to develop and implement this program was to clearly demonstrate a commitment to improved performance in every company operation—even in those which were already regarded as superior in the marketplace.

The success of this program was publicized throughout the company. Workshops were then conducted in other hotels to train the management staff in the methods necessary to implement this training approach. As a result, similar skills training programs were developed and implemented for other food and beverage operations, as well as for front office and other rooms departments. In each case, the first step was to analyze the jobs for which the training would be provided, and then develop the job lists, job breakdowns, and job performance standards upon which the training would be based.

Uses of Job Breakdowns

Once job breakdowns are written, they should be edited, revised as necessary, and typed if possible. Then they should be inserted into three-ring binders and indexed according to job categories (for example, food servers, room attendants, receptionist, etc.). There should be a complete set for each non-management position in the hospitality operation. Job breakdowns have several uses and functions as follows.

Planning Training. The development of job breakdowns is the most time-consuming part of the detailed planning process for an effective technical training effort. This is where many training design efforts fall apart and leave trainers without specific documents upon which to plan their training programs. The results are predictable: inefficient training that is totally dependent on the ability of the trainer to think on his/her feet. Important details and standards of performance will likely be overlooked through this approach.

Outlines for Teaching. Job breakdowns should be viewed as lesson plans for training or learning guides for self-directed learning. The instructor who uses the job breakdowns as lesson plans will have a logical flow of instruction that progresses from the simple to the more complex. The self-directed learner will also be able to visualize the flow of work throughout the steps in the breakdowns. When it is necessary to use the same job breakdown to train more than one category of employee, a copy of that breakdown should be made and indexed according to the employee category to which it applies. For example, "the ability to set tables" may be included in the job list and breakdowns for host/hostess, food server, and busperson (see the second footnote on Exhibit 2.1). The result is a complete set of training guides which can be used for training each category of employees.

Standards for Evaluation. Job breakdowns also provide an objective basis for observing and evaluating the work performed by experienced employees. Such evaluations will often reveal that experienced employees have slipped away from standard operating procedures and are performing parts of their jobs using methods that are less efficient than those in the job breakdowns. Evaluation can show where retraining is needed to realign performance with standards.

Outlines for Manuals. The easiest way to develop a standard operating procedures manual is to write job breakdowns. The breakdowns systematically specify what is to be done and how it should be done to meet the desired standards. In effect, a standard operating procedures manual has the same goal. The logical sequence of repeatedly considering these two elements of each operational duty makes writing of the procedures simple and complete. Many organizations put off training design until they have developed a set of operating manuals. This is the hard way to write manuals; the easy way is to write the job breakdowns first, and then use the breakdowns as the outlines. By adding a few details, it is a relatively easy writing task to transform the outline into a narrative format that is suitable for an operating manual.

Audiovisual Scripts. Audiovisual technical training programs should be carefully planned to ensure the optimum use of visuals and to determine the time available for the audio script. Job breakdowns simplify this process. The "what to do" steps guide the planning for the visuals while the "how to do it" steps guide the writing of the script. The "additional information" is then used to round out the script and to emphasize the intangible aspects of the activity.

Developing Job Performance Standards

All employees need to know how well they are expected to perform their jobs. Employees need to know what standards managers will use and what managers will be looking for so that they can measure their own performance against the manager's "yardstick."

How do managers know when a job is being done well or not so well? By constantly observing and analyzing employees' current and past performances and matching them against what staff members have been trained to do. Performance standards are needed in order to do this. The next Case in Point illustrates the difficulty of getting managers to quantify and qualify what they mean by performance measurement.

A Case in Point: Standards of Performance

A restaurant manager in a large hotel was complaining about the sandwich maker to a hotel consultant. The consultant asked the manager how many sandwiches the sandwich maker was expected to prepare in an hour. The manager replied, "Well, a lot more than he does." The consultant then asked, "How many sandwiches does he make in a busy hour?" The manager replied, "Not nearly enough."

Exasperated, the consultant once more tried to get some more facts by asking, "How many sandwiches does a good sandwich maker make in a busy hour?" The restaurant manager gave the final word by saying, "A lot more than he does!"

Managers must have specific and objective standards against which to measure work performance. It is gross mismanagement when employees do not know exactly what is expected of them. Until managers measure employee output, it is impossible to analyze costs intelligently, regardless of how many reports are available through computerized management information systems.

In this discussion of job performance standards, it is essential to never lose sight of guest satisfaction. Every training program must be focused on efficiency and effectiveness, but the concern for the guest must motivate each training decision. No training in the hospitality industry is complete that overlooks the intangible elements of friendliness, warmth, courtesy, helpfulness, and responsiveness to guest needs. These qualities of performance are part of every well-written job breakdown for guest service skills. When they are not inherently obvious, these qualities should be stressed in the additional information column of the job breakdowns—explaining *why* the skills should be performed in the specified manner. Guest satisfaction indicators should also be stressed in the written job performance standards. Cold, insensitive execution of skills is *not* hospitality, and is not the goal of the job analysis process.

Definition of Job Performance Standards

Job performance standards are statements that describe or clarify the levels of employee performance that are acceptable to the organization. They may be expressed as *minimum* performance levels or as *desired* performance levels. Once established, they provide specific goals for training and specific guidelines for performance reviews. Without defined performance standards, employees work in constant anxiety, never knowing whether their work is pleasing or substandard. This is not an atmosphere that fosters development of full potential or proficiency.

Managers must learn to think about standards as they observe employees performing duties and as they plan job assignments. This requires conditioning to become sensitive to performance standards. As one authority says:

> We can get more practice for the training jobs we will have as a supervisor if we acquire the habit of thinking about standards of performance. The only way we'll ever be successful as trainers is to teach a standard. The only way we are able to know if an employee is below standard is to have a standard, and the only way we'll know if we've been successful in our training efforts is to see whether the employee can now meet the standard.[4]

Job performance standards are nothing more than job breakdowns in a different form; they are merely translated into more measurable terms, and should be written as workable tools such as checklists, written examinations, or observation guides. The more precise the units of measurement, the better off managers will be when it is time to review performance with the employee. When developing standards, it helps to begin with the statement, "Performance is considered good when . . . ," then list the specific indicators or measurements which are used to tell how effectively the job is being done. The list should include guest relations indicators that measure guest satisfaction.

Examples of Job Performance Standards

Exhibit 2.6 illustrates how performance standards can be set using both quality and quantity measures. If it is not possible to develop measurable units to define standards of performance, then it is not fair to hold employees accountable for the quality or quantity of work performed in that area of responsibility. Measures can take a variety of forms, including:

- A smile when greeting a guest
- The number of units to be processed in a given time
- The speed of response in solving a guest problem
- A date or time by which a specified action must be completed
- A verbal invitation for the guest to request assistance at any time
- An acceptable replacement cost figure on breakage or waste
- An acceptable number of rejects or complaints over a given period
- The number of rooms to be cleaned during a certain period
- The appropriate positive communication in each guest contact situation

Sometimes it is impossible or impractical to apply numbers to performance standards. In such cases, standards should describe how management can tell when a desired action has taken place, and describe what will be used to indicate that the job has been performed properly. The frequency of correct performance is equal in importance to the accuracy in relation to established standards.

Writing Job Performance Standards

The Individual Approach. Every good manager has a clear picture of what he/she expects from employees and is able to communicate this to the staff. The ability to write clear performance standards requires some skill in written communications. Sometimes, the clear idea is muddled when it is put on paper by the inexperienced writer. For this reason, the written version should be reviewed for clarity and understandability—even when managers work independently and write their own performance standards for their staff.

The Team Approach. A team approach can also be used to develop performance standards. It is very important that the management staff and the team work together so that everyone will agree on the standards and will have been involved in establishing them. When this is done, there is greater likelihood that the standards will be accepted and achieved without great resistance.

When the group meets, the manager should confirm that performance standards serve three important purposes:

1. To ensure high levels of guest satisfaction
2. To help employees become more proficient at their jobs

Exhibit 2.6 Sample Job Performance Standards: Food Server, Lunch Shift

Job Performance Standards: Food Server, Lunch Shift

A food server's performance in taking care of assigned tables for the lunch shift is considered good when the server performs the following duties according to the procedures documented in job breakdowns that were covered during training:

1. Arrives in the dining room by 10:30 a.m., rested and ready for work in a complete, clean uniform.

2. Has all assigned tables fully set up with tablecloths, napkins, glass and silverware, condiment sets, ashtrays, and matches by 11:15 a.m.

3. Greets guests cordially. Approaches the table as soon as guests are seated to provide necessary service.

4. Suggests a cocktail order while guests are deciding on food selections.

5. Engages in positive communications with the guests concerning daily specials and other menu selections; attempts suggestive selling of food and beverage offerings.

6. Attempts to sell a bottle, carafe, or glass of wine with lunch.

7. Writes orders on guest checks legibly, correctly using approved abbreviations.

8. Places orders in kitchen as soon as they are taken, following the kitchen call system for orders.

9. Picks up and delivers orders promptly; serves orders to all guests at a table at one time.

10. Serves food plates from guest's left side with left hand whenever possible.

11. Serves beverages from guest's right side with right hand whenever possible.

12. Serves wine and cocktails according to approved procedures.

13. Serves standard condiments with food orders without guests having to ask; serves special condiment requests quickly and pleasantly.

14. Checks back on each guest often for refills of beverages and to be sure that all guest requests are quickly filled.

15. Clears china, glassware, and silver from tables as guests complete courses; clears quietly from guest's right with right hand, removing serviceware to a tray on a sidestand nearby.

16. Attempts to sell desserts to all guests.

17. Offers coffee service at the end of the meal for all guests.

18. Presents the guest check promptly as soon as final course has been served.

19. Thanks guests for coming.

20. Immediately clears and resets table as soon as guests leave the dining room.

3. To help the organization meet its quality and productivity objectives

The objective is not to overwork employees but to make them more capable. By raising the average performance closer to the top performance, the guests will receive better service and the business will be successful.

Group members are ready to begin once they understand that they will be developing standards of performance for different jobs in their department. After the group chooses a job with which to begin, the detailed job list and job breakdowns should be reviewed so everyone knows exactly what the job entails.

The Manager's Role in the Group Process. The major role of the manager in the team approach is to lead the group into discussing *measures of performance* rather than *requirements of the job*. To begin the discussion, the manager should ask how an outsider, who knows nothing about the job, could tell if the job is being performed correctly and how well it is being performed. The group's suggestions should be recorded on a flip chart. It may not be necessary to quantify every part of the job, but the most important parts should have clear standards. The job lists and job breakdowns should be used as a resource by every group member to indicate those duties for which performance standards are required.

Suggestions should not be challenged or discussed until the group runs out of ideas. Many of the suggestions will probably deal with how the job is done (duties) rather than how well it is done (standards). When discussion begins, this will become obvious to the group, and they will propose changes.

There are a few basic questions that will help the group members focus on their objective:

- Is this really a measure of performance or just another way of saying what the person does on the job?

- What evidence is there that each part of the job is being done properly?

- Can terms be more specific than just "on time"? For example, how many minutes should it take to do a specified job?

- Is there a good balance between guest relations skills and technical job skills?

The biggest job in writing job performance standards is to transform generalities into specifics. The non-management employees in the group should do this themselves to the greatest extent possible. The group may need direction, and sometimes the manager may have to disagree. This is fine. The employees may even find that they agree with the manager— or they may convince the manager that their point is valid after all.

As the discussion develops, the manager will probably begin to notice members correcting themselves and each other on what is important in a job and what isn't. This insight gives them a better appreciation for the job as it should be done. It often makes members see areas in which they can improve their own performance. Participation on a standards-setting team is a great learning experience in and of itself.

Cautions in Setting Performance Standards

When setting performance standards for the first time, it is important to be realistic. The standards should not be set too high or too low. Of course, more experienced employees may be able to easily exceed the standards, but newer and less experienced employees should have to work up to them. It is also a good idea to emphasize that performance standards are not work quotas or conditions of employment; they are targets or goals in achieving excellence in performance.

Any standards of performance for an employee must represent a level to which he/she can agree without reservation. An "absolute" standard such as "there will be no guest complaints" is unrealistic and should not be stated. The goals must be realistic, attainable, and compatible with the employee's workload, capabilities, and working conditions. These yardsticks should be established to measure the rate of each employee's development or performance.

Managers may later want to raise standards or train individuals to assume higher performance levels. If the operation has a high turnover rate or draws primarily on unskilled labor to fill vacancies, both minimum and desired standards should be established. Otherwise, managers will have to change the performance standards frequently. **Minimum standards** are performance levels that cannot be sacrificed without changing the character of the operation (or without appealing to a less demanding clientele). **Desired standards** are performance levels for which every employee is expected to strive. Achievement of the desired standards would be regarded as excellent performance, while achievement of the minimum standards might be regarded as average performance. Performance standards serve a very real and practical purpose.

Performance standards are not just for non-management employees such as buspersons, room attendants, receptionists, food servers, and cooks. They should also be applied to supervisors, department managers, and general managers. Individuals in positions of top management should help lower-echelon managers set job performance standards with their own peer groups. Like job lists and job breakdowns, job performance standards should be periodically re-evaluated and updated as necessary.

Work Simplification: Making Jobs Easier

When the requirements of a job are established, the job steps should be logical and simplified as much as possible so that the work can be accomplished with the least amount of effort. As one authority states:

> Work analysis is really a system of studying work with the idea of making employees more efficient. The purpose of work analysis is to identify and correct factors having a detrimental effect on productivity in the work system.[5]

As managers prepare each of the documents in the job analysis process (job lists, job breakdowns, and job performance standards), they should carefully study every aspect of the job. Then the following questions should be asked about each job element:[6]

- Can the job step be eliminated? If the step is not really needed to effectively perform the job, then it should be eliminated.

- Can the job step be combined with another step? If it makes more sense to treat a particular step as part of another step, or to combine duties into larger, more meaningful units of work, the step should be revised.

- Can the sequence of job steps be changed? When writing job breakdowns, the flow of job steps should be logical and sequential, beginning with simple steps and building toward more complex advanced steps. Think about how the job is performed when it is done in the most efficient manner possible.

- Can the job step be improved or simplified? Is there a better way to approach the job? Does the job seem unnecessarily difficult? It may be helpful to have someone who knows nothing about the job read the materials. Then that person can describe how he/she thinks the job should be performed. Such an explanation will often reveal unnecessarily complicated steps which can be simplified.

The Job Analysis Foundation

An employee training program without job analysis is like cooking without recipes, or assigning rooms without any record of which guest is assigned to which room. No one knows where the training is at any point or where it is going. Any manager who has had difficulty controlling training is probably operating without the tools of the trade.

Throughout the rest of this book, many activities related to planning, conducting, and evaluating training will refer to the job analysis process. Job analysis is the underlying foundation and focal point of an effective job training program, especially with respect to the teaching and learning of the technical duties of each management and non-management employee. "Shortcuts" to training which reduce the up-front planning effort are, in reality, "detours" from quality training experiences.

A Special Note About Job Analysis

Readers are cautioned that there is not an "all-or-nothing" relationship between complete job analysis and the execution of training. While job analysis is essential to the overall design process for effective training, there will be times when the detailed analysis process may be modified or scaled-down to meet an immediate emergency training need. In other words, if a manager observes an isolated problem which can be resolved through training, it is not necessary to do a complete job list, a complete set of job breakdowns, and a complete identification of all job performance standards before training can begin. Rather, these tools can be developed as they are applied to the problem at hand. It is completely appropriate to focus on duties related to the positions and problems of immediate concern, develop the job breakdowns for the appropriate duties, and establish job performance standards for these duties. Training can then be undertaken to immediately correct the problem. These job analysis tools can later be incorporated into a more complete training program when the analysis process is completed for all the duties of the position.

By taking this approach, management can do "stopgap" training while undertaking the long-range activities of planning for training. For example, if employee theft is discovered, or if there is a sudden increase in the number of guest complaints, these problems must be corrected when identified. The manager should not wait for lengthy pre-training analysis of all duties of the employees involved before dealing with such emergency problems. In these situations, the approach presented in this chapter should be applied to the specific problem. The trainer can prepare the job lists, job breakdowns, and job performance standards required to resolve the situation. Later, this information can be incorporated into a total training plan as it is designed for training employees to be fully competent in all duties required by their positions.

Notes

1. J. R. Grossman and Charles Martinez, "The Missing Link: A Bridge Between Task Analysis and Training Strategy," *Performance and Instruction*, Vol. 27, No. 2, February 1988, pp. 26–28.
2. Lewis C. Forrest, Jr., "Training for Hospitality," Project Hospitality Series (Chicago: National Restaurant Association, 1980). Article demonstrates how knowledge, skills, and hospitality attitudes are integrated in job breakdowns.
3. V. R. Buzzotta, "Does 'People-Skills' Training Really Work?" *Training*, Vol. 23, No. 8, August 1986, pp. 59–60.
4. Martin M. Broadwell, *Moving Up to Supervision*, 2nd ed. (New York: Wiley, 1986), p. 171.
5. John P. Daschler and Jack D. Ninemeier, *Supervision in the Hospitality Industry* (East Lansing, Mich.: The Educational Institute of the American Hotel & Motel Association, 1984), p. 67.
6. A detailed discussion of work simplification principles is beyond the scope of this chapter. Interested readers are referred to: Edward A. Kazarian, *Work Analysis and Design for Hotels, Restaurants, and Institutions* (Westport, Conn.: AVI Publishing Co., 1969).

3 Hiring Trainable Employees

Training effectiveness is measured largely by the success with which employees master the knowledge, skills, and attitudes that are essential to job performance. In this respect, managers should ensure that the most qualified applicants are recruited for vacant or new positions within the hospitality operation. Employee selection must go hand in hand with training if management wants to develop a competent staff that consistently pursues excellence.

Employees represent the ownership and management of the operation to the guest. One goal of training should be to develop employees into acceptable "ambassadors" for the operation. The job performance of the employees should reflect the owner's and manager's concept of hospitality. For this to happen, training efforts must be closely aligned with selection activities. A major goal of personnel selection is to hire individuals who will develop into good hospitality representatives. This can only happen when managers understand that selection and training are complementary activities.

Service organizations must have customer-oriented employees.[1] In the hospitality industry, the guest experience is directly affected by the attitudes and behaviors of the staff. Selecting guest-oriented people, who demonstrate outgoing, warm personalities and behaviors in the interview, is the first crucial step in ensuring that guests will be properly treated.

The goal of recruitment should be to find the best possible people to fill vacant or new positions. There are several possible sources of applicants for positions within the operation. Only staff members who have proven themselves capable should be considered for promotions and transfers. Procedures to identify the best applicants for further consideration must be effective.

It is essential for the human resources and operating departments to work closely together for the good of the entire hospitality operation. The result of this mutual effort must be to bring trainable employees into the operation—employees who are interested in the job, meet the job requirements, and are willing and able to master the skills of the positions for which they are selected.

Getting these new employees off to a positive start on their jobs is the role of orientation. The orientation process should be based on a "guest philosophy." As such, it should emphasize guest relations techniques and endorse the attitude that guests are never a problem. A major message of orientation should be that guests are the reason the hospitality operation—and the employee's job—really exists.

A well-planned and executed orientation program is necessary to retain the new employee's "trainability." A properly selected employee will arrive at his/her new job with a positive attitude. Unfortunately, this attitude can quickly be turned around by unfavorable initial impressions during the first few days of employment. Performance problems can result not just from poor selection procedures (meaning that the employee should not have been hired), but from negative experiences a new employee may have during his/her early relationship with the operation.

In preparing to be an effective trainer, a manager must first review basic principles of employee recruitment, selection, and orientation. Training, regardless of how well it is planned, cannot be effective when it is addressed to the wrong people or to those who will not remain with the operation long enough to make a useful contribution. Training should be fun. This is more likely when the right people are hired and when orientation really creates a desire to help the organization achieve its goals.[2]

The Need for Effective Selection

Most employed individuals can be trained. However, not all people share the same interest in, or capacity for, learning. Selection relates to training because of the need to screen applicants carefully so that the most trainable individuals are hired.

Selection is not limited by racial, ethnic, or cultural barriers, nor is it affected by them. Within every group of the population, there are individuals whose environment has fostered a strong work ethic; there are others who believe that they do not need to work nor put forth the effort to match the income they receive. Even though many hospitality positions require rather simple skills, high levels of productivity are impossible when turnover rates are high. Employees need time to develop confidence in their skills and to develop production speed. Confidence and speed can never be achieved if employees leave before they have mastered their jobs. The positions will always be filled by trainees.

The Warm Body Syndrome

The greatest cause of high turnover and low productivity in the hospitality industry is probably the "warm body syndrome." Tight labor markets and unexpected employee turnover often create stress on the manager—and that can result in hiring the first person who walks in the door looking for a job. The consequences can be disastrous when a manager hires someone who rejects training, snubs all efforts aimed at getting him/her to work more effectively, and complains constantly about being overworked and underpaid. The following Case in Point demonstrates how effective selection can reduce costs and increase productivity.

A Case in Point: Effective Selection Saves Money

A restaurant had been using part-time workers to wash dishes, pots and pans, and perform several utility duties for a period of 22 months. Within these positions, turnover was high and productivity was low. Since management felt that the positions did not warrant a formal selection effort, the first available applicant was usually hired. Most of the employees in these positions were male college students, and there were regular problems of tardiness and below-standard performance. Three part-time employees usually filled the positions.

Circumstances caused the three part-time employees to resign simultaneously. Time was allocated for recruiting, and the decision was made to seek a full-time person to replace the three part-time people. It was expected that one part-time employee would also be needed to assist the full-time employee during busy periods.

The operation ran newspaper ads and conducted interviews for three afternoons between 1:00 and 5:00 p.m. The turnout was heavy and more than 30 applicants were interviewed. There was a temptation to stop the interviews after two days and make a selection, but this plan was vetoed. On the third day, management selected the last person interviewed—a young divorced woman with five small children. This woman had never worked in a restaurant as a dishwasher before, but her desire for the job and her enthusiasm, plus her solid work history in other semi-skilled positions, made her stand out above the other applicants.

This new employee was trained by the restaurant manager and performed the job in an outstanding manner. She never gave the manager any problems or unsatisfactory performance. She did not need an assistant, and her self-motivation and morale were always high. The manager of this restaurant scheduled valuable time to select and train the right person for a very basic position. The payoff made it worthwhile.

Planning for Selection

Efficient management is based on planning. Effective planning and the effective integration of selection and training can ensure productivity and reduce turnover and labor costs.[3] Even in operations where turnover is low, the need for careful personnel administration practices is just as important as in high turnover situations. New talent should be brought into the operation through a planned recruitment and selection process.

In large hotels or restaurants, a human resources department may screen applicants for positions and maintain an active file of potentially good candidates. In smaller operations, managers must do their own screening and maintaining of candidate files. In either case, the ultimate decision to hire should rest with the manager of the department in which the employee will work. The decision to hire should take into consideration how that candidate will fit into, and make a positive contribution to, the work group.

Most hospitality operations depend on the coordinated efforts of many people to meet the needs of guests. This means that people must work together. They must be able to communicate with one another and depend upon one another. The selection and training of every employee should build and strengthen team unity. This will lead to a more contented, productive, and stable work group.

Most operations experience some seasonal fluctuations in staffing needs. These needs are generally predictable and allow the manager to plan for recruitment, selection, and training. Even when there are no vacancies in an operation, it is a good practice to interview candidates who have completed an application. The three primary benefits to this approach are:

1. It maintains an active file of candidates from which to draw when the need occurs.

2. It provides management with an opportunity to keep interviewing skills sharp through practice.

3. It provides a basis for comparing potential employees with actual employees.

Planning for potential vacancies can offset the panic brought on by unexpected employee resignations or other hiring needs. By keeping an active file of applicants, management provides itself with ample time and alternatives for making sound selections when vacancies arise.

Promoting Positive Human Resource Practices

Almost every hospitality organization claims to be people-oriented and to believe in human resource development. In practice, a much smaller number follow through on these claims, especially in terms of investing time and money in effective training and development. Limited resources, stiff competition, and weak management all contribute to ineffective training or no formal training at all. For selection to result in the hiring of trainable individuals with high potential for success, an operation must implement an active, positive plan for human resource development.

Commit to Employee Development

The organization that sincerely commits itself to human resource development has the opportunity to set itself apart from the competition. An operation must organize, plan, and implement various elements of a human resource system and stick to them through thick and thin. It is not sufficient to simply pay "lip service" to these concepts. During the developmental stages of designing and implementing training programs, the per-employee cost is higher than it will be in later years. The investment returns are not always directly correlated to expenditures. However, managers should recognize that returns *will* come from a human resource approach—often in terms of improved marketability that attracts the "crème de la crème" of candidates for positions.

Stress Orientation and Training

The selection process should emphasize the importance the organization places on orientation and training. Orientation and training booklets should be available during interviews as one indication of the organization's commitment to human resource development. Training certificates and other performance awards should be clearly displayed to demonstrate that learning and good performance are recognized and rewarded.

Since the results of training are not always obvious, orientation and training should be promoted to guests as well as to future employees. Most guests are not trained in what to look for and may only see the superficial results of a costly training program. In addition, guests may not be aware of the complexity of the industry and that many positions require years of training to ensure competence. Pointing out the behind-the-scenes training that keeps the hospitality operation running smoothly builds interest and loyalty among guests and results in repeat clientele. The following Case in Point looks at a unique training program undertaken in a full-service hotel.

A Case in Point: Employees Train Guests

In one full-service hotel, employees participated in a guest relations program to promote the hotel and the expertise of the staff. The employees who participated were selected by the hotel's staff and management based on strict criteria for excellence in the performance of their day-to-day job responsibilities. On a courtesy basis, the employees conducted "training" sessions for in-house guests. These sessions were well attended, especially when the hotel was experiencing high occupancy from conference and convention groups that planned activities for spouses of the attendees.

A variety of classes were provided. The executive chef and several of the sous chefs conducted cooking classes. The hotel even invested in a demonstration unit for teaching cooking, complete with an overhead mirror to permit the audience to see the preparation steps more clearly. The servers from the dinner restaurant presented classes on tableside food preparation, and on the selection and service of wines. The beverage staff presented classes on the preparation of exotic drinks, both alcoholic and non-alcoholic. The sales staff presented classes on general sales techniques such as how to arrange appointment calls, how to make sales presentations, and how to close sales. All departments could participate in the program by proposing programs by their "master performers."

Each session was publicized in each guestroom. Guests were required to reserve a seat in the class. This made it possible for the banquet department to properly support the activity with the appropriate setup and refreshments. The general manager or an assigned member of the executive operating committee was always there to welcome the guests, to introduce the employee who would be the trainer, and to review the employee's background and training with the audience before the session began. Each attendee received a brief resume of the employee. The program emphasized the hotel's commitment to excellence and served as an internal incentive to support the ongoing training of staff.

Emphasize High Expectations

Every applicant should be informed from the start that the organization holds high expectations and that only those individuals who desire to meet those expectations will be selected. Employees must also realize that guests have high expectations and that these expectations must be accepted by each employee in order for the operation to be successful.

Expectations clarify appropriate behavior. Guests expect to find a supply of clean towels in the bathroom on a daily basis—which is perhaps a higher expectation than they have in their own homes. They expect hot food to be served hot and cold food to be served cold. They expect cocktails to be garnished with standard traditional garnishes unless they ask for something else—and in that case, they expect the garnish requested without any critical comments from the server or the bartender. Likewise, managers have a set of expectations that are influenced by their perception of what guests expect, and from their own schooling in the hospitality industry.

Emphasize Personal Accountability

It is reasonable to expect employees to be accountable for their personal behavior on the job. Applicants should be told during the selection process that hospitality is a people industry and that serving guests in a responsible manner is essential to success in *all* positions.

Individuals who have difficulty accepting responsibility for their actions and try to blame others for their personal failures should be screened out early. The cost of the human resource commitment needed to operate an organization known for its excellence in performance is too great to waste on individuals who are unwilling or unable to accept responsibility.

Promote a Culture of Excellence

Every operation in the hospitality industry has its own standards of performance. Various organizations have attempted to recognize operations that truly excel in performance with stars, diamonds, or some other designation.

Some operations have never been nor ever will be rated at the top or "five-star" level by any outside rating organization because their marketing plan does not place them within the type of operations considered by such organizations. That does not mean that the operation does not achieve excellence. The only way to rate performance is against goals and standards. The philosophy of the hiring company relative to excellence should be clearly communicated and marketed during the selection process.[4] Consider how the operation in the upcoming Case in Point achieves its own form of excellence.

A Case in Point: Excellent by Local Standards

Consistency and customer satisfaction are the very foundation of any rating of excellence. An independent restaurant in the Southeast demonstrates its own form of excellence through consistency. The restaurant specializes in pork barbecue, prepared by the old-fashioned pit-cooking method, seasoned with pepper-vinegar and finely chopped with a cleaver before service. The barbecue is served with an intentionally overcooked mixture called brunswick stew, paprika-seasoned boiled potatoes, cole slaw, and cornbread sticks which are first baked and then deep-fried. With the exception of the cole slaw, all the food is brown in color, and the meal is served on a brown, sectioned, plastic plate. The cole slaw is served in a side dish, family style for each table.

Why is this restaurant cited for its excellence? Because, for the past 14 years, the service and the food have never changed—the consistency is almost unbelievable.

The servers are young men and boys ranging in age from 16 to 25 years. They wear ordinary jeans, white gym shoes, and a white short-sleeved shirt as their "uniform." A white cook's towel hangs from the right hip pocket of each server and is used for wiping tables and other spills. Parties normally find their own tables as they enter the restaurant and sit at any station they please. During busy times like Sunday lunch, one of the owners stands at the entrance and points customers toward a cleared table. The bare-top tables are cleared between parties and wiped down with a wet cloth but are not reset. It is quite normal to sit down while a tabletop is still wet.

Within seconds of being seated, the server brings each person in the party a six-ounce paper cup of chilled water from the water cooler, plus a paper pouch containing a stainless fork and knife. A napkin dispenser is on each table, along with sugar, artificial sweetener, salt, pepper, bottled ketchup, hot-pepper vinegar, Tabasco sauce, and a laminated 5" by 8" menu card.

Since serving is always done from one corner of the table, the server places the water and flatware by reaching across or passing items to all members of the party. As soon as the server completes this task, he rests his order pad on the table and asks for the order. Most people order without looking at the menu because they have been to the restaurant so many times. First-time customers sometimes ask for explanations since the simple menu choices are listed as "Barbecue Plate," "Barbecue Dinner," "Small Combination Plate," or "Large Combination Plate." The servers explain what is included in each selection.

After taking the order, the server leaves the table, goes directly to the kitchen, and is usually back with the food in about three to five minutes. Only one or two menu items are cooked to order. Whenever customers select one of these choices, they are politely informed that there will be about a 15-minute delay. Food is always delivered to the customer's table on a full-size aluminum sheet baking pan. If coffee or iced tea is ordered, an extra pot or pitcher is delivered with the order so the customer can serve his/her own refills. Iced tea is very sweet and contains crushed ice. Soft drinks are served in the bottles, along with a glass of crushed ice. No alcoholic beverages are served.

The food is never garnished and is always the same. It looks the same, tastes the same, is the same temperature, and would rarely be rated as outstanding in taste or appearance. Most customers can name another barbecue restaurant in town that serves better food, but they still loyally return to this restaurant. It is clearly the highest volume barbecue restaurant in the area. In fact, at certain times during every week, people stand in line to get in. All types of people seem to enjoy the consistent predictability of this establishment; its market mix cuts across every economic and social segment of the community.

This restaurant has a clearly defined marketing plan which has probably never been written down. It is successful both financially and as a hospitality center for the community. In the past 14 years, the greatest change in the front-of-the-house operation occurred in early 1988 when the old wooden dining room chairs were replaced with a new style of wooden chair. The menu selections, the polished vinyl tile floors, the painted cinder block walls, the uncoordinated collection of framed prints of pigs and other farm scenes, and the casual warm friendliness of the owners and staff remain the same.

Excellence is not always doing things in a fancier way than others. It is doing what you set out to do in the most consistent manner possible to reach the goals and results you hoped to achieve. The restaurant described in the Case in Point achieves its own form of excellence and for that, it should be recognized and commended.

Live Up to Promises

There is a temptation when interviewing candidates for employment to oversell the opportunity. The interviewer may promise training and development activities which are not really planned for the position being filled. Making promises that cannot be kept once the person is hired can result in distrust and low morale for the new employee. Some promises may constitute contractual obligations—especially if they are made in written form or are witnessed by others. It is important to stick to the facts and to avoid making promises which will not be met.

Use of Job Analysis Tools

The job analysis tools discussed in Chapter 2 provide standards for conducting employee interviews. They also provide the basis for discussing the kinds of information that will be addressed in individual orientation and training sessions. If they exist at all, traditional job descriptions are too often filed away and rarely used. They become outdated or inadequate for selection, orientation, or training. The selection process should match people with jobs. The more clearly the job requirements are stated, the more effectively the interviewer can compare the applicant with them. The job analysis tools provide very specific information concerning job requirements.

Recruitment and Training

Recruitment and training are linked, since the objective of the recruitment effort should always be to identify trainable employees. The wording of help-wanted ads, the processing of applications, and the sincere execution of a promotion-from-within policy all communicate the operation's commitment to the development of people. Everyone likes to grow and develop. Most people who are looking for a new job are doing so because they are tired of what they have been doing. If all an ad communicates is that the new job will be the same as the old job, a person will have little or no incentive to make the change.

Dare to Be Different

One good way to plan a recruitment campaign is by reading the employment ads of competitors, as well as the recruitment ads of non-hospitality businesses. Which ads catch your attention, and which ones sound dull? Try to plan ads that communicate your standards of excellence and your commitment to people. If you believe that work is fun, and that employees who work in your operation should have a good time and develop strong friendships with co-workers, then that philosophy should be stressed in the employment ads.

Ads that state "no experience necessary, we will train you to do it our way" often belong to operators who recognize that the best way to have good people is to select people who want to learn, who have the ability to learn, and then to develop them according to the standards established for the operation. This is far different from the ads that specify "only experienced applicants should apply." What these ads reveal are organizations that are willing to accept the habits and standards set by someone else. The ads that specify "experience may be helpful, but we will train and develop you to meet our standards" are much more appealing to most people, even those applicants who have some experience.

Classified employment ads should be marketing-oriented. An example of a marketing-oriented classified ad for a hotel is shown in Exhibit 3.1.

The Selection Process

The selection process begins when an applicant arrives at the hospitality operation seeking a position. One of the first steps in that process is for the candidate to complete an application form.

The Application Form

Some applicants will provide a neatly typed or printed resume. Even if a candidate supplies a resume, it is a good idea to require the applicant to complete an application form for three reasons:

1. By completing the application form, the interviewer will be able to judge the applicant's handwriting skills, neatness, and accuracy, all of which may be important in the job being filled.

Exhibit 3.1   Sample Classified Advertisement

```
The Skyview Towers
555 Skyview Road

Exciting Hotel!
Beautiful Guestrooms!
Great Restaurants!
Striking Architecture!
Satisfied Guests!

The Best Employees in Town!

We have openings in several departments.
Drop by for a screening interview.

Mon.-Wed.-Fri.      2:00–4:00 p.m.

No experience required.
We will train you if you are selected.

Equal Opportunity Employer
```

2. Resume services are now available which will write a resume for an applicant. These resumes are intended to present the candidate in the best light, and tend to gloss over weaknesses while emphasizing strengths.

3. The application form should be designed for the needs of the employer. By securing a completed application, comparable information is obtained from all applicants for a position.

The information that the applicant provides on the application form helps the interviewer make efficient use of interview time. The interviewer can quickly scan this basic information and then concentrate on probing for information that will reveal attitudes about work and past work habits—both of which are helpful indicators of future performance and willingness to learn.

The Screening Interview   An application form should gather information that relates to the requirements of the job. A screening interview should be the first step in processing the application form. Even if no job opening exists at the time the application form is completed, a brief screening interview may be conducted to determine whether the application should be held in a "high potential" prospect file. A screening interview has four purposes:

1. It confirms the accuracy of the information supplied on the application form.

2. It determines the applicant's interest level in seeking a position.

3. It can be used to form some initial impressions of how the applicant might fit into the organization.

4. It provides an opportunity to emphasize the benefits and features of working for an organization that has a strong

commitment to the development of people, even if a vacancy does not exist at the moment.

Brief notes should be made and filed with the application for future reference when a job vacancy occurs. In large properties with a separate human resource department, screening interviews are routinely conducted by the staff in that department to maintain an active candidate file.

When an applicant is screened for possible employment and it is clear that the individual is not qualified for any position, the interviewer can save time by tactfully informing the applicant that he/she is not qualified. The job list, job breakdowns, and job performance standards should be on hand to specify the requirements of the job. The decision to say no should be based on an objective comparison of the job requirements and the applicant's capabilities and experience. It is important to tactfully end the process rather than to give the applicant false hope.

When the screening interview identifies someone who seems to be a qualified candidate, the individual should be told that the application will be kept on file and that he/she will be contacted when there is an opening. The applicant should also be told how the selection process will proceed in the case of an advertised opening. A second interview of high-potential applicants allows the interviewer to go into more depth and decide whether the applicant's background and potential match specific job requirements.

The Interview Process

Interviewing is an important aspect of the personnel development process. The way managers handle interviews can influence the attitudes of employees who are hired. Being able to screen out unqualified individuals is only one purpose of the interview. The most important concern is to select individuals who can make the greatest contribution to the objectives of the organization. According to one reference:

> Finding good employees is the primary objective of selection. Even though the final decision is in part a subjective one, the selection procedure can be systematized to make certain that all of the information helpful in making that decision has been collected.[5]

Even in organizations where a human resource department conducts the initial recruiting and screening, company policies should require that the position's supervisor interview all applicants who pass the initial screening before a job offer is made. The human resource department will sometimes rank and then send forward only the top candidates for a vacant position, thus saving time for the manager.

The Formal Interview. The goal of the formal interview process is to select trainable employees who will be able to contribute the most to the goals of the organization. For selection and training to go hand in hand, the interviewer in this case should be the manager who will be responsible for the new employee's training. Formal interviews for a vacant position should be conducted for each applicant who is judged eligible as a result of information gathered through the application form and the preliminary screening interview.

Interviews should be structured to gain the most information in the least amount of time. The interviewer must be prepared to ask pointed questions and to control the question and answer process to stay within the topics of importance. The applicant must be provided the opportunity to talk to reveal strengths and weaknesses in background and abilities. An interviewer who does not control the interview will waste time asking irrelevant questions or will allow the applicant to control the interview. This is likely to bias the discussion to the applicant's strengths while avoiding any discussion of weaknesses.

The interviewer should prepare for the session before the applicant arrives. This preparation should include selecting a place to conduct the interview in private, and reviewing the individual's application, the job analysis tools for the vacant position, and any other available information. A review of the job list and the set of job breakdowns for the position will help focus attention directly on the requirements of the job. The interviewer should also consider what specific personality traits and abilities are the most important for the person who will fill the position.

Once the applicant arrives, the interviewer should be friendly and engage in a limited amount of small talk to put the applicant at ease. The interviewer should then begin asking questions by reviewing the key information supplied on the application form. The manager should direct the interview in a methodical fashion, moving from the candidate's earliest work experience to his/her present employer. This enables the interviewer to see how the applicant grew and progressed.[6] The manager should then begin to probe for in-depth information about specific training, prior education, work experiences, and work attitudes. This information will help in assessing capabilities, competence, learning abilities, and attitudes that will be useful in planning the training if the person is hired.

Questions should be worded to encourage the applicant to talk about his/her strengths and weaknesses in specific areas of performance. The applicant should be asked to give very specific examples of how he/she handled various situations at work or school which are comparable to the situations which might arise in the new position. Four types of questions which are recommended for effective interviews include:[7]

1.   Open-ended (require a broad-based answer)

2.   Direct (require facts or yes/no answers)

3.   Probing (follow up to gain deeper understanding of facts)

4.   Hypothetical ("what if" questions)

By the end of the interview, the applicant should have talked more than 50% of the time. If this was not the case, the manager probably dominated the session and failed to get necessary information. While it is important to present the benefits and features of the position, overselling the job or the organization during the selection interview is a mistake. The purpose of the interview is to provide the applicant a structured opportunity to "sell" his/her capabilities. Interviewers should recognize there will be plenty of time to expound on the wonderful aspects of the work environment when it is clear that this is the right candidate for the position.

The purposes of the formal interview, in order of importance, are:

- To enable the manager to find out about the applicant

- To assess the applicant's *interest in* and *potential for* successful performance of the job

- To answer the applicant's questions

- To tell him/her about the job and the company

- To provide any other information which will help the applicant determine his/her interest in working for the company or operation

Examples of Interview Questions. The hardest part of interviewing is knowing what to ask and when to ask it. The order of questions is important because it will affect how much the applicant opens up and gives in-depth answers. The application form should provide the springboard for going from simple to more complex questions. The questions should begin with confirming factual information and then probe for deeper understanding of the facts (within guidelines for non-discriminatory interviewing). Then the interviewer should ask questions that go *one step further* into the applicant's personal feelings about past education, training, hobbies, leadership activities, and job experiences as they might relate to the current job opportunity and planned training.

Questions asked in a good interview should have the objective of determining work history, patterns of loyalty, success in previous endeavors, as well as attitudes toward work, other employees, and honesty. At best, interviewing is a subjective process. Answers have to be interpreted for specific information, shades of meanings, and attitudinal considerations. Practice improves the interviewing process, especially when each interview is planned in advance of the candidate's arrival.

Predicting Success in Selection

Attempts are sometimes made to design scoring devices for evaluating candidates and determining who should be hired. A score is assigned to each response; scores are then added or otherwise calculated by some weighted formula. When a candidate scores within acceptable parameters, he/she is selected for the position. This process is very difficult to set up and maintain because of the subjectivity of the interview process.

In reality, interviews should lead to a *prognosis* rather than a quantitative score. For example, a physician takes a blood pressure reading, a temperature reading, a pulse rate, and several other related but isolated assessments of health indicators. He/she does not assign a weighted score to each of these, sum them up, and then arrive at a health score. Rather, the physician considers each piece of data separately, and then combines all the data and makes an educated guess as to the condition of the patient. The guess is referred to as a prognosis.

A manager needs to feel comfortable about making a prognosis following the selection interview. Will the applicant be capable of performing the duties of this position at a level that is in line with the documented standards, following a reasonable period of orientation and training? If so, the person should be extended a job offer. If not, no offer should be made.

Overall, the interviewer should have more than 90% confidence in the applicant's ability to succeed or it will probably be a mistake to hire the individual. Granted, there are exceptions that could be cited, where a "late bloomer" who had somehow been held back from his/her full potential suddenly began to excel after a history of mediocre or unsatisfactory performance. Nevertheless, it is an unsound business decision to hire an individual in hopes that such a miracle will occur. It is better to consider the facts assembled through the interview process, make a prognosis that is as objective as possible, and go with the results of that decision.[8]

The best single indicator of how an employee will perform in the future is how that individual has performed in the past. A self-starter who has demonstrated personal goals of excellence in other walks of life will probably bring those attitudes into the job. If the applicant has no previous work history, school experiences are good indicators of performance. If the individual made good grades, participated in extracurricular activities, filled leadership positions, and had a variety of interests, it is generally safe to conclude that the person is self-motivated and capable of mastering the competencies required for most jobs.

Checking References

Reference checks of former employers should be a routine part of the selection process. Reference checks are sometimes performed by the human resource department on high-potential applicants before referring individuals to department managers for further interviews. In other cases, the departmental managers will conduct the reference checks since they are more familiar with the specific job duties and the areas which may be glossed over in the interview process.

Employers today are hesitant to voluntarily give negative information about former employees because of fear of lawsuits for defamation of character or invasion of privacy. Properly conducting reference checks requires good interviewing skills and a great deal of diplomacy.[9] With this in mind, reference checks should focus on:

- Confirming factual information in the application
- Emphasizing the positive abilities of the person

Normally, reference checks should be made after a formal interview indicates that the applicant appears to be a "finalist" for the position. In order to obtain useful information concerning past training or work habits, it is advisable to contact the former supervisor. If an individual is still employed but is looking for another position, he/she may request that the present employer not be contacted since it might jeopardize job security. Such a request should be honored and other references contacted to determine as much as possible about past performance.

The reference check can reveal favorable or unfavorable information about prior training and work performance that did not come out in the formal interviews. Conflicting information concerning such matters as the length of time worked and whether the person would be considered for rehire give clues to job stability and performance. All clues to hidden background information should be followed up directly with the applicant before making a decision to hire.

Most former employers will *verify* information pertaining to an applicant's employment with their organization—especially when the applicant has given permission for the reference to be checked. If the applicant has provided false or misleading information concerning his/her employment experience, most former employers will want to "set the record straight," provided they feel that they can do so without placing themselves in a libelous position. If the reference check includes verifying information from documented records, the former employer may state, "that information is inconsistent with our records on Mr. Smith," thus indicating the need to recheck that information with the applicant.

It is essential not to reveal the sources of negative information to other former employers *or* to the applicant. Also, this information should not be recorded on the documents which will become part of the applicant's human resource file if he/she is hired. Such information could be mishandled by someone who does not have all the facts and could be potentially damaging to the reputation of the employee. If the negative information results in the applicant being unsuitable for the position for which he/she has applied, it is sufficient to note in the file that "the individual was not qualified for the position due to information revealed in reference checks."

The human resource staff and managers who are conducting the selection process and checking references should never tell an applicant that he/she was turned down for a position because "his/her references did not check out." It is sufficient to state that "someone more qualified was selected for the position" or that the applicant did not meet the "specific requirements for the position." Employers are never obligated to tell applicants all their reasons for not extending a job offer. However, it is essential that the decision not to hire an applicant is not related to discriminatory factors specified by law.

Selection Tests   Selection tests are controversial in the field of human resource management. Caution must be used in giving written aptitude, attitude, or psychological tests. In some cases, the courts have ruled that such tests discriminate against minorities because of language and environmental biases. Also, it may be difficult or impossible to show a direct relationship between test scores and job performance. Therefore, before administering such tests as a screening procedure, employers should confer with their organization's legal counsel.

Performance tests are acceptable if the applicant is required to perform job duties for areas in which he/she claims prior experience or for areas that will be part of the job. An applicant for a cook's or chef's position can be required to go into the kitchen and produce selected foods that are typical of the operation's menu. Clerical and secretarial applicants may be required to take a typing or word processing skill or speed test. This process provides the opportunity to judge skill level, technique, neatness, and organizational abilities. Without the performance test, the manager must generally rely on the applicant's explanation of his/her ability to execute these essential skills; sometimes there may be a great difference between that perception and actual ability. In all cases, managers should ensure that any selection test is completely appropriate to use for the position under consideration.

The Decision to Hire   The application form, interview, and reference checks provide the basis for assessing the qualifications of the applicant. If the candidate is from within the operation, managers already have had an opportunity to observe his/her job performance. The candidate's human resource file will provide further information concerning the individual's work history. The final selection decision should be made by department management, with the approval of upper management—not by the human resource department alone.[10]

After all the applicants have been interviewed, the manager must consider each applicant's ability against the requirements of the job in order to make a selection decision. The applicant who is selected should be notified immediately. It is recommended that all job offers be made in writing, or if made over the phone, be confirmed to the applicant in writing. Such notification communicates a sense of professionalism and also provides a permanent record of the terms of the offer. It should cover information such as starting date and time, beginning wages, wages following initial training, performance review dates, probationary periods, policies concerning progressive discipline, the name and phone number of the new hire's immediate supervisor, and an overview of the plan for orientation and training that will take place during the first few days and weeks of employment.

It is also good public relations to notify other applicants that someone else was selected. This notification can be in the form of a postcard or letter, and should clearly thank the applicant for his/her interest in the position. The only reason that should be given for not hiring the applicant is that "someone more qualified was selected."

The Orientation Process

New employees should be given a thorough orientation that begins the first day they arrive for work.[11] Many new employees arrive with a great deal of enthusiasm about their position; this presents an ideal opportunity for the operation to instill pride in the organization and its goals.

Orientation should usually be conducted at two distinct levels: the *general level* and the *departmental or job level*. At the first level, topics of relevance are presented to all employees; at the second, topics are described that are unique to the new employee's specific department and job.[12]

There are operating rules and policies that affect all employees in every organization. The orientation session is the appropriate time to cover these matters so that the employee will not unknowingly break a rule and be embarrassed because of the mistake. Orientation should include at least the following types of information:

1. **The company**—its history, present size, scope, key management or executives, plans for growth, marketing emphasis, and company policies.

2. **The benefits**—wages, payroll procedures, timekeeping procedures, insurance, employee discounts, vacations, paid holidays, employee lockers, and uniforms.

3. **The hospitality operation**—reputation for service, type of guests, names of key management personnel, hours of operation, sales collateral, public outlets, menus, a tour of the facilities, etc.

4. **The position**—what the new employee's job consists of, how it fits into the total organization of the operation, performance standards, and what will be expected of the employee.

5. **The working conditions**—training schedule, training materials and booklets, performance reviews, probationary period, work schedule, breaks, meal periods, overtime, safety, security, and social activities. (Any necessary tools should be made available.)

6. **The work group**—introductions to fellow employees within the new employee's department, explanation of key responsibilities of positions within the department, and who reports to whom in the operation's hierarchy.

7. **The rules and regulations**—regarding, for example, smoking, entry and exit, disciplinary action, parking, etc.

8. **Emergency situations**—location and use of fire suppression equipment, evacuation procedures, safety committee roles, individual responsibilities for safety, emergency plan assignments, etc.

Time should be set aside on the first day to complete all tax withholding, insurance, and similar forms. If a uniform or locker is to be provided, it should be ready for the new employee. As indicated, a tour of the facility is in order. At this time, the manager can introduce the new employee to fellow workers. During the tour, it is important to point out cleaning standards, guest amenities, safety and emergency equipment, and any off-limits areas for this particular employee.

Some operations develop employee manuals or handbooks which highlight many of the preceding concerns. If a manual or handbook is available, it should be provided to the employee during orientation. It is not sufficient to give the new employee the handbook, tell him/her to read it, and then to consider that orientation has been completed. Even new management personnel need personal orientations their first day on the job.

When the orientation is completed, the person conducting the orientation and the new employee should complete an orientation checklist. This checklist documents when orientation took place and what matters were covered (see Exhibit 3.2). After completion, the checklist should become a permanent part of the new employee's human resource file. Management then has a record of the rules, policies, and procedures that were covered with the employee should there ever be any questions.

If the new employee is to be involved in an ongoing training program for new staff members conducted by someone other than his/her immediate supervisor or department head, it is appropriate to introduce the employee to the person responsible for this activity. The importance of training should be communicated throughout the selection and orientation process.

A well-planned and organized orientation will help a new employee get off to a good start in a new job. The orientation communicates to the employee the feeling that management cares. If this attitude is also conveyed in training and in performance evaluation, the employee will develop positive attitudes and is likely to become a productive worker. Employees need to know that their presence in the organization is important and that their performance makes a positive contribution to organizational goals. As one authority observes:

> All employees need orientation. Everyone likes to feel important. The orientation meeting is the official welcome from the company. It should be conducted with warmth and understanding. The first days on the job are filled with doubts and fears. New employees need assurance, confidence, and a nudge in the right direction until they find their own way.
>
> The ideal orientation program gives new employees confidence and pride in themselves and in the company they work for. It makes them feel part of the company team. The meeting, properly handled, is hardly ever forgotten by the employees.[13]

Managers should encourage new employees to become involved in the organization from the very start, and to ask questions whenever they do not understand something. The first days on a new job are filled with anxiety and excitement for most employees. The employee feels like a stranger in an unfamiliar environment and wonders whether co-workers will help him/her to succeed or will make the job more difficult.

The employee's immediate supervisor should take full responsibility for the departmental orientation process, and do everything practical to convince the new employee that everyone is seriously interested in his/her success. The goal of orientation is to make the transition into the new job as smooth as possible. The orientation process should include some time for the supervisor and the employee to discuss events as they occur over the first few days. After the initial orientation, the supervisor should maintain close contact with the new employee and answer any questions that may arise. The orientation, when properly planned and professionally conducted, provides a firm foundation upon which to launch the individualized training for the new employee.

Exhibit 3.2 Sample Orientation Checklist

Orientation Checklist

____ Welcome to the new employee

____ History of the organization

____ What we will expect from each employee

____ What employees can expect from us

____ Our philosophy of guest relations

____ Organizational structure of the company

____ Organizational structure of the operation

____ Payroll and timekeeping procedures

____ Gratuities and tip reporting

____ Wage rates, raises, and incentive pay

____ Work schedules, breaks, and meal periods

____ Meals and employee discounts in outlets

____ Uniforms and dress code

____ Locker, lock, and employee dressing area

____ Probationary period

____ Performance reviews

____ Progressive discipline

____ Employee rules of conduct

____ Grounds for dismissal

____ Promotions and transfers

____ Breakage, unintentional loss, and errors

____ Housekeeping and sanitation

____ Safety and emergency procedures

____ Loss prevention and risk management

____ Holidays, vacation, and sick leave

____ Excused absences and special leaves

____ Employee insurance benefits

____ Tuition reimbursement benefits

____ Employee of the month

____ Staff relationships, nepotism, and dating

____ Personnel appeals procedures

____ Training, coaching, and evaluation

____ Induction paperwork

All the above topics were covered with me and I was encouraged to ask questions to ensure full understanding. I feel that I have a basic understanding of each of the topics that I have initialed. I agree to abide by all policies and employee rules covered in this orientation.

Signed _____ Date _____

Conducted by _____

_____

Notes

1. Robert L. Desatnick, "Building the Customer-Oriented Work Force," *Training and Development Journal*, Vol. 41, No. 3, March 1987, pp. 72–74.

2. It is not the purpose of this chapter to cover everything that might be discussed in administering a complete human resource program. Readers interested in more detailed information are referred to David R. Wheelhouse, *Managing Human Resources in the Hospitality Industry* (East Lansing, Mich.: Educational Institute of the American Hotel & Motel Association, 1989).

3. For a more complete discussion of how to control turnover, see *Reducing Employee Turnover* (East Lansing, Mich.: Educational Institute of the American Hotel & Motel Association, 1982).

4. Recommended references on the pursuit of excellence include Thomas J. Peters and Robert H. Waterman, Jr., *In Search of Excellence: Lessons from America's Best-Run Companies* (New York: Harper & Row, 1982); and Thomas J. Peters and Nancy K. Austin, *A Passion for Excellence: The Leadership Difference* (New York: Random House, 1985).

5. Jerome J. Vallen and James R. Abbey, *The Art and Science of Hospitality Management* (East Lansing, Mich.: The Educational Institute of the American Hotel & Motel Association, 1987), p. 187.

6. William T. Leonard, "The Employment Interview," in *Handbook of Human Resource Administration,* 2nd ed., edited by Joseph J. Famularo (New York: McGraw-Hill, 1986), p. 14-5.

7. Leonard, pp. 14-6–14-7.

8. Leonard, p. 14-5.

9. Robert L. LoPresto, "Recruitment Sources and Techniques," in *Handbook of Human Resource Administration,* 2nd ed., edited by Joseph J. Famularo (New York: McGraw-Hill, 1986), p. 13-23.

10. LoPresto, p. 13-25.

11. Joan P. Holland and Beverly W. George, "Orientation of New Employees," in *Handbook of Human Resource Administration,* 2nd ed., edited by Joseph J. Famularo (New York: McGraw-Hill, 1986), pp. 24-1–24-35.

12. Lloyd L. Byars and Leslie W. Rue, *Human Resource Management,* 2nd ed. (Homewood, Ill.: Irwin, 1987), p. 193.

13. Holland and George, p. 24-26.

Part II

Training Methods

4 Principles and Concepts of Learning

For the purpose of this book, **training** is defined as any activity that results in learning. It seems important, then, to consider exactly what learning is and what trainers can do to positively influence it. There is considerable disagreement over which theory best explains how learning occurs. There is, however, a consensus on the definition of learning and the goals of a learning process.

It is not within the scope of this book to attempt an exhaustive review of the many learning theories available. Rather, this book addresses the need to incorporate adult learning principles into the process of planning and implementing training programs. To facilitate that process, some principles of learning are reviewed.

Most employees (and, therefore, trainees) in the hospitality industry are adults. Every trainer has been influenced greatly by the way he/she was taught as a child. The trainer's beliefs and past experiences concerning learning may need to be modified when making plans for teaching adults. The effectiveness of employee training programs is affected by the extent to which basic principles of adult learning are recognized and applied.

What Is Learning?

Learning is essentially the acquisition of knowledge, skills, or attitudes. In other words, if people perform differently after formal training, and their revised activity conforms to the training objectives, learning is said to have taken place. Learning can also be defined as a change or modification in behavior resulting from factors in an individual's environment or situation.[1] In this sense, if a planned or unplanned life experience leads to a lasting change or modification of behavior, then the experience is said to be a "learning experience."

Defining Reinforcement

A concept that is widely used in teaching and learning is **reinforcement.** Trainers must learn how to use reinforcement to effectively bring about desired performance responses. Reinforcement is an action that occurs in close proximity to a behavioral response and, when associated with the response, has a tendency to either:

- strengthen the probability of the response being repeated, or

- strengthen the intensity of the response.[2]

Reinforcement can be either positive or negative. **Positive reinforcement** is simply a reward for performing in the desired manner. In a management sense, positive reinforcement consists of supportive feedback and incentives which employees receive when their performance meets the desired standards.

The easiest reward that a manager can use to reinforce learning is **recognition.** Recognition may be verbal, non-verbal, public, or private. It may be in the form of an approving smile, a pat on the back, a monetary bonus, or public recognition such as "employee of the month." Training can also serve as a form of recognition. As one authority observes:

> Whether the purpose of training is to develop, maintain, strengthen, or improve performance, training itself can be a reward. It is recognition of an employee's potential and the chance for expanded growth.[3]

Positive reinforcement should be used when predictable behavior is desired. Whenever a manager routinely observes the performance of his/her staff and consistently gives supportive feedback, the employees will do the right things more often and will continually seek higher levels of excellence.

Managers can also give positive reinforcement in more formal ways by offering bonus programs or other tangible incentives. For such programs to be effective, the rewards must be perceived by the employees as desirable and of real value—and they must be clearly associated with the behaviors that the manager wants repeated. Whenever the perceived value of reinforcement diminishes, the response being reinforced will also weaken in intensity and be less likely to occur in the future.

While positive reinforcement may be viewed as a reward for correct performance, **negative reinforcement** may be seen as a negative response to the learner's performance. Negative reinforcement may consist of threats, punishment, or the withholding of recognition. This type of reinforcement is often used by managers who believe that employees will perform in the desired way to avoid these negative consequences. In some situations, negative reinforcement can encourage desired behaviors—particularly in the absence of positive reinforcement. However, the outcome of negative reinforcement is very unpredictable. Negative feedback is very likely to lead to undesirable behavior and may even reinforce unacceptable behavior through the creation of rebellious attitudes. Managers who are pursuing excellence should avoid using negative reinforcement. Better results will always be achieved through the consistent use of positive reinforcement.

Probability of Repeat Behavior

When an employee demonstrates a desired behavior and receives positive reinforcement, there is generally a high probability that this behavior will be repeated in the same or similar situations. Consider, for example, the case of a receptionist. A desired behavior for this employee is to respond to the guest with a smile and appropriate greeting at the front desk. In turn, the guest is likely to *reinforce* the response by returning the smile, complimenting the receptionist for the pleasant greeting, and continuing to communicate in a cooperative manner. The positive response of the guest has reinforced the behavior of the employee. The employee is likely to behave toward other guests in a similar manner and to expect a similar reinforcing response.

Training is considered effective when learning occurs; learning is considered to have occurred when there is a high probability that the desired behavior will be repeated in similar situations. The degree to which the employee responds appropriately to similar situations which were not actually covered in the training is referred to as **transfer of learning.** This type of learning is a very desirable outcome of an effective training effort.[4]

The manager who is involved in training wants to establish desirable behaviors so that they become predictable work habits requiring little thought on the part of the employee. To develop this degree of behavioral predictability through training and coaching, effective positive reinforcement must be used over and over again.

If reinforcement is used consistently, strong response patterns can be developed that are lasting and resistant to change. In practice, there are two elements that affect the relationship between reinforcement and response strength: (1) the frequency of reinforcement and (2) the time between response and reinforcement.

Frequency of Reinforcement. The more times that an appropriate behavior is followed by positive reinforcement, the stronger the response will become—and the more difficult it will become to change the response. The greatest increase in response strength occurs when the first reinforcement is received. When only one form of reinforcement is used repeatedly, each successive reward strengthens the response less and less; after many repetitions, little strength is added. This reduction in value can be overcome by using different forms of reinforcement.

Since positively reinforced behaviors are more likely to be repeated, it would seem that every correct behavior should be rewarded in some manner. This, however, would be highly impractical. It would be equally impractical to give reinforcement on a fixed time basis such as every three minutes, ten minutes, or half hour. It would also be impractical to reinforce on a fixed schedule—that is, after every third, fifth, or tenth occurrence of a behavior. Fortunately, reinforcement is more effective when it is not used on such a completely predictable basis.

Experts recommend reinforcing behavior on a variable time basis to achieve the highest level of learning and retention.[5] If the employee cannot predict the exact time that the manager will reinforce a correct behavior, his/her performance will be rather stable to increase the likelihood of being found performing according to established standards. In the same way, when the employee does not know the exact number of correct responses necessary for reinforcement, there is a tendency to work with more speed and consistency to achieve and maintain the standards.

Time Between Response and Reinforcement. The trainee must be able to associate the reward with a specific behavior in order for that response to be strengthened. The shorter the time between the desired behavior and the reinforcement, the greater the strength of the response. Conversely, the longer the time between the desired behavior and the reinforcement, the less the strength of the response. The following Case in Point looks at potential problems associated with delayed reinforcement.

A Case in Point: Delayed Reinforcement

A receptionist was busy working at the front desk of a hotel, checking in guests during the evening shift. A gentleman approached the desk and, without any show of emotion, stated his name and indicated that he had a reservation. The receptionist warmly greeted the guest, welcomed him to the hotel, and quickly located the reservation record. Without any delay, the receptionist confirmed the details of the reservation, established the guest's credit with his credit card, assigned a room, signaled the bellperson for assistance with the guest's luggage, wished the guest a pleasant stay and a good evening—all within less than two minutes. Meanwhile, the guest stood solemnly throughout the procedure and barely grunted his responses to each of the receptionist's efforts to elicit a smile. As the guest dutifully followed the bellperson to the elevator, the receptionist felt as though she had done something wrong since she had not been able to get any indication that the guest felt properly welcomed.

About two hours later, the guest entered the lobby and passed by the desk on the way to the restaurant. As he passed, he turned to the same receptionist, smiled warmly, and said, "Hi Mary, thanks for the help on check-in. You really know your job." Mary was baffled. For the past two hours her overall performance had been affected by her inability to reach this guest with her efforts at hospitality. Now she was concerned as to whether her preoccupation with this guest had been evident in her communications with the other 20 or more guests she had checked in. As she thought about the situation, she realized that her entire evening would have been so much better if she had received a warm response from this guest when she was checking him in.

In this case, the employee expected the reinforcement to come from the guest when she exhibited the appropriate behavior. When it did not, it affected her overall performance. If the manager had been present and observed this scenario, he/she could have complimented the employee on her excellent check-in performance and commented that this guest was preoccupied, extremely tired, or perhaps a very disagreeable fellow. Mary's concerns about her performance would have been eased had she heard at the right time that she had done her job well.

Reinforcement is needed to maintain high standards. Managers should always be alert to the ever-present need of employees to receive a steady diet of rewards for their hard work and good performance. Reinforcement promotes learning and good work habits, and helps excellence become a reality.

Behavior Modification The practical application of positive reinforcement techniques in the workplace, in schools, and in other non-laboratory settings to bring about desired performance is often referred to as **behavior modification.** Training should always focus on how behavior can be analyzed and how employee behavior can be reinforced when it meets training and performance goals. The result is that behavior is modified or shaped to be consistent with the mission and performance standards of the organization.

People learn through the use of five senses—seeing, hearing, feeling, tasting, and smelling. The senses are the channels through which information is received by the brain. A trainer has objectives which describe how the trainee should behave after his/her senses are stimulated in the learning process. The chances of learning taking place are better if as many senses as possible are stimulated.

When telling someone about a particular method or procedure, the trainer is using only the sense of *hearing*. When the trainer combines *hearing* with *seeing*—through the use of colorful visual aids, vivid demonstrations, active participation, and dramatic presentations—there is an even greater chance of effective learning taking place. For example, an individual can learn something about cooking by *listening* to an audio recording of a culinary lecture. He/she can learn more from *seeing* a demonstration about cooking on a video monitor, along with the audio recording of the lecture. Learning will be further enhanced if the individual has the raw materials at hand, and can *feel* the texture of the ingredients, *see* what they look like, *smell* their aromas, *taste* their flavors, and *hear* the sounds of cooking.

Trainers should be aware that all behaviors are the result of sensory responses to stimuli. With this in mind, a trainer can help employees consider how to respond appropriately in order to meet the organization's goals and performance standards. In behavior modification, the emphasis should be placed on the probability that the desired behavior will occur. One measure of employee competence is the consistency with which an employee responds in an approved way to the work situations.

Adult Learning Principles

What must the manager know about teaching adults in order to effectively train them? What basic learning/training/teaching concepts should be incorporated into the training efforts? Trainers tend to teach as they have been taught. The formative years of most adults were spent in a school environment where they were passive learners, closely controlled by the teachers. In training adults, it is important to know that adults want to be treated as adults—not as children. Trainers should be aware of the following concepts that affect the adult learning process.

The Desire to Learn First, adults must want to learn or they will reject the instruction as a waste of their time. Children will do a certain amount of learning in response to external requirements. They will, for example, take a course simply because they are told to or because it may be required. The desire to make good grades or the fear of failing will induce some children to work hard to master subjects which do not appeal to their interests. Adults are less affected by such factors as threats, grades, or even the fear of failure. They must feel a personal desire to master the new behaviors because they see how the learning will benefit them in a personal way.

Adults will usually resist learning anything merely because someone says they should. They learn most effectively when they have a strong inner motivation to develop a new skill or to acquire a particular type of knowledge. They must be ready to learn. It is seldom effective to force training upon adults without explaining, defending, and justifying the need for training and how it will be of benefit to them. This means that it is often a waste of time to push employees into required training courses. Managers can require all the employees to participate in training that is designed to improve their knowledge, skills, or attitudes, but the employees who master the training first and at the highest levels of performance will probably be those who would have volunteered for the training.

Trainers need to demonstrate the benefits to be derived from training. If this is done—and if the training experiences are interesting and challenging—trainee attitudes may be modified. This can result in a desire to learn that replaces a passive disinterest in the training being presented.

The Need to Learn

Second, adults will learn only when they feel a need to learn. Children can be induced to learn many things for which they can see no immediate use. Long-range goals, such as preparing for the future or being accepted at a good college, are often sufficient motivators to keep youngsters studying courses in which they have no immediate interest.

Adults, however, are much more practical in their approach to learning. They want to know, "How is this going to help me right now?" Sometimes they can be persuaded to learn things that will help them in the future—such as when a promotion is pending. However, adults learn best when they expect to get immediate benefits and when the knowledge or skills they are trying to acquire will be directly useful in meeting a present responsibility.

Training is sometimes resisted because of this interest in practical, short-range benefits. Adults usually aren't satisfied with assurances that they will eventually learn something useful from a course of study. They expect results from the first session and from each additional element of the training. Adults have little patience with a trainer when the trainer insists on providing a lot of preliminary background, theory, or historical review before getting down to the topic at hand.

If a trainer wants adults to learn, he/she must teach them concisely and directly. Adults want the trainer to say: "This is what you do; this is how you do it; and this is why it works." If adults decide that the training has no relevance to their personal needs, they will probably drop out—physically if the training is voluntary, mentally if attendance is required.

Learning By Doing

Third, adults learn best by doing. Active participation in the learning process is essential for adults. People will forget much more of what they learn passively (reading a book, listening to a series of lectures) than what they learn actively. Learning is much faster and retention is much higher when adults have immediate and repeated opportunities to participate in the learning process and to practice using what they are expected to learn.

Practicing some skills will cost money. For example, a chef might argue that the operation cannot afford the luxury of trainees practicing because it would "upset the food cost." The chef could easily become frustrated over how to bridge the gap between the demonstration of the correct procedure and the trainees' mastery of the skill. In the chef's mind, it may not be possible to justify wasting expensive ingredients that the trainees might ruin. As a result, the chef will probably have little success in developing a competent staff. Practice may cost something, but it is essential to developing competence.

A Realistic Focus   Fourth, adult learning must focus on realistic problems. Adults respond well to being taught a general rule or principle and then being shown how the principle applies to specific situations. Adults will learn best if training begins with specific problems drawn from business experiences, and if they are allowed to solve the problems and identify for themselves the principles they learned from the problem-solving exercise. The trainees can then use the principles to resolve other problems in similar situations.

The importance of realism in adult training cannot be over-emphasized. Many adults simply will not bother to figure out a problem which is clearly contrived for training purposes. When any situation differs from their experience, they assume that it is a "pretend" situation which could not occur in the real world. Adult interest in training increases when it is built around real, rather than pretend, problems.

Relating Learning to Experience   Fifth, experience affects adult learning. A big difference between adults and children as learners is that adults have had a lot more experience with life. This can be an asset, but it can also be a liability.

Adult learning must be related to, and integrated with, the accumulated results of a lifetime of learning experience. If the new knowledge does not fit in with what the adults already know, the knowledge will probably be rejected. In fact, past experiences may actually prevent the adult from absorbing the meaning of newly presented information or from perceiving it accurately. For this reason, adults must be given every opportunity to interrupt, to ask questions, or to disagree with the trainer. Through give-and-take, the trainer can determine the experience of the trainees and the viewpoints they have acquired. Then the skillful trainer can present new ideas in such a way that the adults' experiences will reinforce, rather than contradict, the new information being presented.

An Informal Environment   Sixth, adults learn best in an informal environment. Efforts by the trainer to treat trainees like school children or to "manage the classroom" will be met with resistance. Adults want the classroom to be orderly, but they also appreciate an informal environment. If the training occurs away from job stations, trainees may expect permission to smoke, to use their own judgment about whether to take notes, and to otherwise exercise privileges which they may not have back at their work stations.

Managers will find their leadership and training roles much easier and more pleasant if they deal with employees as *professional colleagues* rather than as *subordinates*. Staff members often act as they think their supervisor expects them to act. If they believe that they are expected to be immature and childish, then they may well act that way. Frequently, this response to expectations is not a conscious response. It just seems to happen. When managers treat employees like colleagues and expect them to assume adult responsibilities, employees are more receptive to achieving organizational goals.

A Variety of Methods

Seventh, a variety of methods should be used when teaching adults. Learning occurs most quickly when information reaches the learner through more than one sensory channel. A demonstration, movie, filmstrip, flip chart, or other audiovisual aids can do much to heighten the impact of a training presentation.

In addition to reaching trainees through different communication channels, there are other considerations in using a variety of methods when teaching adults. The methods should be selected by considering exactly what the trainer wants to accomplish. If the main purpose of training is to bring about a change in the trainee's conduct, attitudes, or ideas, then the trainee must be actively involved in the process. In this case, a participation method must be used.

Other methods may be practical if factual knowledge is the desired result. In any instance, procedures which enable the trainer to say the same thing in different ways should be used. Likewise, it is advisable that the trainee be an active participant in the training session rather than a passive observer. Consider, for example, the effect that a participatory approach has on the trainee's viewpoint in the following Case in Point.

A Case in Point: Learning from a Master Performer

In a two-week workshop for managers of public school cafeterias, one of the classes focused on how to make soft yeast rolls with the flour supplied through the government surplus commodity program. Many participants were convinced that the commodity flour was inferior in quality to the name-brand flour they could purchase if they were not "forced" to use the surplus flour.

The instructor for the course was a university professor whose specialty was food service management. He also taught basic, advanced, and quantity food preparation. In his teaching at the university, he had been using name-brand flour and had no firsthand experience with surplus commodities.

After discussing the quality of the commodity flour with the school food service supervisors, the instructor was convinced that the flour was not the problem. The difficulty was that many employees were prejudiced against the non-labeled product. By informally talking with the supervisors and other participants, the instructor also learned that one of the cafeteria managers was known for her outstanding soft rolls.

The strongest critics of the surplus flour insisted that she was really using name-brand flour or was mixing name-brand flour with the surplus flour. She assured the instructor that she was only using the surplus flour and was following the standard recipe supplied by the school food service system. The instructor decided to have this successful manager teach the lab session on soft rolls rather than teach it himself.

The session started with the manager opening a new bag of the surplus flour in view of all of the students. Several students made derogatory comments about the flour. Then she proceeded to demonstrate how she made her wonderful rolls. Each student had a handout copy of the standard recipe to verify her procedures and ingredients. The rolls she baked were outstanding. Everyone had the chance to enjoy them hot from the oven, buttered with a generous portion of surplus-commodity butter.

Some of the critics of the commodity flour were visibly shaken in their position and agreed that the problem might be the baker or the technique, rather than the quality of the ingredients. A few began to blame the humidity of the climate for their lack of success with the flour. Others blamed it on their kitchen equipment.

Following the demonstration, all of the students were required to prepare a batch of soft rolls using the commodity flour and following the standard recipe. The results were not all the same, but the differences were due to differences in the baking skills of the trainees.

Behavior is not easy to change in adults. In the preceding case, a sizable percentage of the learners experienced a change in attitude due to the high degree of realism during instruction, the actual participation in the learning process, and the reinforcement received during the preparation, baking, and consumption of the delicious rolls.

Guidance, Not Grades

Eighth, adults want guidance, not grades. Competition may be an incentive for academic achievement among children, but this is generally not true among adults. Some adults are apprehensive about their learning capacity since they have been out of school for some time. If they are confronted with tests, grades, and other devices for comparative evaluation of their progress, they may withdraw from the entire experience for fear of being humiliated.

At the same time, adult learners want to know how well they are doing. Before they continue learning, adults need to know whether they are learning correctly, if they are performing correctly, and how well they understand the basic ideas. Adults tend to set exacting goals for themselves; often they are impatient with their errors and become easily discouraged about their ability to learn. They need as much praise as the trainer can honestly give them. If it is absolutely necessary to criticize an adult learner, the criticism should be constructive and given privately, in a pleasant and helpful manner.

Factors Affecting the Learning Process

People are individuals and, as such, they learn at different speeds, in different ways, and have different levels and types of abilities as well as different needs. Their backgrounds differ in terms of capabilities and life experiences.

An adult learning activity will not always guarantee the desired changes in behavior. Trainers should realize that just because people are adults doesn't mean that they will automatically be good learners. Trainers should also recognize that adults will not always be motivated to learn—even when the training focuses on their job. Training programs must have the flexibility to accommodate the individual differences of all participants. An important step toward dealing with individual differences is to be aware of some basic factors that affect the learning process.

Interest Level

A good trainer should pay close attention to the trainees. The trainer must watch and listen to the trainees and attempt to gauge their level of interest and responsiveness. If the trainees seem uninterested and bored, or if they reject the training, the trainer should attempt to regain interest by discussing the goals and objectives of the training.

Understanding the Reasons

People learn faster when they understand the correct methods and the reasons behind them. Failure to understand why a particular procedure is important will block the trainee from paying attention to all the details.

Employees will not respond favorably to training if the only reason given is "because the manager says you must." Adults demand a certain amount of respect in learning. They learn what makes sense to them, what they want to learn, and what they are convinced they need to know.

Attention Span

People learn best, and remember longer, when the presentation or training activity does not exceed their span of attention. Therefore, as the length of training time increases, trainers must use a variety of techniques to keep renewing interest. In spite of the creativity of the trainer, there will still be a point of diminishing returns beyond which learning efficiency is no longer achieved. Learning must be efficient for training to be effective.

Sometimes managers think they cannot afford to allocate time for training. When they do schedule a training session, they feel they have to cover everything in one session. After the session, they become frustrated because employees do not apply much of the knowledge, skills, and attitudes that were stressed during the training. One reason for the lack of application may be that too much was covered at one time. The training should be broken up into short sessions that focus on a few skill or knowledge areas. Then, the next training session can build on what was learned in the first session, and the employees can gain experience practicing what they have learned.

People learn best when the training is spaced. For example, four one-hour sessions are usually better than one four-hour session. An exception to this principle is made when a specific learning objective requires intensive experience. For example, culinary training that teaches the technique of braising cannot be completed in one hour, as most braised meats require two or more hours of cooking time. Breaks can be used to help refresh the trainee as training time increases.

Sequence of Instruction

In skill areas, trainees learn best when the training is sequenced from the simple to the complex. In problem-solving areas, sequencing is dependent on the learning styles of the trainees. Trainees should be permitted to have a say in arranging the sequence, and should be given opportunities to learn from their mistakes.

People learn procedural skills best when steps are presented in a consecutive manner. For example, front desk employees should know about room types and rates before they learn how to register a guest or how to prepare guest accounts. The trainer can ensure progress by making each step easy to master, easy to complete, and worthwhile. The job analysis process provides a means for arranging training steps in a logical order based on the way the work is actually performed and on the increasing level of difficulty.

It helps the trainee when he/she is shown an entire duty before it is broken down into its smaller parts. Elements of any job responsibility should be practiced separately only after the individual has a feel for the whole task. After showing the trainee a complete duty, the trainer should then break it down and begin training with simple steps. The trainee should learn the basic steps before the more complex variations.

Individualized Learning Rates

People learn at different rates of speed. When faced with a new task, people will usually start by making rapid progress, then move into a period when little or no progress is made. Sometimes trainees actually regress during this leveling-off period. This is very common when trainees are learning tasks or the steps in a job. They may temporarily forget what was learned or perform more slowly than when they first began.

Trainees usually accelerate again and make further progress. During training, it is advisable to have individuals improve their own performance rather than to gauge it against other trainees. Competition between trainees may lead to conflict and reduced learning.

Some trainees will learn faster than others. When a trainee is slow, the trainer should be patient and attempt to determine the cause so that the trainee can be helped. If the trainee suspects that the trainer is impatient or irritated, his/her confidence can be destroyed and progress will be slowed even more.

Learning takes time for many employees. Sometimes trainers fail to remember that employees may not have the same background, education, or experience that they do—and may attempt to teach too much too fast. Employees should be allowed time to grasp the concepts and skills before moving on. The time spent in training will be repaid many times when employee performance improves.

Accuracy Before Speed

People remember best what they learn first. If errors are made in acquiring speed before accuracy, those habits may be difficult to break. Therefore, accuracy should be stressed before speed. The goal of training is effectiveness and efficiency, but effectiveness should be achieved ahead of efficiency.

Spaced Repetition

People learn information faster, and remember it longer, if it is repeated several times. For example, words, phrases, and symbols are repeated several times in advertising. Such repetition may seem annoying, but the slogans are not quickly forgotten. Even a good joke will not be remembered unless it is told several times soon after it is heard. Saying the same thing several different ways can serve to reinforce and review the most important aspects of content in a training session.

Repetitions are less annoying and still very effective when spaced by some time during each training session and between sessions. It is especially important to repeat the learning objectives and the standards for performance several times throughout a training session to establish these expectations clearly in the minds of the trainees.

One training expert emphasizes that repetition is most valuable when memorization is required. It is less useful in conceptual learning where reasoning is called for, unless it is necessary to learn a formula or procedure which must be applied in the reasoning process.[6]

Repetition by the trainee is also important when mastering knowledge or skills. Repetitions are more effective when each repetition provides a different way of looking at the same situation or concept. For this reason, it is advisable to have different trainees explain their understanding of what has been taught.

A good rule of thumb is that every key principle or procedure that is scheduled for a training session should be repeated at least two to three times during the session. The trainer should explain each procedure once to introduce the behavior, and then repeat the procedure along with a demonstration for the second repetition. Next, the trainee should repeat the demonstration while verbally reviewing the procedure for the third repetition. For complex, hard-to-master skills, five or six repetitions may be necessary to clearly establish the behaviors.

Further repetition is provided through coaching when the supervisor stops by the job station and restates expectations regarding procedures or standards. Whenever an employee has a question regarding a procedure or standard, another repetition is in order. If employees are expected to perform according to established standards, it is essential that the details regarding those expectations be kept clearly before the employees during and after training.

Intrinsic Motivation

Intrinsic motivation is motivation that comes from within the individual. People learn best when they want to learn. Since learning is largely self-motivated, a trainer is limited to how he/she can motivate a trainee. The trainer can help the trainee become motivated to learn by following the principles of learning during the training process, and by relating training to the trainee's interests and needs. The actual amount of learning that takes place, however, depends largely upon the trainee's internal motivation to learn. A trainer should show the trainee the advantages of learning the subject or the skill. This activity relates to the principle of readiness—adults must want to learn. It is difficult to have trainee readiness when the immediate need is not apparent.

Patience and Tact

Trainers should be patient with slow learners, seemingly unmotivated trainees, and careless workers. The behavior of these employees can be irritating, but the trainer's loss of temper and inability to cope with the situation will interfere with learning and solve nothing. Patience during training and coaching activities is always the best approach.

Tact, like patience, requires maturity on the part of the trainer. Trainees learn best when the training enhances their self-image. If the trainer responds to questions without consideration for the trainees' feelings, the trainees may withdraw from the learning process.

Active Participation

People learn and develop skills best by actual hands-on experience. For example, a person who wants to learn how to prepare flambé dishes might read a book on tableside cookery and then watch a maitre d'hôtel prepare a flaming dessert. However, the skill will not be developed until the person actually prepares a flambé dish, ignites the liqueur, and then serves the dish to guests. When participation is not included in training, the result is often "knowledge about" rather than the "ability to apply" the knowledge, skills, and attitudes for which training is being offered.

Visible Progress

Employees learn best when they can see progress being made. Learning that is useful on the job serves as a stimulus for further learning. Trainees gain satisfaction from feeling that they are progressing.

Follow-Up

Follow-up encourages employees to apply what was learned and to maintain performance standards. A trainer may do everything right—plan the training based on a real need, present the training with an excellent demonstration and visual aids, allow trainees to demonstrate the skills, and answer questions to ensure understanding. But then, the trainer may ignore the trainees' performance until months later when he/she is required to complete a formal performance appraisal. The trainer may discover that the procedures learned in training have not been followed since shortly after the training was concluded.

A successful training effort does not end with the last session. Rather, it extends to the actual work situation where the alert trainer or manager follows up by looking for employees who are doing things right and, at the same time, doing the right things. In both situations, the manager will be complimenting and otherwise rewarding appropriate behaviors, making sure that employees know that it does matter that they apply what they were taught during the training process.

Interpersonal Relationships

An individual's learning is influenced by the members of his/her peer group. The individual's relationship with the trainer also affects learning. The trainer should be aware of what trainees think and feel about each other and how they feel about him/her as the trainer.

Application of Past Experience

Everything people learn is based upon something they already know. The trainer must begin with this known information and build from there. Learning is the result of direct and indirect experience. The latter—learning from and through the experiences of others—is the most difficult. New and stimulating learning experiences should be planned so that trainees will recognize the possibility of achieving their own success and growth.

Friendly Competition

It is usually better if the trainee competes with himself/herself rather than with other trainees. However, it is natural for employees to feel some competitive spirit in a lively results-oriented training environment. Within reason, this is not harmful and can add interest if it is not allowed to get out of control. The manager should monitor competition closely to make sure that it is beneficial.

Knowledge of Requirements

The trainer should hold the trainee responsible for a definite amount of achievement. Among other measures, achievement can be gauged in terms of a specified attitude toward guests, level of quality, speed for completing a task, number of items to produce, sales quota, and sanitation level. The trainee should have the opportunity to evaluate his/her own behavioral changes and achievement in relation to the expected levels established by the trainer.

Comfortable Environment

A trainer faced with the need to conduct training on a hot day and in a room with poor ventilation can at least win the goodwill of trainees by doing his/her best to make them comfortable. The preparation of the training environment is the trainer's responsibility. He/she should do everything possible to remove or avoid any environmental barriers to learning. In addition to temperature, ventilation, and lighting, trainees need ample physical space to work with any training materials which are provided.

The following Case in Point illustrates the impact that the training environment can have on the learning process.

A Case in Point: Learning Environment

A training team went to an army post in southern Thailand on the Gulf of Siam during the Vietnam conflict to conduct a food and beverage course for the staffs of three military clubs. The course was scheduled months in advance and the team had requested a function room for the class. However, due to war demands, another training activity had been scheduled at the post for the same week and every available room had been rescheduled for that training. The food service training team had not been informed of the change and arrived on schedule with a senior instructor, an assistant instructor, and a highly-skilled executive chef from Japan who was to conduct actual cooking demonstrations.

Efforts were made to find a suitable room for the food and beverage training but nothing was available. The weather was forecast to be pleasant for several days, so the class was set up outside on the lawn. Extension cords were run to the site, and a makeshift demonstration kitchen was set up using a propane burner and a microwave oven. Chairs were provided for the participants and a flip chart was used instead of the planned overhead projector slides. The team had brought along movies on food preparation and service. Since these could not be shown outdoors, the movies were run in the club lounge during happy hour for the class participants—along with the club members who were enjoying their five o'clock refreshments.

Although the weather was clear and sunny, the glare of the bright sunlight bothered the trainers and the trainees. The gentle breeze blowing off the Gulf of Siam caused the training handouts and trainees' note papers to blow away, the cooking burner to blow out, and the flip chart pages to rustle. In spite of the trainers' best efforts to overcome the physical problems, the class was distracted by the environmental factors and unable to concentrate on the instruction.

A year later, the same team returned to that post to conduct another training class. Needless to say, there was very little evidence that the team had been there a year earlier. The food items demonstrated in the outdoor kitchen had not been added to the menu, and few if any service improvements were apparent in the three operations.

For training to be effective, it must be conducted in an environment that encourages learning. The distractions and lack of realism in the training situation described in the Case in Point guaranteed a low return on the training investment.

Trainer Effectiveness

The trainer must radiate enthusiasm. He/she must be sold on the subject, the standard operating procedures, and the performance standards. The trainer should also possess and display physical vitality, have a thorough knowledge of the subject, and be technically competent in the skill areas. Training should be carefully planned and administered—or it should not be offered at all.

Management should view the tasks that are being learned from the trainees' viewpoint. Peeling potatoes and cleaning out grease traps may be "easy jobs" to many managers, but very few of them actually do these jobs themselves. Employees have to learn some undesirable tasks as well as those that are more pleasant. Whether the task is pleasant or unpleasant, simple or complex, it may be the first time that the trainees have been exposed to it. Trainees who are having difficulty learning tasks or accepting the responsibility to perform undesirable tasks do not want managers to talk about how simple or easy they are. Trainees appreciate empathy from the trainer.

Perhaps the most common mistake made by managers who carry out their training responsibilities is the failure to prepare adequately for the training. There is a common misconception among managers that, because they know about performing most of the skills in their operations, they also know how to teach those skills to others. In order to ensure successful training, smart managers will learn as much as they can about how to prepare for training and about how people learn.

Notes

1. Clark Lambert, *Secrets of a Successful Trainer: A Simplified Guide for Survival* (New York: Wiley, 1986), p. 36.

2. G. S. Reynolds, *A Primer of Operant Conditioning*, Rev. ed. (Glenview, Ill.: Scott, Foresman, 1975), p. 1; and Irvin L. Goldstein, *Training in Organizations: Needs Assessment, Development, and Evaluation*, 2nd ed. (Monterey, Calif.: Brooks/Cole Publishing Co., 1986), pp. 71–75.

3. Marlene B. Young, "Organizational Training: Benefit or Obligation?" *Personnel Administrator*, Vol. 32, No. 10, October 1987, p. 30.

4. Goldstein, p. 21.

5. James Deese, *The Psychology of Learning*, 2nd ed. (New York: McGraw-Hill, 1958), pp. 64–68; and Reynolds, pp. 65–86.

6. Dugan Laird, *Approaches to Training and Development* (Reading, Mass.: Addison-Wesley, 1978), p. 169.

5 Individualized Training Methods

Training programs in the hospitality industry are frequently offered on the job in a one-on-one situation. Such on-the-job training (OJT) programs can be effective *if* they are planned and structured to incorporate many of the training principles described in this book.

In order for on-the-job training to be effective, a planned sequence of activities must occur. First, there must be adequate *preparation;* second, the *presentation* must be given; third, the employee must be able to *try out* what has been learned; and fourth, *follow-through* is necessary to reinforce the learning. This sequence of training activities is referred to as the **four-step training method** and is detailed in this chapter. Finally, all training should be designed to meet individual needs; this is more likely to happen when training is done through an individualized method.

Individualized Instruction

Individualized instruction is the process of custom-tailoring instruction to fit a specific learner. *What* the employee needs to know should be taught at his/her best pace, using the most appropriate method. Individualized instruction may include one-on-one instruction, independent study, mentoring, team teaching methods, programmed instruction, computer-assisted instruction, learner-controlled instruction, and coaching, as well as other personalized techniques.

Individualization occurs when learning activities are consistent with the learning style of the trainee, and when the trainer responds to the trainee's requests for assistance, clarifies questions, checks progress, and offers individual assistance. A training program is individualized to the extent that the trainee:

- Feels that progress depends upon his/her own efforts
- Can help determine which task should be learned next
- Decides what assistance or interaction with others is needed
- Selects resources to suit his/her own learning style

- Views supervisors and other employees as learning resources and as a support group rather than as bosses or competitors

- Exhibits an active, self-directed, purposeful approach to learning with minimal supervision

- Feels that the performance standards are relevant and attainable

- Is evaluated on an individual basis according to specific evaluation factors

- Is given information about his/her progress and status relative to the learning goals

Hospitality operators may reject individualized learning because they see it as a loosely controlled system in which employees learn what *they* want to learn rather than what management needs. Managers must be willing to describe in writing what they expect employees to be able to do as a result of training. These standards serve as goals for learning and refining skills, and they create positive attitudes about the job requirements.

Individualized learning programs sometimes fail, but not because the trainees are unwilling to assume responsibility for learning. Among the reasons some programs are unsuccessful is that expectations are not clearly communicated to trainees. They fail too because learning materials that describe what to do, how to do it, and why it is important are not available or up-to-date. Third, programs will fail when performance standards are inadequate or non-existent.

Individualized approaches to training use principles of adult learning covered in Chapter 4. The use of job breakdowns and the four-step method of training can be paced to meet individual needs.

Trainee Advantages

Individualized approaches to instruction offer advantages for both the trainee and the trainer. Some advantages for the trainee are:

- The learning pace is individualized. Trainees learn at their own speeds without becoming bored from a pace that is too slow or being left behind by a pace that is too fast.

- A wide range of learning resources can be used. When managers recognize the effectiveness of individualized instruction, they can provide resources such as industry books, magazines, and self-instructional audiovisual aids for trainees to use *on their time, at their pace.*

- A variety of learning styles can be accommodated. The more independent the adult's personality, the more resistant he/she may be toward non-individualized approaches to training. Adults like the freedom to learn according to their own styles.

- There is greater opportunity for learning to be personalized. Employers need to establish uniform standards, but they do not need robots. They need employees who can meet the standards while exhibiting their own personalities.

Trainer Advantages

With most individualized approaches, the trainer performs more resource and guidance activities and fewer teaching or instructing activities. The trainer works with the employee to shape the program to the employee's individual needs. Therefore, the employee begins at a level equal to his/her ability, and the trainer guides the employee toward progressively higher levels. Some advantages for trainers who use the individualized approach are:

- More time is available for working on other management responsibilities. The manager responsible for training can accomplish other duties while being available to the trainee as a resource person.

- More satisfaction is derived from seeing employees assume responsibility for developing skills that meet the performance standards. Very few managers enjoy training employees who are not motivated to learn. Individualized methods stimulate self-motivation and trainees become personally committed to standards.

- More time is available for the development of good work habits through coaching and counseling. Management's role as a coach and counselor is emphasized when individualized learning methods are used.

- Trainees can be encouraged to seek assistance from managers and experienced employees who are the "best" in each skill area—instead of just from the assigned trainer (who may be weak in certain skill areas).

A chief justification for individualized instruction is that it provides every trainee with an opportunity to achieve mastery of the tasks he/she attempts. The factors which affect mastery are linked to specific performance standards or learning objectives. Job analysis provides the basis for developing performance standards and lets employees know what is expected. Performance standards lead to the development of observable and measurable learning objectives; they set the level of achievement or advancement that the trainee is expected to attain. Sequencing the objectives, standards, or tasks may simplify learning by requiring mastery of lower level skills before progressing to higher level skills. Whenever possible, sequencing should *not* be inflexible. Adjustments to accommodate individual learning needs will probably be necessary because of each employee's experience.

On-the-Job Training

In most one-on-one training, the employee is placed on the job and a manager or experienced employee shows him/her how to do the job. This training is often called **on-the-job** training (OJT) and should be conducted according to a definite, structured program by using job lists, job breakdowns, and job performance standards as learning guides or lesson plans.

One form of OJT—"the buddy system"—pairs new employees with experienced employees. In this system, the experienced employees are simply told to train the new employees. These experienced employees are not given any specific guidelines about what should be covered or how the training should be conducted. This sad excuse for training has resulted in a bad reputation for OJT in the hospitality industry. This approach to training is also referred to as "shadowing," "trailing," and "following." Perhaps the best description of this approach is suggested by the label it is sometimes given: "the drag system." In other words, training consists of an experienced employee "dragging" a trainee around the operation for a few days; the trainee is expected to be competent at the end of that time.

OJT has great potential if it does not resemble the drag system. In fact, when effectively conducted and based on carefully prepared job analysis materials, OJT is perhaps the most cost-effective method of skills training available; it requires few special training skills. In addition, since OJT is a form of individualized learning, the trainer can design and pace the training to fit the needs of each employee. It can be supplemented with audiovisual aids, but there is actually no better method than providing the motivated trainee with the opportunity to "learn by doing." For OJT to be efficient, the process must be structured, and both the trainee and trainer must be clear as to the expectations and objectives of the OJT activity.

When properly structured, OJT provides maximum realism and wastes no time. The trainee can directly benefit from the training because the immediate application of his/her new job skills is so clear. The trainee focuses on performing the skills which are required according to stated job performance standards. The trainee also receives immediate feedback on job performance from the trainer and has an instant opportunity to practice what was learned.

A disadvantage to this type of training is that it requires a one-on-one relationship; this ties up a trainer for a considerable amount of time with one employee or a very small group. On-the-job training relies on the trainer to follow the job breakdowns to ensure that standard procedures are taught. There is always the possibility that the trainer will ignore the job breakdowns and teach the trainee bad habits or unapproved techniques.

Despite any possible disadvantages, this method can result in the development of a highly skilled staff on a very individualized basis if it is followed through and reinforced by coaching and counseling. Employees are usually positive about this kind of training because it is so specific to the needs of their work. Since learning occurs on-site, there is no difficulty in transferring learning to actual application. *Structured OJT* is highly recommended as a primary training method for ongoing training within any hospitality operation that has a high commitment to training.

Procedures for Conducting On-the-Job Training

A basic and simple model can be used to implement an OJT program. The model is general enough to be used in group training programs as well (see Chapter 6). This basic model is referred to as the **four-step training method** and is explained below.

Step 1:
Preparation

Many trainers think they know the skills required of employees so well that they can teach them to others without any thought or preparation. However, it is easy to forget important details if training is approached without adequate trainer preparation. The training session will be most effective if the trainer is skilled in the area being taught. The trainer should be willing to follow the job breakdowns closely so that the skills are presented in a logical sequence. When this is done, the trainees are better able to understand and remember the steps which are necessary in order to perform the job. All trainers should be involved in the following preliminary training activities.

Develop the Job List. Every position requires a job list. This is the list of duties or tasks that the employee must master and perform in carrying out the job. The job list serves as the index or directory of what is going to occur in the training process. When training is implemented, the job list serves as a checklist of what duties or tasks have been mastered.

Write Training Objectives. The manager preparing to train should state in writing what behaviors and skills the employee will be expected to demonstrate at the end of the training session. This should be done for each item on the job list. The performance level and conditions under which each behavior or skill is demonstrated should also be stated. The procedures for writing training objectives are covered in Chapter 8.

Decide on Teaching Methods. When planning the training sessions, the manager must determine which teaching and learning methods will be most useful, which learning principles are appropriate, and how the principles should be applied.

Develop Job Breakdowns. Each duty or task on the job list should be broken down into steps of execution and arranged in logical order. These job breakdowns also specify how to perform each step and provide information to explain why details are important. When writing job breakdowns, a manager should regard them as lesson plans or training session outlines. During actual training, the appropriate job breakdown should be used to direct the instruction and to ensure that no critical points or steps are overlooked.

Establish a Timetable. An important part of trainer preparation involves planning an appropriate timetable. The trainer should know approximately how long the instruction of each duty or task will take. Based on the time required and the daily work flow, a timetable can help determine when the instruction should take place. When possible, OJT should be conducted when there is a minimum amount of interruption or distraction. The trainer should select times when training can be most effective and schedule these times for training.

Teach Just a Few Procedures or Tasks Each Day. When preparing for training, managers should keep in mind that a trainee can only retain a limited amount of information at one time without becoming tired and frustrated. The trainer should teach what the trainee can reasonably master in one session and allow time for practice. More material can be taught in later sessions until all job responsibilities are covered. The following Case in Point illustrates the application of this important principle.

A Case in Point: Simple Effective Training

In one fast-food company, a complete job list was developed for each employee position, along with a detailed job breakdown for each item on each job list. These materials were typed and laminated with a waterproof plastic coating. Then they were arranged in a three-ring binder with dividers separating the job list and accompanying job breakdowns for each position. One copy of this training manual was placed in each restaurant.

All restaurant managers were required to complete a one-day training session on how to use these materials and how to conduct one-on-one training using the simple four-step training method. When the managers returned to the restaurants, each existing employee was retrained using the materials and the four-step method. All new employees were taught a few skills each day until they mastered all of the duties of their job.

To ensure the continued application of the materials, the area supervisor and director of operations would routinely talk to all new employees and have them explain what they had been taught that day. On occasion, these managers would even have the new employees "teach" them the skills they had mastered through the program in order to reinforce the program's importance and to see the learning that was taking place. Managers were very pleased with the approach because it was so well-defined and so simple to administer. A fifteen-minute training session each day was sufficient to keep most new employees on track in mastering their duties in a reasonable period without teaching them too much too quickly.

Select the Training Location. Whenever possible, job-related training should be conducted at the appropriate work stations. The manager must consider when the training can best occur without interfering with operating demands. Before starting the actual training, the trainer should make sure that the trainee is standing or sitting in a location where all of the demonstration can be seen. Also, the trainee should be able to see the demonstration from the position in which he/she will actually be performing the task. If the trainee is observing across the table from the trainer, then every movement will be the reverse of how it is actually performed. This may seem like a minor point, but it can become so frustrating that the trainee may resist the training and experience difficulty in mastering the duty.

Assemble Training Materials and Equipment. The job breakdown form should provide a space for listing the materials and equipment that will be needed for teaching that particular duty or task. Time can be saved in getting everything together by identifying the necessary materials and equipment when job breakdowns are prepared. Having all materials and equipment at the training site when the session begins will avoid confusion for the trainee.

If a work station will be used to train, it should be set up and stocked exactly as it would be for normal operations. Each piece of equipment should also be positioned in the way the employee is expected to learn and maintain it.

Prepare Training Aids. Carefully selected training aids are useful supplements to the teaching-learning process. It is often difficult to teach complex procedures by lecturing or even by demonstrating. Training aids can be used to amplify and clarify difficult points in the procedures being covered. They can also arouse or hold the trainee's interest since people remember things they see and hear much better than information they only hear.

In training broiler cooks, for example, the trainer could prepare a rare, medium, and well-done steak. These steaks could then serve as training aids to teach cooks how to judge doneness and to demonstrate the desired pattern of broiler grate markings on the meat's exterior. In training food servers to read wine labels, a trainer could prepare a handout that uses a clearly marked illustration to point out the critical information on a wine label. Trainers could also use different wine bottles to relate bottle shapes to the information on the wine labels.

If the trainer is interested in a high level of understanding and retention, a variety of training methods and aids should be used to appeal to as many senses as possible and practical. The choice and use of training aids depends on their contribution to meeting the objectives of the training program. Chapter 7 presents more suggestions on using various training aids that range from simple handouts to complex interactive video systems.

Rehearse the Session. There is a big difference between performing a task and teaching someone else how to perform it. For this reason, it is important for the trainer to rehearse each training session. This is best done at the work station by going through the job breakdown and practicing the demonstration. A serious rehearsal can ensure an outstanding performance when the session takes place.

Prepare the Trainee. The trainer should give the trainee an overview of the training before any actual instruction begins. This orientation will let the trainee know what is expected of him/her during the session, and what will be expected after the training. This can be accomplished by explaining the training objectives for the session. The trainee should be told why the training is important and what specific skills will be developed. The trainee needs an explanation of how the skills relate to the total responsibilities of the job and how to make immediate use of the techniques and information being presented. In order to reduce any anxiety that the trainee might have, the trainer should explain that perfection will not be immediately expected.

Use Job Lists and Job Breakdowns. The trainer should have the job list and the job breakdown available when the session begins. Routinely, the trainer should show the trainee that the duty or task that is about to be taught is on the job list for his/her position. This will also give the trainee some perspective on the amount of training that remains. The trainee should be provided a copy of the job list as well as a copy of each job breakdown as it is to be covered in a training session. The trainee should take these materials home and review them to further reinforce the learning.

Interact with the Trainee. There is no universal method for putting an employee at ease. Each trainee must be approached differently. Some time should be spent learning about the trainee and how he/she feels about mastering the duty that is about to be covered. The trainer should try to make the learning situation as natural as possible.

While finding out how the trainee feels about mastering a duty, the trainer should also find out what the trainee already knows. If the trainee has difficulty applying concepts from previous sessions, it may interfere with the instruction that is about to occur. The trainer may also inquire whether the trainee has had experience with the duty and determine what correct or incorrect things the trainee already knows. If the trainee has performed this duty before, the trainer should try to relate what the trainee is about to learn to his/her experience.

Step 2: Presentation

Once the trainer and trainee have been prepared for training, the actual process can begin. The following are guidelines on how to present the training.

Begin the Training. The trainer should use the job breakdown as a training guide. The trainee should be encouraged to look at the job breakdown so that he/she will know that the standards are documented. The trainer should then simply follow the sequence of each step in the job breakdown, telling the trainee what to do, how to do it, and why the details of each step are important.

Demonstrate the Procedures. While explaining each step thoroughly, the trainer should demonstrate how to do the procedure correctly. The trainee will understand and retain more if he/she sees a demonstration while listening to the explanation. The trainee should be encouraged to ask questions any time he/she does not fully understand. People learn through all five senses, and it often takes more than "showing and telling" to train someone. The trainer must avoid the pitfalls of communicating messages such as, "If you want to learn how to do this job, just watch me," or, "Now listen carefully, because I only have time to explain this to you once."

Speak in Simple Terms. The trainer should use words that the trainee can understand. Training should be simple without being simplistic. If the trainee is new to the job, technical terms that may be familiar to the trainer and to other employees will seem like a foreign language. The same applies to industry jargon, abbreviations, and acronyms. The training message is lost when the terminology is not clear to the trainee.

Take Adequate Time. Presentation should proceed slowly. The trainee may be seeing and hearing a lot of things for the first time. The trainer must carefully show and explain everything the trainee should know about each step.

Be Patient. It is difficult for many trainers to slow their pace and maintain it at the trainee's level. The trainer must try not to become frustrated if the trainee does not grasp each step as quickly and as well as expected.

Check Visibility. The trainer should continuously check to make sure that the trainee can see every move from the proper angle.

Establish a Model. The trainer should take the trainee through the entire sequence of the duty or job task to establish the overall job procedure. The logical flow or sequence of steps is important to mastering the processes of the task.

Repeat the Sequence. After going through the entire sequence once, the trainer should go through it a second time to ensure that the trainee sees the process completely. When repeating the process, the trainer should ask the trainee questions to check comprehension and tell the trainee to interrupt at any point where he/she does not clearly understand the procedures. The trainer should follow the job breakdowns and repeat the steps as many times as necessary until the trainee knows the procedure.

Step 3: Trial Performance

After the trainee feels he/she knows how to execute the duty or task in an acceptable manner, the trainer should allow the trainee to perform the procedure alone. The following are guidelines for carrying out Step 3 in the training sequence.

Require the Trainee to Repeat the Demonstration and Explanation. The trainer should not assume that the trainee knows how to do something just because he/she has no questions or because he/she says, "I know how." A repeat demonstration by the trainee will reveal any misunderstandings that might lead to the formation of bad habits. The trainee must be required to demonstrate and explain each step that was presented. This, in addition to asking questions, will help the trainer check for comprehension.

Require the Trainee to Practice. New skills which are properly demonstrated and explained, followed by immediate and continuous practice, lead to good work habits. The trainer should strive to increase the trainee's skill level by carefully observing the trainee's performance and by helping him/her to smooth out any awkward motions.

Coach the Trainee. Every effort should be made by the trainer to help the trainee gain the skill and confidence necessary to perform the job without assistance or supervision. As a coach, the trainer should compliment the trainee immediately following correct performance and assist the trainee as soon as problems in performance or understanding are observed. It is important to prevent the formation of bad habits at this stage of training since unacceptable practices may be difficult to overcome in the future. The trainer should be sure the trainee understands the "why" of each step.

Test the Level of Mastery. Before the formal training is completed, the trainer should test the mastery level of the trainee. This may be done orally if the trainer has planned the questions and has determined ahead of time what will constitute acceptable answers. The trainer may also ask the trainee to complete a written test. To ensure trainee competence, oral or written questions should be planned which measure knowledge, skills, and application. The trainer should also pay close attention to the trainee's attitude to see if it meets performance expectations.

Performance testing should be routine in all OJT. It should not, however, be taken for granted just because the training is a hands-on approach. The basis for performance testing comes from the quality and quantity aspects of almost all duties which will be taught. It is not sufficient just to *learn* the correct procedures for performing a job task. The trainee must be able to *accomplish* the desired results in an acceptable length of time. The criteria for evaluation should be written in the job performance standards which were prepared well in advance of the OJT session.

**Step 4:
Follow-
Through**

This step can be part of—or should immediately follow—the training session. Regardless, the trainee should continue to perform the new duties on the job after his/her trial performance to gain further speed and accuracy.

Continue Coaching On the Job. The trainer's coaching responsibility continues even after formal training ends. The trainer assumes some responsibility for the productivity of employees—especially for employees who have not achieved mastery and competence. While a new employee is a member of a department's team, he/she is not yet a fully functioning member. The trainer must observe the employee to ensure that the job is being done the proper way. The trainer should tactfully correct the trainee when performance goes astray and re-emphasize procedures and performance standards. If the trainee is using an unsafe practice, immediate corrective action is essential.

The trainee should know where to go for help in the absence of the trainer and should be encouraged to ask questions. Ways to improve performance and efficiency should be discussed. The trainer should gradually reduce coaching as the trainee learns to perform within the set standards. However, the trainer should periodically check back on the employee and continue to help the trainee develop a high degree of confidence in his/her ability to perform according to the trainer's expectations.

Continue Positive Reinforcement and Feedback. When the trainee deviates from prescribed procedures, the trainer should compliment the person for those tasks which have been performed correctly, and review the procedures that need additional attention. This technique will result in improved employee performance and the development of a *positive attitude toward training*.

Verify Competence and Record Progress. Competence should be acknowledged and recorded on the trainee's individual training record each time the newly trained employee consistently meets a performance standard. It is reinforcing to formally recognize competence throughout training; it also demonstrates that training will be an ongoing process. The individual training record should be part of the permanent human resource file for the employee.

Emphasize Mastery and Craftsmanship. The employee should be encouraged to view learning as a process whereby he/she masters a craft. This viewpoint will instill pride in performance and provide motivation through the work itself.

Independent Study

Independent study is one of the most cost-effective ways to present continuous training on an individualized basis. Every operation that is fully committed to life-long learning should provide an employee learning resource center to encourage independent study. The learning resource center should contain current hospitality industry trade magazines and journals and a good selection of industry-related books and manuals. Basic to a good resource center is an up-to-date set of the organization's departmental operating manuals, as well as operating manuals on all equipment.

In addition to printed materials, the learning resource center could also contain self-operated audiovisual equipment and films, slide-sets, videotapes, and computer hardware and software. The more materials available, the more interest the center will hold for employees. A recordkeeping system should be established to monitor the use of the facility and the progress of individual employees.

To encourage use of the learning resource center, managers should develop both written and non-written performance tests on work-related topics and should give assignments for independent study on those topics. The organization may use its own judgment concerning whether employees are permitted to check out materials for home study or are required to use the materials only at the workplace. All assigned independent study that occurs at the workplace must be considered as scheduled work hours. Furthermore, managers may not require an employee to master materials through independent study at home in an effort to avoid paying for training time.

Mentoring

A **mentor** is a trusted counselor or guide who informally tutors others in their learning. Employees who are taught to perform at a high level of excellence tend to view their trainer in a very special way. The trainer has invested in them, and they trust the trainer to help them if they ever have difficulty on the job. Mentoring benefits the mentor and the learner—and contributes to the career success of both.[1]

Mentoring is the natural outcome of an effective training relationship, and provides for the continued growth and development of the learner. On the other hand, mentoring places the trainer in a position where his/her actions can have an immeasurable effect on the learner's career. The selection of mentors is a serious matter because of the far-reaching effects the mentor will have on the learners. The application of mentoring as a management training and development approach will be discussed more in Chapter 10.

Correspondence Courses

Individuals who are interested in self-improvement can take correspondence courses on subjects applicable to the hospitality industry. Correspondence courses are available from the Educational Institute of the American Hotel & Motel Association, the Educational Foundation of the National Restaurant Association, and the American Management Association.

Correspondence courses are taught with materials that trainees read and study alone, on their own time. Trainees complete examinations and submit them for feedback and credit from the organization that is offering the course. Correspondence courses are appropriate for adults because they are self-paced, individualized, voluntary, and self-directed. An unlimited number of employees within an organization can enroll concurrently, yet each person proceeds at his/her own pace. Since employees completing correspondence courses engage in the training on their own time, employers do not have to pay employees for the training. In addition, correspondence or home study does not take time away from the job. Employers should consider adding realism to the training by encouraging employees to practice applying what they are studying while they are at work. The following Case in Point describes the opportunities available to independent learners through one educational foundation.

A Case in Point: Educational Institute Courses

The Educational Institute of the American Hotel & Motel Association offers more than twenty-five hospitality courses for independent learning that cover every major functional area of hotel/motel operations. For successful completion of a course, the employee is awarded an attractive certificate of completion. Students may also take a five-course series leading to certificates of specialization in Rooms Division Management, Food and Beverage Management, Marketing and Sales Management, Accounting and Financial Management, and Engineering and Facility Management. Further coursework may lead to the Institute

Diploma, while a combination of coursework and industry experience qualifies some professionals for industry-recognized executive level certification, including the Certified Rooms Division Executive (CRDE), Certified Food and Beverage Executive (CFBE), Certified Hospitality Housekeeping Executive (CHHE), Certified Human Resources Executive (CHRE), Certified Engineering Operations Executive (CEOE), or—the most prestigious designation awarded—the Certified Hotel Administrator (CHA).

Institute courses increase the competency levels of employees and provide an organized way for staff members to train themselves on their own time. Each student paces his/her own rate of learning without the structure of a classroom to hold back the highly motivated learner. Thousands of employees and managers in the hospitality industry have taken advantage of this effective way to raise their level of competence.

Programmed Instruction

In programmed instruction, a trainee views printed or visual materials called "frames" or a sequence of frames called "vignettes" which explain or demonstrate a concept or procedure. The learner is then quizzed on what he/she learned. If the learner responds correctly, he/she is permitted to continue forward with the next frame or vignette. However, when the learner responds incorrectly, the program tells the learner to recycle through previous instruction or it "branches" the learner off in a different direction to cover some remedial training before returning to the main path of instruction. This approach to individualized instruction became very popular in the 1960s and 1970s and was usually conducted through the use of printed manuals.[2]

Computer-Assisted Instruction

With the advent of the personal computer, much of the application of programmed instruction is communicated through computer programs. The concept of programmed instruction is still the same; the communications medium has changed. The use of the computer as a training tool has increased in direct proportion to the increased use of computer systems in hospitality operations. Computers can also be used to perform other training tasks such as problem-solving simulations, development of training plans and budgets, and management of multimedia training systems.

Managers do not need to become computer programmers to accomplish their responsibilities as trainers. In operations where computer terminals and computerized point-of-sale units are part of the work stations, it is easy to see how computers can be used to teach people how to use computers. In work situations that do not normally involve computer systems, more creativity is required to see how the computer can be used to enhance individualized learning.[3]

It is a mistake to overlook the value of the computer as a training tool. The use of the computer to simulate reality in a training setting expands the classroom far beyond the traditional chalkboard or flip chart. Software packages that simulate lodging and food service functions are being developed to teach such areas as decision-making, marketing, and problem-solving. The computer may be the most significant addition to the tools of the trainer to come about in this century.

Interactive Video. One of the latest developments in computer-assisted instruction is interactive video. This form of individualized instruction involves the traditional computer-assisted instructional format with a video component. The computer serves as the controller of the learning process while a video provides an appropriate taped demonstration when necessary. Learners respond to questions at various points throughout the program to evaluate their understanding of the concepts demonstrated through the video. Depending on their responses, learners are advised to repeat a sequence in the program or to advance to another segment of the program. More information on interactive video is provided in Chapter 7.

Learner-Controlled Instruction

Learner-controlled instruction (LCI) is a specialized form of individualized learning that has been used with great success in several large lodging and food service organizations. LCI differs from traditional "instructor-controlled" approaches to training in several ways; the most obvious is that the *trainee* manages and controls the learning process.

Self-motivation increases when adult learners are given the opportunity to direct their own learning. It appears that what adults learn through their own self-direction is learned more deeply and permanently than what they learn while under the control of other people.[4]

LCI was first introduced to the hospitality industry in 1971 by Marriott Hotels and Resorts; its application in that organization came to be known as their "Individual Development" (ID) program. Other industry leaders such as the Holiday Corporation, Long John Silver's, Pizza Hut, Red Barn, and Tia Maria Restaurants followed the Marriott example and designed LCI programs for management training during the 1970s.[5]

Since the late 1970s, Stouffer Hotel Company, Radisson Hotel Corporation, Omni Hotels, Doubletree Hotels, Hardee's Restaurants, Darryl's Restaurants, and others have implemented the concept. LCI has been applied internationally by SAS Catering of Copenhagen, Denmark, for use in their operations throughout Europe, the Middle East, and in Japan.[6] Companies that continue to use LCI regard it as part of their corporate culture and consider it a demonstration of their total commitment to the application of adult learning principles in their training programs.

Most LCI programs used in the hospitality industry have the following nine features:

1. The trainee directs the learning process within guidelines established by the organization.

2. The learning outcomes are expressed in performance terms, requiring on-the-job performance testing.

3. The program makes extensive use of "contract learning" techniques to provide some structure for the self-directed learning process.

4. The learning environment is the actual job setting, and everyone in the training setting becomes a resource for the learner.

5. The learning activities are supported by printed materials and information so that standard operating procedures and job performance standards are clear to the learner.

6. The learner is formally recognized each time he/she masters a defined competency with its specified skills and knowledge.

7. Feedback on progress and performance is provided on an immediate and continuous basis by individuals who serve as coaches, counselors, and resource people to the self-directed learner.

8. The trainee controls the pace and sequence of learning activities, being required to demonstrate continuous progress under his/her own management of the learning.

9. The trainee may challenge and bypass learning activities leading to mastery of behaviors that he/she has acquired from past experiences.

LCI is discussed in more detail in Chapter 10 where it is specifically applied to management training and development. The use of LCI is not limited to management training. However, its application for training non-management personnel is somewhat more difficult to implement due to current fair wage and salary laws. These laws require that non-exempt salaried employees must be compensated for time worked over a base number of hours. Since the laws are complicated and changing, specific questions about "overtime" pay for salaried employees should be addressed to officials in state and/or federal fair wage and hour law departments. Potential problems can be overcome by budgeting a generous amount of overtime, or by limiting the trainees to specified times within which they may manage their own learning.

Organizations with properly designed and managed LCI programs have reported higher levels of learner achievement and subsequent competence than were attained from using any other training method.[7] Training time was also reduced in these organizations. Increased competence and reduced training time occurred because training was designed to meet individual learning styles. LCI is considered one of the most efficient methods of individualized training available.

Notes

1. Jerry Wilber, "Does Mentoring Breed Success?" *Training and Development Journal*, Vol. 41, No. 11, November 1987, pp. 38–41.

2. For examples of programmed texts produced for the hospitality industry, see the three examples prepared by Bolt Reranek and Newman Inc., Cambridge, Mass., entitled *Today's Waitress, Today's Busboy,* and *Today's Dishwashing Machine Operator* (New York: Chain Store Publishing Corp., 1971).

3. For a more detailed discussion of computer-assisted instruction and computer-assisted learning, see C. Dean and Q. Whitlock, *A Handbook of Computer-Based Training* (New York: Nichols Publishing Co., 1983) and D. Godfrey and S. Sterling, *The Elements of CAL* (Reston, Va.: Reston Publishing Co., 1982).

4. Malcolm Knowles, *The Adult Learner: A Neglected Species,* 2nd ed. (Houston: Gulf Publishing Co., l978), p. 198.

5. Mershid Nazmi-Ansari Cox, "A Learner-Controlled Instruction Program in Food Production Management for the Foodservice Practicum" (Master's thesis, East Carolina University, 1977), pp. 37–42.

6. The application of LCI in these organizations was designed and implemented by this author, Lewis C. Forrest, Jr., on a consulting arrangement.

7. Cox, pp. 37–42, and Frank T. Wydra, "Learner-Controlled Instruction: How Allied Supermarkets Made it Work," *Training Magazine* (August, 1975), pp. 32–39.

6 Group Training Methods

Group training can reduce training time and costs when several employees are to be taught the same task or information. At times, group training is more practical and appropriate than individualized training. For example, a group session may be the most efficient method of instruction when implementing a new service procedure that affects a large number of employees. Likewise, when the primary purpose is to dispense information on such topics as new and changing policies, a group session can inform all employees in the shortest amount of time.

Sometimes, group training will take place in a function room where a classroom environment can be arranged. More often, the group training will occur in a job setting, such as in the dining room of the restaurant, within the kitchen, behind the front desk, or in a guestroom. Effective group training does not require a formal classroom environment or the use of visual aids, podiums, or large blocks of time. Group training is simply that training which effectively conveys desired learning objectives to several employees at once—and which effectively achieves those objectives.

Principles of planning and implementing group training sessions should be understood by the manager who is preparing to conduct group training. If effective procedures are followed from the initial training design through the presentation, evaluation, and follow-up, the likelihood of achieving the desired objectives is enhanced.

The Group Trainer

The manager who is conducting training serves as a mentor. As noted earlier, a mentor is a personal counselor who is entrusted with the education or training of another person. Employees normally look to their managers for this personal guidance and instruction. When managers prepare to conduct group training, they often feel that their role has shifted from mentor to "professional instructor." This should not be the case. Managers should understand that group training is actually **group mentoring** and should accept the continuing responsibility for the personal development of each trainee.

Trainers should always view themselves as **facilitators** of learning, whether the learning takes place through an individualized or group method. This means that the trainer—rather than simply communicating new information or procedures—helps others learn from their own resources and past experiences.

Group Training Techniques

Managers should understand their role in group training and understand the advantages and disadvantages of each group training method. No single method works best in all situations. Managers must consider training objectives and use the methods that are more likely to achieve those objectives.

This chapter presents nine group training techniques. Some of the approaches overlap, but each is unique and can be a useful training tool. The group methods described include lecture, demonstration, seminar, conference, panel, role playing, case study, simulation, and project-based approaches.

Lecture Method

The lecture method is characterized by spoken instruction from one person. The lecturer talks, explains, and teaches. The lecture method may include limited opportunities for trainees to ask questions. Usually the lecturer answers the trainees' questions and does not open the discussion to other members of the class.

The lecture method can be used when specific information must be presented in a short amount of time to a large group of people. It is not very effective when used alone and, therefore, should be used in conjunction with other group training methods. When material is taught totally by lecture, much of the information may be forgotten very quickly by the trainees. It is possible to record a lecture on audiotape or videotape for later replay and review.

Despite the problem of low retention, the lecture method does have its advantages. It is useful when general familiarity with the subject matter is required by a large number of people but recall of specific information is not necessary. In addition, the lecture method usually requires the least amount of trainer preparation. If the trainer knows the subject, he/she can lecture with only a set of outline notes, or even without written aids. No audiovisual aids or demonstrations are required. The manager who has become a true expert in his/her field may be able to organize thoughts as he/she speaks and present an effective lecture.

The main disadvantage is that the lecture method does not appeal to many of the senses through which people learn. The method relies primarily on hearing. Gestures can add some visual emphasis to what is being said, or handouts can be supplied to the trainees for review.

A strict lecture method provides no opportunity for an exchange of ideas. It does not give the trainees the chance to practice what they have been taught. Trainees can forget material very quickly when they are not given the opportunity to practice what they are learning.

Demonstration Method

Demonstration is probably the best method for teaching most procedures and employee skills in the hospitality industry. In a group setting, demonstration may be combined with lecture to increase the trainer's effectiveness. It can be conducted, enhanced, or standardized by using audiovisual aids such as filmstrips, film loops, movies, or videotapes.

A trainer uses the demonstration method when he/she performs a job procedure as outlined in a job breakdown. Demonstration is a means of teaching the correct steps and rationale for performing that job function. Each step should be explained as it is performed.

When giving a demonstration, the trainer should always be certain that the trainees have a clear view of what is being shown. There should be a comfortable amount of space in the room for the demonstration and for the trainees. Trainees should be checked from time to time to make sure that they understand what is being done.

The four-step training method (Chapter 5) is a proven approach to incorporating demonstrations into training. Step three of that method emphasizes the importance of checking comprehension. The trainer can judge the effectiveness of the demonstration by asking questions. In a group, comprehension can also be checked by having each employee repeat an entire demonstration for the group. To save time, and to reinforce learning, it is also possible to have individual trainees successively perform segments of the procedure, with one trainee picking up and continuing the demonstration where another trainee left off. Another way to check comprehension is to divide the training group into smaller groups in which each trainee repeats the demonstration for a few co-workers.

When using the demonstration method, trainers should be careful to teach only one set of related operational procedures at a time. Trainees should master each duty or task in the sequence of the job breakdown before they are exposed to another. This is true for any method of presentation that is controlled by an instructor. Instruction should focus on each specific duty or task and move methodically and logically from duty to duty, instead of presenting the total job function at one time.

Occasionally, the trainer may be tempted to digress in order to answer a trainee's question. At such times, the trainer should handle the question with as little interruption as possible and return to the demonstration without being discourteous. If the question is important—but would disrupt the demonstration if it were answered at the time—the trainer should indicate that the question is good enough to be saved for a complete discussion. A good technique is to write each question or a key word on a flip chart or chalkboard and then return immediately to the demonstration. After the demonstration is completed and comprehension has been verified, the trainer can then return to these questions.

It is not a good practice to demonstrate incorrect procedures in order to point out unacceptable methods. Such demonstrations are a waste of time and may encourage trainees to use the incorrect procedures as alternatives to the correct methods. If the correct procedures are presented in a clear and logical manner—and if the importance of each step is explained—the trainees are likely to achieve the desired performance objectives.

The advantage of the demonstration method is that trainees learn by seeing and hearing. Without demonstrations, trainees must generally rely on what they hear—plus anything they might read. Employees are likely to apply a new procedure through blind trial and error unless they have seen a demonstration. A demonstration will eliminate most of the error since trainees will copy the correct procedure which they have observed.

The disadvantage of the demonstration method is that it requires a great deal of preparation by the trainer. The demonstration should not be conducted without a complete job breakdown of the procedures to be demonstrated. The job breakdown serves as a lesson plan or a demonstration outline. It covers each important step and provides additional information that is relevant to the procedure. Each breakdown also includes a list of all equipment and materials required to perform or demonstrate the procedure.

Seminar Method

Seminars are a planned approach to learning that combines such methods as lectures, discussions, and conferences. In seminars, knowledgeable resource people share their expertise with trainees through lectures, discussions, or a variety of participative learning activities. An exchange of information between the resource people and the trainees is essential in the seminar method.

An advantage of the seminar method is that it fosters involvement by trainees. A variety of training objectives, ranging from skill development to problem-solving, can be achieved using the seminar method. Managers should attempt to design seminars that are creative, challenging, and refreshing. Successful seminars incorporate a variety of learning experiences and make optimum use of the operation's management team as the resource group.

The seminar method has many variations and is very effective when the training objectives specify a high level of trainee involvement. Employees usually enjoy seminars and feel that they benefit not only from the variety of training methods, but also from being able to learn from several resource people who are competent in their fields.

A major disadvantage of the seminar approach is that its design requires a lot of time and considerable skill. Seminars also require more time to conduct than many other training methods because of trainee participation in a variety of learning activities. Managers who participate as resource persons must also be prepared to conduct or participate in these activities.

One manner of conducting effective seminars is similar to the four-step training method. The following steps explain the procedure.

Presentation. The trainer or designated resource person presents information to the entire group of trainees. The information may explain how to perform a particular set of skills, how to carry out a general procedure, how to resolve a guest-related problem, how to deal with employee conflict in certain situations, or even how to participate in a learning activity.

Demonstration. The trainer or designated resource person demonstrates the procedure being taught and may use group members as assistants. The trainer also shows trainees how to carry out the learning activities that have been designed to achieve the training objectives.

Supplemental Instruction. Following the demonstration, the trainer or designated resource person should try to determine the group's level of comprehension. Any necessary supplemental instruction should be provided to prepare the group for the next step.

Application. In this step, the trainees may be divided into small groups or teams that engage in participative learning activities. The activities should be designed to further develop the specific behaviors covered in the earlier steps. These behaviors may include technical or interpersonal job skills such as suggestive selling, resolving employee conflicts, decision-making, and teamwork.

Evaluation. The evaluation can take two forms: (a) the trainer and resource persons evaluate each individual's or group's participation and contribution, and (b) the group members evaluate themselves and each other. The trainers and trainees can also evaluate the program format.

Conference Method

One way to ensure a high return on the training investment is to develop training activities which deal with real performance problems. The conference method is extremely useful in solving problems related to guest hospitality, interpersonal relations, and employee attitudes. It can be equally useful for improving performance in technical skill areas. The conference method involves:

1. bringing a group of people together to discuss a problem which is common to all the members of the group, and

2. finding a workable solution which all group participants will agree to apply in order to remove or overcome the performance deficiency.

In this problem-solving approach to training, it is especially important that the trainer be a *facilitator* rather than an instructor. The trainer should encourage trainees to learn from themselves as well as from other members of the group. When trainees solve their own problems in a training session, they can see how they may apply the new ideas and new behaviors in work situations. The transfer of learning from training to the job setting is thus optimized.

The conference method relies heavily on the concept of **brainstorming.** The effective use of this technique is essential to the conference's success. Brainstorming is a process designed to generate as many ideas as possible about a designated situation or problem. It encourages all group members to participate in a free flow of ideas and to build on the ideas of others.

The outcome of the conference method should be agreement on the solutions to a job-related problem which will be applied when the participants return to the job setting. Agreement does not always mean a unanimous vote. However, the solutions selected should have received more support than a simple majority. At the beginning of the training activity, it is advisable to establish a percentage of agreement that will be acceptable to everyone.

The conference procedure begins with the trainer describing the problem. Once the problem is stated, and all questions are clarified, the leader should ask for volunteers to give their opinions of how the problem can be solved. Everyone in the group should be encouraged to participate. The leader should allow only one person to talk at one time. If arguments arise, the trainer should arbitrate and bring out the views of both sides.

As a group leader, the trainer must keep the discussion flowing and bring out the best contributions of all participants. This is accomplished by asking stimulating questions and by directing the group discussions into areas that seem productive. The trainer must not tell the group how or what to think. Rather, he/she must encourage all group members to say what they think or feel without fear of punishment or criticism. The leader should facilitate a group analysis of ideas generated through brainstorming and help the group summarize the points around which they can reach reasonable agreement.

Some employees or managers may feel that they have more experience or training in the area of the problem and may expect their point of view to "carry more weight." If this occurs, the trainer must tactfully remind everyone that opinions or ideas of every group member carry equal weight. He/she must then emphasize that the final determination of a solution will be based on the rationale behind each alternative, rather than the expertise of one group member.

The leading advantage of the conference method is that it deals with real problems from the job setting. Another advantage is that it involves several employees at once, and contributes to team building. The involvement and participation of the employees in this method builds self-esteem, makes training exciting, builds personal accountability, and results in strong commitment to performance standards and problem solutions. The following Case in Point shows how a convention hotel used the conference method to identify and solve a complex problem.

A Case in Point: Convention Check-In Mania

One problem regularly faced by the front desk staff of a 2,000-room convention hotel in New York City was handling the registration process on days when large convention groups were arriving. It was not unusual at least once or twice each week to see as many as six separate lines of guests backed up for several hours as thousands of people checked in. Needless to say, the guests were not happy about the lines or the time required to process their registrations. In turn, the hotel routinely received hundreds of letters complaining about the inefficiency and even the rudeness of the front desk staff. The corporate office directed that a training program be established to teach the front desk staff how to be nice to guests.

The person assigned to conduct the training performed a needs analysis to determine the skill level of the staff. This study revealed that the staff was highly competent in all skill areas, and that there was considerable longevity for the front desk employees. The newer employees were already receiving skills training through an ongoing program, and the standards for performance were clearly documented in training manuals.

The conference method was selected as a training approach since it appeared that the solution rested in something other than further technical training. The 24 guest receptionists were divided into four training groups in order to staff the desk during training and to accommodate the varying workshifts. As each group met, the problem was explained and sample guest complaint letters were reviewed to focus on the problem from the guests' point of view. Interestingly, it was discovered that this was the first time that employees had been shown any guest letters concerning their performance—either positive or negative. Then the groups were asked to brainstorm how these complaints could be overcome.

The employee input revealed several interesting factors. First, heavy convention check-ins sometimes resulted in long lines for as many as six to eight hours during a morning and afternoon shift. Second, whenever there were lines, the supervisors would not permit receptionists to take breaks—nor would they agree to relieve receptionists for breaks. Supervisors felt they needed to be available to handle guest complaints and solve problems that might arise among the six receptionists and among the front desk cashiers who were checking out guests. It was also revealed that check-in delays were most often caused by errors in reservations, which were out of the direct control of the receptionists.

The complexity of the problem required the formation of additional conference groups made up of reservationists and sales department representatives who were responsible for coordinating convention rooming lists. A number of actions were identified and implemented to turn the situation around. Except for the reservations group, additional technical training was not included as a solution—and then only as it related to accurately transferring information from group rooming lists to reservations records.

The foremost solution to this performance problem was to institute a break policy. This policy required that an additional receptionist be scheduled for heavy check-in periods to relieve other receptionists for rest breaks on a rotating basis. The break policy had an observable positive effect on the attitudes of the employees when they worked during heavy check-ins. A second solution was to create a feedback file at the front desk. This file consisted of a three-ring binder into which photocopies of all letters from guests concerning front desk performance were placed. This feedback alone had a dramatic effect on improving employee performance. Third, the decision was made to order new uniforms for front desk employees. Brainstorming had revealed that there was great dissatisfaction with the current uniforms relating to style and comfort. The employees felt that they would communicate more positively to guests if they felt more positive about themselves. Finally, a program was initiated to recognize and reward each employee who was complimented by name in a guest letter by providing him/her with a complimentary dinner for two in one of the hotel restaurants.

Six months after the solutions to these problems were implemented, the company selected this renewed front desk staff to serve as the role model for front desk training for the entire company. The company created its first videotaped front desk training program—with its model staff serving as the actors.

One disadvantage of the conference method is that a freewheeling group may be hard for a trainer to manage. Some people may get angry if the solution adopted does not reflect their opinions. Another disadvantage is that the approach may result in a solution that is so different from the established standard operating procedures that approval must be sought from high-level management. If acceptance from the top is slow in coming or if the solution is rejected, the morale of the group will drop—and the problem is liable to get worse. The organization's top management must be prepared to support this type of training so that the staff may quickly implement acceptable changes.

Finally, some trainers refuse to accept the conference approach as legitimate because it does not emphasize the acquisition of knowledge, skills, or attitudes through a straightforward instructional presentation. However, trainers who understand that their job is to bring out the trainee's best through training and coaching realize that the conference method should be part of their regular training agenda.

Panel Presentation

A panel can be used to present several points of view on the same subject as a basis for discussion or to consider alternative approaches to the same situation. A panel can also function as a team in implementing the four-step training method. Panel members share the preparation, presentation, and follow-up of the instruction. In many ways, a panel represents a team approach to the demonstration method.

The typical panel has three to five members with one member serving as the chairperson or moderator. Rules should be established beforehand and should specify how time will be divided among panel members for making opening remarks or for presenting each point of view. Rules should also address whether panel members will be permitted to interrupt one another with conflicting viewpoints, how questions from the trainees will be directed and answered among panel members, and how the session will be summarized and concluded. The rules should clarify whether panel members are permitted to present ideas that take exception to organizational policies or standard operating procedures.

Panels are most appropriate for general topics when specific performance standards are not required. Suitable topics include merchandising, handling unruly guests, extending catering sales, or creating repeat business. A panel is probably not the most effective way to teach specific job skills. The number of panel members would probably confuse the presentation and the specific details of the job procedures might be lost.

An advantage of the panel approach is that it can heighten trainee interest because of the different points of view held by the panel members. Employees may also feel that managers are more democratic if they encourage the consideration of several opinions. The panel approach is beneficial in showing that there may be more than one good way to achieve the same result.

One disadvantage of the panel approach is that it needs more preparation than methods that require only one trainer. All the panel members should agree on the training objectives, even if they differ on the content required to meet these specific goals. The panel approach is also difficult to evaluate because the method approves different approaches to handling given situations. The only way to evaluate panel approaches is by evaluating the results—in other words, what happens when trainees apply what they learned.

Role Playing

Role playing is a participative method that gives trainees an opportunity to practice the skills of dealing with people. It is a means of learning the "hows and whys" of job behavior. Trainees have the opportunity to try various ways of communicating and interacting with people. Then they analyze why people act a certain way and how the interactions depicted in the role play could be improved. If other members of the group point out how the behavior appeared to them, trainees are able to judge which behaviors achieved desired results.

An advantage of role playing is that, as the skit or scene is analyzed, other members of the group have a chance to state how they would have played the roles differently. The group can discuss the merits of each approach and accept or reject the suggestions. Another advantage is that the method is very useful for developing human relations skills involved in employee-guest relations. Role playing gives the trainees an opportunity to test approaches to sensitive situations in a safe environment.

Role playing is practicing for results. It should not be confused with a play or skit that is performed primarily for entertainment. It requires the preparation of job scenarios that adequately portray problems that need solutions. Role playing instructions should include character descriptions so that all participants are given some guidance as to the personality and attitude of the individuals they will depict. Participants should not see each other's character descriptions. Observers may be given all character descriptions when the role play begins so that they can evaluate whether trainees follow their given roles. The Case in Point which follows describes how one trainer approached the task of preparing for and conducting role plays.

A Case in Point: Overcoming Guest Complaints

The manager of an Italian-style specialty restaurant set out to train the service staff in how to turn guest complaints into positive guest experiences. He had already conducted an extensive skills training program; all the servers demonstrated competence in skill areas, menu knowledge, and routine guest relations. The only area left was training in difficult guest relations situations. The manager began by identifying the following common guest complaints:

1. Service slow or otherwise incompetent
2. Staff surly, unfriendly, and sometimes rude
3. Food unsatisfactory due to temperature, ingredients, or method of preparation
4. Beverages unsatisfactory due to ingredients or preparation
5. Decor or cleanliness of the room unsatisfactory
6. Prices too high
7. Room too noisy
8. Not enough menu selections
9. Unsatisfactory restaurant location

Next, he wrote cards describing a variety of situations based on one or more of these complaints. Each card provided both an employee role and guest role to play. For example:

Guest Situation: Mr. Genelli is a guest in our restaurant on a busy Friday evening. He calls the server over and begins to complain that the clam sauce contains canned clams. He points out that the sauce is described as "Our own freshly made clam sauce" and argues that the description implies the use of fresh clams. He threatens to sue for violation of the truth-in-menu laws if he is not immediately served sauce with fresh clams "as the menu states."

Guest Situation: Ms. Johnson is a guest in our restaurant for the Sunday brunch buffet. She is a southern lady with a charming accent. After going to the buffet and collecting a selection of small servings of several of the dishes, she returns to her table to begin her meal. She is talking incessantly to her lunch companions, and, after several minutes, she signals for a server. She complains that everything on the buffet is cold, and that she just cannot possibly eat cold pasta.

Guest Situation: Late on a busy Saturday evening, Mr. Richards complains to the server that he failed to note the prices on the menu when he ordered his dinner. Now that the check has been presented, he is shocked to learn of the total tab. He and the three businessmen with him have been at their table since about 7:30 p.m. Along with consuming large dinners, they have had two rounds of cocktails and two bottles of a rather expensive red wine. They are not drunk, but they are also not thinking as clearly as they might have been had they not been drinking. Mr. Richards is becoming rather loud and obnoxious and is making remarks to the server such as: "this is highway robbery"; "we don't want to buy the restaurant"; "you must be working on a commission."

To conduct the role plays, the manager designated each trainee either a "guest" or a "server." He gave a card to the "guests" so they would know what type role to play. The "servers" were instructed to apply their technical training, good sense, and the policies and procedures covered in earlier training to handle each situation. The overriding objective was to turn each complaint into a positive guest experience while maintaining established procedures and company policies.

During the actual role plays, the servers who were not actually engaged in the skit were to critically observe and evaluate how the situation was handled. Following each skit, the entire group participated in a discussion about what they learned and how the situation could have been handled differently, and evaluated whether they felt the server had turned the situation around into a positive experience.

A disadvantage of role playing is that it requires a considerable amount of time to get across points that may seem rather simple. Also, time and some creativity are required to write the job scenes. Some employees will resist role plays if they feel shy acting in front of peers. They may have difficulty feeling the realism of the situation. This does not necessarily mean that they will be ineffective in actual on-the-job situations. Such employees may just have difficulty getting into the roles in a simulated situation.

For most employees, role playing is very enjoyable. It can be used within the seminar method as one type of learning activity that involves a high level of employee participation. It can also be incorporated into the four-step training method as the application step in which trainees act out what they have learned—especially in such areas as restaurant service, front desk service, beverage service, and safety and emergency response.

Role Playing Variations. Progressive role playing involves changing the situation or adding information at predetermined times to add to the complexity of the interactions. For example, John may be playing the role of a receptionist and Susan may be playing the role of Ms. Hancock, a business executive with six large and heavy pieces of luggage who is arriving for check-in for a convention. The situation indicates that John is unable to find Ms. Hancock's reservation and that the hotel is full. This may be all the information that is supplied in the beginning.

John proceeds to greet Ms. Hancock, offers assistance, and then begins to show some frustration over not being able to locate the reservation. In turn, Ms. Hancock becomes impatient with the delay. At this point, the situation is altered by two events which neither John nor Susan are expecting. The front desk phone rings and it is a guest on the ninth floor who is upset because his television reception is not clear. About the same time, the sales manager approaches the desk, warmly greets Ms. Hancock, and turns to John to determine the cause of the delay; he tells John that Ms. Hancock is the meeting planner for the convention which has filled the hotel. How John recovers and handles this situation is important to the learning activity and should be consistent with the instructional objectives which influenced the design of the role play.

Another role playing variation is called the **incident method.** Trainees bring in a written narrative of an event or incident that has confronted them in their work. The event or incident should have elements of conflict, in terms of how the writer sees other persons in the situation. The writer should detail as many facts as possible about the other person or persons in the situation. Real names should not be used. The writer should read the incident to the group. The group can then discuss the problem and ask questions for clarification. When the trainer feels that the stage has been set, another trainee should volunteer to participate in the incident while the writer plays him/herself. The role play continues until the incident is resolved.

Another role play variation is a technique called **dialogue training.** In dialogue training, realistic scripts of on-the-job conversations are prepared and put on overhead projector transparencies, poster boards (cue cards), or duplicated on paper for the trainees. Trainees then act out the situation, closely following the scripted dialogue (see Exhibit 6.1). This type of training is sometimes referred to as **scenario training.**

Typical dialogues may involve interaction between guests and employees. The actual role play dialogue is critiqued by the trainees in terms of what was done right and what was done wrong. A group discussion is held to decide what could have been said to improve the situation. The trainer should prompt the group to respond so that every person is involved in the discussion. The objective of dialogue training is to get trainees to think about what to say and do in day-to-day work situations. Since the scripts are realistic, the training promotes understanding of the effect employee behavior can have on others.

Case Studies

A case study is a description or statement of the history of a real or imaginary (but plausible) situation. The case study should provide enough detail that will enable trainees to suggest possible ways of responding to the situation within the performance standards of the organization. The description should detail the events that have led up to the present state of affairs. The case study is used to stimulate group analysis of what occurred and what might have been prevented or changed. A case may be very brief, with just enough details to focus on a specific problem, or it may be quite lengthy with many complex interrelated variables. A sample case study appears in Exhibit 6.2.

Every situation that occurs within an operation has the potential of becoming a training case. Trainers should begin with short cases (one or two paragraphs) and increase the length and complexity of the situations as they gain experience in using the technique.

Large training groups should be divided into smaller groups of three to five employees. Each group should then be given written copies of the case. The groups should be asked to analyze the case and suggest ways that the situation could have been handled to achieve established performance standards. The purpose is to seek better ways of handling situations and to practice making thoughtful decisions. After a reasonable amount of time, the trainer should ask each group to report its opinions. Then everyone can critique and discuss the various approaches.

In some cases there is no clear-cut way to handle a situation. After alternatives have been considered, the group should summarize the approaches it feels would achieve performance standards. It is some-

Exhibit 6.1 Scenario for Bell Staff

Situation:

The bellperson, being alert to the activity of patrons entering the lobby, should step forward and assist the guest with luggage when the guest completes the registration process; no bell or "front" call should be needed to summon the bellperson. The receptionist should introduce the guest to the bellperson as he/she hands the key and rooming slip to the bellperson (without announcing the room number aloud).

Receptionist Script:

Steve, this is Mr. Smith.

Mr. Smith, I hope you enjoy your stay.

Bellperson Script:

Hello Mr. Smith. Welcome to our hotel. Are these all your bags?

Guest Script:

Yes, these are all my bags.

Situation:

Steve leads Mr. Smith to the elevator, waits for the door, and then steps to the right to allow Mr. Smith to enter first. Once in the elevator, Steve begins to talk to Mr. Smith. The conversation should be tailored to the responses of the guest, but when possible should include a personal introduction and an explanation of the hotel's restaurants.

Bellperson Script:

Mr. Smith, I don't know if you caught my name. I'm Steve, and if I can do anything for you to make your stay more enjoyable, please feel free to let me know. I can be reached by dialing #21 on your phone.

We have three very nice restaurants in the hotel. The coffee shop opens at six o'clock in the morning and remains open until midnight. The Fishmarket Restaurant is open for lunch and dinner and serves fresh fish for moderate prices. The Blue Room is our premier dinner restaurant with a five-star rating. It is outstanding and is only open for dinner. You'll need reservations for dinner in the Blue Room.

Situation:

By now, the elevator should have reached the proper floor. The bellperson should exit first, stepping off in the proper direction toward the guest's room, and then pause to lead the way for Mr. Smith. On the way down the corridor, Steve should point out the emergency exits and equipment.

Bellperson Script:

Mr. Smith, we have an excellent emergency response system in this hotel. Please note the emergency exit that we just passed beside the elevator; there is another one at the end of this corridor. There is a fire extinguisher here in the corridor as well as a fire hose. There is an individual smoke detector in your room, as well as a sprinkler system for the entire building.

Situation:

At the room, Steve should unlock the door and enter the room ahead of Mr. Smith. This is to ensure that the room is clean and in order. Steve should reach in and turn on the lights. Then the door should be opened completely and the guest invited in.

Bellperson Script:

Room 321, Mr. Smith, please come in.

Situation:

Steve should hang up any hangable garment bags and place other luggage on luggage racks. Then he should orient Mr. Smith to the room. The dialogue in the room should vary somewhat depending on the time of check-in and the guest's mood. Information should be appropriate for the time of day, and should be shortened if the guest's mood or reaction indicates disinterest.

Bellperson Script:

You have cable channels on your television, as well as a pay movie system. The operation of both of these is explained on the card on top of the set. The television is remotely controlled from your bedside. I have adjusted the heat for 72°. Mr. Smith, I hope that you find everything to your satisfaction. Is there anything that I can get for you?

(continued)

Exhibit 6.1 *(continued)*

Situation:
Mr. Smith should acknowledge that everything is satisfactory or make any requests. Steve should now proceed to leave the room.

Bellperson Script:
There is a complete directory of all the hotel's services in your desk drawer. Here is your key. I hope you enjoy your stay with us.

Situation:
Steve should leave the room and make sure the door closes securely behind him. He should then return immediately to the bell station in the lobby.

---

times helpful to rank the possible solutions from the one most likely to the one least likely to succeed. This forces the participants to take a stand and to defend their opinions.

An advantage of case studies is that they can represent actual or potential problems in the operation. Employees can project themselves into the situations and consider how they would act. A disadvantage of the case method is that realistic cases are not easy to write. Important details related to the history of a situation must be revealed without obscuring the problem itself. If too much emphasis is placed on background information, the problem may get lost in the discussion of the details.

A second disadvantage is that the analysis can be time-consuming. Since training time is always limited, the trainer must be sure that the information being learned is worth the time. Small cases that focus on specific employee-employee interactions or employee-guest interactions can serve as an interesting training activity for daily ongoing training sessions at least once or twice a week.

Simulations

A simulation might be defined as an imitation of the real world, designed to reflect reality. Role playing is a form of simulation. A demonstration within a classroom setting is another form of simulation. Behaviors can be learned through simulation of real work situations. In a classroom, trainees can be asked to simulate or imitate the behavior that will be performed on the job.

Simulations add realism to training by requiring trainees to become actively involved in the learning process. Employees being trained in hotel reservations techniques, for example, can use training telephones to simulate taking reservations. Managers or experienced employees may play the roles of guests calling in to make reservations. Since they know what kinds of special requests guests make, they can simulate a wide variety of guest situations.

Before opening a new dining room, it is often a good idea to simulate the preparation and service of a complete meal. Employees, friends, and suppliers can be invited as the "guests." Restaurant employees are instructed in all the skills beforehand and are told to treat the invited guests as they would treat regular guests. The guests can be invited to review and critique the experience with the staff in payment for their meal. This type of training may seem costly, but it is extremely effective

Exhibit 6.2   Sample Case Study

Case Study: Crackers in the Bed

Mr. Farnsworth checked into the hotel at 10:45 p.m. after traveling nearly 6,000 miles. He was truly exhausted. The check-in went without a hitch. Mr. Farnsworth had a guaranteed room which had been saved for him, even though the hotel was otherwise full. In fact, he was assigned to the last available room. The bellperson had assisted him with his luggage and had returned to the lobby, pleased with the large tip that he had received.

About 10 minutes passed and the phone rang at the front desk. It was Mr. Farnsworth calling, obviously upset, to complain about his bed. It seems that when he turned back the covers and crawled into the bed, he discovered cracker crumbs between the sheets. Getting out of the bed, he turned on the lights to inspect the situation more closely and realized that the sheets had not been changed from the previous guest. As he described the situation, he became more and more upset and was now demanding that something be done immediately to correct the situation.

The receptionist assured Mr. Farnsworth that someone would be right up to take care of the situation. After hanging up the phone, the receptionist realized that it was almost time for both him and the bellperson to get off work; in addition, no one was on duty in housekeeping. Since he had not been approved for overtime, the receptionist wrote a note for the night auditor who was due to arrive any minute and went back to completing the closing report. His note read:

TO: Night Auditor

FROM: Jimmy—Receptionist

DATE: 9/6   10:55 p.m.

Help! Farnsworth, room 901, crackers in bed. Please handle. He is mad!

Jimmy left the note on the night auditor's desk. When the night auditor arrived, Jimmy greeted him, and then almost in the same breath, said good night and rushed to the time clock to punch out by 11:00 p.m. Not once did he mention Mr. Farnsworth's problem.

At 11:20 p.m., the night auditor received a call from Mr. Farnsworth, who is now furious over the situation and lack of response. The night auditor has been busy since his arrival setting up his cash bank and running occupancy and house count reports on the computer; he has not even seen the note that is on his desk.

*   *   *

What steps should be taken to follow through on the situation at this point?

---

and usually will provide a good return on investment. Many of the mistakes that are associated with an opening can be corrected before regular paying guests are present.

Project Approach

Adults learn naturally throughout their lives by engaging in learning projects.[1] The astute trainer can capitalize on this tendency by helping groups, as well as individuals, plan and execute learning projects which are directed toward the organization's learning needs.

In every hospitality operation, there are areas where improvements are needed in systems and procedures. Most employees will set tougher performance standards for their projects than managers will set for them. The project approach should be a regular, ongoing training activity in hospitality operations.

Many projects can develop in-depth competence in reasoning, analysis, synthesis, and application skills. The creation of a new menu for a restaurant can be an excellent learning project for the entire restaurant staff. The development of annual departmental operating budgets is a great project for teaching cost-consciousness and the relationship of costs to revenues. The development of safety inspection systems is best achieved by a group of employees who are likely to emerge from such a project with a high degree of sensitivity toward the potential hazards in the workplace.

Managers often feel that these improvements are their sole responsibility. Since there are so many day-to-day demands on a manager's time, many improvements are never made. A great way to achieve improvements and facilitate learning is to make projects out of these situations and involve employees in working out the details. The project approach builds teamwork, fosters commitment to group goals, and involves employees in various learning activities. Management must accept the fact that the abilities necessary to contribute positively to such projects are not unique traits of management personnel.

Procedures for Group Training

The ability to manage people and activities is clearly demonstrated when a trainer effectively carries out a plan for group training. In the day-to-day activity of a hospitality operation, production demands and guest service needs provide the necessary stimuli for motivating employees. In a group training setting, it is usually difficult to reproduce the urgency of production or service demands. As a result, the learning objectives may seem abstract and may even be labeled with such vague terms as the ability to "comprehend," "understand," "know," and "appreciate" rather than expressing what the trainees will be able to "do." Training objectives should specify observable and measurable learning outcomes whenever possible, even if trainers are limited in how much concrete evaluation of the learning and application they can do in a training setting. Trainers must design and conduct training that ensures visible results when employees perform their jobs.

The four-step training method is just as applicable for groups as it is for individualized training—especially when the objective is to teach a skill or procedure. Any training activity must begin with planning and must continue with presentation of training, practice by the trainee, follow-through, evaluation, and coaching as necessary.

Planning the Group Training Activity

Trainers must plan the total training activity in detail and must anticipate employee needs and reactions. A training plan prescribes what should occur in the learning situation. The concept of a **lesson plan** which is "borrowed" from education has inherent dangers. Most lesson plans emphasize content; therefore, trainers fall into the lecture trap. Chapter 8 provides examples of several plans that can be used to manage a training session. An effective training plan outlines what should be occurring throughout the scheduled training time and provides for content presentations as well as other necessary training activities. The training plan should be prepared well in advance of the training activity.

As the time for the training activity approaches, the trainer should carefully review the plan. Using the plan, the trainer should determine what preparations need to be made, and develop a checklist of errands and setup activities. Time should be spent actually rehearsing content, presentations, and demonstrations.

Handout material should be prepared well in advance of training. In addition, any equipment that will be needed for demonstrations should be obtained. If other people are assisting with the demonstrations, their roles should be reviewed and rehearsed. Demonstrations depict ideal performances, so every detail should be planned.

Arrangements should be made for audiovisual aids. If slides or overhead transparencies are being produced for the program, ample time should be allowed to avoid situations that may result from last-minute film processing. Extra bulbs should be available for all projectors. The trainer should practice setting up and operating the projector before-hand—which includes changing the projector bulbs.

The trainer should plan for the training location. In hospitality operations, training is often conducted in a dining room during closed periods or in banquet function rooms. Every effort should be made to provide clean, well-arranged, comfortable surroundings with appropriate equipment and furniture.

If training is going to take place in a function room, the trainer may be able to enlist the support of the catering and convention services department to set up the basic furniture and equipment. If this is the case, a function event order should be prepared which informs the staff of the setup requirements.

Arrangements for coffee and other refreshments should be made in advance; ashtrays should be provided if smoking is permitted. To accommodate individual preferences, seating may be divided into smoking and no-smoking areas.

Beginning the Training

When the training begins, it is important for the trainer to state the training objectives and discuss why each is important. The trainer should then present an overview of how the training will be conducted. The trainer should also tell the trainees how they will be involved in the training process and what expectations will be held for them. The methods that will be used to evaluate the training and the learning of each employee should be covered in detail. Evaluation should be an ongoing part of every training activity.

Any other logistic details can be covered at this time. The trainees should be informed of the estimated training time and class rules to remove any questions from employees' minds. Once the group has been fully oriented, the trainer should review what the trainees already know about the subject or procedure. A pre-evaluation should have established the need for the training, but a review of those findings would be appropriate. An open discussion of the pre-evaluation findings and their implications for improvement is important in order to relate the training objectives to the group needs. Trainees should know the reason for training—that it is being conducted in response to a defined problem or need. Trainers should explain the current status of this problem or need and how training will change this status.

Control of the Group

Most people resist change. When objectives are reviewed that specify changes in behavior, employees may tend to resist them. Resistance can be overcome if employees become involved in the learning process and are personally committed to the objectives. The trainer must establish a learning environment in which each individual can relate the training to his/her job.

Individual differences are harder to deal with in a group session, but they affect how each employee feels about the training. Some individuals will sit quietly while others will ask many questions. Some people may oppose and criticize the training objectives. Others may try to monopolize the group by showing off or by ridiculing the training program or the trainer. Some individuals may be unmotivated while others are so overzealous and eager that they must be calmed down. Group conversations may show excitement or resistance. In establishing a productive learning environment, the trainer must set some basic behavioral ground rules. When doing so, it is important to recognize individual differences and the positive effect a mixture of attitudes can have.

Training Aids

Retention is always a problem for both trainer and trainees. The trainer becomes frustrated when trainees do not retain what was covered. At the same time, the trainees become frustrated because they are expected to remember so much. A number of approaches can be used to help trainees remember key points or concepts.

Note-Taking. Some trainees take notes; this practice works well for those who would not remember without them. Several techniques encourage effective note-taking. Note forms can be prepared that state the training objectives and provide space for notes related to each objective. Note forms may also have two columns, with an abbreviated outline of the training presentation or activity in the left column and space for note-taking in the right. Note forms may be prepared in the form of questions; space should be provided for the trainees to write the answers to the questions as the training progresses. Determining the answers to these questions becomes an integral part of the learning process. Still another format for note forms is to list key points that the training will cover, leaving space for the trainee to fill in the details of each point as it is learned.

Handouts. Typed outlines or printed job breakdown sheets can also be used to emphasize points and increase retention. Handouts should be well planned and professionally reproduced either in-house or at a copy center. The availability of photocopy equipment may tempt a manager to photocopy handout materials that are not very helpful. Trainers are sometimes tempted to reproduce entire sections of books or articles from magazines. Copyright laws prohibit such practices. Additionally, such published materials rarely deal directly with the training objectives. It is usually best to prepare handouts that meet the specific training objectives.

Supplemental handouts may be distributed before or during the training. If a handout covers general principles, there is little harm in distributing it before it is needed. However, if a handout describes a case history or the rules for a simulation or role play, it should be distributed when it fits into the planned program. If the trainees read this type of handout ahead of time, the impact of the exercise may be diminished.

Work Assignments. Following a training session, every trainee can be given a specific work assignment which requires application of the learning. These assignments are to be performed outside of the group meeting and should increase involvement and retention. Assignments may be made before, during, or after a training activity. Individual assignments emphasize individual input and should be planned to contribute directly to meeting the training objectives.

Brainteasers. A brainteaser is a lot like a complex riddle. It should be work-related and require application of what was learned in the group session. Brainteasers are useful in building retention. Brainteasers can be problems that may be solved by individual trainees or a small group. They can even be taken home and solved in order to maintain trainee interest from one session to the next. These exercises might deal with food or beverage cost calculations, engineering troubleshooting, writing creative menu descriptions, designing new recipes for food or beverage products, and writing service scenarios. Mini-cases about such potentially problematic duties as handling credit cards and reviewing recipes for missing ingredients provide other possibilities. Brainteasers of any type should relate to the objectives of the specific training program.

Effective Group Leadership

Group trainers must be concerned with the effectiveness of their leadership style. The key to a successful training program of any type is planning, preparation, and rehearsal.

Trainers—especially when lecturing—must speak clearly and with emphasis. Relaxation during public speaking can only come after much practice; it should not be expected right away. Remember that sincerity can offset a beginning trainer's nervous behaviors.

It is essential for a trainer to be able to look into the faces of an audience and be mentally conscious of the group's interest or boredom. As a trainer becomes more comfortable leading groups, the ability to "read" an audience becomes more natural. Interest is easier to maintain when a trainer talks *with* a group rather than *to* a group.

Props can be an aid to the trainer. If the trainer is not familiar with the props, then they become a hindrance and a distraction. Props can be audiovisual materials and aids, demonstration materials, or assistants who have agreed to help in some way. Three good rules for any trainer are: (1) know yourself, (2) know your audience, and (3) know your props.

Humor can either contribute positively to a program or destroy it. Some trainers are good at telling humorous stories or jokes that emphasize key points. However, telling jokes just to entertain the group may interfere with the purpose of the training and make it difficult to attain the learning objectives. Very few people can tell humorous stories effectively. In spite of what many books on public speaking recommend about telling funny stories to relax an audience, there is no better way to turn off an audience than to tell a story that falls flat. It is better not to attempt telling stories; the program will survive without them. Sincerity is much more important to the employee whose job performance and career are at stake. Off-color or ethnic jokes and stories are *never* appropriate. They are the marks of an unprofessional.

How to Ask Questions

The process of asking and answering questions is necessary in employee training. When trainees ask or answer a question, the trainer determines whether the employees understand the material or concepts being covered. When trainees are unable to answer questions raised by either the trainer or other trainees, the trainer should proceed to answer the question and reinforce the instruction. There is no excuse for a trainer to be anything less than courteous and patient when questions are asked or answered. Good feelings must prevail if good learning is to result.

Skillful questioning comes from experience. It is a necessary and important process that is part of a manager's training ability. A question stimulates thought and requires employees to account for what they have learned. The trainer should follow several practices when asking questions.

State the Question Clearly. Questions in a training session are usually related to how and why. Unless the trainees understand the question, there is no way to determine whether they understand the materials covered or the procedures demonstrated. Restate questions asked by trainees to be certain that everyone understood what was asked.

Ask Questions on a Random Basis. When details about how the training will be conducted are discussed at the beginning of the session, one "rule" might be that questions will be asked on a random basis. This plan may keep the trainees alert since they will understand that they might be called upon to answer or discuss a question.

If all questions are asked of the audience in general, a few trainees may respond to all of the questions, and it is difficult to determine the comprehension of the quiet members of the group. If questions are answered by a group, it is impossible to determine which individuals in the group are learning. Group answers create confusion in the classroom and are frustrating to those individuals who are having some difficulty understanding the procedure.

Encourage Complete and Clear Answers. The question and answer process not only informs the trainer about what the trainees are learning, but also helps the trainees learn from one another by listening to the questions and answers of co-workers. If they are unable to hear or understand what is being said, no learning is taking place.

If an individual cannot give an exact answer, ask for some ideas about the question's subject which might be "part of the answer." Attempt to build an answer from the partial knowledge held by the trainee and by various members of the group. Then, summarize the pieces, fill in the gaps, and give the full answer as clarification.

Use "Yes" or "No" Questions Sparingly. The purpose of asking questions is to determine the level of understanding. Questions should be worded so that employees respond by explaining or describing a procedure or rationale.

Follow Through on Employee Questions and Probe for Understanding. Examples of questions which demonstrate this point include:

- Questions which are reversed to the person who asked them originally ("I'm not sure what you mean, Joe. Can you tell me more?")

- Questions which are referred to another member of the group to get him/her more involved ("That's a good question, Nancy. How would you answer that, Joe?")

Ask Only One Question at a Time. It is best to ask questions one at a time. As the question is correctly answered, the next question can then be posed.

Building Confidence

Unpleasant feelings and failures tend to prevent personal development and destroy confidence. A trainee's confidence in his/her own ability is a desirable outcome of training. Anything that destroys confidence should be avoided.

In group as well as individual training, the trainer should be careful not to criticize too much or too often. Instead, the trainer should find ways to commend and build on success. It is not possible to build on failure.

Both pleasant and unpleasant feelings underlie learning situations. Unpleasant feelings interfere with successful teaching and learning. Nervousness, fear, anger, melancholy, and disgust are examples of such feelings. They agitate the entire body and interfere with learning, the development of skills, and the building of confidence. They tend to block judgments of situations, and they often cause accidents.

Not all feelings are exhibited outwardly. Many emotions are expressed internally. It is not uncommon for trainees to experience such conditions as headaches, depression, loss of appetite, and poor digestion when extremely unpleasant feelings are present. Trainees respond to extreme feelings in different ways. Some react more than others, but it is safe to assume that all employees are alike in one respect: unpleasant feelings are detrimental to learning.

Trainees who are easily upset require tolerant, sympathetic attention. Trainers are not always qualified to recognize varying degrees of emotions. Therefore, it is advisable to avoid eliciting the emotions of trainees through ridicule or sarcasm.

The trainer should try to do those things that will build confidence. Confidence is a favorable attitude that will help overcome extreme emotional conditions. The trainer should be calm, have poise, and be firm.

Notes

1. Allen Tough, *The Adult's Learning Projects* (Ann Arbor, Mich.: Books on Demand, University Microfilms International, 1979).

7 Using Audiovisual Aids

Individuals learn through the five senses of sight, taste, touch, smell, and hearing. Often, only one sense is involved because the training is limited to lecturing or reading printed policies and procedures. Understanding and retention can be enhanced by increasing learner participation and by using training methods which stimulate more of the senses. When used effectively, audiovisual aids provide a variety of stimulating approaches and yield very good results.

Different types of projection and non-projection media are available for different training situations. Managers should know the advantages and disadvantages of the most popular types to select the best media for the intended purpose.[1] It is also advisable for managers to be aware of the costs associated with particular media when deciding among alternatives.

Managers should know how to design slides, flip chart pages, overhead transparencies, audio recordings, video recordings, and so on, for the best results. The manager who is preparing to be a competent trainer must learn when an audiovisual aid will increase understanding and retention. Audiovisuals that are poorly planned or incorrectly used only increase confusion and can destroy the manager's credibility as a trainer.[2]

Overview of Audiovisual Aids

Audiovisual aids are teaching and learning materials that have sound *and* visual characteristics. When the term is used in a general sense in this book, it may refer to aids with sound and/or visual characteristics; when materials are specifically limited to either sound or visual characteristics, they will be referred to as audio aids or visual aids, respectively.

Audiovisual aids are tools for both the trainer and the trainee. They can be used by the trainer to help make a point. Also, complete training presentations can be placed on audiovisual equipment and the program can be self-administered by the trainee. This results in self-directed learning; the trainer does not need to be physically present for the training. When a trainer conducts a training session or makes a presentation, it is important to determine the instructional method that will work best to achieve the specified learning objectives.

Audiovisuals can be useful in many training activities, but they do have limitations when used to teach certain skills. For example, a movie, videotape, or slide-sound presentation can be used to train cooks in how to prepare a particular food product; however, the trainees will not experience the taste or aroma of the product until it is actually prepared in the kitchen. The trainees cannot know whether the smell or taste is correct unless someone else who has produced the product before can judge it. To some extent, the same limitations are true for learning the correct consistency, color, texture, degree of doneness, and serving temperature. If the audiovisual is used along with samples of the actual products, or reinforced with actual cooking demonstrations, the training can be very effective because of the variety of human senses involved.

When audiovisuals are used in self-directed learning programs, they can actually substitute for the presence of an instructor. The instructor's presentation is programmed into the particular audiovisual medium. The trainees receive the training from the instructor via the audiovisual equipment. One advantage of using this approach is that the presentation is usually made from a script. In the process of writing and editing a script, there is a tendency to prepare a better presentation than might be the case in a live presentation. The same presentation can also be made with less training time. On the negative side, if a trainer is unavailable, the learner may have no one to ask questions of if he/she fails to understand the audiovisual program.

A common practice in the hospitality industry is to contract the production of audiovisual training programs through consultants and specialized production companies. These programs are tailor-made for the client organization and are supplied along with the equipment for standardization of training. This approach is especially popular in organizations with a number of similar operations. Many of these programs are self-instructional; some involve several audiovisual media. Some programs may be interactive, meaning that the learner responds to questions posed by the media. The responses of the learner activate the particular learning paths taken by the program. While some of these programs are very sophisticated and very effective, they are also very costly. As with any investment, the cost-effectiveness must be considered before purchasing such programs.

Any audiovisual approach has advantages and disadvantages. At this point it is sufficient to say that audiovisual aids are not helpful in every training situation. They do not replace effective needs analysis, training design, and evaluation.

Hardware and Software

Trainers must understand the definition of two audiovisual terms. **Hardware** refers to the equipment that is used in an audiovisual presentation or program. The equipment could be projectors, recorders, flip chart easels, flannel boards, chalkboards, screens, video monitors, or computer terminals. **Software** refers to the programs that are developed and presented through the use of particular hardware; for example, films, 35mm slides, overhead transparencies, pre-printed pads for flip charts, audio or videotapes, or computer programs. Trainers should learn how to use audiovisual equipment, what types of hardware are available, the advantages and disadvantages of the software required for each type of hardware, and the degree of difficulty involved in producing the various software.

The user of any audiovisual aid must never lose sight of the purpose of the training activity. There are many audiovisual aids available that are fun, colorful, and interesting. But unless the instruction presented meets a defined learning need, time is largely wasted, and the cost of the activity is unjustified.

The most complete source of audiovisual equipment and aids will generally be a school or an educational supply company. Such firms are found in most cities. Secondary sources include office or camera supply firms.

Cost   The cost of audiovisual aids varies greatly. A poster is probably the simplest, least expensive visual aid that can be prepared. The cost of producing quality color video programs or color movies can easily exceed $1,000 per minute of program time. Multi-media and interactive programs are even more costly. Some companies have gone to great expense to produce elaborate audiovisual systems, both in terms of hardware and software investments.

The manager who is interested in using audiovisual aids will need to obtain current price quotes in the locale where the production will be done or where the equipment will be purchased. The decision to use an audiovisual aid should not be based primarily on cost nor on whether another hospitality company has decided to use the approach. When selecting audiovisual tools, the major concern should be whether a particular medium is needed to accomplish the training goals and what alternatives are available. Each alternative should be analyzed to determine the most cost-effective approach. There are no hard and fast rules for selecting an audiovisual approach. In many situations, the equipment and materials that make up the work station are all that is needed to achieve the training objectives.

Relevance   Audiovisual aids should be relevant to the training. One of the problems of producing expensive software such as films and videotapes is that the programs may become dated before the production investment is recovered. The hospitality industry is constantly changing because of technological innovations and new developments in the marketplace. Changes in both hospitality industry equipment and audiovisual hardware affect software needs.

Many skills in the hospitality industry are very simple to learn while many pieces of audiovisual equipment are difficult to operate. Whenever trainers or trainees become more concerned about the correct operation of the audiovisual equipment than they are about teaching or learning the simple skills being presented, the learning objective is obscured and the audiovisual becomes a hindrance to the learning process. Simple skills are best taught using straightforward, simple training methods. Audiovisual aids should be no more complicated to master than the skills that they are being used to teach.

Selecting an appropriate, effective audiovisual aid is not easy. Many trainers ignore the possibility that there may be better aids available than those with which they are familiar. Whenever new material is taught, new audiovisual aids should be considered. Even a slight change in a training objective can affect an otherwise useful audiovisual aid. To meet the requirements of changing lessons and objectives, trainers must constantly re-evaluate their audiovisual aids.

Determining Needs

The first and probably most important consideration in planning audiovisual aids is to determine the need. Whenever there are points of instruction that are difficult to explain verbally, an audio and/or visual aid may be helpful. If a verbal description fails to convey a clear and complete image, a visual may be all that is needed to clarify matters for the trainee. Consideration of need should be applied not only to new training programs but to older, established training programs as well.

Audiovisuals also may be used to stimulate interest at appropriate points throughout the training session. However, any audiovisual aid the trainer uses to heighten interest should be related to the material being taught and to the training objective.

When a trainer has decided that an audiovisual aid is needed, the next step is to determine specifically what the aid should accomplish. The training objectives should be reviewed to assess what the trainees must be able to do as a result of the learning. Is it possible to develop the particular competence without an audiovisual aid? What is the mental image that the training is attempting to fix in the trainees' memories so that they will recall what was taught when that information and skill are required on the job?

Selection and Design

Audiovisual aids must be correctly designed, carefully selected, and skillfully used by the trainer in order to be effective. They should last long enough to be reused for training until they become outdated or damaged. This is important because considerable time, labor, and expense are involved in production. In addition, an audiovisual aid should be understandable, simple, accurate, realistic, colorful, and manageable.

Understandable. A visual has to be legible and a sound track has to be audible. The visual must be capable of being seen and understood by all trainees. This involves the overall design, the size of lettering, and strong sharp contrasts. Accuracy, realism, and clarity of detail should also be considered. An audible sound track means that the voice, music, or other sounds are clear, communicate the message in a straightforward manner, and carry well throughout the room. If the sound track is garbled, has static interference, lacks balanced volume, or is otherwise difficult to understand, it will interfere with learning and fail to meet the training objectives.

Simple. An audiovisual aid will appeal to a broad audience if it is simple without being simplistic. If it is complicated, it will generally meet with varying degrees of resistance. This is true of both verbal and pictorial visuals as well as audio aids. Verbal visuals include words that are reproduced on slides, flip chart pads, posters, or a chalkboard. Often, trainers try to put too much information on a single slide or flip chart sheet. The results are confusing. The problem is even greater with photographs and pictorial visuals.

If a visual aid is being used to introduce trainees to specific components of a piece of complicated equipment, these components should be highlighted in relation to the rest of the machine. Trainers should not use slides that fail to show any distinction between the components that trainees should identify and the rest of the equipment. Non-essentials distract and confuse trainees, lessening the effectiveness of the visuals.

Audio aids such as audio cassettes or the audio portion of a video can be ineffective if they attempt to say too much. The trainer should keep the dialogue simple and use background music sparingly. The music should not be entertainment. If the trainees hear a popular tune, they may mentally sing along and fail to hear the training message—unless the message is conveyed through the lyrics. The purpose of music on most audio aids should be to fill up dead spaces in the dialogue and to allow time for the training points to sink in. A trainer should guard against selecting or designing audio aids where the music drowns out the message. In using published music, the trainer must comply with copyright laws which make it illegal to reproduce such music for any purpose without the written permission of the owner of the copyright.

Accurate. Trainees will often reject a training session because of incorrect or obsolete information that is presented through an audiovisual aid. Audiovisual materials should be current, accurate, and precise. When facts, procedures, statistics, specifications, prices, rates, policies, rules, or formulas are presented, they must be exact and up-to-date.

If a visual is designed to a specified scale, it should be designed to the same scale throughout, or should clearly indicate when the scale size changes. This will enhance the explanation and add to a visual's accuracy.

Realistic. A realistic audiovisual aid usually is accepted with a positive response by trainees. Realism allows trainees to more easily transfer what they learned in a training setting to an on-the-job situation. Trainers must select or design aids with realistic details and characteristics. Photographs taken on-site, drawings, graphic designs, flow charts, and actual equipment can be used as realistic visuals. Demonstrations that use real objects from the job allow both trainees and trainers to simulate the work that will be performed following the training.

Colorful. Color is an integral part of vision, so nothing is more important in visual aids than using natural and realistic colors to help trainees learn. Visuals are more realistic when properly colored. A predominant color helps focus attention. For example, the shelf above the change drawer on a cash register could be highlighted with a circle of red on a black and white photo to emphasize where currency should be placed until change is made. Colorful displays, exhibits, or printed materials have more emotional appeal than their drab black and white counterparts.

Of course, there can be too much color. Since color affects the relative importance of items, overcoloring produces confusion. Trainers should always study their training needs and the effect color will have on the trainees, and design the visuals accordingly. In selecting colors, it is important to use natural colors. Purple broccoli, green carrots, and blue apples may be interesting, but such indiscriminate use of colors will not enhance the learning process.

Manageable. Trainers should not devise a visual that is too large or too awkward to handle. Occasionally a full-size model or an oversize reproduction is needed, but smaller substitutes will usually serve the purpose. If large visuals are needed or if an unwieldy visual must be used, the trainer should re-examine the training objectives, the audiovisuals, and the facilities. Relocating instructional space, for example, might solve the problem. If trainees are ready for direct contact with the material, the trainer might substitute actual equipment for the visual. Where instructional site changes are not advisable, models, mock-ups, and small-scale objects can often produce adequate visual impressions.

How to Use Audiovisuals

There are many ways to use audiovisuals for maximum effectiveness. In all cases, these aids must be used correctly in order to function effectively. For example, if audiovisuals are out of sequence or exposed to trainees at the wrong time, they will detract from the presentation. Instruction should be planned so that there is a suitable environment, necessary equipment, and appropriate materials. A trainer will become frustrated when he/she plans to use specific instructional materials and then discovers that the room cannot be darkened for projection or that the visual message cannot be seen by trainees in the rear of the room.

Just as lesson plans are organized in logical sequence, so should audiovisuals be properly arranged. Random use of audiovisual material is equal to a rambling presentation. Trainers should practice using audiovisuals so they become familiar with the sequence, content, and volume of the audio. This also enables the trainer to check on the adequacy of the audiovisuals in the actual training setting.

The following are procedures for using audiovisuals effectively.

Explain the Message to the Trainees. Elaborate audiovisuals are often used to illustrate complicated or technical subjects. Before using this kind of audiovisual, the trainer should briefly explain its purpose and function. Otherwise, the trainees may be distracted by details of the visual and miss part of the audio presentation.

Display at the Appropriate Time. Visuals should be covered or out of view when not in use to avoid attracting unnecessary attention. If a chart or overhead transparency contains lines of print, strips of paper can be cut to cover each line and can be removed one by one at the appropriate time. Key points can be presented using 35mm slides—with one point on each slide. Models and cutaways can be covered with cloth.

Use a Pointer. A pointer can be used to focus attention on a particular part of a visual. It should be held steadily on the part of the visual that trainees are expected to observe. It should also be held in the hand nearest the visual in order to maintain better eye contact with the class.

If the pointer is held across the body, the trainer is likely to speak to the visual rather than to the trainees. To help prevent distraction, the pointer should be put aside when it is not needed.

Use Assistants to Best Advantage. If assistant trainers or volunteers from the class are used to help present the audiovisuals, they should know exactly what to do and when to do it. If an assistant is projecting visuals, a prearranged signal can tell him/her when to change the slides or when to turn off the projector. Any time assistants are used to help the main trainer, it is important that their behavior complements the training and doesn't distract participants in any way.

Display Visuals Smoothly. When using several visuals, trainers should number them in the order in which they will be used. If possible, equipment should be set up before the training session. If not, it should be moved in quietly to avoid disturbing the class. Remote control devices for projectors and video monitors can ease the presentation process. When used effectively, audiovisual aids are beneficial in achieving training objectives; ineffective use causes them to be an interference to the learning process. Consider how audiovisual aids are designed and used for maximum effect in the following Case in Point.

A Case in Point: Excellent Audiovisuals

The U.S. military makes extremely effective use of audiovisual aids to present briefings and training programs. Some of the principles they follow could benefit any trainer.

First, the military plans its visuals well. The trainers effectively use the medium selected, and spend the necessary money to prepare professional quality visuals. Most overhead transparencies are prepared by a graphic artist. The policy is that if the information requires a visual, it deserves a good visual. For many civilian trainers, visuals are just fillers, designed because someone suggested that there should be a visual to spark interest. Not so with the military. Unless the visual communicates the message more clearly than the speaker, the visual is not included.

Audio scripts are prepared for maximum impact. There is no such thing as an ad lib verbal presentation in an audio medium. Even live verbal presentations in briefings and training have carefully planned and scripted messages. Humorous stories and jokes are often included but they are programmed with the main message and are there to make a specific point.

Assistants help with audiovisuals both in terms of setting up equipment and in operating the systems during the presentations. This frees up the primary presenter to concentrate on the message being communicated and the reactions of the audience.

Exhibit 7.1   Front Projection

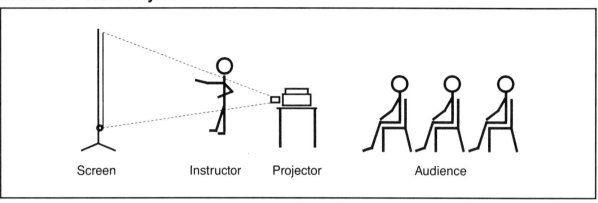

Functions and Types of Audiovisual Media

Good trainers use audiovisuals because they recognize that a training presentation without audiovisuals may be inadequate. Trainers must convert ideas into words when they train. These words are then spoken to the trainees who must decode and convert them into meaningful ideas. Consider the difficulty which even the simplest oral explanation presents: A trainer describes a stairway leading to the top of a lighthouse to trainees who have never been in a lighthouse. He/she describes it as a spiral—like a corkscrew or bedspring. Regardless of how much care is taken to describe the staircase, there is likely to be little uniformity in the way that trainees interpret the description. If the trainer had displayed a graphic visual such as a photograph or accurate drawing, the trainees would have received the intended concept more quickly and accurately.

Good audiovisuals can illustrate the trainer's concept and emphasize essential points when information is difficult to explain verbally, when specific procedures must be performed, and when exact understanding is necessary. A picture is worth a thousand words when trainers try to describe something that trainees have never seen. But, better than a picture may be the real thing if it is readily available. Even then, an understanding of how it works may be more quickly gained with flowcharts, schematic drawings, enlarged photos of the small components, and visuals that show the hidden parts.

Projection Media

It is sometimes difficult for the trainer to gain the trainees' full attention. Projection media can be a powerful means of capturing and holding attention. The concentration of focused light on a screen combined with the images that represent the teaching points can effectively direct and hold the trainees' attention on the training subject.

Two different methods may be used to project images onto a screen. The choice of method will influence the projection system and the mode of instruction. The first method—**front projection**—permits both the projector and the viewers to be on the same side of the viewing screen (see Exhibit 7.1). The image is cast onto a screen or any light-colored wall or surface. To use front projection most effectively, the screen should be

Exhibit 7.2 Rear Projection

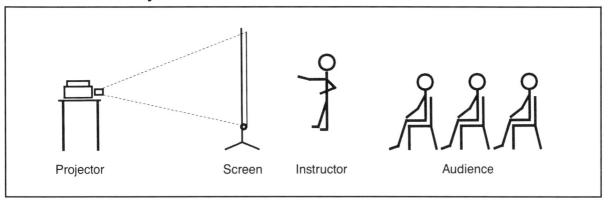

Projector   Screen   Instructor   Audience

mounted above the height of the average instructor or to one side of the room to reduce the likelihood of obstruction of the projector's light beam.

In **rear projection,** the projection equipment and the viewers are on opposite sides of a screen through which the image is displayed (see Exhibit 7.2). Rear projection requires less restriction of natural daylight or artificial lighting within the classroom than front projection. This allows better interaction between the trainer and trainees when the visuals are presented in conjunction with live presentations. With rear screen projection, the trainer can stand in front of the image to point out details without casting distracting shadows onto the screen or blocking the projected image.

Rear projection requires additional space behind the screen so that the projector can cast an image far enough to maximize legibility. Combinations of mirrors or short focal-length lenses can be used to offset the need for a large amount of space (see Exhibit 7.3). However, the short focal-length lenses or mirrors may result in an inferior projected image and increase the cost of setting up the visual aids.

If a screen is mounted flat against a wall or a portable screen is used with the surface of the screen exactly perpendicular to the floor, the image projected on the screen will be wider at the top of the screen than at the bottom. This condition is called keystone effect and results in a distorted visual aid (see Exhibit 7.4). To correct this problem, the center of the projected beam of light must be exactly perpendicular (90° angle) to the center of the screen's surface. This can be accomplished by either of two methods: (1) the top of the screen can be tilted 12 inches forward into the projector's light beam; (2) the screen can remain flat (perpendicular to the floor) and the projector can be elevated to a height directly perpendicular to the center of the screen (see Exhibit 7.5). By following either of these two procedures, the projected image will appear square and undistorted on the screen.

Many types of projection media are available, each having advantages and limitations. Since different media require specific projection devices, each is discussed separately.

35mm Slides. The projection equipment used with 35mm slides is simple to use; the skills required to operate the equipment can be learned in

Exhibit 7.3 Rear Projection Using Mirror and Short Focal-Length Lens

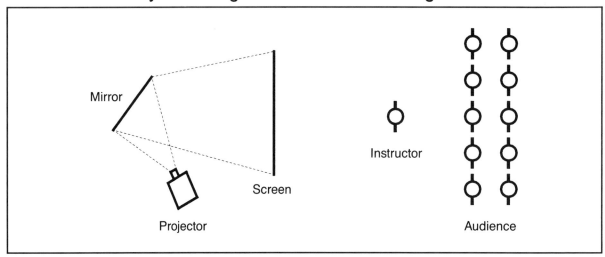

Exhibit 7.4 Keystone Effect on Screen

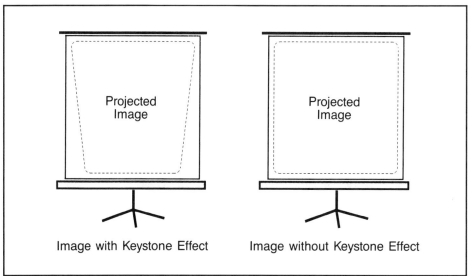

minutes.[3] Modern, automatic 2- by 2-inch slide projectors have round or rectangular trays that serve as storage compartments for slide sets and as part of the slide-feed mechanism. Fully automatic projectors change slides at pre-determined rates, while others operate by remote or manual control. For slide presentations with audio components, equipment is available for programming inaudible (silent) signals onto the audio tape. These signals will automatically cause the 35mm slide projector to advance the slides at the desired points in the recorded verbal presentation.[4]

The 35mm slide itself is a transparent picture or image, individually mounted in a 2- by 2-inch cardboard, metal, or plastic frame. The image is projected onto a screen or other flat surface by passing a strong light through it. Slides are compact and convenient to manage, and they

Exhibit 7.5   Elimination of Keystone Effect

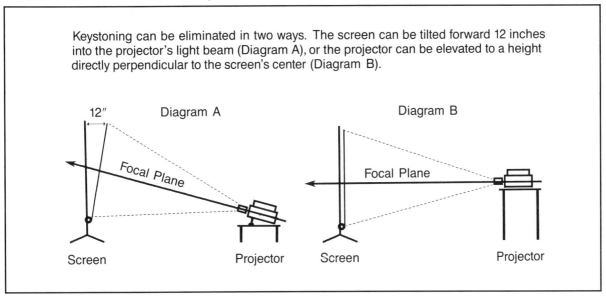

Keystoning can be eliminated in two ways. The screen can be tilted forward 12 inches into the projector's light beam (Diagram A), or the projector can be elevated to a height directly perpendicular to the screen's center (Diagram B).

render clearly detailed images if the photography is of high quality. Message content can be brought up-to-date by replacing individual slides with new ones. Additional or replacement slides can be easily inserted at the desired sequence in the program. Slides that are going to be reused many times should be mounted in frames between thin sheets of glass (referred to as glass mounted) since the heat from the projector may cause the slides to warp. Warped slides tend to jam in the feed mechanism of automatic slide projectors.

Slide sets are most easily handled when stored in the slide tray that will be used with the particular projector. One tray usually comes with each projector, but additional trays are available at a reasonable cost. These trays of slides should then be placed in the boxes that the trays came in, and the training topic or program title marked on the outside.

If 35mm slides are to be shown by direct rear-screen projection, without the use of mirrors, the slides must be reversed (placed front to back) in the feed trays. If this is not done, the images on the screen will be backward. By numbering the slide mounts consistently in the top right-hand corner on the front, it is easy to quickly arrange all the slides in a tray without confusing their orientation to the screen. The front of a 35mm slide can be determined by looking at the slide without a projector; the slide is front side up when the image has the same orientation as a photograph.

Trainers can discuss details with the trainees while showing a slide. As a general rule, a single slide should be exposed to trainees for at least 5 seconds to permit comprehension, but not more than 90 seconds to avoid boredom. If a longer period is needed for explanation, additional slides should be added for variety.

Filmstrips. A filmstrip consists of a series of 35mm single frames processed into a single strip. Filmstrips are wound into rolls and stored in can-like containers approximately one inch in diameter by two inches in length. Each filmstrip is equivalent to numerous 35mm slides, charts, pictures, or drawings. Since the entire filmstrip must be reproduced to change the frame sequence or to update a single frame, trainers should consider using filmstrips only when the subject matter will remain constant for an extended period. It is more costly to reproduce a filmstrip than to replace individual overhead transparencies or 35mm slides. Otherwise, filmstrips do not require much storage space and are inexpensive to mail to various locations in chain-organization training programs.

Overhead Transparencies. Overhead projectors operate on the principle of passing an intense light through a transparent slide. The image is then passed through a mirrored lens and reflected on the screen. The overhead projector slide is made of a transparent plastic, cellophane, or acetate sheet with a size up to 10 by 10 inches. Slides are very versatile and can be prepared without any special photography skills.[5] Tracings, drawings, lettering, and photographic reproductions on these transparent sheets can be projected clearly on the screen. The image will have equal brilliance on front- or rear-screen projection. If the slides are going to be changed by the trainer, front-screen projection is more appropriate. Because of the strong projection light, overhead projection can be used in an area where it is not possible to have total darkness. The overhead projector is usually operated manually. If a projectionist or assistant instructor will be changing the slides, the trainer should review the transparencies before training to make sure the slides are in the right order for presentation.

Trainers can prepare overhead projector slides by several means. The easiest way is to use a grease pencil or an erasable felt-tip pen designed for writing on acetate surfaces. This can be a very effective way to create good visuals if the trainer has good penmanship and some artistic abilities.

Transparencies can also be made by typing the information on a plain piece of paper, and then photocopying the typed information onto a transparency. Normal size pica or elite type is small for transparencies, and should only be used when the training group and training room is small. For larger groups, transparencies should be made with bulletin-size type or on a photocopy machine that has enlargement capabilities. Some dot matrix computer printers can also produce enlarged or double-width characters. Some laser printers produce large-size fonts of professional quality.

Trainers can also create excellent transparencies using transferable letters. Most office supply stores sell a variety of type styles of transferable letters for graphic arts applications. These letters can be transferred to paper or directly to overhead acetate transparencies; they do not require special equipment or artistic abilities. Easy-to-follow instructions are usually included with the letter-sets.

One manufacturer of overhead projectors recommends that transparencies containing only written material be limited to six lines of information and six words per line. This is a good guideline to follow when preparing transparencies.

Many commercially prepared transparencies are excellent in quality.

Trainers should consider the following criteria when purchasing commercially prepared transparencies or preparing their own:

- Does the subject lend itself more to transparencies than to the actual equipment that the trainee will use on the job, or to other visual aids such as posters, charts, mounted photographs or drawings, 35mm slides, filmstrips, videotapes, or computer graphics?
- Is the content accurate and up-to-date?
- Are transparency techniques such as overlays used effectively?
- Are letter size and color quality adequate?
- Will trainee participation be encouraged through the use of the transparency?

In setting up the screen for front-screen overhead projection, trainers should realize that keystoning is usually a greater problem with overhead projection than with 35mm slides. It is important to remember that keystoning should be overcome for the visuals to have maximum impact.

Opaque Projection. The opaque projector reflects light from the surface of the original visual to the screen. Consequently, the projected image is less bright and often unfavorable when compared to direct light projection through a film slide or overhead transparency. The main advantage of opaque projection is that this type of equipment will project all kinds of printed matter (color and black and white) and some three-dimensional objects; it does not require a slide or transparency.

Newer opaque projectors are less bulky to handle and provide more light than older models. Nevertheless, a relatively dark room is needed in order to get viewable results. Both old and new opaque projectors contain projection lamps that generate considerable heat. Paper that is exposed to the light for more than a few minutes may char or even ignite. Also, some types of plastic may soften, discolor, or burn when exposed to the heat for an extended period. Opaque projectors are used infrequently today and should probably be considered only by trainers who already have the equipment available.

Video and Motion Picture Media. Video recordings and motion picture media essentially perform the same functions. Each displays events or a sequence of events with movement as compared to still photographs, overhead transparencies, 35mm slides, or filmstrips. Videos or motion pictures can be substituted for live demonstrations which may require expensive equipment. They should be considered when motion is needed to show how ideas relate to each other, to build continuity of thought, or to create a dramatic impact. For example, the trainer may want to design a training activity with a learning objective that requires trainees to identify the steps in braising. A film clip could show how to sear the meat, add stock, bring the liquid to a simmer, cover the cooking container, and then show the results. Videos or motion pictures could realistically demonstrate this process without a time lapse of two or three hours, which is not unusual when braising less-tender cuts of meat.

Three-dimensional characteristics can also be portrayed quite readily via video or motion pictures. If the trainer wants to show trainees how to decorate a cake, the procedure could be videotaped or filmed to show the cake being turned in various directions as it is decorated. Thus, trainees can learn to identify three-dimensional characteristics from a two-dimensional medium.

Trainers have limited influence on trainees during such presentations due to the pace and structure of motion pictures and television. Their influence is largely confined to what happens before and after the presentation. Trainers can tell trainees what to expect and can help them recall and organize what they saw and heard, but the presentation cannot be speeded up or slowed down. Trainers cannot normally explain, clarify, or correct during the presentation without distracting from the ongoing training.

The videotape system (camera, recorder, and video monitor) has the capability of instant replay, which can be controlled by the trainer and used for performance analysis. Videotape can have a tremendous impact when used to critique trainees' on-the-job performance.

One drawback of video is cost. At commercial rates, professional quality video production costs about $1,000 to $4,000 per minute. This figure can be substantially lowered through in-house capabilities and substantially raised if expensive talent or special effects are involved.[6] Costs consist of such expenses as:[7]

- Recording days (cost of production crew)

- Talent (cost of narrators, actors, directors, etc.)

- Rental of studio (or cost of using a hotel's facilities)

- Editing (cost of time, professional editing equipment, and professional editor)

- Formatting (cost of finalizing, packaging, and preparing supplemental instructional materials)

In addition to production costs, using videotape for training requires expenditures for playback units and monitors for each training location. If the programs are to be used in chain-type hospitality operations, the costs of mass producing and distributing multiple copies must also be included.

Laser Videodiscs. An emerging video technology that has applications for training is the laser videodisc. The principles of use are the same as for videotape. Recordings are made on discs that look much like records or albums without visible grooves. The information is recorded and played back by a laser light process. The primary advantage of the laser video recording method is that the original quality of the audiovisual presentation is much higher. The program can be replayed many times with no observable change in the quality of the audio or visual images. Videotapes tend to wear out with use, and the quality of the audio and video become unacceptable over time. Multi-media applications of video-tape and videodisc are further discussed later in this chapter.

Film Loops. A variation in filmstrips and moving pictures is the continuous film loop—silent or with sound. Film loops are usually made from 8mm movie film and are packaged in cartridges with capacities ranging from about four to thirty minutes. These cartridges are easily inserted in the appropriate slot of a film loop projector. The film appears on a small screen built into the projection unit. Some projectors are adjustable so that the program can be shown on a larger, external screen for group viewing.

The film loop can easily be operated by either the trainer or the trainees. The latter may use the loop projector for individualized instruction without requiring much training space. As a self-instructional device, the film loop has another advantage: the trainee can use it as often as necessary to review or reinforce learning. The same principle applies to the use of videotape recordings.

A disadvantage of film loops is that the cartridges are usually not interchangeable between different brands of projectors. Regular, open-reel 16mm films can be projected using any brand of 16mm projector; videotapes have become standardized into a very few interchangeable tape formats. With film loops, however, the choice of cartridge type dictates the type of projector to be used.

Non-Projection Media

Training aids are not limited to projection media. Various objects can also be used to attain learning objectives. The workplace provides a multitude of training media that can enhance learning by stimulating any of the five senses. Trainers must realize that non-projection media can sometimes serve as an effective alternative to projection media.

Real Objects. Real objects include such things as ingredients, products, equipment, printed forms, and people. In many learning situations no better teaching device exists than a hands-on session with the real object being studied or a face-to-face meeting with the people being served.

For example, a training objective might require trainees to know the various tasks involved in cleaning a guestroom. This objective can best be illustrated in an actual guestroom where the objects concerned with the tasks are in their natural setting. Real objects can also be brought to the classroom. For example, food and beverages or models of food and beverages can be used in a class on dining room service.

The more closely a learning experience approximates the actual job conditions, the more effective and permanent learning will be. Of course, real objects may not always be available, or they may be so large that they cannot be brought into the classroom. Sometimes too, real objects are so small that the trainer cannot use them effectively for group instruction. However, a diagram of a small item can be made into a transparency and projected for a larger view with an overhead projector. Pictures, films, videotapes, slides, and models can be used when real objects are not practical. Even when these media are used to increase size and detail, the real objects could be shown briefly to trainees, then put aside for individual review. No matter how well-made, a reproduction is not as vivid as the object itself.

Cutaways. A particularly effective three-dimensional teaching device is the cutaway. Components of the real object are literally "cut away." The item is opened so that the interior can be clearly seen. Cutaways are useful in training when the inner parts of an item need to be displayed. Cutaways can be used to show how foods such as cantaloupes and watermelons should be selected for quality. They enable the trainees to look at exterior and interior qualities at the same time.

To eliminate the recurring costs of preparation, cutaways are often photographed and processed into an overhead transparency or 35mm slide.

Models. A model is a recognizable imitation of the real object and is often made of plastic, wood, or metal. It may look and work exactly like the original but be smaller or larger. The purpose of making a model is to enlarge or reduce the real object to a manageable size. Models increase the reality of any training session; they help trainees learn to recognize and identify objects.

When making scale models, the craftsman can rearrange or construct individual parts to show relationships to the whole. For example, a model of a hotel ballroom could be presented so that table arrangements are portrayed with scale models of tables and chairs. Since such models can be made larger or smaller than life-size, both trainer and trainees can easily handle and use the materials.

Chalkboards, Posters, and Charts. The chalkboard is inexpensive and requires no special skills. A major disadvantage is that the material presented on its surface has to be erased.

Posters and charts can be retained for future use. Posters and charts must be simple to be effective; the material should be understandable at first glance. Posters and charts are portable, adaptable, easy to store, and economical. Posters and charts require very little special equipment except a crayon or felt marker and a piece of cardboard or poster board.

Flip Charts. Flip chart paper pads are mounted on an easel and provide all the advantages of a chalkboard and poster. Blank pages can be used for jotting down ideas or key points as they are developed by the trainer and trainees; pre-prepared charts can be interspersed to emphasize key points.

Resource People. Besides the training aids mentioned, the trainer should not overlook the possibility of using resource people. A resource person is one who is a specialist in, or has particular knowledge about, the material being covered in the training session. This person could be a guest speaker or demonstrator.

Personalized Multi-Media Systems

A multi-media system is actually a combination of instructional materials that can be used in a learning situation. These materials—often called instructional kits or learning packages—may include written, pictorial, and/or audiovisual media. The possible combinations are limitless depending on the training facilities and on the ability of the trainer to make effective use of a number of interwoven media forms.

Audiovisual equipment is available that facilitates the use of multi-media programs. As discussed in Chapter 5, advances in computer applications have greatly expanded this type of programmed instruction and will greatly affect future multi-media training. Automated and manually controlled operations may be combined to present sound or silent filmstrips, motion pictures, slides, audio and/or videotaped segments, and quizzes. Special control units are available to program the interfacing of the various media used. Training programs can be developed so that the trainee can stop for work assignments or personalized instructions or explanations by a trainer. When the trainee returns to the audiovisual presentation, he/she will be quizzed through the programmed audiovisual medium on what he/she learned in the work assignment or personalized instruction. Based on the responses, the equipment can actually assess the trainee's level of comprehension at that stage and determine what should be taught next.

The following Case in Point describes one type of personalized multi-media system that can be used to train hospitality personnel.[8]

A Case in Point: Interactive Audiovisual Aids

One hotel company uses interactive audiovisual aids in personnel training by combining the use of videotape and the personal computer. This company developed approximately 1,000 policies and standard operating procedures which cover almost any situation that might occur in any of its hotels. The goal of the company's training is to cover the applicable policies and procedures with the employees in a consistent and interesting manner to ensure that the company's standards are always followed.

The computer is programmed to serve as the controller for the program. The policies and procedures of the company are stored on hard disk within the computer. These procedures are cataloged by department with an index system that allows the user to enter a key word through the computer keyboard. The computer searches for the policies and procedures that deal with that topic. The user then selects the policy or procedure which seems to most closely address the area he/she is trying to master. Soon after, the policy and procedure appears on the computer monitor, much as it might in a printed manual.

If the trainee is not clear on how to apply the procedure, the computer monitor will flash a message asking the trainee if he/she needs to see a videotape demonstration that shows the correct way to do the procedures. If so, the learner types in YES and the monitor flashes another message stating which tape to select and insert into the video player. The computer then advances the videotape to the appropriate taped demonstration.

Following the demonstration, the computer asks the trainee a series of questions to evaluate whether the learner mastered the key information in the procedures. If not, the computer is programmed to advise the trainee to repeat the process.

The greatest limitation of an interactive video system is the speed of both the computer search process and the video equipment. In addition, the development of interactive video training programs requires sophisticated skills to maximize the potential value of the technology. Some limitations will be overcome by continued technological development of faster microprocessor systems and the expanded use of the laser disc over slower videotape systems. Many training authorities feel that as the technology is developed and refined, interactive video will make truly individualized instruction possible.[9]

Planning Audiovisual Programs

The planning process for audiovisual aids has two elements: planning the visuals and planning the audio script. An excellent approach to planning visuals involves a technique called "storyboarding." The job breakdown should be the basis for preparing the storyboard. A good way to plan the storyboard is to prepare one card for each point in the first column of the job breakdown ("what to do"). Depending on the complexity of the job task, more visuals may be needed to present various details covered in the second column ("how to do it"). Finally, the "additional information" outlined in the third column may suggest other visuals.

To prepare a storyboard, 3- by 5-inch cards (or larger) can be used. On each card, the trainer should roughly sketch the visual that will be prepared for the program. For trainers with limited artistic abilities, stick figures are sufficient. The rough sketches on cards are guidelines for laying out the series of visuals that will be used for the entire program. Even if the visuals are to be moving in films or videos, the main scenes should be planned before any filming or taping begins. Each visual or scene should illustrate a key point.

The job breakdown should also be the basis for preparing the audio scripts. The purpose of the training is to present the correct way to perform job duties. The job breakdowns document the correct procedures, step by step. If the visuals present these steps in sufficient detail to show the correct procedures, the script should merely describe what each visual depicts. The outlined information in the job breakdown can be easily followed to write the specific script stating clearly what to do, how to do it, and any additional information to round out the instruction. Whether music, humor, or professionally trained narrators should be employed is a decision that is secondary to the basic content of the audiovisual aid. The trainer must never lose sight of his/her primary mission: to improve the performance of the trainees.

Notes

1. Jorgen Roed, "The Use of Audio-Visual Aids in Management Training," in *Management Development and Training Handbook,* 2nd ed., edited by Bernard Taylor and Gordon Lippett (London: McGraw-Hill, 1983), pp. 280–294.

2. For a more detailed discussion of audiovisual materials, see J. E. Kemp, *Planning and Producing Audiovisual Materials* (New York: Harper & Row, 1980); R. H. Anderson, *Selection and Developing Media for Instruction* (Cincinnati: Van Nostrand Reinhold, 1976); and Henry Ellington, *Producing Teaching Materials: A Handbook for Trainers and Teachers* (London: Kogan Page, 1985).

3. Greg Kearsley, *Training and Technology: A Handbook for HRD Professionals* (Reading, Mass.: Addison-Wesley, 1984), pp. 21–23.

4. Lee Green, *Creative Slide/Tape Programs* (Littleton, Colo.: Libraries Unlimited, 1986).

5. Kearsley, pp. 18–21.

6. Kearsley, pp. 36–37.

7. Danny E. Hupp, "Estimating Video Costs," *Training*, Vol. 25, No. 1, January 1988, pp. 43–45.

8. The Educational Institute of AH&MA is in the process of developing interactive video presentations for the hospitality industry. These presentations will provide instruction in such areas as guest relations, front office, housekeeping, dining room service, sales and marketing, and security. Readers who desire more information on these training programs are encouraged to write the Educational Institute of AH&MA.

9. Maureen M. Beausey, "Videodisc Development," *Training*, Vol. 25, No. 2, February 1988, pp. 65–68.

Part III

Training in
Action

8 Developing Training Programs

The general steps involved in planning a training program were presented in Chapter 1. The first step noted was to define or assess training needs. A **training** need is a change that is necessary in an employee's behavior to bring that employee's performance in line with standards and objectives established for the operation. The employee's behavior must change to meet performance standards. Before training, the trainer should state and describe in writing what employee behavior is desired and what standards should be met when the employee is working. During and after training, the trainer can observe the employee's behavior and assess changes to determine if the training objectives were met.[1] The training needs assessment tells the trainer how far actual behavior is from the desired behavior. The training objective states what the employee will be able to do at the end of a successful training activity.

A training plan is based upon the needs assessment. It outlines the total training program that will be developed and carried out to meet the needs of the operation. The training plan describes how the trainer will raise performance levels through the learning process. Following a well-written training plan, the trainer can then do the detailed planning necessary to develop training outlines for individual sessions. Good training is based on good planning, just as are all other management activities.

Four principles of training should be considered when designing a training program:[2]

1. The training content must be relevant to the trainee.

2. The training objectives must be consistent with the work tasks that the training is trying to effect.

3. The training activities must be systematic and relate directly to the training objectives.

4. The training program must involve the trainees so that they can relate it personally to themselves.

The training session outline is a written guide for the activities or strategies that the trainer will use to achieve a specific training objective in a session. This chapter describes how to write training objectives and how to develop training plans and training session outlines that achieve objectives.

Establishing Good Training Objectives

It is important that meaningful training objectives be stated in writing since they specify the ultimate aims of the particular training. Most trainers appear to have some goals in mind that they hope to achieve, but limited time and lack of experience sometimes prevent them from writing training objectives. The following key points help specify objectives for training.

Key Points **Distinguish Between General and Performance-Based Objectives.** Performance-based objectives specify the particular performance or behavior that the employees are expected to do or exhibit as a result of training. General objectives are usually broad goals or platitudes that may or may not specify the desired employee performance.

List the Behaviors that Employees Must Learn to Perform. The trainer should identify and analyze the particular duty or job task that must be performed in order to accomplish the stated goal. This process is similar to preparing a job list. Like a job list, the list of behaviors should serve as an index of training objectives for a position. Sometimes the behaviors involved will seem so automatic or insignificant that it will seem unnecessary to list them. However, behaviors should be listed if they are important in reaching the ultimate goal. When listing behaviors, consider the order in which they will be performed. This is especially important when a particular behavior will affect the ability to perform a later step in the duty or job task. Learning has been defined as a change in behavior; therefore, it is necessary to specify which behavior is to be changed and to what extent.

Identify Evaluation Factors for Each Required Performance. Knowing the trainees builds an awareness of how well each one can perform before the instruction begins. Identifying the competency level and readiness of each individual employee is an important first step in specifying behaviors. If this assessment of each employee cannot be made on the basis of prior knowledge, the necessary information should be obtained through interviews, observations, or other pre-evaluation techniques (see Chapters 12 and 17). The readiness levels of different employees must be considered. Expectations must be flexible to accommodate individual differences. Acceptable performance levels for each employee must be established without compromising the standards of the operation. Likewise, the point at which training goals will be met by each individual employee must be identified. In specifying beginning and ending behaviors and in distinguishing between acceptable and unacceptable performances, evaluation factors will be defined.

Establish Realistic Performance Goals. Evaluation is an integral part of the learning process. The trainer must specify both behaviors and performance levels in terms of appropriate units of measurement or quality descriptions. Examples of units of measurement that can be used to evaluate certain behaviors are time limits, percentage of correct responses, percentage of deviance from standards, and the actual number of errors allowed. Examples of quality descriptions are food temperature, texture, color, aroma, and doneness. The key to successfully building evaluation factors into the performance objectives is to ensure that the evaluation factors are meaningful and realistic in view of how the behavior will be beneficial in job situations.

State the Objectives. The trainer should clearly and precisely define the behaviors expected after training. Objectives may contain one sentence, one phrase, or several sentences. The length of the objective is not important. What is important is that the performance objective be stated in terms of what behavior is expected and what performance level is acceptable. Objectives should be written so clearly that the trainees cannot be confused about the desired outcome. Objectives should then be listed in a logical order with behaviors becoming increasingly complex and difficult as trainees progress through training. This is why trainees should master behaviors that are identified first before attempting harder ones.

Use the Objectives and Provide the Trainees with Copies. Implementing well-planned, well-stated objectives leads to more efficient instruction and learning; both trainer and trainees understand what the trainees are expected to learn.

Employee involvement can make the task of developing and using performance objectives exciting and educational. Employees can identify behaviors that should be learned, and they can establish realistic levels and goals.

Examples of Poor Objectives

Training objectives are not difficult to write; however, writing clear statements does require practice, as is shown in the following examples of poor objectives.

1. At the end of the session, the employee will have developed qualities of rational thought and good employee practices.
   Problem: This objective is too broad to be meaningful. The definitions of *rational thought* and *good employee practices* are open to interpretation.

2. The trainee will gain an appreciation of how important the guest is to the success of the operation.
   Problem: Although the objective limits the content to appreciation, it is still vague. An objective like this does not help in planning the training because it is not measurable. There is no way for a trainer to evaluate how well the trainee learned or whether (or when) the training objective was achieved.

3. The trainee will become familiar with the basic company standards.

   Problem: Again, the action of the objective—becoming familiar—is not observable or measurable. The objective should be clear so that the trainer knows whether it has been met.

4. The training program will improve attitudes.

   Problem: This is a commendable training objective but not observable or measurable. It is difficult to assess attitude change, even when the attitude is specified in relation to the performance of a specific task. It is, therefore, necessary to translate the attitude change into measurable behavior. If, for example, poor employee attitude is judged to correlate with guest complaints (about food quality, cleanliness of rooms, etc.), then effective training (increased positive attitude) might be measured by fewer guest complaints.

5. The trainee will understand the basics of dining room operations.

   Problem: The word *understand* means different things to different people. In addition, the term dining room operations is too broad. Finally, the term *basics* must be defined for the specific operation. What is basic in a gourmet dining room may be very advanced for a family restaurant.

Examples of Good Objectives

Performance objectives should contain words that are easily measured. All training objectives should indicate (a) *observable elements* and (b) the *conditions* under which they will be met. The objective should leave no doubt as to its meaning. The following are examples of well-written objectives.

1. The trainee will be able to identify the four points that are most important when providing excellent guest service in any department.

   Comments: This objective is both observable and measurable. The word *identify* makes the required activity observable. The *four points of guest service* are measurable since they are a company standard by which the trainer can measure performance.

2. The employee will be able to state the procedure to follow in case of an over-ring on the cash register.

   Comments: This objective is stated in terms that are *observable* and *measurable*. The situation in which this behavior will be used is also identified.

3. The employee will be able to assemble the ingredients prescribed by standard recipes.

   Comments: This objective incorporates another important characteristic—the *condition* under which the employee is to perform; that is, when using *standard recipes*. The condition should state any limiting factors under which the behavior will be performed. The condition further limits the interpretation of the expected behavior.

4. A food server will be able to prepare coffee with urn equipment in accordance with procedures outlined in the company's procedure manual for coffee filter, coffee grounds, water temperature, and coffee equipment sanitation.
   Comments: This objective contains the *two key elements* of a training objective. It is stated in terms that will make it possible to *observe* the performance and it specifies *conditions* (. . . in accordance with) under which the performance should take place.

Designing the Training Plan

A training plan is a broad outline of *what* must be done, by *whom*, *when*, and *how*, in order to attain the training objectives that have been defined. The following questions should be answered when developing a training plan.

1. What should be learned and by whom? Is it necessary for all employees to learn or relearn the entire operation, or do the employees need training in just one or a few phases of the total operation? It is helpful to state the general purpose and specific objectives of the training. This statement will indicate the direction and extent to which the employees' knowledge, skills, and/or attitudes need to be developed. The training plan should also specify for whom the training is intended.

2. How much is to be learned? Defining what changes are to be learned will also help define how much is to be learned at any particular session. A trainer must recognize that trainees cannot learn everything at one time. It may be necessary to set up a list of priorities that can be accomplished over several sessions.

3. When should it be learned? Will the entire group of employees be trained before the shift, at the end of a shift, or at another time? Will they be trained in small groups or individually while the operation is open? The nature of the training need will help determine the answer. If many employees are to be trained, it may be effective for the trainer to use a group training method.

4. Where should the training session take place? If the trainer plans to concentrate on a few trainees at a time, the training might be scheduled during slow periods so that a few trainees can be involved without interrupting operations. If training is to be conducted for a large group, the session may have to be scheduled during non-working hours. The location of the training should be conducive to learning and it should be appropriate for any audiovisual aids, props, or equipment.

5. What method of learning is to be used? The trainer must decide upon the method of teaching/learning to be used in order to attain the training objectives. If only a few employees are involved, one-on-one training using job breakdowns as training

guides will generally accomplish the results. This approach was presented in Chapter 5.

If a group approach is appropriate because of the number of employees involved, there are many alternatives that can be used (see Chapter 6). In some group approaches, the trainer acts as a facilitator of learning rather than an instructor.[3] The primary mission of an instructor is to teach; this is usually done by showing, guiding, directing, or telling. Facilitation of learning involves the creation of a learning environment in which the trainee takes an active role in, and the trainer helps with, the training. The decision to act as an instructor or facilitator depends upon the needs of the trainees and their interest in learning. The decision also affects the format and the content of the training plan.

6.   What evaluation criteria will be used? The trainer should identify the criteria that will be used to determine if the training has met the performance objectives. For example, an evaluation criterion might be that a particular problem has been solved as a result of training. Another might be that trainee performance matches specific standards that were taught during the training.

7.   One method of evaluation is to establish a performance checklist of the specific behaviors in which employees were trained. The trainer can use the checklist to observe job performance after training.[4] Another method is to use sales reports and records that provide information which can be tied to specific employee performance. This enables the trainer to analyze changes in data that occur after training. While factors other than employee performance can bias such data, sales per labor hour and guest check averages might be tied to suggestive selling and merchandising techniques which have been taught. Historical trends should be documented, when possible, to serve as the basis for such evaluations. Observing employees on the job and analyzing all factors (including training) are important in assessing the effect that training has had on subsequent job performance.

The following Case in Point describes the effect a well-devised training plan had on one food service operation.

A Case in Point: A Staff of Trainers

In an independently owned fine-dining restaurant, the entire staff was trained in how to conduct one-on-one training according to training plans developed by the owners. For example, each time a new food server was hired, the training plan was adjusted as appropriate for the new employee and then posted on the employee bulletin board. Next to the plan was a sign-up sheet for experienced servers to sign up to conduct the one-on-one training sessions for the new employee. The same procedure was followed throughout the restaurant.

The trainers were required to evaluate the performance of the new employee at the conclusion of each session; the owner verified that standards were being met and maintained. Each training session included off-the-job instruction, role plays, time for practice, and finally actual supervised performance at the job station. The staff clearly understood their responsibility to maintain and communicate the established standards for the restaurant.

"Trainer" hours were kept separate from regular hours and were budgeted at a premium rate of pay. No trainer was permitted to follow his/her own training agenda; everyone followed the training plan for the new employee and the session outlines. Standard job breakdowns were used for each job duty covered in the training. Evaluation included written tests, verbal quizzes, and performance tests in role plays, practice sessions, and on-the-job situations.

The entire staff of this restaurant maintained a high reputation for their commitment to the guests and to the owners. They felt personally responsible for the success of the overall guest experience. The training plan served as the basis for a serious approach to training in which expectations were always very clear.

The Training Plan Format

The format of a training plan can vary according to the style of the trainer. Two examples of training plans are presented in this chapter. One is a plan for improving the performance of a group of hotel receptionists (Exhibit 8.1). The second example is a plan for training individuals, one-on-one, to perform food server skills (Exhibit 8.2).

The training plan generally outlines a series of sessions, each of which relates to logically sequenced objectives. More than one objective may be applicable to a training session. The scope of the plan or activity is determined from the need that is being met by the training effort.

The Training Session Outline

After developing the training plan, it is necessary to prepare a training session outline for each session in the training plan. These outlines may also be called instructors' guides, learning guides, or training contracts. Session outlines describe the specific activities that should take place in order to attain the session's performance objectives.

In individual skills training, job breakdowns can be used as session outlines. The trainer should follow the four-step training method, presenting what is to be done, how to do each step, and pointing out related information for each step.

In group training, the session outlines will aid the trainer in managing classroom activities. They should describe the sequence of events that will occur, the role of the trainer, and the requirements of the trainees. The details of the training plan and session outlines are a matter of personal preference. The amount of information in the training plan and session outlines depends largely upon the method of instruction. In general, the more participative the teaching/learning method, the less detail will be necessary in the training plan and session outlines.

Exhibit 8.1   Sample Group Training Plan for Receptionists

Group Training Plan: Receptionists

Training Objectives

At the conclusion of the training, trainees must be able to:
1. Greet and register guests with all types of reservations according to documented procedures.
2. Follow approved guest credit procedures for all arriving guests.
3. Assign rooms according to guest requests for type of room accommodations.
4. Make effective use of computerized guest history information during the registration process.
5. Perform all computerized registration tasks correctly and accurately while maintaining effective communications with the guests.
6. Effectively handle a variety of oral communications and requests at the front desk by registered guests and other visitors to the hotel.
7. Assist guests with check-out and process all forms of account settlement.
8. Perform all computerized check-out tasks correctly and accurately.

Performance Standards

At the conclusion of the training, trainees must demonstrate mastery according to procedures detailed in specific job breakdowns and accompanying job performance standards.

Employees Involved

G. Harris	B. Conners	H. Bernstein
M. Taylor	H. Snyder	J. Alverez
B. Williams	T. Schmidt	B. Atwood

Schedule of Sessions

Session	Objective	Date	Time	Location
1	1	9/14	2:00–3:00 p.m.	Cherry Room/Front Desk
2	2	9/15	2:00–3:00 p.m.	Cherry Room
3	3,4	9/16	2:00–3:00 p.m.	Cherry Room/Front Desk
4	5	9/17	2:00–3:00 p.m.	Cherry Room/Front Desk
5	6	9/18	2:00–3:00 p.m.	Cherry Room
6	7,8	9/21	2:00–3:00 p.m.	Cherry Room/Front Desk

Methods of Instruction by Sessions   **Trainer**

Session #1: Lecture/Discussion, Four-Step Method, Role Plays . . . . (Obj. 1) Jones
Session #2: Four-Step Method . . . . (Obj. 2) Jones, Taylor
Session #3: Lecture/Discussion, Role Plays . . . . (Obj. 3,4) Jones
Session #4: Four-Step Method, Role Plays, Practice Exercises . . . . (Obj. 5) Jones, Taylor
Session #5: Lecture/Discussion, Role Plays . . . . (Obj. 6) Taylor
Session #6: Four-Step Method, Role Plays, Practice Exercises . . . . (Obj. 7,8) Jones, Taylor

Training Equipment/Supplies Needed by Sessions

Session #1: Reservation slips (examples), registration slips, chart of room types, computer terms and codes, computer menus for registration, role play scripts, Job Breakdowns #301, 302, 303, 304, 305 with corresponding Job Performance Standards.
Session #2: Registration slips, credit policy, credit card imprinter, credit card slips, credit card verification telephone, check-register, computer menus for guest accounting, Job Breakdowns #306, 307, 308, 309, 310 with corresponding Job Performance Standards.
Session #3: Reservation slips, registration slips, chart of room types, computer menu for guest history, room keys, registration cards, role play scripts, Job Breakdowns #311, 312, 313 with corresponding Job Performance Standards.
Session #4: Reservation slips, registration slips, computer menus for registration and guest accounting, role play scripts, Job Breakdowns #314, 315, 316, 317 with corresponding Job Performance Standards.
Session #5: Role play scripts, guest relations policies, directory of guest services and community attractions, city maps, Job Breakdowns #318, 319, 320, 321 with corresponding Job Performance Standards.

Exhibit 8.1 *(continued)*

Session #6: Computer menus for guest accounting, computer terms and codes, credit card slips, credit card imprinter, credit card verification telephone, cash bank, role play scripts, Job Breakdowns #322, 323, 324, 325 with corresponding Job Performance Standards.

Evaluation by Sessions
Session #1: Written test of registration policies and procedures; performance checklist based on Job Performance Standards.
Session #2: Written test of credit policies; performance checklist based on Job Performance Standards.
Session #3: Written test on room types and rates, computer menus for registration, guest credit, and guest history; performance checklist based on Job Performance Standards.
Session #4: Written test on policies and procedures concerning the use and development of guest history information; performance checklists based on Job Performance Standards.
Session #5: Written test on guest services available within the hotel, local community attractions, directions to various places within the city; performance checklist based on Job Performance Standards.
Session #6: Written test on check-out policies and procedures; performance checklist based on Job Performance Standards.

Training Room Setup by Sessions
Session #1: Hollow-square seating, instructor six-foot table, flip chart.
Session #2: Three front desk mock-ups using six-foot tables, flip chart, hollow-square seating.
Session #3: Hollow-square seating, instructor six-foot table, flip chart.
Session #4: Three front desk mock-ups using six-foot tables, flip chart, hollow-square seating.
Session #5: Three front desk mock-ups using six-foot tables, flip chart, hollow-square seating.
Session #6: Three front desk mock-ups using six-foot tables, flip chart, hollow-square seating.

Special Audiovisual Requirements
None other than flip chart and specified front desk equipment for each session.

Session Rules
• No planned breaks due to length of each session.
• No smoking permitted in classroom except during lecture/discussions.
• No smoking permitted while training at front desk.
• All trainees in full uniform according to dress code.

Special Notes or Reminders
Request Cherry Room from Catering Department by 9/1.

Exhibit 8.3 shows one example of a session outline form. This type of outline identifies which topics will be covered, their content, the process or teaching method that will be used, who will be involved in the particular process, and how much time will be devoted to each topic. A beginning trainer can use the same type of form, expanding the information in each content and process block to detail what will be covered and how to facilitate the process. An experienced trainer can use the form as a guide.

The next two examples (Exhibits 8.4 and 8.5) are session outlines taken from a group course for developing energy conservation skills in food service situations.[5] The complete course has ten sessions. The group learning methods vary in the two training lessons in order to encourage class participation and variety. Each lesson includes a pre-class individual assignment that prepares the learner for class participation.

Exhibit 8.2 Sample One-on-One Training Plan for Newly Hired Food Servers

---

Training Plan: Food Servers

General Goal: To train a newly hired food server to perform service skills.

Specific Performance Objectives

At the conclusion of the training, the employee will be able to:

1. Greet and seat guests arriving at the restaurant for meal service, using approved scenarios for greeting and introduction.
2. Present the menu and explain the specials of the day, using approved descriptions of menu items.
3. Assist guests in making menu selections, effectively executing suggestive selling techniques and approved guest service scenarios.
4. Serve food and beverage items according to courses, correct placement, courteous guest contact, and all service standards.
5. Clear courses quietly and neatly, while being courteous to the guests.
6. Sell desserts, coffee, or hot tea, using approved suggestive selling scenarios.
7. Serve desserts, coffee, and hot tea according to service standards.
8. Prepare the guest check accurately and completely and present it to the guest at the proper time.
9. Clear, clean, and reset tables quietly and neatly following tabletop specifications for the meal period.

Performance Standards

Employee develops the ability to perform according to procedures outlined in the Job Breakdowns at a level which equals or exceeds the accompanying Job Performance Standards.

Employee Involved

John Allen

Schedule of Sessions

Session	Objective	Date	Time	Location
1	1,2	2/10	10:00–11:00 a.m.	Cafe (Station #6)
2	3,4,5	2/11	10:00–11:00 a.m.	Cafe (Station #6)
3	6,7	2/12	10:00–11:00 a.m.	Cafe (Station #6)
4	8,9	2/13	10:00–11:00 a.m.	Cafe (Station #6)
5	Evaluation	2/14	10:00–11:00 a.m.	Cafe (Station #6)

Methods of Instruction by Sessions   **Trainer**

Session #1: One-on-one (Four-Step Method)............................(Obj. 1,2) Ms. L. Walker
Session #2: One-on-one (Four-Step Method), Video: "Suggestive Selling" ... (Obj. 3,4,5) Ms. L. Walker
Session #3: One-on-one (Four-Step Method)............................(Obj. 6,7) Ms. L. Walker
Session #4: One-on-one (Four-Step Method)............................(Obj. 8,9) Ms. L. Walker
Session #5: Performance tests and written test .... Ms. L. Walker

Evaluation by Sessions

Session #1: Performance test of skills using checklist; oral test of menu knowledge.
Session #2: Performance test of skills using checklist; oral test of scenarios; written test of menu knowledge.
Session #3: Performance test of skills using checklist; oral test of scenarios; oral test of dessert, coffee, and hot tea knowledge.
Session #4: Performance test of skills using checklist; oral test of guest check procedures and knowledge of desserts, coffee, and hot tea service.
Session #5: Overall evaluation including review of performance in all areas plus written test on menu, desserts, service procedures, suggestive selling, guest check procedures, and guest relations techniques.

Equipment Needed by Sessions

Session #1: Equipment specified in Job Breakdowns #202, 203, 204 with corresponding Job Performance Standards.

Exhibit 8.2 *(continued)*

Session #2: Equipment specified in Job Breakdowns #205, 206 with corresponding Job Performance Standards; VCR and monitor.
Session #3: Equipment specified in Job Breakdowns #207, 208, 209, 210 with corresponding Job Performance Standards.
Session #4: Equipment specified in Job Breakdowns #211, 212, 213, 214 with corresponding Job Performance Standards.
Session #5: Refer to Sessions #1 through #4 for equipment requirements based on the specific performance tests which will be given.

Training Room Setup by Sessions
Session #1: Station #6 set for luncheon service, two tables, four covers each table, side station set with ice water, backup serviceware and linens.
Session #2: Same as Session #1 plus VCR and monitor set up in east corner of Station #6.
Session #3: Same as Session #1.
Session #4: Same as Session #1 plus guest checks set up at cashier's station.
Session #5: Work stations should be set up based on the specific performance test. Set up one dining room station for the written test. Have paper and an adequate number of pencils available.

Audiovisual Requirements
Rent a VCR and monitor for Session #2 on 2/11. Order equipment from rental service by 2/1.

Session Rules
- No smoking during training.
- Employee dressed in full uniform with hair according to dress code.

Special Notes or Reminders
Post note on bulletin board announcing the training so that guests can be seated away from Station #6 in the restaurant during the training times.

The session outlines for the energy conservation course can easily be followed by inexperienced trainers. The format is very similar to the format for job breakdowns. The first example from the energy conservation course is entitled "Session 2: Food Preparation" (Exhibit 8.4). The primary method of instruction is the conference method based on directed questions. The trainer raises questions based on the pre-class assignment and the trainees discuss them. The trainer highlights or reinforces comments made by trainees that emphasize principles of energy conservation. The trainer should plan to ask many questions to involve as many trainees as possible. He/she should also consider the individual differences of trainees and their ability to respond to certain questions.

The second example (Exhibit 8.5) is entitled "Session 9: Energy Conservation on the Job." The group learning method is a seminar approach with a project-based emphasis. Trainees are divided into small groups to develop plans for conserving energy on the job. The trainer acts as a facilitator to bring out key principles and points from the group members.

The final example of a session outline is taken from a training plan for dishwashers (Exhibit 8.6). This example demonstrates how the four-step training method and job breakdowns are incorporated into a session outline. This session outline covers how to use a decoy system for organizing the soiled dishes in the dishroom; it is one in a series for

Exhibit 8.3 Sample Session Outline for Guest Relations

Session Outline

Objective: The ability to handle guest problems that arise at the front desk.

Content	Process	Who	Time
1. Identify five guest problems that have arisen during the past month.	Brainstorm. List problems on flip chart.	Total group	10 min.
2. Discuss ways that the problems could have been prevented or solved.	Brainstorm. Each group takes one problem which has been identified in (1) above.	Small group (3–4/group)	20 min.
3. Compare approaches used by different groups.	Spokesperson from each group reports steps that could have been taken.	One person from each group.	10 min.
4. Identify principles for preventing or solving guest problems.	Brainstorm key points that each group presents.	Facilitator leads with group participation.	10 min.
5. Review organizational philosophy related to handling guests and compare with principles and techniques identified by the group.	Presentation with group participation.	Facilitator presentation with group suggestions.	10 min.

---

dishroom employees. The session to follow would be how to rinse and rack soiled dishes and serviceware.

The effective trainer will plan how to involve the group, how to organize content, and how to use time to meet the training objectives. The entire training process is dependent on effective planning. The manager who attempts to provide training without an organized plan is doomed to mediocrity and inefficiency. There is no replacement for effective planning, and no excuse for not meeting this basic management responsibility. Training is an essential management activity and it requires commitment, organization, and written plans. The following Case in Point shows what can happen when a well-intended training effort is not formally planned.

A Case in Point: Unplanned Training Chaos

The general manager of a large hotel decided that all departments would be required to conduct training sessions for their employees beginning on a certain day. Managers were given no instructions regarding what the training should cover, let alone how it should be prepared and conducted.

The general manager was proud of the new "training program" that he was launching and invited two corporate officers to observe a session. A session for cooks, conducted by the sous chef, was selected. The topic was "how to prepare stocks from scratch."

The seven cook trainees gathered around a large steam-jacketed kettle for the training session. The sous chef had no evident notes or printed training plan. However, since he had prepared stocks so many times in his career, he was confident that he could cover the instruction with no problems in the scheduled time.

He began by explaining why stocks prepared from scratch were better than those made from instant bases, but did not have a sample of either to demonstrate the differences in taste or smell. The trainees were required to use their imagination and take the chef's word for the differences.

Next, the sous chef began to describe what should be included in a white stock. When he began to talk about the bones used for the stock, he sent one of the trainees to the refrigerator to get "about 30 pounds of beef and veal bones." The cook hurried away to get the bones.

The sous chef continued to talk, indicating that onions, carrots, and celery would also be needed. At this point he sent another cook to the refrigerator to get three pounds of onions, two pounds of carrots, and two pounds of celery.

Without waiting for either of the cooks to return, the discussion continued and the sous chef explained the spices that would be needed for the stock. He then sent a third cook to get bay leaves, thyme, whole peppercorns, whole cloves, and some fresh parsley stems.

About this time, the first cook returned to report that he had found some bones but he couldn't distinguish between beef bones and veal bones. The second cook suddenly returned with a large bus pan containing an assortment of the specified vegetables which had not been washed or prepped for the stock. The vegetable preparation sink was in a separate area on the opposite end of the kitchen.

The situation only got worse. The sous chef began to show his nervousness and confusion. His voice became more high-pitched, and on one occasion he spoke sharply to the cook who brought in the unwashed vegetables.

At this point, the corporate officers quietly slipped out of the kitchen and left the general manager there to assist the struggling sous chef in salvaging the new training program.

Plans are essential to good training. Part of planning is assembling the materials required for the training before calling trainees into a session. Good training is the result of a carefully planned and executed set of activities directed toward a clear set of learning objectives.

Evaluation and Feedback

Evaluation must be an ongoing process in training. Trainees must receive feedback on their progress if performance is expected to improve.

Exhibit 8.4   Sample Session Outline #1: Energy Conservation Course

Group Training Session Outline

Pre-class Assignment for Session 2: Food Preparation

Purpose: To have the trainees gather data that will be used in determining whether the food service operation is effectively applying energy conservation principles.

Determine the following before class (write detailed answers on separate paper):

1. Do we cook some foods on our menus in advance of actual guest orders—either partially   Yes/No
   or fully? If so, which food items? If not, why not?

   What types of food items might it be unwise to cook in advance?

2. Are any foods on our menus cooked in volume? If so, which food items? If not, could   Yes/No
   they be?

   What would be the advantages of volume preparation? Disadvantages?

3. Are ovens fully loaded for each baking cycle? Is this practical with our menus? Why or   Yes/No
   why not?

4. After a load of baked products has been removed, is another load put in right away while   Yes/No
   the ovens are still hot? Is this practical in our operation? What would be the advantages
   and disadvantages?

5. Is food cooked at the lowest temperature possible? What are the advantages and   Yes/No
   disadvantages of this process?

6. Does the first person in the production department turn on all of the large cooking   Yes/No
   equipment which will be used for the first meal preparation? Is the equipment preheated
   just before use?

   What are the advantages and disadvantages of these procedures?

7. During slow periods of the day, is cooking equipment turned off or are temperatures   Yes/No
   reduced? What are the advantages and disadvantages of these procedures?

8. Do you know how long it takes for major cooking equipment to preheat to selected   Yes/No
   temperatures? Determine how long it takes to preheat the following:

   Deep fat fryer to 375°F?   _____

   Convection oven to 350°F?   _____

   Broiler to 450°F?   _____

   Pressure steamer to 212°F?   _____

9. Is equipment checked regularly for possible repair needs? How could this result in energy   Yes/No
   conservation?

Session 2: Food Preparation

Learning Objective: At the conclusion of this session, the trainee will have the ability to identify and explain energy conservation principles in food preparation.

Equipment and Supplies: Flip chart easel and pad, felt-tipped marker, pre-class assignments for Sessions 2 and 3.

Resources: Energy Conservation Manual, Section 3.

Exhibit 8.4 *(continued)*

What to Do	How to Do It	Remarks
Before class begins, choose employees to answer questions. Write their names in the second column. Choose alternate employees in case someone is absent or other opinions or inputs are needed.	Select names of employees who are scheduled to attend this training session.	This will make it easy to involve employees in class participation.
5 minutes Administration	Check to make sure that everyone scheduled is present.	Record attendance for training records.
50 minutes Lead a discussion about ways to conserve energy. Try to restrict comments on each subject to five minutes so all areas can be covered.	1. Ask (Name) _____ (Alternate) _____ What are some advantages of cooking foods in advance, and how often is it done in this operation?	Listen carefully to all answers. List key points on flip chart. Emphasize that energy costs can be conserved by cooking during off-peak times when energy rates are lower.
	Ask _____ Alt _____ Name some foods on our menus that can be effectively cooked in advance.	Discuss braised meats, starchy vegetables, pastas, and breads. This is not suitable for fried eggs, fried potatoes, or steaks.
	What are some disadvantages of cooking foods in advance?	Products may lose some of their fresh appearance over time.
	2. Ask _____ Alt _____ What are some advantages of cooking foods in volume, and how is this done in our operation?	Conserves energy by reducing the number of times the cooking equipment must be preheated.
	Ask _____ Alt _____ What are some food items on our menus that could be cooked in volume and some that could not be satisfactorily cooked in volume?	Suitable for pies, cakes, soups, sauces, stews, roast meats, and braised meats. Not suitable for delicate foods since the texture is likely to be destroyed by the volume handling.
	Ask _____ Alt _____ What are some of the disadvantages of cooking foods in volume?	Potential waste from overproduction; reduction in product quality; difficulty of maintaining desired serving temperature without overcooking.

(continued)

Exhibit 8.4 *(continued)*

What to Do	How to Do It	Remarks
	3. Ask _____ Alt _____	
	How effective is our operation in maximizing oven capabilities when baking is performed?	Convection ovens can be fully loaded on all shelves with good results due to the circulating hot air.
	4. Ask _____ Alt _____	
	How effective is our operation in planning successive cooking of baked and roasted products to make optimum use of ovens once they are hot?	By cooking items in succession, energy is saved that would be required to reheat the oven.
	Ask _____ Alt _____	
	When cooking in succession, should the item requiring the lowest temperature be cooked first or last, and why?	Cook low temperature items first to reduce wasted energy waiting for the equipment to "cool down" for the next item.
	5. Ask _____ Alt _____	
	What are the advantages of cooking foods at the lowest possible temperatures?	Less expenditure of energy, less weight loss of meats, less heat loss from cooking equipment, less heat in kitchen for air conditioning to overcome.
	6. Ask _____ Alt _____	
	How far in advance of cooking time should heavy-duty cooking equipment be turned on and why?	Modern equipment preheats in a short amount of time.
	7. Ask _____ Alt _____	
	Who is responsible for turning off equipment that is not in use or not needed during slow periods within our kitchens?	Every food prep employee should conserve energy.
	8. Ask _____ Alt _____	
	Name three pieces of equipment within our kitchen and give the time required to preheat each to a given temperature level.	Explain importance of developing preheating time charts for all large cooking equipment, showing time needed to preheat to certain temperatures.

Exhibit 8.4 *(continued)*

What to Do	How to Do It	Remarks
	9. Ask _____ Alt _____	
	What scheduled maintenance checks are performed on the food production equipment in this operation, and how often?	Discuss importance of preventive maintenance to adjust pilots, clean gas orifices, adjust belts, lubricate motors, etc.
5 minutes Summarize the session and review the learning objective.	Review and summarize key points. Assess how well the training objective was met in this session.	Re-emphasize the high cost of utilities and the importance of energy conservation.
5 minutes Motivate the class to prepare for the next session.	Review the pre-class assignment for Session 3 and answer any questions.	Hand out the pre-class assignment for Session 3.

Evaluation plans are part of the training plan and can be part of each session outline, or they may be handled separately. In the training plan for entry-level food servers (Exhibit 8.2), the fifth session was devoted fully to performance testing and a comprehensive written test that covered the first four training sessions. In the energy conservation course example (Exhibits 8.4 and 8.5), the tenth session was devoted to a comprehensive written evaluation of the learning that took place in the first nine sessions.

It is also recommended that the trainer assess the group after each session by an informal or formal question-and-answer period. When the lessons deal with specific skills, the trainer should require trainees to perform the skills under observation and then evaluate their performance. The primary purpose of evaluation should not be to weed out slow learners. Rather, it should be to develop every individual to his/her full potential. If such an evaluation reveals employees who are unable or unwilling to master the desired competencies, comprehensive evaluation must be undertaken to determine whether those employees should be dismissed (see Chapters 12 and 17 for more on performance evaluation).

Coaching and Follow-Up

A training plan is incomplete unless it includes follow-up. Coaching is planned and directed supervisory communication and it is used to reinforce what was covered in the training sessions. It involves recognizing and commending correct performance, correcting errors by reinstructing employees, discouraging unacceptable behavior, and removing barriers to good performance. Group training is individualized by one-on-one coaching and follow-up (coaching and counseling techniques are discussed in Chapter 16). Follow-up is essential in developing the performance standards specified for the operation.

Exhibit 8.5   Sample Session Outline #2: Energy Conservation Course

---

Group Training Session Outline

Pre-class Assignment for Session 9: Energy Conservation On the Job

Purpose: Review and list ways to conserve energy in the food service operation.

Based on what has been learned in Sessions 1–8 about conserving energy in the food service operation, prepare a list of steps that you could take to reduce energy usage. Bring this list to Session 9.

Session 9: Energy Conservation On the Job

Learning Objective: At the conclusion of this session, the trainees will have the ability to develop an "action plan" for conserving energy in the food service operation.

Equipment and Supplies: Four flip chart easels with pads and four felt-tipped markers.

Resources: Energy Conservation Manual, all sections.

What to Do	How to Do It	Remarks
5 minutes Administration	Check to be sure that everyone scheduled is present.	Record attendance for training records.
15 minutes Divide the trainees into groups and allow them to discuss ways that energy use can be reduced within the food service operation.	Groups should consist of trainees who work in similar job capacities within the food production department. Have each group choose a leader.	Trainees should share the lists they prepared before the session with the group; a combined list should then be prepared on a flip chart.
35 minutes Have the leader from each group present the combined steps agreed upon by his/her group. The leader should explain each step. A means for monitoring progress in energy conservation should be identified for each step, with assistance from all trainees.	The lists from each small group should be posted before the total class for review and comparison. Have the trainees discuss the advantages and disadvantages of each approach listed as well as the practicality of each step. Allow the total group to revise, refine, or discard suggested steps after they have been discussed.	Highlight and reinforce each point that will result in conservation. If necessary, ask probing questions to bring out advantages and disadvantages. Emphasize practical approaches to energy conservation.
5 minutes Summarize the session; review the learning objective.	Review and summarize key points. Assess how well the training objective was met in this session.	Re-emphasize the high cost of utilities and the importance of energy conservation.
Announce that there will be a written test at the next (and last) training session.	Explain that the test will include all materials covered in Sessions 1–9. The test will be multiple choice, short answers, and one discussion question.	Tell the trainees to review past pre-class assignments and their personal notes in preparation for the test.

A Close Look at the Trainer

Any study of employee training must also consider the trainer since he/she is critical to the effectiveness of the training effort. Earlier chapters have established that not everyone will be a good trainer—even though

Exhibit 8.6 Sample Session Outline for Dishwasher Course: Use of Decoy System

Session Outline: Use of Decoy System for Sorting Dishes

Learning Objective: After this session, the trainees will be able to sort and place dishes and glasses correctly using a decoy system to improve organization of the sorting process and to reduce breakage in the dishwashing activity.

Equipment and Supplies: Three each of all dishes and glasses used in the food service operation; washable felt-tipped marker.

Trainer: John Lee

Time Required for Session: 30 minutes

Location of Training: Dishroom

What to Do	How to Do It	Remarks
Before Session: Inform a.m. dishwasher crew about training to take place at 10:15 a.m.	Post training schedule on employee bulletin board.	Post training notice one week prior with weekly work schedule.
Make sure dishroom is clean and in order.	Delegate to a.m. Utility Shift Supervisor	Supervisor should assign to a.m. shift.
Assemble equipment and supplies.	Delegate to a.m. Utility Shift Supervisor	Supervisor should assign to a.m. shift.
10:15 a.m.—5 minutes Administrative duties	Make sure everyone is present.	Record attendance on training records. Start on time. This communicates the importance of the training.
	Cover the purpose of the training. Quickly go over training rules.	Emphasize that trainees should ask you questions as they arise.
10:20 a.m.—5 minutes Define the problem and clarify the training objective.	Explain why employees should be concerned about clean dishes and the costs of dish breakage:	
Review the cost per piece of china and glassware.	a. Breakage costs are estimated at $1,100 per month—occurs mostly in the dishroom.	May want to use washable felt-tipped marker and write replacement cost on face of each dish and glass to emphasize cost.
	b. Dish replacement costs are increasing.	Relate specific cases of careless handling and high breakage.
	c. Budget for dish replacement is 20% more than last year.	Compare the percentage increase in budgeted replacement to the budgeted percentage increase in guest counts and revenues.
10:25 a.m.—15 minutes Teach use of decoy system for sorting.	Explain why the decoy system will: a. Organize the sorting process b. Reduce breakage	Emphasize that this system will help buspersons as well.

(continued)

Exhibit 8.6 *(continued)*

What to Do	How to Do It	Remarks
	Explain and demonstrate the procedures for using the decoy system: a. What to do—cover each step b. How to do it—explain each step c. Additional information—emphasize why each step is important; emphasize safety and efficiency.	Follow Job Breakdown #8 very carefully. Use the four-step training method. For each step: —Prepare the learners —Present the instruction —Try out performance —Follow through (coach)
	Select employees and have them repeat the steps in the process of using the decoy system. They should demonstrate the process and explain why steps are important.	Watch all trainees for signs of understanding. If a trainee looks confused or distracted, that employee should be asked to demonstrate and explain the process.
	Tell the trainees to begin using the decoy system immediately and that you will be checking with them throughout their shift for problems in making the system work under rush-hour conditions.	Be available during lunch for follow-through and on-the-job coaching.
10:40 a.m.—5 minutes Questions and closing	Clear up any questions about the decoy system.	Try not to leave anything unanswered.
	Answer any questions about future training.	Be positive about the values of training.
	Remind the group that a training session on dish racking and rinsing will be held tomorrow at 10:15 a.m.	End on a positive note.
10:45 a.m.—Adjourn		Always try to end on time.

many managers equate seniority, experience, or ability to perform a skill or task with the ability to train.

Whenever possible, the manager who is directly responsible for supervising the employee should be the trainer. When this is not possible, the manager must delegate the training task. As a start, the manager should identify key management or non-management employees in each department who will be responsible for training.

Managers must recognize that the trainer must have both the required job competence and the desire to train in order to do it well. In addition, the person selected must know how to train or be willing to learn. Trainers should be instructed in the four-step method of training or a similar approach to on-the-job training so that the training will be presented in an organized, structured, and effective manner. Likewise, trainers should be taught some of the basic principles of adult learning so that these principles can be effectively applied. The procedures for training and developing employees to be skilled trainers are the same as the procedures for any other skills training activity. One-on-one or small group methods are best for developing a trainer's instructional abilities.

Managers should create a job classification for non-management employees who have been certified as competent trainers within their areas of expertise. This job classification might carry a higher rate of pay than classification for similar employees who have not been trained to be trainers. This concept blends with the idea that people should be recognized for their high levels of performance—and for the extra effort which they expend for the operation.

Leadership Abilities

Good trainers must be good leaders. Regardless of how highly skilled a person may be, if the individual is unable to get others to willingly follow his/her example and instruction, the person will never be a successful trainer.

The staff of every department needs leadership from within to function effectively in the absence of the manager. The non-management trainers in the department should provide that leadership in the absence of a manager. There should rarely be any concern over the direction in which the staff is going as long as a trainer is present to provide direction.

Professional Standards

Trainers must demonstrate consistent respect for organizational performance standards and must personally demonstrate a strong commitment to excellence. The cost of employee training is too high to waste resources on sloppy training by individuals who will pass on as many bad habits as they will new skills.

More is expected of a trainer. The standards of behavior expected by management, peers, and other bystanders are more critical than for other employees. The person selected to be a trainer tends to be observed more carefully in the execution of all work activities. When anyone wants to know how to perform a certain skill, the trainer in that area should be the model for performance.

Personal Competence

Trainers should have a documented record of personal competence. The trainer's own human resource file should contain verification that he/she has been evaluated and judged to be competent in every area that he/she will teach. When it is clear that only those individuals who have verifiable competence are allowed to be trainers, more employees and managers will work to prove their level of mastery in order to be considered as trainers.

Trainers must respect rules of personal behavior that apply to everyone in the department. If smoking is not permitted at the work station, then the trainer must not smoke; furthermore, he/she must not complain about the rule. The same applies to other areas of personal behavior such as arriving for work on time, taking only approved breaks, being productive on the job, and following approved standard operating procedures. The example set by the trainer will be followed by all the employees he/she trains, whether through formal or informal training.

Exhibit 8.7   Potential Sources of Training Assistance

Colleges, Universities, Vocational, and Technical Schools
Hospitality Management Faculty
Foods and Nutrition Faculty
Business Administration Faculty
Marketing Faculty
Education Faculty
Audiovisual Faculty
Continuing Education Faculty
Externship/Internship Coordinator
Trade Associations
State Hotel and Restaurant Trade Associations
National Hotel and Restaurant Trade Associations
Local Chapters of Hospitality Industry Trade Associations
Sales Representatives
Food and Beverage Suppliers
Chemical Suppliers
Computer Hardware and Software Suppliers
Linen Suppliers
Equipment Suppliers
Emergency and Safety Equipment Suppliers
Manufacturers' Representatives
Equipment Manufacturers
Supply Manufacturers
Community Organizations
Chamber of Commerce
Local Fire and Rescue Department
Local Law Enforcement Agencies
Local Red Cross Chapter
Local Public, University, and Technical College Libraries
Toastmasters, Rotary International, Civitan Club
Government Agencies
Small Business Administration
Local Health Department
Federal or State Supported Job Training Programs
Professional Training and Education Societies
Council of Hotel and Restaurant Trainers
Council of Hotel, Restaurant, and Institutional Education
American Society for Training and Development
National Society for Performance in Instruction
Educational Institute of the American Hotel & Motel Association
Labor Unions
Apprenticeship Programs
Competitors
Successful Hospitality Operators
Special Counseling Services
Community Mental Health Clinics
Religious Counselors
Licensed Counseling Professionals
Outside Consultants
Training Consultants
Operations Consultants
Audiovisual Consultants
Packaged Training Programs
Generic Films and Videotapes
Generic Training Books and Manuals
Generic Multimedia Training Packages

Training Resources

Many resources are available to help the trainer. Some are costly but many are free or inexpensive. Trainers should realize it is usually not cost-effective to develop programs and materials if the same or similar resources already exist and can be adapted for use. Many local, state, and national organizations are ready and willing to share information or provide professional assistance that may be useful to trainers. Locating and using appropriate resources can reduce the time spent "reinventing the wheel." Exhibit 8.7 presents a guide that trainers can follow to develop their own resource lists.

When selecting outside resources, the trainer should ensure that the assistance available will contribute directly to the goals of the training program. Trainers are always tempted to use outside speakers, books, manuals, or audiovisual aids when they are free or inexpensive and readily available. These efforts can prove to be the most expensive training approach if they do not lead to improved performance. The time managers and employees spend in "bad" or unnecessary training cannot be justified. Therefore, trainers must first determine exactly what they want the training to accomplish. Methods and materials should be selected which will help accomplish these training goals.

In some instances, the advantages of "getting one step ahead" in the training process by purchasing materials may be worth an additional expense. Purchasing materials or other outside resources does not remove management responsibility. While consultants can be brought in to assist in designing or implementing training, the ultimate responsibility for the results of the program will always rest with the manager.

Notes

1. Lloyd L. Byars and Leslie W. Rue, *Human Resource Management*, 2nd ed. (Homewood, Ill.: Irwin, 1987), p. 199.
2. James T. Chapados, Deborah Rentfrow, and Louis I. Hochheiser, "Four Principles of Training," *Training and Development Journal*, Vol. 41, No. 12, December 1987, pp. 63–66.
3. Carl R. Rogers, *Freedom to Learn* (Columbus, Ohio: Merrill, 1969), pp. 104–126.
4. B. S. Deming, *Evaluating Job Related Training* (Englewood Cliffs, N.J.: ASTD/Prentice Hall, 1982), pp. 41–42.
5. Lewis C. Forrest, Jr., *Energy Conservation in Foodservice: A Course for Foodservice Personnel* (Raleigh, N.C.: Department of Community Colleges, 1979) pp. 7–10, 29–30, 73, 89.

9 Ongoing Training

Training must be an ongoing process in a hospitality operation. Since most hospitality operations are open over several workshifts, it is difficult to get all employees from a department together at one time to participate in a training session. This reality of the hospitality industry makes it essential for training to be planned and executed during each shift. Emphasis should be placed on individualized approaches to learning and structured on-the-job training.

Training *can* be accomplished in a busy hospitality operation. The secret lies in the commitment of management to develop and maintain a high level of staff competence. This chapter addresses the many considerations in establishing and maintaining an effective ongoing training effort. The concept of ongoing training includes the initial training of new employees, the retraining of experienced employees whose skills and knowledge require improvement, and the teaching of new procedures to employees as changes occur within the operation.

Management Commitment to Continuous Training

Managers must be convinced that training is a cost-effective use of their time. They must be convinced that their personal career will be enhanced by a management style that supports training as a daily and weekly routine. Finally, managers must be convinced that their personal reputations are strengthened when their staff consistently achieves established standards.

Training should be viewed as an investment in improved efficiency, increased job satisfaction, and reduced staff turnover. The return on this investment will come, as long as competence is consistently developed, evaluated, and improved. The way a manager views training is directly related to the degree of commitment he/she makes to the development of competence.

Management commitment to training cannot be dictated by corporate policies and procedures for training. It must come from within each individual manager. A manager who is personally committed to training will never be willing to accept mediocrity or inferior results from his/her personal efforts, or from the efforts of his/her staff.

Daily/Weekly Training Routines

Every business has certain activities that occur every day and certain activities that occur on a weekly basis. These activities may include certain routines related to purchasing, taking inventory, controlling cash, or ensuring guest satisfaction. For a hospitality operation to develop and maintain a highly competent staff, training, too, must become an established daily and weekly routine.

The first step in this process is to establish a set time every day for training activities. The management staff should agree on the established time for each department and should respect each other's commitment by not scheduling other activities during this dedicated training time. In shift operations, a training time should be established for each shift.

If possible, it is good practice to establish the same time for training in all departments. This way, every manager will know that this time is dedicated to training and is not available for other purposes. Furthermore, a uniform training period builds cooperation among managers as they work together to make the most effective use of this training time.

Just because there is a daily training time does not mean that every staff member is trained on a daily basis. New employees may receive more attention since they have more to learn to become competent. However, every employee, no matter how experienced, should participate in a training session at least once each week. This is essential to making the training commitment a reality for every member of the staff.

Where dedicated training time is part of the daily routine, it is important for each department manager to plan for each day of the coming week or month. Daily sessions may be delegated to qualified trainers within the department. The manager should list the topics that will be covered each day, as well as who will be responsible for conducting each session. Exhibit 9.1 is an example of a department's ongoing training schedule.

Training that takes place within an operation can be classified according to type or objective. For the remainder of this chapter, training will be discussed under the headings of general training, departmental training, and specialized training. These three classifications of training are not mutually exclusive; in fact, they may overlap heavily in some cases. The training discussed here is primarily intended for the non-management staff although management personnel should also attend.

General Training

General training refers to training required for all personnel in the hospitality operation, or at least personnel from more than one department. The topics addressed are broader in scope than those of individual departments. These sessions may be conducted by the general manager, human resources director, a training manager, or a member of the management team. In some cases, an outside resource person may supplement the instruction given by management.[1] Operational managers should always be directly involved and attend the general training sessions. These managers must know what has been taught to their staffs to effectively reinforce and follow up on training.

Exhibit 9.1 Sample Monthly List of Ongoing Training Topics

Food Server Training Topics for February

Training Time: 2:45–3:15   Location: Dining Room

Date	Topic	Trainer
2/1	Setting Up Stations	LF
2/2	Sidework	LF
2/3	Greeting Guests	LF
2/4	Seating Guests	JJ
2/5	Check-Writing Procedures	JJ
2/6	Selling Food and Beverage	JJ
2/7	Alcoholic Beverage Service	CS
2/8	Describing Menu Selections	LF
2/9	Selling Wines with the Meal	LF
2/10	Serving Food Selections	CS
2/11	Serving Still Red Wines	CS
2/12	Serving Still White Wines	CS
2/13	Selling Valentine Specials	CS
2/14	Serving Sparkling Wines/Champagne	LF
2/15	Selling Dessert Selections	LF
2/16	Serving Dessert Selections	JJ
2/17	Selling After-Dinner Drinks	JJ
2/18	Serving After-Dinner Drinks	JJ
2/19	Closing Out	JJ
2/20	Presenting the Check	JJ
2/21	Processing Guest Payment	JJ
2/22	Assisting Guests upon Departure	LF
2/23	Handling Guest Complaints	LF
2/24	Restaurant Incidents Log	LF
2/25	Assisting Sick or Inebriated Guests	BR
2/26	Reporting Accidents and Injuries	BR
2/27	Emergency Fire Procedures	BR
2/28	Shift Closing Procedures	LF

The most appropriate time to schedule general training is during the dedicated training times that have been established for all departments. If the designated daily training time differs between departments, then management will have to decide on the most convenient time.

As with all training, it is essential for the assigned trainer to make the best use of the scheduled time. Wasting time with poorly planned or poorly executed training is irresponsible and sets a bad example for the employees. The general manager, the human resources director, and the individual department heads must all monitor the general training sessions to ensure that they accomplish the desired results in a cost-effective manner. The following topics are among those which fall under general training.

Guest Relations

The total hospitality operation must be concerned with positive guest relations. This topic must be integrated into departmental training, but it also warrants special attention on an interdepartmental basis.

Equal to the content of this training is the credibility of the trainer. Guest relations training should be conducted on a regular basis by the general manager, or be rotated according to an established schedule among designated senior-level managers. This training must come from a clearly established leader who exemplifies the principles taught in his/her day-to-day contacts with guests.

A good way to cover guest relations is to plan the training around recent actual cases, letters, or written comments received from guests. Sessions may be devoted to small group discussions on ways to overcome specific instances of dissatisfaction, or on ways to capitalize on instances of extreme guest satisfaction. Each case-analysis session should be summarized and the key points listed on a flip chart to reinforce the best ideas for achieving guest satisfaction.

Another good way to teach guest relations is through role playing. For this approach, it is important for the trainer to develop the role plays ahead of time, using actual guest situations. Role plays are most effective when separate instruction sheets are prepared for each participating trainee. In this way, each participant has little idea of what to expect and must draw upon his/her guest relations skills to handle a simulated—but true to life—situation. Following the role plays, trainers should encourage constructive criticism from all trainees.

Speeches or lectures on guest relations often fall on deaf ears. It is great to express the total commitment of the management staff to a great guest experience, but until those concepts are applied, they are nothing more than lofty ideals.

The goal of guest relations training is to develop the ability to deliver pleasing guest experiences. This includes the ability to turn around a situation that is causing dissatisfaction and emerge with a happy guest. To develop this skill requires the use of practical true-to-life examples. Top management must also be willing to admit mistakes that have been made in dealing with guests. In this honest and practical environment, trainees are more than likely to learn the necessary knowledge, skills, and attitudes to achieve positive guest relations.

Sales and Marketing

Employees should be trained in the operational philosophy and application of sales and marketing. They should be familiar with the operation's sales and marketing plan and should receive monthly updates on upcoming efforts involving major market segments, advertising, promotions, sales campaigns, and product positioning.

For too long, the sales and marketing effort has been surrounded by mystique, almost as though it were separate and apart from the main thrust of the operations side of the business. Successful operations understand that a business must be market-driven—that marketing must be the foundation upon which all sound operating decisions are made. For a business to be truly market-driven, its staff must be part of the marketing process. In a successful hospitality operation, each staff member is informed about the way the operation does business and how each employee's efforts fit into the total picture.

The general manager and the director of sales and marketing are the logical individuals to conduct this general sales and marketing training. The training must be planned and executed with a straightforward approach, and must relate the information in an understandable way to all affected departments. Handouts that list upcoming key events and feature profiles of target client groups or market segments are helpful in getting the information across.

Like all forms of training, it is important to allow time for questions and answers. The learning objective is one of understanding and attitude development, rather than skill. The purpose is not to teach the staff how to market the operation, but to help them see their contribution to the product being marketed.

Suggestive Selling

Selling is the direct responsibility of many members of the staff. It is both a departmental skill and a general skill of every staff member whose position requires regular guest contact.

Sales are a measure of productivity. Sales per guest, sales per hour of the day, sales per labor hour, sales per seat in the restaurant, sales per occupied room, sales per square foot of banquet space, and sales per dollar spent on advertising are but a few examples of ways that sales can be used to measure productivity across departmental lines. Too often, members of sales and marketing see their function as specialized to room sales, banquet sales, outside sales, or group sales. However, when a sales staff is successful, they have mastered the skills of selling almost anything.

Sales skills are applicable to almost all products. Departments that generate sales should rely heavily on sales experts to provide general training in effective sales techniques. General training does not replace the need to integrate suggestive sales training into the job breakdowns for departmental training. It does, however, provide a broader perspective of the sales techniques and establishes selling as a critical function of all guest-contact employees.

Role playing is an effective way to teach suggestive selling skills. After the trainer has outlined the principles of effective sales presentations, staff members can actually act out sales situations using the sales techniques. Prepared scripts or sales scenarios are also helpful to a trainee who wants to practice the best way to suggest a product and to close the sale. The director of sales should work closely with the department heads in developing scripts and scenarios. This helps ensure that the sales situations are realistic, and result in selling items which are most likely to increase profitability and guest satisfaction.

Safety and Emergency Procedures

The Occupational Safety and Health Act (OSHA) of 1970 sets standards and regulations related to the safety and health of workers throughout the United States. Severe penalties are imposed on employers who do not comply with these standards and regulations. OSHA has forced the hospitality industry to consider the role of training and job analysis in establishing effective accident control programs.

Every person who works in a hospitality operation must be concerned about the safety of guests and the staff. Safety should be emphasized in departmental training as it relates to work practices and emergency procedures. In a broader sense, general safety training should be covered in interdepartmental training so that *all* employees feel confident that everyone is safety-conscious. The general manager should be involved in this training and should endorse its importance.

The hospitality operation should have a written emergency response plan to follow in the event of a fire, bomb threat, assault, robbery, utility outage, various kinds of storms, or other unusual events that might endanger life or property. These procedures should be communicated in training sessions by the person who coordinates the plan in the operation. Safety training should include evacuation drills and should inform employees about where to report during a major emergency. Employees should also learn to identify situations where aid to the injured is appropriate. The importance of following pre-planned courses of action should be stressed. Trainers should emphasize that trying to be a hero by taking action that is not according to the established plan might actually result in more people being injured.

All accidents, injuries, or work-related illnesses must be reported to the department head and appropriate workers' compensation forms must be completed. These procedures should be covered in training so all employees have a clear understanding of how and when to report such situations.

Training should include a tour and demonstration of the building's emergency and safety systems. This instills employee confidence in the safety system, and ensures that each employee knows how to activate all manual systems. The session should also cover the appropriate use of safety log books for documenting any and all situations where safety is involved. Safety log books provide a record for investigation should any situation require a review of the facts surrounding the incident.

A record should be kept of all employees who complete this training. Such records are important in the event of a major incident resulting in bodily injury and possible liability claims. To ensure that safety knowledge was acquired in this crucial area, a written test should be administered with a high minimum standard of performance (90% to 95%). The tests should be filed in the personnel folders of each employee when he/she successfully completes the training.

Sanitation

Sanitation training is crucial in a hospitality operation—particularly the specialized departmental training that focuses on the causes and prevention of food-borne illnesses. But, in a broader sense, every employee must be sensitive to the standards of cleanliness, and should be instructed to correct or report any unsanitary or otherwise potentially hazardous situations that relate to cleanliness.

Sometimes employees do not know what to look for in identifying potentially hazardous, unsanitary situations. Other times, they find an unsanitary situation but feel that it is not their responsibility to correct the matter or to report the condition to the appropriate person. These feelings must be overcome so that immediate action is always taken by the first employee who spots an unsanitary situation.

Sanitation training is best addressed as a two-step process. First, principles of cleanliness and sanitation should be covered in a classroom setting. This can be done through lecture/discussion, problem-solving, or brainstorming. Second, employees should be taken on a tour with a prepared inspection sheet and actively look for unsanitary conditions. As each condition is identified, the employee should indicate on the inspection form what immediate action can be taken to correct the situation. Afterward, the group should return to the classroom setting and review the findings.

Sanitation training should be conducted by the general manager, by senior management, or by a representative of the local health department. It is very important for employees to see senior management setting or endorsing the criteria for cleanliness and sanitation.

Personal Hygiene and Grooming

The general manager must be the ultimate role model for personal hygiene and grooming. The management team follows the leadership of the general manager; likewise, supervisors and employees follow the example set by the management team. For this reason, the general manager and senior management staff should be actively involved in the training sessions concerning standards for personal hygiene and grooming. When management does not make hygiene and grooming a matter of priority in general training, the faddish norms of the community may become the standard for employee appearance.

Outside resource people are available to assist in such areas as selecting complementary clothing, hair and nail care, and specialized hygiene concerns. Most standards of personal hygiene and grooming can be effectively covered by the management staff without outside resource people.

Departmental Training

The department head is directly responsible for departmental training. The planning and execution of an effective ongoing training program is essential to the success of the department. A department that maintains an ongoing training commitment and brings it to life on a daily basis for every shift is a fun place to work; everyone grows and feels the importance of his/her contribution to the overall guest experience.

The single most important ingredient for effective departmental training is genuine departmental pride. The department that has pride in its work will be actively involved in training and cross-training. Training will be a daily topic of discussion, and it will be central to the way the department is managed.

Training Matrix by Position

One tool for planning department training is a carefully prepared training matrix by position (see Exhibit 9.2). One side of the schedule should list all the topics to be covered; the other should consist of the various employee groups to be trained.

Some topics are required for some positions and not for others. Still other topics may be required for all department employees. The matrix should list the job titles across the top of the form. Then, the department head must go down the list of topics for each job title and indicate which topics must be mastered by staff members who hold that position.

The purpose of the departmental training matrix is to aid the department head in selecting training topics for the daily training routines. When the weekly employee work schedule is prepared, it is important that employees who need certain blocks of training are scheduled to work on the days that those blocks will be covered.

Exhibit 9.2   Sample Departmental Training Matrix by Position

Training Matrix: Housekeeping Department

Topics/Tasks	Positions		
	Room Attendant	Laundry Attendant	Public Area Attendant
1. Housekeeping Organization	X	X	X
2. Housekeeping Terminology	X	X	X
3. Linen Identification	X	X	X
4. Linen Soil Sorting	X	X	
5. Linen Pre-Soaking		X	
6. Linen Washing		X	
7. Linen Drying		X	
8. Linen Folding		X	
9. Scheduling Laundry Operations		X	
10. Folding and Steaming		X	
11. Linen Running	X	X	
12. Stocking Linen Closets	X	X	
13. Stocking Linen Carts	X		
14. Entering Guestrooms	X		
15. Removing Waste from Guestrooms	X		
16. Preparing to Clean Guestrooms	X		
17. Stripping the Bed and Removing Soiled Linens	X		
18. Dusting the Guestroom	X		

Employees who need to sharpen skills that have slipped away from the standards should be scheduled to work on the days when appropriate training blocks are planned. The training topics should be posted along with the employee work schedule. This emphasizes that formal training is an ongoing daily routine and will be a consideration when employees ask to trade work days with other employees.

Not all employees will attend every daily training session. Managers should highlight the names of employees on the work schedule who need to attend a particular session. The training session, if well prepared and efficiently presented, should probably not last more than 30 minutes to an hour.

Effective Use of Shift Meetings

The shift meeting—or shift line-up—is an excellent concept and should be used in every operations department such as the front office, housekeeping, and food and beverage. The purpose of the shift meeting is to check attendance, check employee appearance, and to communicate anything that will help the employees do a better job during that shift. It may include reinforcement of standards, review of changes in standard procedures, and brief instructions concerning anything that calls for immediate attention.

Shift meetings should always be planned as positive reinforcement sessions. They should be disciplined but interesting and informative. Nothing is worse than starting a shift with a lecture about what was done wrong during yesterday's shift. Each day, the meeting provides a great opportunity to praise employees who are doing an outstanding job.

The shift meeting should be a cheerleading session, designed to send employees off to their stations excited and motivated to be at work. A good shift meeting lasts about ten minutes and ends on a happy note. It is well planned, concise, and fun. The meeting should take place away from interruptions and should be strongly focused on the communications at hand. These meetings are one of the easiest tools for a department head to use to demonstrate a clear, positive leadership style.

In some operations departments, employees begin work according to staggered shift starting times. In these cases, the shift meeting may require some creative scheduling or may be done in conjunction with scheduled breaks. The daily shift meeting is for all employees and should not become the daily ongoing training time. Training needs of individual employees vary as indicated in the departmental training matrix (see Exhibit 9.2). The shift meeting should be held every working day (including weekends) for each shift. Since the department head does not work every shift and normally has certain days off each week, the responsibility for conducting the meeting at those times should be delegated to an assistant manager or shift supervisor. A weekly plan for the meetings should be made for all shifts and should be coordinated among all management personnel.

Organized Training Materials

Organized training materials are essential to effective ongoing training. The training matrix described earlier includes a list of all topics that are routinely taught in departmental training. For each of these topics, there should be clear, concise training materials. For those topics that involve skill acquisition, there should be job breakdowns that detail what to do, how to do it, and why each step is important.

For training sessions where the goal is knowledge and understanding, clear outlines of the information which will be covered should be available. It is a good idea to have prepared handouts that support the lecture/discussion sessions for this type of training. In all cases, the trainer should be organized and have all materials prepared in advance of the actual training session. A pre-class checklist can be helpful in making certain that all important details have been taken care of beforehand (See Exhibit 9.3).

Some operations develop training manuals or training booklets for employees. It is important to have these available and to make sure that the information taught during the actual sessions agrees with the printed information. The following Case in Point describes the extent to which one hospitality operation approached the development and use of such training materials.

A Case in Point: Training Booklets

Most hotel and restaurant companies develop training manuals or booklets for guest service and housekeeping employees. One new hotel company made a commitment before opening its first property to develop a training booklet for every position. Booklets were developed that clarified the duties and expectations and that detailed how to perform the most critical skills. Every new employee, transferred employee, or promoted employee was provided with a booklet for his/her position the first day on the job.

Booklets were written and provided for every employee classification, including secretaries, maintenance assistants, banquet setup assistants, night auditors, cooks, and bookkeepers, as well as the more visible guest service areas such as food servers, cocktail servers, bartenders, housekeeping room attendants, receptionists, reservations, and bell staff. There were 21 non-management job classifications in this company's hotels, and there were 21 different training booklets.

Management training booklets were also written for each of the 10 management classifications, based on the learner-controlled instruction model. In addition, 11 policy and procedure manuals were written to provide detailed documentation to back up all training materials. An extensive four-hour orientation program was developed for each employee's first day. This program was supported by a complete orientation booklet which became the property of the employee after the orientation session.

Accurate Training Records

Accountability is a two-way street. For anyone to be held accountable for something, it must first be proven that the person knew what was expected of him/her. That is why training records are so important. Records document mastery and competence; they indicate the training status of any given employee on any given day. Training records should be maintained for each employee. All that is required is a form for recording what training took place, the dates that mastery was achieved in each area, and the signature or initials of the person who verified the employee's mastery (See Exhibit 9.4).

Training records are of no value if performance is not tested for each employee. Too often, training is presented in a group setting and attendance is equated with mastery. In reality, some employees who attend may master the concepts taught or demonstrated. Others probably cannot perform the skills according to the standards. Evaluation of mastery should be individualized.

Specialized Training

Some training is best conducted by outside resource people because of the highly specialized nature of the content. With enough training and experience, department managers may be able to conduct some or all of this training. However, to rule out certain topics just because there is nobody on staff who is competent enough to conduct the training could lead to incompetence in critical operational areas.

The general manager should have the authority to call in outside specialists for certain training situations. If a department head needs the assistance of a specialist, it is appropriate in most operations to request such assistance through the general manager. A written statement should be provided that honestly describes the limitations of the depart-

Exhibit 9.3   Sample Pre-Session Training Checklist

Pre-Session Training Checklist

Training Plan

Clearly stated training objectives?   _____

Job Breakdowns for each procedure to be taught?   _____

Evaluation instruments for each objective?   _____

Individual training records for each employee?   _____

Training Room

Adequate lighting?   _____

Adequate seating?   _____

Adequate tables or writing surface?   _____

Free from unnecessary distractions?   _____

Room scheduled for the training?   _____

Training Aids

Audiovisual equipment?

     List _____   _____

           _____   _____

           _____   _____

           _____   _____

           _____   _____

Training manuals?   _____

Handouts?

     List _____   _____

           _____   _____

           _____   _____

Other training aids?

     List _____   _____

           _____   _____

Trainers?

     List _____   _____

           _____   _____

           _____   _____

Miscellaneous

Ashtrays?   _____

Refreshments?   _____

Pencils/pens?   _____

Note pads?   _____

Other miscellaneous?

     List _____   _____

           _____   _____

           _____   _____

Exhibit 9.4   Sample Individual Training Record

Individual Training Record: Food Server		
Employee's Name _____		
I hereby confirm that the above-named employee demonstrated mastery of each of the following areas of training on the date indicated:		
Competency Area	**Date**	**Verified By**
Restaurant Service Concept	_____	_____
Guest Relations	_____	_____
Food Sanitation	_____	_____
Cocktail Service	_____	_____
Wine Service	_____	_____
Menu Knowledge	_____	_____
Service Preparations	_____	_____
Sidework	_____	_____
Guest Reception	_____	_____
Restaurant Breakfast Service	_____	_____
Restaurant Lunch Service	_____	_____
Restaurant Dinner Service	_____	_____

ment management in presenting a certain topic and why the help of a specialist is needed. Specialists may or may not charge for their services. If there is a charge, the cost should be included in annual budgets, and planned for like any other training expense. It is important, too, to integrate specialized training into the general and departmental training of the operation. These three areas of training must be viewed as one master design for achieving high levels of competence.

Training by Outside Specialists

Whenever an outside specialist comes into the operation to conduct training, the training sessions should be attended by appropriate department heads. This ensures that the reinforcement given at the departmental level is consistent with the training. Furthermore, after the specialist has left the premises, employees will look to their department head for assistance when they have problems applying what they learned.

With ongoing training, the biggest problem in using outside resource people is the difficulty of scheduling employees. Sometimes it is necessary to schedule several sessions of the same training to catch all employees. If an employee misses the specialized training due to vacation, sickness, or other approved absence, it is very difficult to make up the instruction, since the management staff has already admitted they are not expressly qualified to teach the topic.

One way to ensure that presentations made by specialized trainers are available for employees who missed those sessions is to videotape the presentations. Make-up sessions can then be scheduled. It is also possible to videotape the presentations for the entire staff in advance of any scheduled training sessions. Sometimes this taping is done at the specialist's "home base"—thus making it unnecessary for the specialist to travel to the operation. This can reduce the cost of specialized training, especially in chain organizations with many operations that need the same training. Of course, it is important to note that video production costs can be high if too much emphasis is placed on the glamour of the production. Simple, straightforward presentations can be very cost-effective.

Corporate Trainers. Some hospitality organizations—such as large chains or small companies—have a training manager or director on the corporate staff who specializes in presenting certain types of instruction. This is particularly true in the presentation of seminars and workshops for the management staff. Corporate training specialists may also be available to teach such high-tech subjects as point-of-sale control systems, computer systems, food preparation, wine service, or any other topic which requires specialized skills.

Whenever a corporate trainer conducts training for any segment of the staff, the management staff of the operation should maintain control over the scheduling and evaluation. The corporate trainer should be viewed as a resource person who assists the management staff in getting their job done. After the corporate trainer leaves, the management team will be held accountable for the desired results. This responsibility cannot be shifted to the corporate trainer just because he/she conducted the training.

It is important to learn the capabilities of the corporate trainers so that their assistance can be used effectively. These individuals are on the company payroll; their services do not normally cost the operation any more than is already being contributed to support corporate office overhead. Furthermore, corporate trainers have a vested interest in the success of the training; as company employees, they have concern for the continued survival of each operation.

Consultants. Consultants are available who specialize in every aspect of hospitality operations. Some specialize in one or two operational areas and others specialize in the total range of operational needs. Consultants usually charge for their services on an hourly, daily, or project basis.

Consultant services may be expensive. It is important to determine whether such expertise is actually needed or whether the desired training can be provided by another means at a lower cost. Good consultants offer seasoned experience in their areas of specialization, and are able to view operational situations objectively. Because their survival depends upon their ability to sell their time and services, consultants normally work very hard at pleasing the client—and at delivering the results that were agreed upon when they were retained.

It is important when hiring consultants to have a written agreement specifying what the consultant agrees to do, how results will be evaluated, what the financial arrangements will be, and what guarantees are expressed and implied. A consultant cannot read the client's mind. A consultant must be told in clear terms what is needed and what the end results must be. The same is true for the client; the consultant should know exactly how the management team will be involved in the training process. These matters should be negotiated and specified before the signing of any contractual obligations.

The following Case in Point illustrates how one hospitality operation effectively uses the services of a consultant at a particular time each year.

A Case in Point: Consultant Trains Trainers

Every December, a large country club in southern Florida hires more than 400 employees to work the busy winter months until the operation slows down in May. This necessitates intensive training in every department in order for the staff to perform according to the high standards expected by the club's exclusive clientele.

To meet this need, the country club brings in a consultant each December to train managers and supervisors in how to train employees. This training expert effectively prepares the management and supervisory staff for their seasonal start-up with optimum efficiency. While this training could be conducted by the human resources director or a senior staff member, the club's top management feels that the presence of a consultant emphasizes the importance of the training task. Furthermore, the human resources director and senior management are extremely busy at this time of the year with the mass hiring activities.

Purveyor Representatives. Many suppliers, manufacturers, and service companies have personnel who provide specialized training in their area of expertise. These suppliers may offer their services as part of the routine service package or may charge a fee. The cost should be clear before an agreement is made with a purveyor to provide specialized training.

Again, like all outside trainers, the activities of these specialists must be monitored to ensure the highest return on the training investment. The cost of time for training employees is real and adds up quickly, especially with large groups.

Other Outside Resource People. There are various sources of outside resource people available to the management team that is totally committed to developing a competent staff. Public agencies such as the fire department, police department, American Red Cross, local rescue squad, and Chamber of Commerce can provide specialists on areas of interest to hospitality operations.

The management team should always be concerned about the quality of the training. It is a good idea to ask all outside resource people to list references and places where they have recently conducted training. These references should be called to determine how well they feel their training needs were met by the training provided. Some of these references may indicate that the trainer was entertaining, fun, exciting, flamboyant, charismatic, and that the staff really enjoyed the session. This is fine and may even be important, but more important, did the training result in the desired competence? What did the learners master as a direct result of the training? Was there an observable improvement in performance that could be directly linked to the training? Managers should analyze these references carefully to ensure they are making the best choice.

Specialized Training Topics

Each operation has to decide what training can effectively be done by the management team or experienced non-management personnel. After doing so, the management team must determine the best way to conduct specialized training that exceeds the technical expertise of the staff. Topics will vary between organizations, but some of the areas that are often covered by outside specialists will be briefly discussed here.

Computer Training. Most hospitality operations that make extensive use of computers have their software programs written to their specifications by a software company. When software packages are first installed, or when major changes are made in software programs, it is customary to have the software company send in specialized trainers to teach the staff about the new programs. This service is usually done for a contract price and consists of an agreed upon number of hours or days of training.

The individuals who conduct this training are usually very competent; some may even have worked in an actual hospitality operation. Sometimes these trainers have standards that exceed or fall below the standards of the operation. If this seems to be a problem, the trainers should be called aside and the standards should be clarified. This ensures that there is no discrepancy between what is being taught and what the staff will be held accountable for later.

Training groups should not exceed three trainees at any given time. Training should also be done at the actual computer terminals to allow for maximum hands-on practice with the software. If too much computer instruction is covered in one day, little will be retained. To maximize retention, each trainee should not undergo more than two hours of software training during a shift. It is not uncommon for software training to range from 14 to 18 hours for some positions. In these instances, it may be necessary to have the computer trainers available each day for two or more weeks to effectively cover the training. Exhibit 9.5 gives a sample chart of computer training hours for the front office staff of a 200-room hotel.

Point-of-Sale Equipment Training. Similar to computer training, training on computerized point-of-sale equipment is often provided on a contract basis by the supplier or from the developer of the software. The same caution applies here that applied to computer software training in terms of maintaining established standards. For example, if the training is conducted in the dining room, and the operation does not permit the staff to smoke in the dining room while on duty, then the trainer should not smoke while conducting the training. The trainer should support all standards of the operation. This means that the trainer must be fully briefed as to the client's expectations.

Telephone Switchboard Training. In most modern hospitality operations, telephone switchboard training is actually computerized telecommunications console training. Such high-tech equipment requires the

Exhibit 9.5   Sample Specialized Training Schedule

Front Office Computer Training Schedule

Position	Training Hours	Topics*
Front Office Manager	24	All Menus
Asst. Front Office Managers	24	All Menus
Reservations Manager	18	2,3,4,5,7,10,11
Guest Reservationists	16	3,4,5,7,10,11
Guest Receptionists	14	3,4,6,7,8
Night Auditors	18	2,3,4,6,7,8,9

***Key to Training Topics**

1. Front Office Maintenance Menu
2. Report Menu
3. Front Office Menu
4. Reservations Menu
5. Group Booking Menu
6. Housekeeping Menu
7. Guest Accounting Menu
8. Shift Closing Menu
9. Night Audit Menu
10. Guest History Menu
11. Travel Agent Menu
12. Accounts Receivable Inquiry Menu

same type of technical emphasis given to computer and point-of-sale training.

Generally, the telecommunications console is the command center in the emergency response plan. Training on this important system is often done by an expert who can instill confidence in the staff that they can handle incoming and internal communications under the most adverse conditions.

The expert makes the operation of this sophisticated piece of equipment seem simple. Emphasis can then be placed on the most important aspect of telephone training: the conversations with callers. The training of staff who operate the main telecommunications console should incorporate scripts or scenarios that have been prepared by the management team or corporate office. These scripts should reflect the approved verbiage for answering calls and responding to frequently asked questions. In addition, training should cover the approved procedures for placing calls on hold—with proper emphasis given to public relations.

Job breakdowns on the actual operation of the console will expedite training when the outside expert is not available to train a new-hire. Training on telephone switchboard procedures should be scheduled as part of ongoing department training.

Fire Safety Training. The local fire marshal will usually be able to recommend someone who specializes in fire safety training. Among the items covered in this type of training are the use of portable fire extinguishers and fire hoses that are installed within the building; the procedures for evacuating the building; and the operation of fire alarms, sprinkler systems, smoke detectors, internal emergency public address systems, and other safety devices.

Fire safety training must be consistent with the emergency procedures established for the operation and covered in the internal emergency response plan. Therefore, it is necessary to have the fire safety instructor review the emergency response plan before the training to ensure the compatibility of instruction. This training must be viewed as essential for all personnel.

Fire safety training often includes tours of the building to point out the location of fire alarms, fire suppression equipment, and evacuation routes. Tour routes should be planned in order to minimize the time involved and to provide minimal interference with guest and employee activities.

First Aid Training. Basic first aid should be taught to all personnel who work in hospitality operations. This training should cover the emergency treatment of cuts, abrasions, and minor burns. Employees who complete the training satisfactorily should be certified by the training organization; this certification should be recognized by the American Red Cross and other emergency care agencies.

In all cases, first aid training must be conducted by a certified instructor. The local chapter of the American Red Cross may be willing to provide this training. If not, it is probably available from the local rescue squad, fire department, or a supplier of emergency oxygen equipment. If a member of the management staff is a certified instructor in first aid, he/she may conduct the training.

Cardiopulmonary Resuscitation Training (CPR). Many hotel companies require all personnel—particularly those in management and guest-contact positions—to be certified in CPR. Often, the fate of the guest who suffers a heart attack is dependent on the ability of the staff to provide emergency aid. Like first aid training, CPR training must be provided by a certified instructor.

This training usually takes about five hours and can be taught in one or more blocks. Scheduling will require more effort than simply plugging the sessions into the daily ongoing training times. Since it involves employees from various departments, CPR training should be coordinated through the general manager's or human resources director's office. Certification should be recorded in each employee's personnel file.

Heimlich Maneuver Training. The ability to provide emergency assistance to a person who has something lodged in his/her windpipe is important in hospitality operations—especially in restaurants. The Heimlich Maneuver is a medically approved technique for removing the item which is causing the blockage of air to the lungs. This training must also be conducted by a certified trainer, coordinated through the general manager's or human resources director's office, and recorded in the employee's personnel file. This training is sometimes combined with

CPR training since the object of both is to help a victim restore normal breathing.

Financial Management for Non-Financial Managers. The successful hospitality manager must be competent in financial management. This training should not focus on basic bookkeeping, but on financial analysis and interpretation. Managers are often required to write variance reports to explain unacceptable deviations from financial plans, and to take a more active role in preparing and monitoring budgets. When financial performance in the controllable aspects of their department is substandard, managers are expected to recommend actions to correct the situation.

Most employees want to know more about the financial performance of the businesses in which they work. In response, some hospitality companies routinely share income and expense information with all employees in confidential monthly meetings. This emerging trend makes it important to teach management and non-management personnel how to read, analyze, interpret, and react to financial information.

Training in financial management for the non-financial staff may require specialized assistance from an outside resource person. For one, financial knowledge of the management team may not be adequate to provide effective training. Second, the expertise of the controller or accounting manager may be too technical for personnel who have not been trained in bookkeeping and detailed accounting practices. This training must be at a level that is comprehensible. Many managers lack a sound understanding of how to analyze and interpret financial information because it was taught to them by a technician who talked over their heads. They failed to grasp the concepts and the practical application of the tools available to them in making better management decisions.

The best tools for teaching financial management are the operation's annual budget and the monthly income and expense statement. Some companies generate statistical analysis reports on a monthly basis. These computerized reports reduce the need to calculate mathematical equations to analyze and interpret financial data. The more basic business training is administered to the staff, the more conscientious the staff will be in managing revenues and costs. The purpose of this block of specialized training is to remove the mystery from this critical area in order to increase the competence of the management and staff in managing the assets of the enterprise.

Wine Product Training. Wine sales can increase revenues in most food and beverage operations. There is a difference between wine knowledge that is used to sell the products on the wine list and wine knowledge that is possessed by a connoisseur or wine expert. The hospitality operator must know the market segments served by the operation and must develop the amount of wine knowledge that will optimize sales.

Food and beverage managers may have sufficient wine product knowledge to train the service staff in the departmental training sessions. However, outside resource persons are available from wine distributors and vintners to provide this specialized product training. The key concern is to match the product knowledge to the market segments. Guests are easily offended by inadequate knowledge of the available wines as well as by a server who comes across as a wine snob.

Alcohol Awareness Training. Recent liability suits have led to a special emphasis on responsible beverage service within the hospitality industry. In many cases, the courts have ruled that if a person is involved in an accident that results in bodily or property injury following the consumption of alcohol, the business or employee who served the drinks can be held partially liable. This situation is a form of third party liability. In many states, these laws are referred to as "dram shop laws" or "alcohol-related third party liability laws." The shift in liability laws and court rulings has made special staff training essential where it was often ignored in the past.

Responsible beverage service training may be conducted by the beverage management staff; it is important that employees know that top management is supportive of the training. The staff must be trained in how to detect symptoms of intoxication and how to refuse further service of alcohol in a positive and tactful manner. A well-planned, competently executed, and thoroughly documented training effort should be mandatory in all hospitality operations which dispense alcoholic beverages.

The Educational Institute of AH&MA publishes an excellent training resource and produces a complementary video program which suggest guidelines on how servers may properly serve and monitor alcohol consumption. *Serving Alcohol with Care* is designed for both managers and servers and can be helpful in providing useful information which can make alcoholic beverage service a pleasurable experience for guests and staff.[2]

Cleaning Chemicals Training. Under current OSHA regulations, employees are entitled to training on chemical hazards in the workplace. In hospitality operations, most hazardous chemicals are used in conjunction with cleaning and sanitizing. OSHA requires hospitality operators to inform employees about hazardous materials that employees may need to handle to do particular jobs. Employees should be trained concerning general chemical hazards and the specific hazards associated with particular chemicals.

Departmental management must be thoroughly trained in safe chemical usage and in emergency treatment for individuals who have been exposed to a dangerous chemical. OSHA provides specific regulations for this training and for the mandatory recordkeeping involved. Until the management staff is fully competent to provide this training, it is advisable to use outside resource specialists who have the training and credentials. This can protect the employees from injury and reduce the likelihood of liability suits by individuals who are injured through improper handling of these substances.

This specialized training should be coordinated with the departments that use these chemicals. Department heads will usually schedule outside trainers, especially if they are provided as a part of the regular follow-through service of a chemical supplier or manufacturer. This training can be scheduled as the daily ongoing training session for certain days each month.

Specialized Equipment Training. Outside resource people can also teach the use and care of specialized equipment within the operation. Such equipment includes dish machines, laundry machines, office machines, computerized time clocks, and trash compactors. Outside resource persons bring both technical expertise and credibility to training. Specialized equipment training should be scheduled by department heads in conjunction with ongoing departmental training.

Accountability for Performance

Every individual who works in a hospitality operation should be held accountable for his/her performance in accordance with clearly communicated standards. But, as is the case in many walks of life, a few people are usually expected to accept a large share of the blame when things do not go according to plan.

The lion's share of responsibility for failures in the hospitality operation falls on the management team—specifically those managers whose departments did not achieve the desired results. The career of a management person rests largely on his/her ability to get the job done through the combined efforts of his/her staff—and to get it done according to the established standards.

Employees are not mind readers. They cannot be expected to know what management wants unless it is clearly communicated to them through orientation, training, and regular coaching and counseling. Upper level management may direct their attention to the corporate structure of the company, but, as the requirement for accountability filters through the ranks, the buck will stop with the management team—and not departmental employees.

It is imperative that the management staff accept the personal responsibility for training, and make every effort to ensure that each staff member is performing at his/her full potential. This is the only way that the management team can guarantee the results that are expected by the owners and corporate management of the organization.

Notes

1. The Educational Institute of AH&MA produces dozens of videotapes which can be used to supplement hospitality training. These tapes cover several topics and range from conceptual introductions to specific procedural demonstrations. For more information, contact the Educational Institute, P.O. Box 1240, East Lansing, MI 48826.
2. Van V. Heffner, *Serving Alcohol with Care*, 2nd ed. (East Lansing, Mich.: Educational Institute of the American Hotel & Motel Association, 1988). Readers who desire more detailed information are encouraged to write the Educational Institute, P.O. Box 1240, East Lansing, MI 48826. A videotape is also available which complements this training program for owners.

10 Management Training and Development

Training managers is just as important as training other employees. One big difference between management and non-management training is the degree of personal responsibility a trainee must assume for his/her own personal development. Management development is actually manager development; it addresses the individual development of managerial knowledge, skills, and attitudes. The individual manager must recognize the need for training and development, and must have the desire to achieve a higher level of excellence.[1] Within most industries, manager development is largely a self-directed process that follows a different pattern for each individual.

Management training and development may include formal activities such as classroom sessions and directed field training experiences. However, the process should recognize and accommodate the learning that occurs through participation in ongoing management tasks. Learning by doing is a legitimate development process if it is accompanied by objective feedback and an opportunity to correct mistakes and learn from experience. As one authority notes:

> The entire approach to management self-development is based on the belief that the best managers are not those who have attended numerous training courses. Rather, they are those who, on their own, take every opportunity of increasing their knowledge and/or modifying their behavior in order to work more successfully with others, for their mutual benefit.[2]

In this chapter, the learner is often referred to as a **management trainee.** The term **trainee** carries no connotation of age or experience. Trainees can be managers at any level. Managers need to be involved in training throughout their career—not just when they are new to an organization.

Overview of Management Development

Management development deals with the overall professional growth and improvement of the manager. The organizational goal of the process is to increase productivity and bottom-line profits. For management development to be effective, it must meet the personal goals of the manager and the business goals of the organization.[3]

With this in mind, management development activities should:[4]

- Be geared toward self-development

- Be tailored to the specific needs of the individual

- Provide actual practice in applying knowledge and using the new skills on the job

In addition, the managers involved should know their development priorities and what information or skills they are expected to master within a certain time. The trainee's manager must be completely supportive of the development effort. He/she must allow the individual trainee to experiment on the job with newly learned knowledge and skills, and should provide counseling on mastering these techniques when necessary. Finally, the organization's climate and culture itself must support each manager's acquired knowledge and skills.[5]

While job lists, job breakdowns, and related materials are primarily used to train non-management staff, these materials can also be used to develop the technical proficiency of managers in specific areas.

Establishing a Competency Model

An organized program of management training and development should always start with a list of specific competencies which the manager must master and demonstrate. This list is sometimes referred to as a **competency model**.[6] It may be helpful to group functionally related competencies under subheadings. Several competencies may be listed under a single heading to serve as the basis for planning formal or informal learning activities within that functional area. Lists may vary among hospitality organizations for the same management titles. It is difficult to arrive at a universal list for the hospitality industry because different organizations hold different expectations.

The competency list is similar to the job list developed for non-management training except that competencies are much broader than technical tasks. A competency consists of a group of interrelated tasks that are performed and supervised as a unit. This distinction between a competency and a task is important in designing management training.

Approaches to Management Training

Not too long ago, it was widely believed that management development did not require a formal structure and that the best leaders would rise to the top.[7] Fortunately, this "survival of the fittest" philosophy has lost ground. Now, most successful hospitality organizations support some formal approach to the management development process. Despite this shift, it is still important to emphasize that most management development must be self-development.

Many approaches can be used to support the management development process. They range from individual to group or classroom training approaches. The following list identifies many approaches to consider when planning or expanding management development activities:[8]

1. **In-house training**—conducting organized training activities within the organization, such as the four-step method for teaching technical skills; usually instructor-controlled.

2. **External training**—sending managers to courses or seminars offered for a fee by outside agencies.

3. **Training centers**—sending managers to centralized training facilities that are part of the corporate structure and away from the manager's day-to-day operation.

4. **Career development**—providing counseling and information services as part of self-directed learning; directing activities toward specific areas that need improvement.

5. **Job rotation**—shifting managers to other jobs to learn from experience; includes lateral or vertical assignments.

6. **Temporary assignments**—assigning projects within or outside the organization; examples include loaning managers to other internal departments or outside organizations such as government agencies, financial institutions, or civic groups.

7. **International assignments**—exposing managers to cross-cultural experiences, with or without structured training activities.

8. **Consultants**—using the services of internal or external experts in management specializations; examples include using corporate trainers or private consultants to conduct courses, facilitate projects, and evaluate programs.

9. **Counseling**—focusing on personal growth, personal problems, and management adjustment.

10. **Coaching**—providing on-the-job assistance through supervisors and/or trainers; job-specific individualized instruction.

11. **Task forces (Project groups)**—assembling cross-departmental groups to address organizational problems.

12. **Seminars**—conducting teach-each-other events (participative learning activities facilitated by a trainer) that pool the experience of participants.

13. **Exchange consulting**—sharing of expertise among managers on technical, managerial, or personnel problems.

14. **Group training programs**—conducting a type of in-house training that is subject-matter or task-oriented; usually instructor-controlled.

15. **Self-study courses**—taking correspondence courses for credit or certification of completion.

16. **Computer-assisted instruction**—being tutored through a computer terminal and software; consists of simulations or programmed instruction.

17. **Personal research and inquiry projects**—using resources of local libraries for adult learning projects; conducting actual research surveys; experimenting with two or more different operational procedures or methods; personal investigation of areas of interest on a need-to-know basis.

18. **University or technical college courses**—completing courses in defined areas or pursuing a degree that relates directly to job responsibilities.

19. **Directed reading**—participating in a planned program of reading in subject areas that are pertinent to management responsibilities; participating in a management reading group or professional organizations that encourage the exchange of ideas through reading forums or topical seminars.

20. **Assessment centers and performance reviews**—evaluating managers according to a goal-oriented management structure; developing individual growth plans; promoting self-directed learning.

21. **Mentoring**—formally assigning senior managers to assist new managers in growing into their jobs; encouraging informal mentor-trainee relationships within the organization.

22. **Learner-controlled instruction (LCI)**—offering a specialized type of self-directed on-the-job training in which the trainee controls the training schedule and sequence of learning activities; the trainee also chooses the resources, trainer, and procedures within a prescribed competency-based structure.

These approaches may be used individually or combined to accomplish training goals. All training should focus on efficiency and effectiveness. The last three approaches on the list will receive detailed treatment because of their potential for effectiveness and, in the case of mentoring, its current popularity as well. LCI—the last approach on the list—provides a framework that is especially suited to adult learning and the goals of management training. The LCI framework can incorporate any of the other approaches to increase the effectiveness and efficiency of the individual training activity.

Assessment Center Programs

For managers to grow, they must recognize the need to grow. Performance reviews are one means of assessing the strengths and weaknesses of managers. This process is discussed in general in Chapter 17.

One specialized form of management review that is directly related to the management development process is the **assessment center** approach. An assessment center is not a place; it is a technique for identifying an individual's potential and his/her training and development needs. Some training experts feel this approach is superior to all other approaches—including traditional performance reviews—for assessing management development needs. Participation in the activity itself is considered an outstanding management training experience.[9]

In a typical assessment center program, participants take part in exercises that identify important behaviors for management personnel. The exercises further point out strengths and weaknesses in the execution of these important behaviors, and provide a more objective basis for designing training and development for each manager.

Assessment centers are also useful when a person is being considered for a promotion or transfer since the exercises can include simulations of behaviors that will be required in the new positions.

In most assessment center applications, the assessors are responsible for evaluating the work performed by the managers. The assessors prepare a detailed report of their judgments and recommendations for the management trainee to use in further self-development.

Some possible assessment center applications follow:

1. A manager's ability to analyze financial reports and plan operational adjustments based on financial analysis might be assessed by providing the manager trainee with:
   - A set of financial statements covering the past three accounting periods (to show short-run trend history and current state of performance)
   - The financial reports for the same three accounting periods last year (to compare performance patterns)
   - The financial reports from last year that correspond to the upcoming three accounting periods (to predict short-run trends)
   - The annual budget with quarterly updates and adjustments for the current year

   Using these items, the trainee would be required to prepare and submit a written analysis and give an oral briefing on findings and recommendations.

2. As another example, a manager's ability to investigate and document an employee performance problem might be assessed by giving the trainee a fictitious employee file and a case description of an employee who is about to be terminated.

   Using these materials, the trainee would be required to prepare a written analysis of the case. This analysis would discuss all pertinent documentation within the employee file, and recommend whether the employee should be terminated or not based on the documented evidence. The written analysis should also suggest step-by-step actions that could be taken instead of termination, as well as appropriate instructions for what to do if termination is unavoidable.

Assessment exercises can be developed to cover every management competency, including technical abilities as well as the less defined areas of leadership and decision-making. The objective is simple: to identify strengths and weaknesses which can be analyzed to prescribe appropriate training or to increase the efficiency of other human resource actions.

In the absence of assessment centers, management training needs should still be based on as much objective data as possible. Performance reviews should always be viewed as a development activity that provides objective feedback in order to identify areas that need improvement.

Mentoring

Mentoring has gained popularity in recent years as a formalized training method. The approach has existed for centuries in many cultures as an informal activity in which an experienced and wiser colleague grooms a junior protégé for higher levels of performance and maturity. One authority describes mentoring as follows:

> A mentor is a very special person with regard to an individual's career and personal development. Mentors take their protégés under their wings and invite them into a new occupational world where they show them around, impart wisdom, sponsor, and criticize in a constructive manner. A mentor can help control the "luck" variable in the success equation. Mentors put in a good word for their protégés, tell them about new opportunities, and encourage them to aim for goals that seem out of reach. They are extremely influential people in the lives of their protégés because they help them reach their major goals in life. They often have the power, through who or what they know, to promote the younger person's welfare, training, and career.[10]

Many people in hospitality management are not familiar with the formal concept of mentoring, although they recognize individuals who have contributed directly to their career growth. For organizations to endorse and foster mentoring as a management development approach, management personnel must take time to understand the historical and current bases for mentoring, and its benefits.

Mentoring is difficult to evaluate on a skill or organizational level because it is so individualized; the sharing process between the two individuals is rarely formalized to the point of having clear-cut objectives. While mentoring can be a valuable learning experience, it is not without certain risks. It should not be the only training method used to develop managers. On the negative side, the mentor may look out for his/her own career more than the career of the younger manager. Some other managers within the organization may also dislike the young manager simply because they dislike the mentor. In this case, the young manager could be very vulnerable to attacks on his/her performance should the mentor be transferred or leave the organization.

The best mentors are individuals who have had the benefit of a mentor and who now desire to adopt the mentor role. While it is possible to train someone from scratch to be a mentor, it is far easier to ask someone who has had a mentor to be a mentor. A good mentor should enjoy teaching, guiding, and training.[11]

A mentor is not expected to be a professional trainer. He/she is expected to use career experiences to guide a less experienced employee in his/her current position and to help the junior manager prepare for future assignments.

For mentoring to be successful, the junior manager must be a willing participant, respect the wisdom and skills of the mentor, and desire to emulate the mentor's successes. The trainee must be willing to carry his/her part of the relationship by giving as well as taking. Mentoring is a fun way to learn—and for two people to become great friends and colleagues. The following Case in Point illustrates the learning and maturation which can occur in an effective mentoring relationship.

A Case in Point: Mentor, Master Teacher, and Friend

A young man entered active duty in the U.S. Army after acquiring a graduate degree in education. He had been commissioned through the Reserve Officer Training Corps in college. He was assigned to be an open mess training officer for Army clubs throughout the Pacific and Far East and was stationed in Hawaii. Since he had not been formally educated in hotel or restaurant management, the Army enrolled him in its intense club manager training course before sending him to the Pacific. He reported for his assignment barely knowing the basic terminology of the business he was to teach, let alone the technical or managerial nuances.

Upon arriving for duty, the young lieutenant was assigned to work alongside a seasoned 59-year-old club executive who was a civilian employee and coordinator of the club training department. This man had managed hotels, restaurants, and clubs in Las Vegas, Puerto Rico, Japan, and many other places. His career had been full and his knowledge spanned every facet and function of the industry. He prided himself on having been an innovator, and he had trained and developed a long list of loyal followers over the years.

The young lieutenant—green as they come—and the old industry warrior became close friends. Their first joint project was the revision of three training manuals for club personnel that had been written some time before by the senior member of the new duo. The educational background of the lieutenant proved useful in improving writing style and flow, while the experienced civilian provided the meat for the content.

For two years, the two men were inseparable. They traveled together to Korea, Japan, Thailand, Taiwan, Okinawa, and South Vietnam and conducted training courses and management analysis of army clubs for officers, non-commissioned officers, and enlisted personnel. For the young lieutenant, every day was a school day. The civilian took on the role of mentor and teacher and carefully tutored his young friend in everything from the basics to the finer points of successful hospitality management.

The mentor had amassed a complete personal library on every subject related to hospitality which he made available to the lieutenant. Anytime the lieutenant had a question about anything, he would ask his mentor, who would patiently explain it step by step. Often the lieutenant had to ask the same question two days in a row, not because the explanation was inadequate, but because it was so detailed and thorough that it was difficult to absorb it in one session. For a young man who had a sincere love for learning, it was a joy to work with and to learn from his wise and respected friend.

The friendship between these two men has grown and lasted for the past 18 years. At the end of his two-year Army obligation, the young man was discharged and went on to pursue his career. In time his old friend retired. Today, they are both still very active in the hospitality industry and keep in touch to continue sharing their lives.

Learner-Controlled Instruction

Learner-controlled instruction (LCI) is a structured application of self-directed learning that incorporates concepts such as mastery learning, self-pacing, performance-based evaluation, and the effective use of a wide range of learning resources. In fact, this form of training provides a structure for turning the total work environment into a system of learning resources.

As noted in Chapter 5, LCI has been used within the hospitality industry with great success since the early 1970s. The management selection, training, and development philosophy of the hospitality companies with LCI programs have all been positively shaped by their commitment to this form of self-directed learning. The benefits of LCI have established it as a superior approach to the development of competent managers. Research on LCI and other individualized learning models indicate that LCI is more effective as a learning model than any other available approach.[12]

When explaining LCI, it is important to note that LCI is a form of on-the-job training; management trainees master the competencies of their future assignments within an actual operation. However, when all facets of LCI are considered, the approach is actually much more than traditional on-the-job training programs.

In the execution of an LCI program, the trainee is given full control over scheduling activities and pacing the amount of time required to master specific job duties. LCI trainees perform best when they are given considerable freedom in determining their training hours—and are permitted to spend as many hours as they desire in their pursuit.

Characteristics of LCI Users

Individuals who are naturally self-motivated will learn much faster using the LCI approach. Not all individuals who seek a management career are self-directed. Individuals who lack self-confidence will have difficulty progressing in a learner-controlled environment. They will also have difficulty accepting management responsibilities later on because of their unwillingness to take risks and make decisions. Individuals who do not succeed in a learner-controlled training environment usually do not succeed in management assignments—even when they are trained through instructor-controlled methods. The LCI approach performs a vital secondary role since it screens out those individuals who are most likely to fail in management assignments.

Fortunately, most management candidates bring a solid record of self-directed achievement. Many have reached their present state in life by overcoming difficult barriers. Some have had to work to help pay for their education or have developed a sense of self-reliance from other experiences. Others have developed their own form of self-direction from experiences in sports, social pursuits, or early work experiences. The vast majority of successful leaders in business, government, or any other segment of society have a strong sense of self-motivation. For these self-directed types, LCI is the ideal way to help them master new management responsibilities with the least amount of time and the greatest feeling of accomplishment.

How LCI Differs from Traditional Training

In LCI, learning is not equated with time spent in training; it is measured by demonstrated performance according to written standards. Conversely, traditional on-the-job management training is **time-based.** The trainee rotates from one station to another and spends a specified amount of time at each station observing performance and assisting with duties. When the allotted time has passed, the trainee moves to another station for a similar activity. At the end of this rotational schedule, the trainee is regarded as competent and fully trained to assume his/her next management assignment.

Time-based programs must be scheduled for the average learning speed or the speed of slower learners. Fast-paced learners are held back and may become bored by the pace of traditional programs. Such expressions of boredom are often misinterpreted as a lack of interest in the job, when they should be seen as an indication of ineffective management training.

Many time-based rotation programs are limited to the duties performed by hourly workers. It is important for management training to develop competence in decision-making, risk management, and actual problem analysis. This is difficult through time-based training because the trainee is not given control of the learning process. Development in true managerial responsibilities such as interviewing, counseling, coaching, scheduling, risk management, guest relations, motivation, leadership, disciplinary actions, performance reviews, terminations, financial analysis, and budgeting are often covered in classroom sessions—or not at all. These classroom sessions make extensive use of role plays, simulated situations, and hypothetical problem-solving. This is because time-based rotation programs do not adequately provide the systems or the resources for learning many interpersonal and analytical skills.

In LCI, the *total* scope of management responsibility can be incorporated into one field-based program. The results are often superior to those achieved in any combination of training and classroom training. The key is that while individual management training methods can accomplish some management training goals, LCI can provide the best of all worlds since numerous methods can be incorporated into the learner-controlled model.

Elements of an LCI Program

The LCI Manual or Document. The trainee who is assigned to complete an LCI program should be given a manual or other document to serve as a learning guide. With today's technology, the manual can take many forms ranging from typical paper and print to computer disc or interactive video. The communications medium will change with changing

Exhibit 10.1 Sample List of Management Competencies

Management Competencies

Basic Skill Level Competencies
1. The ability to set up the dining room for service
2. The ability to perform busing duties
3. The ability to set up, operate, and clean service equipment
4. The ability to perform table service
5. The ability to perform hosting duties

Administrative Competencies
1. The ability to write food descriptions and menus
2. The ability to forecast restaurant sales
3. The ability to schedule employees
4. The ability to prepare the weekly payroll
5. The ability to prepare all cashier's reports

Personnel Management Competencies
1. The ability to recruit, select, and hire employees
2. The ability to orient and train employees
3. The ability to coach and counsel employees
4. The ability to conduct formal performance reviews
5. The ability to administer employee discipline

Financial Analysis Competencies
1. The ability to troubleshoot food and beverage control systems
2. The ability to interpret the effect of hotel banquets on restaurant traffic
3. The ability to perform a food and beverage audit
4. The ability to prepare restaurant budgets
5. The ability to analyze and interpret monthly financial statements

Operational Supervision Competencies
1. The ability to supervise the opening of the restaurant
2. The ability to supervise the restaurant during all meal periods
3. The ability to handle guest complaints and/or compliments
4. The ability to handle emergency situations in the restaurant
5. The ability to supervise the closing of the restaurant

Note: The above list is not intended to be complete. Rather, it shows the possible scope of an LCI training approach. A complete list of competencies for an assistant restaurant manager might include 40 to 50 competencies.

---

technology; in all cases, however, the following learning elements should be present.

Introduction. The manual should begin with an overview of learner-controlled instruction. It should describe how LCI differs from traditional instructor-controlled methods, and should provide guidelines for progressing through the program as a self-directed learner. The introduction should also explain each component of the training materials and how the trainee will work with other individuals in the hospitality operation to master the prescribed competencies.

Competencies. The manual or document should also inform the trainee of the competencies he/she must master to complete the training. Exhibits 10.1 and 10.2 provide sample competency lists for two management positions that could be part of an LCI trainee guide.

Suggested learning activities. For each competency, the manual

Exhibit 10.2   Sample List of Management Competencies

The Director of Catering must demonstrate the ability to perform each of the following according to the standards prescribed.

Catering (Specific Specialization Training)

Perform an analysis of catering markets and the strength of competition within each market.

Describe the total catering product for the property including each menu item, style of service, setup, and theme or decor package.

Apply sales administration policies and procedures as they relate to catering activities.

Prepare a catering sales reference manual with appropriate sales collateral materials.

Coordinate the setup and service of all types of catering functions routinely provided by the hotel.

Describe the duties of convention services and the interrelatedness of banquet and conference service.

Manage all available function space to optimize catering revenues.

Prepare and process function billings including presentation of the bill and settlement of the account.

Prepare written communication to clients and to other departments concerning catering activities.

Explore areas of new business, evaluate prospects' needs, and determine appropriate follow-up action.

Make sales calls (solicitation and appointment calls) that result in profitable bookings.

Conduct in-house tours with catering clients that result in profitable bookings.

Finalize and communicate all details for food and beverage catered functions through the function event order system.

Plan and conduct catering staff meetings.

Catering Financial Analysis

Prepare the 10-day, 30-day, and quarterly banquet forecast.

Analyze the financial performance of the catering department and its contribution to the overall performance of the hotel.

Prepare quarterly and annual catering operating and revenue budgets.

Human Resources Management (Supervision)

Explain the detailed supervisory procedures behind each human resources policy covered in the employee handbook.

Perform the department head's roles in the selection and hiring process.

Conduct departmental orientations and skills training for catering and banquet service personnel.

Conduct formal performance reviews (written and oral) for catering personnel.

Conduct employee problem analysis and counseling sessions.

Perform all steps of the progressive employee discipline and development process.

Perform investigations related to the employee work suspension and/or termination process.

Basic Hotel Familiarization (Manager-on-Duty Competencies)

Food and Beverage (General)

Explain local food and beverage sanitation regulations.

Describe the kitchen organization and production capabilities of the food production department.

Describe the mission of each public food and beverage outlet, including room service.

Describe the organization of the stewarding department and the support procedures for banquets.

Describe the organization of the banquet service department and the styles of service available.

(continued)

Exhibit 10.2 *(continued)*

Front Office (General)

Explain the reservations procedures for the hotel.

Explain the registration and check-out procedures for guests.

Explain the function and operation of the hotel telecommunications console.

Explain the functions and duties of the hotel's guest services department.

Engineering (General)

Explain the functions of the engineering department and the procedures for requesting engineering or maintenance assistance.

Security/Risk Management (Total Hotel)

Respond to all breaches in security within the property.

Take appropriate emergency response steps in the event of a major emergency or disaster.

Apply appropriate first aid and emergency care procedures to ill or injured guests or employees.

Manager-on-Duty (Total Hotel)

Perform the role of Manager-on-Duty including full documentation in the Manager-on-Duty log.

---

should describe specific on-the-job learning activities which the trainee may use to gain mastery. These should not be role plays or business games. The activities should be actual business situations which the manager will be expected to personally perform or supervise on a regular basis when the training is completed. The self-directed trainee is expected to "plug into" these business situations and master them under the actual demands of the job situation.

While the approaches to management training listed earlier can be incorporated into an LCI program, the use of instructor-controlled methods should be kept to an absolute minimum. First, they are less effective, except in pure skill areas such as those taught through the four-step training method. Second, when applied to groups, instructor-controlled methods are paced to the average learner's speed and fail to meet individualized needs.

Outside seminars and correspondence courses are appropriate learning activities for the learner-controlled environment. Other legitimate learning activities for the self-directed learner include projects and special assignments. The use of internal and external consultants can also be easily incorporated into the suggested learning activities. Some hospitality organizations have created centralized learning centers where all instruction is learner-controlled. The centers provide a complete array of training resources, mock-up equipment, and trained individuals to act as learning facilitators rather than as teachers. The LCI model provides great flexibility for applying most every effective learning strategy.

Criteria for evaluation. Each suggested learning activity should be evaluated based on certain criteria. This helps the trainee know exactly what constitutes mastery for the competency being sought.

Selected printed resources. Appropriate policies, procedures, and other documents should be listed which will help the trainee gain the desired knowledge in each competency area.

Format of the LCI manual or document. Exhibits 10.3, 10.4, and 10.5 provide sample formats for specifying the learning experiences, criteria for evaluation, and resource lists. When contract learning is discussed later in this chapter, it will become clear why these forms are designated as *training contracts*. For now, it is sufficient to think of them as *learning guides* that are used to structure the mastery of each prescribed competency. In other words, the manual or document should consist of a series of training contracts or learning guides which specify competencies and provide guidelines for acquiring and demonstrating mastery.

The document serves as the rule-book for the LCI experience. Everyone who works with the trainee is expected to follow the rules to ensure that the trainee achieves results that are consistent with the organization's performance standards.

The Training Advisor. Each trainee should be assigned a "training advisor" at the beginning of the program. This individual should be a manager with experience in the areas and responsibilities the trainee will be assigned after training. Assignment as a training advisor should be treated as an extra duty reserved for the *best* managers in the organization.

The training advisor is not expected to be a teacher in the LCI model, or to set and control the trainee's schedule. Rather, the training advisor should be a friend, counselor, and role model throughout the learner-controlled experience. This concept is, in essence, a formalized approach to mentoring within a competency-based training program.

The training advisor should give suggestions and act as a sounding board for the trainee to try out ideas and approaches to the learning process. However, the ideal advisor will never tell the trainee what to do or when to do it. The trainee needs to constantly assess the operation's activities and determine when and how to most effectively use the business environment as a learning center to master the required competencies.

Contract Learning

The individuals who train through LCI should not look to professional trainers for help in mastering the designated competencies. Rather, trainees should identify the master performers within their organization and "contract" for assistance in learning specific job duties. This concept is referred to as **contract learning.**

When this contract learning relationship is established, the master performer should be regarded as a **contractor** and accept responsibility for helping the trainee. This assistance may be in the form of demonstrating, coaching, teaching, or explaining; it should include the final evaluation of the trainee. The contracting process itself should be somewhat formal. Experience with LCI has shown that informal verbal agreements are often disregarded or misunderstood and hinder rather than facilitate learning. Both parties should sign a statement when the contract is made. The contractor should sign a second time when the trainee achieves mastery according to specified evaluation criteria. Refer

Exhibit 10.3 Sample Training Contract #1

Training Contract

Competency: The ability to register guests.

Strategies for Developing Competence

1. Meet with the contractor and discuss the following:
   a. Work flow at the front desk
   b. Forms used for registering guests
   c. Front office terminology
   d. Market segments
   e. Check-in scenarios
   f. Procedures for handling other than normal reservations
   g. Procedures for handling different guest personalities and attitudes

2. Observe front desk operations during heavy check-in periods.

3. Work as a receptionist and room as many of the following categories of guests as possible:
   a. Transients with reservations
   b. Airline personnel
   c. Walk-ins
   d. VIPs
   e. Pre-registered groups
   f. Mini-vacations
   g. Special unit packages
   h. Complimentary rooms

4. Work as a receptionist and process:
   a. Folios
   b. Rack slips
   c. Telephone slips

5. Meet with the contractor and review the procedures for registering guests plus any unusual problems encountered and resolved during the learning experience.

Guidelines for Evaluating Performance

1. A meeting with the trainee to review the following points:
   a. Trainee had reviewed all resources
   b. Trainee asked questions that demonstrated a desire to be fully oriented to the registration process
   c. Trainee could answer questions raised by the contractor, demonstrating an understanding of each point discussed

2. Based on observations, trainee could describe how receptionists handled various guest situations; what he/she saw that should not have occurred; what he/she observed as missing from guest check-in practices.

3. Trainee handled each market segment according to recommended procedures; followed correct scenarios; resolved all problems that arose in a professional manner. Trainee registered a sufficient number of guests to demonstrate proficiency in handling most check-in situations and procedures, as judged by the contractor.

4. Trainee completed and processed all forms correctly and completely; could explain the importance of accurately handling the processing of each form and problems that could arise because of errors.

5. Trainee could answer any questions asked by the contractor relative to registration procedures to demonstrate a complete understanding of the function and the specific procedures.

Resources

Corporate Front Office Manual
Property Front Office Manual
Brochures on Special Packages

Property Marketing Plan
Job Description: Receptionist
Skills Training Guide: Receptionist

Agreement and Mastery Declaration

I agree to assist the trainee in developing mastery of the competency identified in this training contract.

_____   _____
        Signed—Contractor   Date

I confirm that in my best judgment the trainee has satisfactorily performed the strategies and developed mastery of the competency identified in this training contract.

_____   _____   _____
   Signed—Training Advisor   Signed—Contractor   Date

Exhibit 10.4 Sample Training Contract #2

Training Contract

Function: Purchasing

Competency: The ability to purchase and requisition food and supply needs.

Key Points

1. How does the company's central purchasing system operate?
2. Under what conditions are items purchased from local sources?
3. How and when are deliveries made:
    a. from central warehouse?
    b. from local sources?
4. How is billing and payment for food and supplies handled?
5. What procedures are followed for stock rotation?
6. What control procedures are followed for receiving food and supply deliveries?
7. What course of action should a manager follow when unplanned shortages of product occur?
8. How is payment for C.O.D. (cash paid-out) items made?
9. How are products transferred from one store to another and how are transfers documented?
10. What action should be taken when products delivered do not meet standards for quality?

Strategies for Developing Competence	Guidelines for Evaluating Performance

1. Assist the store manager in taking the food and supplies inventory.	1. Trainee was able to:
	  a. Accurately record the inventory on standard form.
	  b. Identify how different food and supply items are packaged.
	  c. Identify par levels for all food and supply items.

2. Schedule yourself to take the food and supplies inventory and order/requisition needed items.	2. Trainee was able to:
	  a. Correctly take and record the inventory.
	  b. Order needed direct purchases such as eggs, milk, and chicken.
	  c. Determine how to requisition additional food or supply items beyond the standard par level.

3. Schedule yourself to receive direct purchase items and perform quality and quantity checks on items received.	3. Trainee was able to judge products received for approved quality and correct quantities and refuse all unacceptable deliveries. Documentation of products received or refused was complete.
4. Store items received from warehouse and from direct purchases.	4. Storage was in proper locations and approved rotation procedures were followed.

Resources

R-113 Receiving, Storing, and Rotating Inventory (Quality Section)
R-114 Inventory Forms   R-115 Chemical Supply Order Form

Agreement and Mastery Declaration

I agree to assist the trainee in developing mastery of the competency identified in this training contract.

_____   _____
Signed—Contractor   Date

I confirm that in my best judgment the trainee has satisfactorily performed the strategies specified to develop mastery of the competency identified in this training contract.

_____   _____   _____
Signed—Training Advisor   Signed—Contractor   Date

Exhibit 10.5 Sample Training Contract #3

Training Contract

Position: Director of Sales

Competency: The ability to conduct sales tours of the hotel.

Knowledge and Understanding of the Competency

1. State four very clear and observable business objectives of an effective sales tour of the hotel.

2. For each of the following areas, describe how ongoing activities in the hotel affect the plan for the tour in terms of what area is shown and at what time:
   a. Front office
   b. Housekeeping
   c. Food and beverage public outlets
   d. Function areas
   e. Pool, health club, and recreational facilities

3. What are the steps in planning for an effective sales tour?

4. What are two benefits and two positive features of each facility or service that will be shown during the tour which can be drawn to the attention of the touring client?

5. What follow-up steps should routinely follow each sales tour with respect to each of the following?
   a. Follow-up before the client leaves
   b. Follow-up after the client leaves

Suggested Learning Activities

1. Meet with the current Director of Sales and obtain a complete orientation to the facilities and services available to clients in the following categories:
   a. Function space
   b. Guestrooms and suites; number, sizes, rates
   c. Public food and beverage outlets; menus, hours, capacities
   d. Special amenities; restrictions, hours, guest charges

2. Assist in planning and conducting a minimum of four sales tours including the following:
   a. Two tours conducted for clients by the Director of Sales or a member of the sales staff
   b. Two tours conducted by you for clients while accompanied by the Director of Sales or a member of the sales staff

3. Plan and conduct sales tours for clients on your own until you are successful in booking a meeting group for the hotel requiring guestrooms and function space. Document each tour on a Sales Call Report form and identify the appropriate follow-up action for each tour conducted.

Guidelines for Evaluating Performance

1. Trainee reviewed all policies and procedures pertaining to sales calls and could correctly answer 90 percent or more of the questions asked about these matters by the contractor.

2. Trainee demonstrated a clear understanding of the purpose of sales tours, the steps and procedures in planning good tours, and the interdepartmental communications and cooperation required for a successful tour.

3. Trainee could identify benefits and features of each area of the hotel included in the tour.

4. Trainee demonstrated the ability to overcome client objections and offset such resistance with a positive feature or benefit of the facilities or services.

5. Trainee was successful in qualifying each client as to the desirability of the group's business in relation to the overall sales plan for the hotel.

6. Trainee was successful in booking a profitable piece of business and appropriately documented the transaction including the contract and confirmation.

Exhibit 10.5 *(continued)*

Printed Resources

1. Sales plan for the hotel
2. Sales policies and procedures
3. Hotel floor plans and diagrams
4. Promotional materials for the hotel
5. Current rate listing for groups

Agreement and Mastery Declaration

I agree to assist the trainee in developing the competency described in this training contract.

_____   _____
      Signed—Contractor   Date

I confirm that in my best judgment, the trainee has mastered the competency described in this training contract within the spirit of the evaluation criteria.

_____   _____
      Signed—Contractor   Date

_____   _____
      Approved—Training Advisor   Date

---

to Exhibits 10.3, 10.4, and 10.5 for examples of formal contract agreements and corresponding sign-off statements.

Master performers are the keys to the success of the LCI approach. Potential contractors are available within every organization. Most people enjoy being recognized for their achievements, and are ready to aid anyone who sincerely wants to learn from them. Master performers are automatically reinforced simply by being asked to assume the role of contractor.

Time Requirements for LCI Training

The time required to complete an LCI program varies with each individual since the trainee controls the scheduling and pacing. This creates some inconvenience for the organization in planning when the trainees will be ready to assume their management assignments. This inconvenience, however, is easily offset by the benefits of the program.

Experience has shown that once an organization adjusts its hiring practices to select only self-directed individuals, these trainees master the total job in *less* time than is required to complete time-based field training and supplemental classroom training. Consider the discoveries made by one organization during and after the implementation of an LCI program.

A Case in Point: Rewarding Self-Motivation

A small fast-food chain faced a situation where about half of its managers seemed motivated to do a good job and the other half seemed unmotivated. The owners felt that the cause of low motivation was a lack of sufficient training. None of the managers had been formally trained by the company. The motivated managers were trying harder and were getting better results, even though their performance needed much improvement.

A learner-controlled instruction program was developed and implemented. All managers and assistant managers were required to participate. Each manager was informed that to remain a store manager, he/she must successfully complete the training. While there was no specified time for the training, the company made it clear that everyone would be expected to show steady progress each week.

By the end of the second week, it was obvious that the same unmotivated managers were not making any progress, while the motivated group was moving steadily ahead. Among the assistant managers, some were making good progress and others were procrastinating and dragging their feet.

Weekly counseling sessions were held with each of the managers. These sessions focused on determining what problems were arising in the training, and how the managers were overcoming their problems. The unmotivated managers kept complaining that they would prefer a training program where they were told what to do and were responsible for making fewer decisions. By the end of six weeks, the motivated group and about two-thirds of the assistant managers had completed their training. Meanwhile, the unmotivated group was far behind; some had hardly started.

A meeting was held and everyone was reminded that an individual could no longer be a store manager unless he/she completed the training. Four more weeks were allowed and progress was again assessed. Again, little progress had been made by the unmotivated group. It was obvious that there was no intent on the part of most of that group to complete the training. The store managers who had not completed the program blamed the delay on their busy schedules. At this time, each of these managers was relieved of his/her store manager duties and replaced by those assistant managers who had completed the training.

The managers who were relieved of their store manager duties knew that if they had not completed the training by the end of the tenth week, the assistant manager assigned to run their store would become the permanent store manager. None of the store managers in this group completed the training.

Within three months, all of the unmotivated managers and assistant managers who had not completed the training had been phased out of the company. Selection procedures were altered to only select individuals with a strong history of self-motivation.

The LCI format served two purposes in this company. First, the LCI program provided a consistent standard for competence. Second, it provided a means for identifying individuals that lacked self-motivation. There was a direct relationship between the failure of the unmotivated individuals to succeed in the self-directed learning environment and their failure to succeed as managers. Training will rarely motivate individuals who lack self-motivation. Even though such trainees are likely to complete the instructor-controlled training, they will rarely be anything more than unmotivated managers.

Experience with numerous LCI programs within the hospitality industry provides some indication of average completion times for self-directed learners. In hotel situations, an entry-level manager within a department can be expected to take 12 to 16 weeks to fully master the competencies required for the position. A hotel department head can be expected to take three to six weeks if he/she is promoted from within and has completed an entry-level LCI program; about twice the time will be required if the individual was hired from outside. Typical LCI programs for managers and assistant managers in free-standing restaurants usually require about four to eight weeks. Department heads within airline catering operations average about 8 to 10 weeks for mastery of their responsibilities.

Again, these averages are based on a large number of individual trainees. People learn at different paces and should learn within a system that accommodates individual learning speed and style. It is a mistake to limit LCI trainees to a set number of weeks based on the above averages. When this occurs, the overall effectiveness of the approach is greatly reduced. Self-motivated learners will master each area as quickly as they can and will be anxious to move on.

Training must be a life-long process. While it is a mistake to rotate trainees out of an area before they have confidently mastered the duties for which they will be held accountable, it is an equally serious mistake to keep managers in a training classification for longer than absolutely necessary. It is much better to have a complete training system which permits every manager to pass through a self-directed, competency-based, mastery-learning experience *each time* he/she makes a career move. This promotes an ongoing self-development process and avoids placing individuals in situations where they are likely to get off to a bad start, make costly mistakes, and even fail.

Benefits of LCI

With LCI, there is never any guesswork as to what managers are expected to master in the training process. Each competency is clearly specified in the training contracts and learning materials. There are no grades and each trainee operates on a "pass-incomplete" basis.

The cost benefits of LCI are numerous. There is no need for costly staff trainers who are expected to be experts in everything that a manager must know. LCI usually takes less time than other training approaches to achieve competence, and the competence achieved is higher in quality. This is because competency is achieved under the actual demands of the job situation, rather than in a simulated environment.

Experience shows that management turnover is reduced in organizations that give wholehearted support to self-directed management development. Managers see that their careers will advance on more solid footing in such an environment. An LCI program places a trainee in a position where a high level of organizational involvement is required. This results in an increased sense of loyalty which also contributes to management stability.

The contract learning process helps the manager develop important skills related to motivation. **Recognition** is a strong motivator. In LCI, the trainee experiences first-hand how to apply recognition to get the assistance needed to master essential competencies. The entire LCI model applies the principles of positive reinforcement (see Chapter 4), since the manager is reinforced each time he/she is certified as competent in a particular area. The manager repeatedly experiences practical application of behavior modification in the management of people.

The importance of clear expectations cannot be overemphasized in the management training process. Managers are expected to clearly communicate expectations to employees, yet the organization is often unclear in communicating expectations to managers. This is largely overcome through the LCI approach to management development. The design process requires top management to clearly state expectations and to explain plans for evaluating results. This clarification benefits the entire organization and makes business goal-setting much easier. Expectations define individual roles and group norms. Successful organizations have a clear sense of direction because they have willingly gone through a process of clarifying their expectations.

The LCI model emphasizes performance standards. Competency goes beyond being able to do something in a so-so manner; it means doing it right, according to established standards, and in a way that contributes to the organization's goals. The LCI approach leaves nothing to chance. If a manager is going to be held accountable for a specific area of responsibility, it is only fair that the organization provide the opportunity to gain competence in that area.

The LCI structure leads the manager through a complete orientation and mastery of every job duty as well as interpersonal and analytical responsibilities. This results in managers fully understanding the organization's performance standards and the employees which they will later supervise.

Every management discipline can be incorporated in an effective LCI program, either as a competency to be mastered or as a learning process that must be applied. For example, decision-making is learned by making decisions about the training activities. Time management is learned by being responsible for schedules, appointments with contractors, and timely completion of the program. Throughout the period that the trainee masters each of these abilities, he/she receives feedback from other people in the operation. Gradually, such skills as effective decision-making and time management become learned abilities as the trainee is reinforced each time he/she demonstrates the appropriate behaviors.

A person who sets out to design an LCI program should believe that all forms of manager training can be incorporated into a single LCI program. The designer needs to believe that every job responsibility can be mastered in a learner-controlled environment if learning activities and evaluation criteria are adequately specified.

The designer must resist the temptation to assign fixed amounts of time or to establish a sequence of learning activities in an LCI program. The same is true for assigning the contractors or trainers for the LCI trainee. Much of the learning in the LCI approach is gained through the trainee managing and controlling the learning process. An LCI program loses much of its value in teaching such abilities as decision-making, time management, motivation, and leadership when it is time-based, when the sequencing of learning activities is rigid, or when the trainee is not required to arrange his/her own contracts. Learning how to be a manager is largely accomplished by managing the learning process.

Leaders should be trained using a learning system which recognizes their self-direction and reinforces their willingness to take risks and make decisions. No other approach to training does this as well as the LCI model. Management training and development is essential to the pursuit of excellence. Managers and leaders are not born; they are made through a lifelong process of training and development.

Notes

1. Peter F. Drucker, *Management: Tasks, Responsibilities, Practices* (New York: Harper & Row, 1974), pp. 425–429. For a somewhat different point of view, see Ferdinand F. Fournies, *Coaching for Improved Work Performance* (New York: Van Nostrand Reinhold, 1978), pp. 19–27.

2. Tom Boydell, *Management Self-Development: A Guide for Managers, Organizations and Institutions,* Management Development Series No. 21 (Geneva, Switzerland: International Labour Office, 1985), back cover.

3. Gary L. Schulze, "Management Development," in *Handbook of Human Resource Administration,* 2nd ed., edited by Joseph J. Famularo (New York: McGraw-Hill, 1986), p. 23-3; and Lloyd L. Byars and Leslie W. Rue, *Human Resource Management,* 2nd ed. (Homewood, Ill.: Irwin, 1987), p. 232.

4. Schulze, p. 23-5.

5. Ibid.

6. Schulze, p. 23-49.

7. Douglas McGregor, *The Human Side of Enterprise,* (New York: McGraw-Hill, 1960) p. 190.

8. John E. Jones and Mike Woodcock, *Manual of Management Development: Strategy, Design and Instruments for Programme Improvement* (Brookfield, Vt.: Gower Publishing Company, 1985).

9. William C. Byham, "The Use of Assessment Centres in Management Development," in *Management Development and Training Handbook,* 2nd ed., edited by Bernard Taylor and Gordon Lippett (London: McGraw-Hill, 1983), pp. 222–223.

10. Howard Adler, "Mentoring and the Management Development Process," in *The Practice of Hospitality Management II: Profitability in a Changing Environment* (Westport, Conn.: AVI, 1986), pp. 271–280.

11. John Lawrie, "How to Establish a Mentoring Program," *Training and Development Journal,* Vol. 41, No. 3, March 1987, pp. 25–27.

12. Lewis C. Forrest, Jr., and John H. Cox, *The Theoretical Basis for Learner-Controlled Instruction,* Training Research Series (Greenville, N.C.: Hospitality Consulting Associates, 1979).

11 Pre-Opening Training

The opening of a new hospitality operation is always exciting. Construction is frequently behind schedule or pushing completion right to the final hour. Suppliers are coming and going, delivering furniture, fixtures, equipment, and operating supplies, or merely seeking the opportunity to be a regular purchasing source for the operation. Communications are often difficult because of construction noise and incomplete telephone systems. It is always a hustle-bustle situation.

Training is usually a high priority during this time. In addition to the management staff, personnel from the corporate headquarters or representatives of the owners assist with the staffing and training activities. Further assistance may be available from hired consultants and from various purveyors who are supplying equipment, computer software, and other products.

The goal of pre-opening training is to be ready for the first guest, and to convince that guest that every employee is prepared and in complete control. For an opening to go smoothly, it must be planned down to the most minute detail. Everything that might go wrong must be taken into consideration, and alternative plans must be available in case such situations occur. The manager who can oversee a smooth opening has mastered the hardest planning task that a trainer can undertake. This chapter will discuss the many elements which must be included in a pre-opening plan and how to carry through on that plan despite construction constraints and other inconveniences.

Expansion in the Hospitality Industry

The hospitality industry is growing at a phenomenal rate. In most cities in the United States and in many cities worldwide, new hotels, motels, restaurants, and other hospitality enterprises are under construction or renovation. Each of these operations undergoes a period in which it readies itself for the public. A vital part of that preparation is pre-opening training.

It takes a great investment to construct a new facility and furnish it for operation. The same applies to operations under renovation or under a change in management or ownership. The cost of pre-opening training will be very small when compared to the total investment. It is utterly foolish to attempt an opening of a new or renovated operation—or of a property undergoing a conversion or change in management—without a thorough training program.

New Construction

Opening a brand-new hospitality operation is almost like unveiling a masterpiece. The color schemes, ambience, product mix, and market positioning of the enterprise are the results of months of planning. And yet, the success of the operation will ultimately rest in the hands of the staff, and how well they deliver the guest experience which was envisioned from the project's inception.

Usually, the staff of a new hospitality operation will consist largely of people who never worked for the organization. Training must begin from scratch, cover all standards of performance, and develop competence in every job. The training task in the opening of a new facility is probably the most comprehensive project that a trainer will undertake in the hospitality industry.

Conversions

A **conversion** is a hospitality operation that is purchased, leased, or otherwise taken over by another owner or management company. The new owner may drastically change the operation's identity, product mix, market mix, or other factors. Some renovation or alteration of the facility is usually involved. The new owner or operator may replace part of the staff, but some of the former staff will probably be retained in the same positions or reassigned.

Pre-opening training is important in a conversion; it clarifies the performance standards of the new owners or management company. It is extremely important to carefully assess the competencies of all retained employees. These employees may have developed bad habits under the former operator and may think they know more than the new operator or the new employees. Since these employees may resist training, it is critical that pre-opening training be well planned to gain their confidence and respect.

Changes in Ownership or Management

Changes can occur in ownership or management that do not entail a conversion of the property's basic identity, but merely change the property's operating procedures and standards. This situation also calls for pre-opening training to facilitate the smoothest possible transition. Like a conversion, changes in ownership or management often mean changes in staffing and expectations.

Renovations and Re-Openings

A **renovation** refers to repositioning the enterprise in the marketplace by restructuring the physical facilities; it does not necessarily involve a change in ownership or management. A **re-opening** refers to the opening following a renovation, or the repositioning of an existing operation without renovating the physical facilities. An example of a re-opening would be closing and re-opening a restaurant with an entirely new menu concept.

Planning for the Opening

Planning an opening may begin months in advance of the soft opening date. It is very important to have a schedule of all pre-opening activities that identifies critical completion dates and benchmarks for tracking progress. This schedule is often referred to as the **master plan** for pre-opening activities. The master plan should be overseen by one person who serves as the overall coordinator.

Any plan that is connected to an opening must be flexible, especially if there is new construction or renovation involved. The person who oversees the planning for pre-opening training must be able to recover quickly from any setback and maintain the overall schedule in order to be properly prepared for the soft opening. The **soft opening** is the day that paying guests are first served in the operation. At this time, the traditional ribbon cutting usually takes place that signifies that the enterprise is officially open for business.

The soft opening is different from the **grand opening.** The grand opening usually occurs several weeks after the soft opening. It is a gala event to attract publicity and to honor special guests. The grand opening is usually an elaborate party that demonstrates the full capabilities of the staff. Sufficient time is usually scheduled between the soft and grand openings to allow the staff to smooth out any problems that may have arisen during the early weeks of operation.

Backplanning

Backplanning is especially useful in planning an opening. Everyone backplans to some extent when planning everyday situations such as dinners or vacations. Backplanning simply involves visualizing the desired outcome of a series of actions before taking the necessary steps to achieve that outcome.

When applied to the pre-opening plan, backplanning begins by thinking ahead to the day of the soft opening. The person in charge of the pre-opening training should envision what will be happening in each department on opening day if everything is going perfectly. When doing so, it is a good idea for the planner to write a narrative description of what the activities "look like" in each situation. The ability to see that day in a realistic way is very important to planning the activities, and setting the goals and objectives, which will make everything fall into place.

The second step in the backplanning process is to work back from the soft opening date one day at a time and to envision what must be completed by the end of each day for the operation to be ready on the soft opening date. This is a better approach than picking some arbitrary starting date and trying to fit everything in. The latter usually results in too much or too little time for the pre-opening activities and creates waste or confusion. As the backplanning process moves backward, day by day, a natural starting point will be found for the training and staffing activities required to develop the entire pre-opening plan.

Construction Constraints

In any opening where construction is involved, the individuals coordinating the training must know the rights of the building contractor and their crews relative to control of the building. The master plan should take into consideration the schedule of construction activities. Construction contracts will specify anticipated completion dates for the various construction projects. Contracts usually include penalty clauses that assess a certain fee if the work is not completed on time. The contractor usually has control of the building until he/she willingly relinquishes it to the management or training staff. Anything in print with regard to completion dates serves only as a general guide for planning.

While construction is still underway, several things can happen which can affect the training process. Common inconveniences associated with construction may include:

- Interruptions or shutdowns in electrical power
- Testing of fire alarms
- Inoperable telephones
- Computer malfunctions due to electrical fluctuations or construction dust
- Closed restrooms due to incomplete plumbing
- Closed public areas due to carpet installation
- Limited access to and from the building

A trainer who has never worked around construction situations may not know what potential problems to expect. In these cases, it is important to ask the construction supervisor and general contractor what they feel could go wrong. Other management personnel may have experienced openings and, if asked, will probably relate some "horror stories." Consider the problems encountered by two separate facilities in the following Cases in Point.

A Case in Point: Lost at Sea

During the opening of a deluxe hotel, the installation of the front desk computers was held up due to the late delivery of the Italian marble needed for front desk construction. The order was traced and found to be delayed at sea on a ship coming from Italy. Since it was determined that the marble would not arrive before the soft opening, the contractor arranged for the construction of a temporary front desk until the marble could be installed. Training at the front desk was delayed about three days while an alternative site was arranged. Several weeks after the hotel opened, the marble arrived.

A Case in Point: Elements of Panic

On the day before the soft opening of a new continental-style dinner restaurant, the final health department inspection revealed that the dish machine had a problem elevating the rinse water temperature to the required 180°F for sanitizing serviceware. Training was complete, dress rehearsal had gone very well, and now it appeared that the opening might have to be delayed. The health department agreed to issue a temporary permit to open, provided that all food and beverages be served with disposable serviceware, and that no china or silverware be used until the equipment could be repaired. The owners could not see serving continental food and fine wines in paper, Styrofoam, or plastic serviceware. The electrical and plumbing contractors worked on the problem until nearly midnight and finally found the problem. Someone had connected the electricity to the booster water heater before the booster tank was completely filled with water, and had burned out three of the seven heating elements. Therefore, the booster was working but would only heat the water to 140°F rather than the required 180°F. Replacement elements were installed, the health department came back the next morning and issued the permit, and the restaurant opened on time to a full house.

Selecting the Trainers

During the pre-opening process, training may be conducted by specialists who can get the job done in a limited amount of time. The selection of the trainers depends on the size of the operation, the nature of the ownership or business organization, the training policy of the organization, and the resources available to support the pre-opening costs. Several groups frequently participate in pre-opening training activities, including corporate trainers, consultants, purveyors, government or community representatives, operational management, and training teams.

Corporate Trainers. Larger organizations which own or manage several hospitality operations customarily have a corporate training staff. These trainers serve as resource specialists for the whole company and may participate in pre-opening activities that range from planning and executing the entire pre-opening plan to conducting certain orientation and training sessions. Operational management should not feel threatened or intimidated by the presence of corporate trainers. Good corporate trainers will help the management team overcome operational problems and will discreetly cover gaps in expertise until the management team is in full control.

Consultants. Like corporate trainers, outside consultants may be hired to plan and coordinate the entire pre-opening training process, or may be retained to handle certain specialized instructional tasks. It is always advisable to have written contracts specifying the consultants' roles. The control of the pre-opening may be delegated to a consultant, but limits should be set in terms of the consultant's role in setting operational standards, managing or disciplining employees, interacting with the management team, and making operational decisions.

There should be close teamwork between the consultants and management to ensure that the staff does not rely on the consultants for leadership in areas where management has the responsibility for the results. The management team of the operation must be viewed by the staff as a competent group to whom they owe respect and loyalty. The consultants will leave once the operation is open and running.

Purveyor Representatives. The suppliers of equipment, operating supplies, raw products, merchandise, and computer software often have training specialists available to assist with openings. These individuals can teach the staff how to effectively use the equipment or products that they represent, and are very helpful in teaching specified blocks of instruction. Purveyor representatives should not be given the responsibility for coordinating the opening training. These trainers must be carefully managed to ensure that they use the session to train the staff on approved items—not to promote other products. If an organization sees a real need for training by purveyors, such logistics as time, location, fees, and other support considerations will have to be negotiated.

Government and Community Agency Trainers. Local government and community agencies may be able to provide training on such topics as fire safety, security, first aid, cardiopulmonary resuscitation (CPR), local community attractions, telephone techniques, sanitation, and general job safety. Like purveyor representatives, these individuals must be scheduled based on a real need—not on their availability.

Even if there is no specific fee for the training by an agency, it is not free. The costs of labor and other training support make it imperative that pre-opening training be restricted to those competencies that will be required to serve the guests and to achieve high levels of service and satisfaction on opening day. Lower priority, "nice to know" training can be covered once the operation is in full swing and there is some slowdown of activity following the opening.

Operational Management. The management team should definitely be involved as trainers in some parts of the pre-opening activities. If necessary, corporate trainers can pick up general orientation and training, as well as some specialized training. Consultants may be used to conduct specialized training and to reinforce departmental training. However, the bulk of departmental training should be conducted by the management team which is going to stay with the operation beyond the opening.

Training Teams. A popular practice within the hospitality industry is the use of training teams for pre-opening training. These teams may consist of corporate trainers, consultants, purveyor representatives, the management team, and selected personnel from the new operation or from other operations within the same company.

Using a training team from the new operation can guarantee a smooth transition from pre-opening to post-opening activities. The fewer trainers who have to leave after the soft opening, the better. This lessens the chance that some staff members will feel as if they have lost the necessary support and confidence to handle any situation which might arise.

Chain-type organizations sometimes transfer employees from one hospitality operation to the new operation to help with the pre-opening training. Non-management and management personnel can work together to teach company policies, procedures, and standards. Sometimes, too, an opening provides the company with an opportunity to recognize and reward outstanding employees. These high performers are invited to be part of a training team to go to a new operation for a period of one to eight weeks to conduct training sessions and help start up the new operation. These individuals may be management or non-management personnel.

As another option, the corporate office may provide a team to conduct the planning and most of the training for new operations. These teams usually report to the vice president of human resources between openings, and are assigned to the vice president of operations during the actual pre-opening. A good corporate training team develops and continually refines a plan that can be used over and over again as new operations are started up.

Organizations with a corporate training staff frequently supplement a corporate training team with high performers from other company operations. While these team members may be excellent in their jobs, they may not be skilled trainers. Unlike corporate trainers, these individuals will be unfamiliar with how to effectively use the company's training system and materials. It is still important to provide training sessions for the entire team so that the team functions smoothly in a unified effort to achieve the desired results on opening day.

The Master Plan

The accomplishment of predictable results begins with a carefully thought-out plan. Without a written plan, pre-opening activities will be disorganized and reactionary, and the results will be inefficiency and ineffectiveness.

A well-designed plan serves as a road map for activities leading to defined goals. The master plan must show the flow of activities that will occur from the date that the plan is kicked off until the date that the operation is scheduled for the soft opening. Exhibit 11.1 is a recommended outline for the contents of the master plan.

The development of the master plan for the pre-opening process should be a joint effort. Participants should include representatives from ownership or corporate management, operational management, and the designated training team. Leadership should be provided by the person appointed as the overall coordinator of the pre-opening training and other human resources activities. In some situations, one leader will coordinate orientation and training, while another leader coordinates staffing and personnel administration. In this case, it is important for one of these leaders to report to the other, or to have a single leader to whom both of these individuals report.

Once the plan is written and approved, copies should be made for all concerned so that everyone knows what to expect. The master plan should be prepared on a word processor so that changes can be easily made and corrected copies can be distributed each time the plan is altered.

The master plan should specify a kickoff date that signifies the countdown to the soft opening date. The kickoff should begin with a meeting of all key decision-makers and the members of the management team who have been hired up to that point. Everyone present should have a copy of the plan. This will help communicate the magnitude of the pre-opening process and the number of details that will be involved.

Exhibit 11.1   Sample Master Plan Outline

Master Plan Outline

1. Purpose of the plan
2. Objectives, goal statements, or mission statement
3. Pre-opening team organization with statements of responsibility and authority
4. Checklist of key events
5. List of outside resource people with statements of their responsibility and authority
6. Mass hiring plan
7. Scheduling procedures for management training
8. Scheduling procedures for non-management training
9. Scheduling assumptions
10. Specialized training schedules by trainer
11. Master schedule for all activities
12. Evaluation plan by departments
13. Packing lists
14. Miscellaneous pre-opening notes
15. Pre-opening budget

The master plan should be reviewed by decision-makers and the management team week by week. It is a good idea to start the briefing with a description of what will happen in each department on the soft opening day if the pre-opening plan is a success. As the plan is reviewed, the individuals involved will be able to see how each piece of the plan is leading up to the goals described for opening day.

The Overall Coordinator

The person designated as the overall coordinator of the pre-opening training and other human resources activities must be an effective leader. The plan is only as good as its execution; the strong leadership of a respected professional is essential to success. The general manager or director of human resources from the new operation may be assigned this role, but it will be difficult for either of these individuals to coordinate all the pre-opening human resources activities and meet the demands of their primary assignments.

A better approach is to select an individual from the corporate staff or an outside consultant. The effective coordinator will recognize the need to work closely with the general manager and director of human resources, but will have the necessary freedom to respond effectively to unforeseen difficulties as they arise and keep the plan on schedule.

Control of the Plan

Regardless of the number of leaders involved, the plan must be non-negotiable, non-disputable, and the absolute guide for the pre-opening activities once it is developed and approved. There will be times when the plan must be altered, but this alteration must be under the control of the overall coordinator. That assigned power must not be overruled or ignored by anyone, regardless of their level of responsibility. Once the training activities move into the new facility, the overall coordinator of the master plan should not be scheduled as a trainer. He/she must be available to attend to any training need and to manage any scheduling adjustments which may be necessary because of construction. The coordinator may, however, conduct any training activity that occurs off the premises during the early weeks of the training plan.

Once the approved master plan is implemented, it is essential that every trainer and trainee knows who controls the plan. The decision-making structure must be established early in the pre-opening plan. The authority of the overall coordinator must be defined, especially as it relates to hiring and dismissal of staff, and the appointment or dismissal of anyone on the training team. The overall coordinator must be available and accessible to answer questions concerning logistics, scheduling, training materials, and any construction-related situation which delays a training session.

The corporate officers and representatives of ownership may not be directly involved in the pre-opening human resources activities. It is imperative that these individuals be regularly briefed on the master plan and its progress. Failure to communicate the plan to these key decision-makers before implementation and at predetermined stages can result in their panicking and stepping in to redirect the training activities. This can be disastrous to the master plan and to the overall pre-opening process.

The Pre-Opening Training Budget

The coordinator and key decision-makers of the master plan must know how much can be spent on the pre-opening training and other human resources activities. Until the operation actually opens to guests and begins to generate revenues, the owners must foot the bill for these expenses as a capital expenditure. Failure to budget and set aside funds for pre-opening staffing and training is a mistake.

Every person involved in the pre-opening activities must be held accountable for controlling costs. There is no free ticket in an opening situation, even if the costs of starting up an operation are to be written off as the costs of getting into business. Someone pays for these costs, whether it is the operation through an amortization of pre-opening expenses, or whether it is the owners who cover these expenses with working capital and never charge the operation. Pre-opening expenses that are paid for from start-up capital should be recovered over a long period according to a planned schedule for return on this important investment.

Development of the Budget   In many situations, the pre-opening budget will probably not be limited to training. It should include all labor costs, material costs, and other staff-related operating expenses. In order to arrive at such a budget, a staffing and hiring plan must be prepared that shows the starting date, salary, and the costs of benefits and employment taxes for each employee. The sample budget form in Exhibit 11.2 shows the variety of pre-opening costs which might be included in the pre-opening budget.

Exhibit 11.2   Sample Pre-Opening Budget Form

Pre-Opening Budget (Six-Month Period Prior to Soft Opening Date)		
Expense Category	**Weeks Prior to Opening**	**Salaries/Wages**
MANAGEMENT PAYROLL		
General Manager	26	$_____
Director of Sales	26	_____
Sales Manager	20	_____
Director of Food and Beverage	8	_____
Director of Rooms	8	_____
Director of Accounting	8	_____
Catering Manager	6	_____
Maintenance Manager	6	_____
Reservations Manager	6	_____
Executive Housekeeper	6	_____
Food Production Manager	6	_____
Restaurant Manager	6	_____
Restaurant Manager	6	_____
Total Management Gross Salaries		$_____
NON-MANAGEMENT ADMINISTRATIVE PAYROLL		
Executive Secretary	26	$_____
Sales Secretary	26	_____
Total Non-Management Administrative Gross Wages		$_____
NON-MANAGEMENT OPERATIONS TRAINING PAYROLL (60 HOURS PER EMPLOYEE)		
Front Office Department Payroll	2	$_____
Housekeeping Department Payroll	3	_____
Food and Beverage Department Payroll	2	_____
Maintenance Department Payroll	2	_____
Accounting Department Payroll	2	_____
Total Non-Management Operations Wages		$_____
PAYROLL-RELATED EXPENSES—ALL EMPLOYEES		
FICA		$_____
FUTA		_____
State Unemployment		_____
Vacation Accrual		_____
Workers' Compensation Insurance		_____
Employee Insurance		_____
Total Payroll-Related Expenses		$_____
Total Pre-opening Payroll and Payroll-Related Expenses		$_____
TRAINING AND HUMAN RESOURCES-RELATED OPERATING EXPENSES		
General Training Supplies		$_____
Training Food Supplies		_____
Training Beverage Supplies		_____
Training Printing		_____
Human Resources Forms		_____
Training Equipment Rental		_____
Training Consultant Fees		_____
Training Consultant Travel		_____
Labor Relations Attorney Fees		_____
Labor Relations Attorney Travel		_____

Exhibit 11.2 *(continued)*

Purveyor Trainer Fees	_____
Purveyor Trainer Travel	_____
Government/Community Agency Training Fees	_____
Government/Community Agency Travel	_____
Corporate Training Team Chargeback Fees	_____
Corporate Training Team Travel	_____
Other Training Team Chargeback Fees	_____
Other Training Team Travel	_____
Rental of Hiring Hall	_____
Employment Advertising	_____
Signage for Mass Hiring	_____
Total Training-Related Operating Expenses	$_____

NON-TRAINING PRE-OPENING OPERATING EXPENSES (26 WEEKS)

Accounting and Data Processing Allocations	$_____
Advertising Media	_____
Brochures and Folders	_____
Car and Gas Allowance	_____
Computer Supplies	_____
Dues and Subscriptions	_____
Entertainment by Staff	_____
Equipment Rental	_____
Executive Office Overhead	_____
Executive Search/Relocation	_____
Furniture/Office Rental	_____
Liability Insurance	_____
Maintenance Contracts	_____
Miscellaneous Expenses	_____
Office Supplies	_____
Postage	_____
Printing and Stationery	_____
Public Relations Agency Fees	_____
Sales Promotion	_____
Reservations-Makers Club	_____
Special Mailings	_____
Telephone	_____
Travel—Staff	_____
Utilities	_____
Yellow Pages Listings	_____
Total Non-Training Pre-Opening Operating Expenses	$_____
TOTAL SIX-MONTH PRE-OPENING BUDGET	$_____

Note that the budget in Exhibit 11.2 covers the pre-opening costs of the general manager and the sales and marketing staff, all of whom are scheduled to begin their employment six months before the scheduled soft opening. Since some of this time may not be under the control of the master plan coordinator, it is probably wise to make a distinction between those pre-opening costs that occur before the beginning of the master plan and those incurred under the execution of the plan.

Management of the Budget

The general manager should be held accountable for managing the non-training and non-human resources portions of the pre-opening budget; the coordinator of the master plan should be held accountable for managing the training and human resources portions. The budget form in Exhibit 11.2 includes all pre-opening expenses, but it is possible to separate the budget into the two areas of responsibility. Of course, if the general manager is appointed to be the coordinator of the master plan, as is often the case in smaller independent operations, he/she should be held responsible for managing the total budget.

Elements of Pre-Opening Training

Training is only one of the critical human resources activities which must be completed before the soft opening. Just like most property-wide training efforts, pre-opening training applies to both management and non-management personnel. In a general sense, training is conducted for the new operation as a whole; in a practical sense, it is broken down by department and specialized training topics. All elements of training should be specified in the master plan.

Orientation should be treated as one part of pre-opening training. The training of new staff includes so much orientation to new policies, procedures, co-workers, and to the operation itself, that it is difficult to separate the functions of orientation and training. For this reason, the person who is responsible for planning and scheduling pre-opening training should also schedule all orientation activities. In this chapter, orientation and training will be viewed as complementary activities under the control of the same leader.

Management Training

The training and development of managers is a lifelong process. The management team that is selected to start up a hospitality operation must be oriented and given refresher training to prepare team members to function effectively.

It is a good idea to conduct most of the pre-opening management training before the non-management staff is selected. This helps to better prepare the management team for hiring individuals who have the greatest potential and fit the needs and philosophy of the organization.

Policies and Procedures. The training of the management team in an opening situation should begin with a thorough indoctrination in the organization's policies and standard operating procedures. Organizations vary greatly in how much of this information is available in written form. Where the documentation of policies and procedures is limited, key representatives of ownership or top management should participate in the instruction to orally review the established operating rules. This provides a uniform beginning upon which to build training and to communicate standards to the operational staff. The expectations of the top leadership must be clear if managers are going to be successful in achieving organizational goals.

Some organizations have clear, written policies and procedures which must be followed by all personnel. Others have corporate policies and procedures, or corporate mission statements and minimum standards for their operations. In the latter cases, the management team for each hospitality operation is expected to develop appropriate policies and procedures for the staff. When this situation exists, much of the time scheduled for management training before the opening must be devoted to the development of these policies and procedures since they will serve as the foundation upon which the staff training will be conducted.

Basic Managerial Skills. The pre-opening management training should include a review of the principles of human resources management including recruitment, interviewing, reference checking, and selection. It should emphasize how these concepts will be applied in selecting non-management staff for the new operation. Training should also include a review of the application of such concepts as motivation, leadership, problem-solving, decision-making, progressive discipline, performance reviews, coaching, counseling, and time management.

In reviewing management skills, it is important to stress the importance of effective communications with the staff and with other managers. This review should include written communications, oral communications, non-verbal communications, and listening skills (see Chapter 13). Another skill which should be reviewed is the ability to evaluate performance. The value of continuously evaluating each individual's performance should be stressed, as well as the value of assessing the performance of each department.

Administrative Procedures. The new operation will have many forms that are unfamiliar to new managers. It is essential that pre-opening management training include a detailed review of all forms including their purpose, the policies and procedures that support them, and actual practices for completing the forms.

Training should be based on those forms and administrative procedures which must be completed daily, weekly, at the end of each accounting period, and on a situational basis. Forms and administrative procedures that are required on an annual basis can be covered later through ongoing training when it is time for them to be completed.

Team Building. An important part of pre-opening management training is uniting new management personnel in a team that believes in common goals and standards—and in each other. To accomplish this, management training should emphasize participation and should include projects that new managers complete together.

Unity in the management team is extremely important to the operation's success. If there is an individual in the group who resists being a team player, it will show up in the training sessions—and the group will have an opportunity to overcome the problem. If the problem cannot be overcome, the training coordinator and the person who makes hiring and dismissal decisions must determine whether the person should be replaced.

By the time the management training phase of the pre-opening process is completed, the managers should be on friendly terms and have mutual respect for one another's professionalism. Some social interaction between the managers is beneficial to the team-building effort. Chapter 10 provides further suggestions for implementing a management training and development program in a hospitality operation.

Departmental Training   Department managers should conduct the bulk of the skills training within their departments. An exception to this is specialized training on computer systems, point-of-sale equipment, and telecommunications consoles. Such training will probably be conducted by a purveyor representative, consultant, or corporate trainer. In order for departmental training to be effective, the managers must be fully prepared before the training begins.

Preparation of Trainers. Every management and supervisory person who is scheduled to conduct training during the opening should receive instruction and practice in how to train others. This type of training is often referred to as "train-the-trainer." Such training is usually conducted by the corporate training staff or by consultants. It is important that these sessions be based on the use of the job lists, job breakdowns, job performance standards, and related materials which will actually be used during the pre-opening training sessions. Train-the-trainer sessions should not focus on theoretical discussions but should focus on how to develop specific skills as efficiently and effectively as possible.

Training in training methods should include role plays in which the managers practice training each other. While one manager serves as the trainer, other managers serve as "employees." These role plays may be videotaped and played back for analysis and critique in an all-out effort to get the management team prepared for its training assignments.

Preparation of Training Locations. The best place for training to occur is at the job station. This ideal is not always possible during an opening since the final stages of construction may interfere. In order to have the construction completed in critical training locations, it is essential to plan in advance for the spaces and locations that will be needed.

The trainer should develop a good working relationship with the general contractor and with the hospitality company's project engineer or supervisor. Developing rapport can ensure that everyone understands the need for training on the premises about two to four weeks before the soft opening date. A written request for the specific spaces on certain dates should be provided by the trainer to the project engineer. The trainer should supply extra copies of the request for the engineer to pass on to the general contractor and appropriate sub-contractors.

When requesting spaces for training, it is important to request that the specific facilities be available at least 24 hours before they are actually needed. Construction workers are often putting on the finishing touches until the very last minute. Time will be required to clean up the construction debris and to set up the area for the training.

In some municipalities, training may not occur in the building until the local building inspector approves the building for safety and issues a certificate of occupancy. Trainers should investigate the attitude of the local authorities far in advance so that alternative arrangements can be made if occupancy is going to present a problem. In other municipalities, it is necessary for everyone in the building before the actual opening to wear a protective safety helmet. "Hard hat training" can be conducted, but someone must plan for the availability of the required number of protective helmets.

Exhibit 11.3 Checklist of Specialized Training Topics

		Specialized Training Topics
Yes____	No____	Computer Training for Front Office
Yes____	No____	Point-of-Sale Equipment Training
Yes____	No____	Fire Safety Training
Yes____	No____	First Aid Training
Yes____	No____	Cardiopulmonary Resuscitation Training
Yes____	No____	Heimlich Maneuver Training
Yes____	No____	Wine Product/Service Training
Yes____	No____	Chemical Use Training (OSHA Training Topics)
Yes____	No____	Laundry Equipment Training
Yes____	No____	Telecommunications Console Training
Yes____	No____	Health Insurance Administration Training
Yes____	No____	Computerized Time Clock Training
Yes____	No____	Train-the-Trainer Training
Yes____	No____	Interview and Selection Training
Yes____	No____	Preventive Labor Relations Training
Yes____	No____	Labor Relations Training (Unionized)
Yes____	No____	Swimming Pool/Whirlpool Maintenance Training
Yes____	No____	Workers' Compensation Administration Training
Yes____	No____	Security Procedures Training
Yes____	No____	Audiovisual Equipment Operation Training
Yes____	No____	In-Room Movie Equipment Operation Training
Yes____	No____	Carpet Shampoo Equipment Training
Yes____	No____	Responsible Alcoholic Beverage Service Training
Yes____	No____	Sanitation Training
Yes____	No____	_____
Yes____	No____	_____
Yes____	No____	_____

Preparation of Departments. In addition to preparing the staff for opening day, each department must be set up so that business can be conducted. Departments are usually set up around the same time training activities take place. Usually, new staff participate in this activity by opening boxes and crates, storing supplies, cleaning up behind the construction crews, and checking out all equipment to be sure that it operates properly.

The coordinator of the pre-opening schedule must determine whether to budget the hours required to complete these tasks as training hours or as extra setup hours. Some of this activity can be regarded as training, but much of it is just work that will not normally be part of the daily or weekly schedule. Nevertheless, this work must be scheduled and taken care of as part of the operation's pre-opening activities.

Specialized Training

The master pre-opening plan should specify areas needing specialized training and the designated trainers. Exhibit 11.3 is a checklist of possible specialized topics. Details on several of these topics can be found in Chapter 9.

In preparing the master plan, it is important to determine what specialized training should be conducted by:

- A member of the management team
- Corporate trainers
- Experienced employees or managers from other operations within the company
- Outside consultants
- Purveyor representatives

In rapidly expanding companies, it may be advantageous to develop internal specialists for pre-opening training. For example, the company may develop a training specialist in point-of-sale equipment by sending a staff member to special classes offered by the manufacturer or supplier. Cultivating internal specialists provides better quality control over specialized training and can reduce the costs of using outside resource people.

A great way to recognize the excellence of an experienced employee or manager is to ask that person to become a trainer. This also provides for the further development of in-house experts in various areas of the operation. It is a good idea to help these people prepare for the training since it is one thing to be an outstanding performer in a skilled area, and another to be a trainer.

Training Techniques and Rehearsals

If used, role plays, case studies, or simulations should be scripted as part of the planning process. In role plays or simulations that involve several trainees, it is a good idea to write descriptions of the characters they will play. If participants are not permitted to see the character descriptions of the other participants, the learning experience will take on more realism.

Videotaping role plays, case studies, simulations, and other problem-solving exercises can add an effective dimension to this learning activity. Following the exercises, trainees can view themselves on the monitor and critique their performance. This is an ideal way to refine human relations and communications skills.

It is advisable that one person be designated as the video specialist, camera operator, and equipment caretaker. This equipment requires special care to operate properly—especially in a construction environment. Also it is important in the planning stages to determine whether the video equipment will be purchased, rented, or borrowed from the company that has been contracted to provide rental audiovisual equipment for the new facility. The effective use of various learning activities and audiovisual aids is discussed more completely in Chapters 6 and 7.

A complete pre-opening plan includes time for rehearsals in which the staff can apply what is being learned. These rehearsal sessions must be scheduled in the master plan. Practice sessions might include serving meals in the restaurants to groups of employees and other individuals acting as "guests," cleaning and making up guestrooms occupied by trainers and company executives during the pre-opening period, and role playing registration and check-out at the front desk.

Integrating All Human Resources Activities

The person who is responsible for planning and coordinating the training may or may not be held responsible for the functions related to staffing and human resources administration. These activities must be coordinated with the training plan; one person should be the overall coordinator of all pre-opening human resources activities. This is the only way to ensure a logical flow of all pre-opening activities related to preparing the staff for the soft opening. The master plan should clearly show how all human resources activities will be accomplished, and how training will serve as the focal point of the pre-opening activities of the new staff.

Staff Recruitment

The plan should show the approaches that will be used to recruit a staff of high-potential, trainable employees. In an opening situation, it is customary to have some sort of mass hiring activities to interview as many people as possible from which to select the best possible staff.

This activity may be held away from the new facility (especially if construction is not complete) in a public meeting hall, convention center, or other facility that will accommodate a large applicant turnout. The facility used for the mass hiring should provide plenty of parking, and, when possible, should be accessible by public transportation. On the day of the mass hiring, tables should be set up in one section so that applicants can sit down to complete the application forms. Pencils or pens should be available, as well as handouts on the new operation and brief descriptions of all the available jobs. It is also a good practice to have local telephone directories available and to require applicants to put the telephone number of each local employer reference on the application.

In planning for the mass hiring, it is important to plan every detail in advance so that the best possible impressions will be made on the community and the applicants. Exhibit 11.4 is a sample mass hiring plan which could be included in the master plan.

Recruitment plans should include a schedule of advertisements for newspapers, radio, and television that announce employment opportunities, the location and times that applications will be accepted, and when interviews will be conducted. Handouts with abbreviated descriptions of the available positions and a schedule of starting wages by position should be available for applicants' review.

Staff Interviews

The master plan should include a schedule of employment interviewing. The plan should state how many managers will interview each applicant and who will make the final hiring selections for each department. Plans for refresher training for managers in interviewing techniques should also be included. More detailed information on interviewing is provided in Chapter 3.

Reference Checking

Every applicant who is seriously considered for a position should provide the names and telephone numbers of former supervisors. The pre-opening plan should include a schedule for checking references and an indication of who will perform this activity. Forms used in reference

Exhibit 11.4   Sample Mass Hiring Plan

Mass Hiring Plan

Schedule for Mass Hiring

The mass hiring process is scheduled to take two weeks, beginning with three days of intensive interviewing at a large hiring hall reserved for this purpose. The nature of the labor market affects the type of hiring hall which should be selected. If the labor market is tight with low unemployment, the number of applicants will be smaller than if unemployment is high. While the rental charges for the hiring hall can affect the decision of how many days are needed, the hall should be reserved for enough time to process a sufficient number of applicants to allow for selection based on a qualified pool of candidates. For this 200-room hotel with a staff of 100 non-management employees, three days are scheduled for mass interviewing, three days for reference checking, and four days for sending out offer letters and rejection cards—thus making up a two-week period.

Hiring Hall Specifications:

Location: _____
_____
_____
_____

Capacity: _____
Inclement Weather Plans (Alternative Plans): _____
_____
_____
_____

Times Reserved: _____
Cost of Rental: _____
Contact: _____
Logistical Support
  Number of Chairs: _____
  Number and Size of Tables: _____
  Availability of Restrooms: _____
  Availability of Refreshments: _____

  Signage: _____
_____
_____
_____
_____

Mass Hiring Recruitment Plan

Schedule of Recruitment Ads

Newspapers: _____
_____
_____
_____
_____

Radio Spots: _____
_____
_____
_____

Agency Listings: _____
_____
_____
_____

Exhibit 11.4 *(continued)*

Mass Hiring Interview Assignments

Application Processing: _____

_____

_____

Initial Screening: _____

_____

_____

High-Potential Screening: _____

_____

_____

Final Decision Interviews (Department Heads): _____

_____

_____

_____

_____

Reference-Checking Assignments (Only for applicants who successfully completed final decision interviews):

_____

_____

_____

_____

_____

Assignments for Preparing Offer Letters and Rejection Cards: _____

_____

_____

_____

_____

---

checking should be reviewed with the management team so that everyone is informed of the reference-checking procedures.

It is often difficult to obtain information from former employers other than verification that the person did work there between certain dates. This is especially true when contacting the human resources director of former employers. More helpful information can often be obtained from the person's former supervisor, especially if the applicant has given the former supervisor permission to give out information when called for a reference check.

Staff Selection

The selection of the individuals who will open a hospitality operation is critical to the property's ultimate success. The high costs associated with hiring and training make it critical to minimize employee turnover by assembling a team that will work well together and remain with the organization.

A positive personality and a strong work ethic are important in every position. Applicants with a work history of successive job failures should be avoided in favor of more qualified candidates. Past work history and personal habits are indicators of what an individual can be expected to do in the future.

Management Selection. It is extremely important in opening situations to select management personnel with experience in personnel training.

Some of the management training will include sessions designed to train trainers. However, a manager with no training experience will not have enough time to become a competent trainer under the pressures of the opening. The manager with training experience will be able to take the specified materials and assignments and follow through with the necessary departmental training during the pre-opening process.

The general manager may be selected by the owners or the corporate staff; selection of other managers is usually a joint decision-making process that involves owners or corporate executives and the general manager. As managers are selected, they should be briefed on the master plan. They should be encouraged to devote whatever time they have to clearing up as much personal business as possible before the final weeks of the pre-opening process. If the offices for managers are ready early, the new managers should settle in so they have a place to work during the pre-opening activities.

Non-Management Selection. The management team for the new operation should be involved in recruiting, screening, interviewing, reference checking, selecting, hiring, and processing the non-management staff. Executives representing the owners or corporate staff may be available to assist with these activities, but the bulk of the work should fall on the management team. By doing so, the management team will develop a good working knowledge of the labor pool and be able to best select the individuals they will ultimately train and supervise.

Employment Offers

The hiring process in a new operation should be viewed not just as a human resources activity but as a marketing and public relations activity. The mass hiring procedures can establish the reputation of the new operation as a good place to work where selection is taken seriously and handled professionally. In keeping with this attitude, it is a good idea to notify all applicants of the status of their applications.

Applicants that do not meet the hiring criteria should be notified by a letter or postcard within five days following the decision not to hire them. This is possible even in a large mass hiring activity if each applicant is required to fill out a peel-and-stick address label. Notifying the applicant can be as easy as affixing the address labels to pre-printed postcards.

Individuals who are selected should be notified by letter. The letter should congratulate the person and review the position and starting wage. In addition, instructions should be given about reporting for work, the pre-opening training plans, and any other information that will help get the new hire off to a good start. In the case of tipped employees, it is not unusual to pay a training rate until the operation actually opens and the employee has the opportunity to earn gratuities. This, too, should be explained in the offer of employment letter. All these plans should be reviewed with the decision-makers and managers so that everyone is clear on how job offers will be made, who will be authorized to sign offer letters, and who must approve each new-hire decision.

Follow-Up. In a pre-opening situation, it is very important to know whether the applicants who are offered positions are going to accept the

Exhibit 11.5   Sample Portion of a Master Training Schedule

Master Training Schedule*		Day <u>Tues.</u> Date <u>3/3</u> Page <u>1</u> of <u>5</u>

Position	Name	8	9	10	11	12	1	2	3	4	5	6	7	8	9
General Manager	_____	O	O	O	O			O	O						
Exec. Secretary	_____	O	O	O	O			O	O						
Dir. of Sales	_____	O	O	O	O			O	O						
Sales Manager	_____	O	O	O	O			O	O						
Sales Secretary	_____	O	O	O	O			O	O						
Dir. of Acct.	_____	O	O	O	O			D	D						
Bookkeeper	_____	O	O	O	O			D	D						
Maint. Manager	_____	O	O	O	O	O		D	D	U	U				
Maint. Assistant	_____	O	O	O	O	O		D	D	U	U				
Executive Hsk.	_____	O	O	O	O			D	D	U	U				
Asst. Exec. Hsk.	_____	O	O	O	O			D	D	U	U				
Housekpng. Supv.	_____	O	O	O	O			D	D	U	U				
Housekpng. Supv.	_____	O	O	O	O			D	D	U	U				
Guest Room Attn.	_____	O	O	O	O			D	D	U	U				
Guest Room Attn.	_____	O	O	O	O			D	D	U	U				
Guest Room Attn.	_____	O	O	O	O			D	D	U	U				
Guest Room Attn.	_____	O	O	O	O			D	D	U	U				
Guest Room Attn.	_____	O	O	O	O			D	D	U	U				
Guest Room Attn.	_____	O	O	O	O			D	D	U	U				
Guest Room Attn.	_____	O	O	O	O			D	D	U	U				
Guest Room Attn.	_____	O	O	O	O			D	D	U	U				
Guest Room Attn.	_____	O	O	O	O			D	D	U	U				
Publ. Area Attn.	_____	O	O	O	O			D	D	U	U				
Publ. Area Attn.	_____	O	O	O	O			D	D	U	U				
Laundry Attn.	_____	O	O	O	O			D	D	U	U				
Laundry Attn.	_____	O	O	O	O			D	D	U	U				
Laundry Attn.	_____	O	O	O	O			D	D	U	U				
Laundry Attn.	_____	O	O	O	O			D	D	U	U				
Laundry Attn.	_____	O	O	O	O			D	D	U	U				
Laundry Attn.	_____	O	O	O	O			D	D	U	U				

*Key to Abbreviations
O = General Orientation
D = Departmental Orientation—By Department Heads
U = Uniform Fittings

positions. It is a good practice to include a pre-printed acceptance form or postcard with all offer letters. The form or card should be pre-addressed to the hospitality operation and stamped as a convenient and time-saving measure. If there is not enough time to wait for a reply by mail, the applicant can be required to telephone with his/her acceptance by a specified deadline. If the applicant fails to call by the specified time, the offer should be extended to another candidate.

Scheduling Training

As decisions are made concerning new hires, and names are placed in each position in the staffing chart, it is important to also plug these names into the master plan. By doing so, the master plan will show what every employee is scheduled to do each hour of his/her day during the pre-opening activities. Exhibit 11.5 provides a partial schedule for one day of pre-opening activities. From the master plan, each department head can then prepare individual training schedules for each employee in his/her department based on individual work schedules.

Orientation

New-hire orientation should be scheduled for the first day of employment. In a pre-opening situation it is important to have employees begin work on the same day or in groups to facilitate the scheduling of orientation sessions. An employee handbook or neatly prepared handouts should be prepared in advance that highlight employee benefits and state policies and procedures. Each new employee should receive a personal copy of these materials. It is a good practice to have each employee sign for these materials as a permanent record of their issue. The orientation session should be upbeat, thorough, and fast-paced. This creates an air of excitement, and emphasizes the need for everyone to give their best effort.

The use of audiovisual aids should be carefully planned to help convey the most information in the shortest possible time. Charts, overhead projector transparencies, and 35-mm slides are inexpensive to prepare and can add much to the presentations. If the president of the company or the equivalent top executive cannot be present to personally give a warm welcome, such a welcome speech can be videotaped in advance and viewed during the orientation.

Human Resources Files

In conjunction with orientation, the new employees should complete all necessary forms to establish their payroll records and create a human resources file. These documents might include such items as tax withholding forms (federal, state, and local, as applicable), insurance benefit enrollment forms, or proof of eligibility to work within the country. Forms should be available as well as pens and a suitable place to write the required information.

Time can be saved in setting up human resources and payroll files if the file folders are prepared in advance of the first session. Forms can be reviewed for completeness and accuracy as they are turned in and then placed into each new employee's file.

Everything placed in employee files should be punched at the top with a two-hole punch and attached to the folder with wing clips. This reduces the possibility of losing important documents and keeps the file orderly. Documents should be filed in reverse chronological order—meaning that the most current document is on top when the file folder is opened.

Pre-Opening Payroll

One of the foremost concerns of employees on their first day is when they will be paid and how they will receive their checks. In an opening situation, the accounting department may not be completely functional on the day that employees begin work. Plans must be made for how employees will be paid before the actual soft opening date. This should include the procedures for timekeeping, preparing payroll reports, issuing checks, and funding bank accounts to cover the payroll.

As mentioned earlier, some employees may be hired for tipped positions that allow payment of less than the federal minimum wage.

These employees may require a special training rate of pay during the pre-opening activities. This should be determined before employment offers are made. When payroll procedures are explained during orientation, the special rate should be announced. It is important to be very clear as to how long this special rate will be in effect, and at what point the regular rate based on tip credits will begin.

Uniforms, Lockers, and Special Tools

Most hospitality operations furnish employee uniforms. It is important for staff morale that uniforms fit properly. In order to be ready for guests on opening day, uniform fittings should be scheduled early in the pre-opening process. Once sizes are known, arrangements must be made with the uniform supplier for a quick turnaround on uniform orders. A local alterations service should handle the fittings, make necessary alterations, and ensure a perfect fit for each employee's uniform.

A sufficient quantity of uniforms should be ordered to allow for proper cleaning and care, and to permit the employees to wear a fresh uniform each day. Some uniforms may be laundered by the employees and some will require the care of a professional laundry or dry cleaning establishment. It should be determined how uniforms will be cleaned and maintained before the employees begin so they will know their responsibilities when the uniforms are issued.

Arrangements should also be made for preparing individual name badges. Employees should be asked how they prefer their names to appear on their name badges. Some employees prefer appropriate nicknames and others prefer more formality. The use of an employee's preferred name is important to employee morale and communications.

Lockers for employees to store personal items should be available by the time indicated in the master plan. Lockers and locks should be assigned early in the pre-opening process, preferably on the employee's first day. Combinations for locks should be recorded before locks are issued. The rules concerning locker use should be covered during orientation. Items which may not be stored in lockers should be clarified.

In addition to lockers, some employees may be assigned special equipment to perform their jobs. For example, a cook may be assigned a set of knives. The rules for storage and security of these items should be determined in advance and covered during orientation.

Employee Meals

Most hospitality operations provide meals for the staff on a free or reduced-price basis. In an opening situation, the kitchen is usually not fully operational. Kitchen staff, too, must be trained. Furthermore, the fire department may not permit the use of any kitchen equipment until the certificate of occupancy is issued. Even if employees are not provided meals by the operation, arrangements must be made for employee meals during the pre-opening process. One option is to give the staff sufficient meal breaks for them to leave the premises and buy their meals. If the hospitality operation is remotely located, other arrangements will be required. In these cases, a catering service, mobile canteen truck, or other arrangement may meet food service needs.

Evaluating Learning

The coordinator of the master plan should monitor the evaluation procedures being used in each department. Learning should not be assumed just because training was provided. It is important to objectively assess knowledge, skills, and attitudes along the way. If paper and pencil tests are given after blocks of training, these tests should be developed before the departmental training begins. Because time is such a factor during pre-opening training, it is suggested that paper and pencil tests consist of multiple choice, true-false, and short answer questions. Discussion-type questions take more time to score and should be reserved for ongoing training after the operation is open for business. Chapter 12 provides many suggestions for how to develop effective evaluation instruments.

Individual training records can serve as the basic guide for specifying the areas for evaluating learning and verifying competence. Training record forms should be prepared in advance for each employee by job position. A checklist should be developed that serves as a record of the competencies which are mastered through training. Chapter 9 provides several sample forms which can be adapted for pre-opening purposes.

The status of this verification process should be discussed by the coordinator with the trainers on a daily basis. Open and honest assessments are essential so that there are no surprises. If any of the new members of the staff are encountering difficulties, the coordinator must know so that steps can be taken to correct the matter. Individual training records will continue to grow as additional competencies are mastered through ongoing training; the department head is responsible for recording these accomplishments as they occur.

Transition from Pre-Opening to Actual Operation

A series of activities should be devised so that the transition from pre-opening to actual operation is smooth but well-defined. Some activities should be planned to make a clear distinction between the formal orientation and training that takes place during a pre-opening, and what will begin on the soft opening date. Employees need to understand that they have completed the planned pre-opening program, and have contributed to the achievement of the training team's objectives. It is also important to recognize people who have taken part in the pre-opening activities but will not be staying on as part of the staff.

Pre-Opening Training Awards

It is a good practice to present training awards or certificates at the conclusion of the pre-opening training to people who successfully completed the program. The specific areas of competence should be determined when the master plan is prepared so that everyone agrees what the training certificate represents. To further build team spirit, awards can be given for such attributes as the fastest learner, the friendliest new employee, the best team player, the best sport, and the best helper. Trainers should also be recognized for their hard work.

Awards and recognition should never be given in such a way that makes anyone feel bad because they had difficulty mastering job skills. These individuals should be counseled privately to determine whether the obstacles can be overcome. If they cannot, termination of employment may be necessary before the training awards are presented.

Training certificates and awards should not be presented to individuals who did not master their duties. If they are recognized and rewarded for having successfully completed the training, and then are terminated a week later for failure to perform, the termination may be viewed as unfair and may have a detrimental effect on group morale. Furthermore, the terminated employee may have cause for a grievance or complaint for wrongful dismissal that could lead to a lawsuit or other charges.

Shifting Responsibilities

Beginning with the first shift on soft opening day, the operational management team assumes full responsibility for decision-making. On that date, too, many trainers assume staff roles. Now, the training team must work through the operational management team to complete any unfinished pre-opening training or human resources activities.

During the pre-opening training, the department head or a skilled trainer is always around to answer questions and to back up the inexperienced staff. However, this is not the case once the operation opens for business. The training personnel who were not slated to assume staff roles disappear at or around the time of the soft opening. Someone is usually designated to supervise the departmental operations during each shift, but the person in charge may not have the level of expertise that instills confidence. This is a big change from the pre-opening training environment and can confuse the staff unless a definite announcement is made on the transition of leadership.

The general manager and the coordinator of the master plan should clarify management organization through a joint announcement, either at an employee meeting or by a memo. This transition is extremely important; it should not be assumed that it will happen on its own.

The master plan should include a schedule for the departure of all outside trainers. This makes it possible to inform the staff when each specialist will leave; any assistance that is needed in an area of specialization should be obtained before the trainers leave. This helps in the transition from dependency on the specialized trainers to achieving self-sufficiency.

The Arrival of Guests

Staff should be briefed on the number of guests expected on opening day, and any extra amenities or special treatment that guests will receive. On opening day, guests may receive a gift, complimentary food or beverages, or special rates. Consider the special amenity provided by one operation on its first official day of business.

A Case in Point: Inaugural Cruise

The first guests are usually recognized in some special way during the opening of a new hospitality operation. During the inaugural voyage of a luxury cruise ship that sailed from New York City to the

Caribbean, each of the passengers was photographed shaking hands with the captain. They were then presented a certificate for being part of the inaugural cruise, given a copy of their photograph with the captain, and given a photograph of the ship sailing out of New York Harbor with the Statue of Liberty in the background.

It is not unusual to have photographers take pictures of the first guests, and to have representatives of the press available to interview guests and employees. The press is usually interested in events that affect the community and may run a special article that features the staff and their preparation for the start-up. This is an excellent public relations opportunity to showcase the efforts of an operation's staff. The astute training team will make full use of the natural excitement which surrounds an opening to further communicate to each employee and to each guest that they are special.

Establishing Staff Schedules

On opening day, staff schedules must change according to the scheduling system which will be used for the ongoing operation. Most operations use some sort of base and variable staffing system. This ensures that a base number of staff will be present to open the business to the public each day. It also provides a variable formula for additional staff depending on the guest forecast. Hotels operate 24 hours per day, while restaurants often operate 12 to 16 hours. This necessitates shift scheduling, since a typical shift does not exceed eight hours.

Employees who enjoyed training together may end up on different shifts, and seldom see each other except at employee meetings or social functions. This is important to discuss during the transition from pre-opening to actual operation. If employees discover that the peers they depended on during training will be working different shifts, it can shake their confidence and interfere with their performance.

Department heads will be held accountable for scheduling their staff within the operating budget, using the scheduling system that they are taught during the pre-opening management training. After having all department staff present for training, the actual number of employees called for by the scheduling system on opening day may seem very small. There may be a temptation to ignore the operating budget and to schedule heavier than usual since the new staff is inexperienced. Department heads should rest assured that the new staff will be ready to handle their duties if the pre-opening training was thorough.

If a department is overstaffed during the opening week, it sets a precedent; when the staffing is cut back to the prescribed formulas, the staff will complain because there is too much work. They will insist that it is impossible to meet the organization's standards unless more people are routinely scheduled. The result is an intolerable over-budget situation that will ensure the failure of the new operation.

Ongoing Training

Ongoing training should be initiated immediately after pre-opening training; there must not be a gap. As discussed in Chapter 1, training can be grouped according to priorities—A, B, and C, or essential, desirable, and expendable. Because of budget restraints, most pre-opening plans can only accommodate essential training.

The department head should have plans for the implementation of priority B training the first week the operation is open for business. By the third or fourth week of operation, the ongoing training effort should have advanced to the priority C training topics and objectives. As employee turnover occurs, the department head must be prepared to begin the entire training cycle again for the new staff replacements. Chapter 9 covers detailed procedures for ongoing training.

Administrative Follow-Through

The coordinator of the master plan must work closely with the general manager, department heads, and human resources director (if there is one) to establish the human resources administrative systems during the pre-opening. Good personnel files are essential to a well-managed business in order to track the growth and development of staff and to comply with government regulations.

Budget vs. Actual Costs

The coordinator of the master plan should track actual expenses against the pre-opening budget at every stage of the plan. When the operation goes through its soft opening, it will shift from the pre-opening budget to the operating budget which includes revenues as well as expenses. At that time, the coordinator should prepare a detailed budget analysis to determine whether the plan was executed within the budget, and to identify the causes of all unacceptable variances.

Revisions and Refinements

The best time to analyze how the plan could have been improved is within the first two weeks of the new operation. During this time, the coordinator should objectively observe performance in each department to assess which areas needed more attention during the pre-opening training. The coordinator may also identify competencies which were considered priorities during the pre-opening and which actually could have waited until after the opening. This helps free up time for more emphasis on the areas which seem to have needed more attention.

Each trainer should be evaluated to determine whether he/she should be used as a trainer in the future or whether he/she needs additional training and coaching skills. This is critical if a weak trainer is a department head and is now expected to conduct ongoing training.

The coordinator should be very critical of his/her own performance as a leader. The coordinator should seek candid evaluations from others concerning the execution of the plan and the leadership provided throughout the process. If excellence is the honest goal, then everyone must be willing to address weaknesses and document how the process could be improved.

Turnover of Relevant Information

Throughout the pre-opening process, the responsibility for supplying training materials, administrative forms, and training aids rested with the coordinator of the master plan. As the training responsibilities shift to the management team, it is important that all training materials be transferred to the department heads and management staff. This should be an organized process—not just passing along boxes of materials which were used during the pre-opening training. The coordinator should provide an inventory of the materials that are turned over to each manager. This helps managers make immediate use of the materials.

For materials produced at the corporate office or purchased from a purveyor, instructions should be provided for re-ordering. Management should also know which materials may be reproduced by the operation either internally or by a local printer. Copyright materials must be re-ordered and not reproduced, unless permission has been given in writing by the owner of the copyright.

Final Analysis and Report

Unless he/she is the owner of the business, the coordinator of the master plan should prepare a written report of the opening for the owner or management executives. Since owners and executives received a "report" when the plan was implemented, they should now receive a report that documents problems and solutions, analyzes the budget, and makes recommendations for future openings.

The report should address the strengths and weaknesses of the master plan. The coordinator's honesty and objectivity in writing the report is essential to making it a worthwhile document. Any attempt at covering up weaknesses, or trying to blame problems on someone else, will hamper the effectiveness of the report as a future planning tool. It is sufficient to state the facts surrounding each of the problems, how each problem was resolved, and how each problem might be prevented or sidestepped in the future.

The final report should be distributed to the appropriate executives; an additional copy should be filed and made available as a reference and planning resource. Filed with the report should be a copy of the original plan and a copy of the revised plan. If the master plan is not revised at this time, the file should include clearly written notes that suggest alternative approaches if the plan is used again. Organizations that open many operations should continue to refine their pre-opening plans. There will still be enough unexpected events in future openings without repeating the same problems and weaknesses encountered in the past.

12 Evaluating Training Programs

Everyone uses evaluation daily.[1] Evaluation can be so casual or automatic that the evaluator is hardly aware of the process—looking out the window to check the weather and deciding whether to carry an umbrella, for example. At the other extreme is scholarly or scientific research under laboratory conditions. Somewhere between casual observations and controlled research falls the evaluation that determines the effectiveness of employee training. Three steps are involved in most any form of evaluation (Exhibit 12.1). First, observations are made or information is collected. Second, comparisons are made between observations and previously developed standards. Third, judgments are formed about the comparisons that lead to conclusions or decisions.

Evaluation is a critical element in the overall training and coaching process. Managers can use evaluation results to improve the effectiveness of their training programs. The information necessary to conduct the evaluation can be collected easily if procedures are built into training activities. There is no need for continuing or repetitive problems which stem from lack of evaluation. The more prepared trainers are to do training evaluation, the better the training results will be. The techniques presented in this chapter are intended to improve evaluations by minimizing the errors in the evaluation process.

Evaluation: Part of the Manager's Everyday Job

Managers sometimes assume that training is effective without looking beyond their casual observations. Casual evaluations are often misleading because of errors in observation and interpretation. When employee performance begins to slip, the tendency may be to go back and retrain, using the same methods as before. Many factors can influence a person's performance on a given day. If systematic evaluation is not used, it is impossible to know whether performance problems are the result of insufficient training, inadequate training, or other factors.

Training is far from the only job-related activity which managers must evaluate. Managers must also evaluate employee performance

Exhibit 12.1   Overview of the Evaluation Process

> **The Evaluation Process**
>
> 1. Collect information
> 2. Compare information to standards
> 3. Draw conclusions based on comparisons

during the normal course of supervising and coaching on the job. Casual, everyday evaluation can be improved by recognizing the difference between objective observations and observations that are clouded by personal feelings or biases. The following tips can help to improve evaluations of training or other activities.

1. Be critical of observations—even when they are your own.

2. Consider the possibility of bias—even when you are the observer.

3. Withhold conclusions until observations have been checked and rechecked.

4. Look for justifiable causes of substandard behavior and make allowances for them.

5. Allow the information to present the facts objectively rather than using it to prove your point.

6. Establish written criteria or standards against which to judge performance.

7. Check to be sure that products reportedly produced by employees are their own work.

8. Give credit for correct performance when identifying substandard behavior; few people are total failures.

9. Determine whether the observations represent the "real" situation and if they are a fair basis for decision-making.

10. Consider the consequences of acting on the information before making a decision.

By following these ten suggestions, a manager can blend objectivity into the day-to-day supervision of employees. A biased manager will destroy morale and create an unproductive environment.

Managers should also consider four special areas when evaluating a training program.[2]

1. **Reaction**—How do the trainees feel about the training program?

2. **Learning**—To what extent have the trainees learned new information or skills? How have their attitudes changed?

3. **Behavior**—How has behavior changed on the job because of the learning which occurred?

4. **Results**—How have profits, sales, costs, product or service quality, etc., been positively affected since the training took place?

Managers do not need to be scientific researchers. They should be reasonably unbiased observers, capable of using some basic tools to increase their objectivity. Perfect accuracy is not necessary—or attainable—even in scientific research.

Why Evaluate?   The benefits of evaluation go beyond the basic concern for training effectiveness. Effective evaluation procedures can positively affect the work environment by encouraging the following conditions.

An Objective Working Climate. When business is conducted without objectivity, it lacks a sound foundation. Managers cannot make good decisions unless they know the facts, can look at them objectively, and know what to do next. The results of the objective decision-making process must be evaluated to determine if, and to what extent, business decisions were correct and whether additional attention is necessary. Employees will work harder to meet operational goals if managers continuously evaluate performance and overall progress. They will be more aware of performance standards and management expectations. They are also likely to be more productive and better self-disciplined.

A Constant Needs Assessment. Evaluation is a process of objectively determining whether certain activities actually do lead to the anticipated results. Good evaluation provides a framework for ongoing assessment of training programs. An objective evaluation process must be the basis for any changes if improvements are to be verifiable.

A Basis for Feedback. Employees can become so involved in their jobs and so concerned about their effectiveness that they doubt their accomplishments. Objective evaluations of employee performance provide factual information on how well the job is being done so that employees can work toward improving their performance.

Improved Employee Relations. Objective evaluations encourage fairness and honesty. Employees see that decisions are based on factual information rather than on favoritism. Employees like to know "where they stand," but they want judgments to be objective.

Improved Management. Evaluation promotes professionalism in management. Managers are likely to develop a more logical approach to developing and following through on plans when they (1) state objectives in a systematic fashion, (2) specify desired changes, (3) analyze the training activities designed to accomplish the objectives, (4) appraise the results, and (5) determine the need, if any, for further action. Eventually, the overall management process will become more objective. Systematic procedures for human resource development and techniques to measure the results of staff performance will become the norm.

Stages in Evaluation

There are two stages in the evaluation of any training program. First, it is important to evaluate the *methods* used to achieve the specified objectives. These methods include training materials, instructors, audio-visual aids, and the criteria established to evaluate the training results. Carefully evaluating proposed methods before training can save time and money since it can reveal deficiencies in the training program. Failure to evaluate training methods is one reason why programs are often ineffective and training is criticized.

The second stage is the evaluation of the training program *results*—or the improvements in performance that result from training. The evaluation should assess changes in knowledge, understanding, attitudes, skills, and overall abilities of trainees who were involved in the program.

Three activities must be completed for a meaningful evaluation of methods and results. The first activity is fact-finding. This involves assembling measurable information which the trainer can use in the evaluation process. The second activity involves comparing the information with expectations about training methods and training results. The third activity requires the trainer to draw conclusions based upon the comparisons. Evaluation is not finished until the trainer completes each of these activities.

Responsibility for Evaluation. If possible, evaluation should be done by the managers who are responsible for the training program. The people who will probably benefit the most from the evaluation are the actual trainers. They will be able to see the effect of the methods and procedures firsthand, and will immediately see the success of their training efforts.

Sometimes the complexity of a problem makes it impossible or impractical for managers to conduct an independent evaluation. Corporate trainers or outside consultants can be enlisted to help set up or conduct the evaluation. Managers should still be heavily involved in the evaluation process since it is ultimately for their benefit and since they will have to make decisions based on the results.

Questions for Evaluation

A few simple questions can be applied to almost any situation requiring evaluation. The trainer will need to answer these questions when devising a program for evaluating training methods and results.

What Do You Want to Know? The trainer must decide exactly what he/she wants to find out in order to determine where to begin. What are the questions that the evaluation will attempt to answer? These questions must be determined very carefully since they will guide the content of the evaluation, and since the answers will help measure the training program's effectiveness. Once the trainer knows what information is desired, he/she can develop questionnaires, tests, or other devices that will be used to collect the information.

Where and How Will the Information Be Obtained? From what source will the evaluator obtain the information? Will it be from trainees, guests, managers, or corporate observers? What about outside inspection agencies such as the health department, fire department, or management consultants? Will the information come from everyone in a group or from a sample? Other sources of information are sales records, internal inspection reports, yield test reports, financial statements, and audit reports. *How* the information is obtained refers to such activities as observations, questionnaires, tests, checklists, score cards, case studies, and interviews. Forms should be prepared on which to record the information as it is collected. This will help summarize and process the information; it is risky to rely solely on memory.

Who Will Collect the Information? Based upon where and how the information will be obtained, the decision must be made as to *who* will actually collect the evaluation data. If the individuals selected are not directly involved in conducting the training or designing the evaluation, they must be trained to perform this job task correctly.

How Will the Information Be Analyzed? The questions asked in step one determine how the information will be analyzed. The information must be organized to provide factual answers to the questions and to determine the effectiveness of the training.

What Does It Mean? What implications do the data have for the training program? In what ways can the program be improved? After knowing the results, what changes should be made in future programs? What areas of employee performance were unsatisfactory due to weak spots in the training program? What steps should be taken to remedy these problems?

Often the changes are not major. Many times the program can be improved by a demonstration, by simplifying written material, or by allowing more time to practice the program.

The Evaluation Process

The most common argument against formal evaluation is that "everyone knows what we are trying to accomplish, so let's get on with the job." Training objectives should be written and carefully evaluated at the beginning of the training program. In reality, managers often fail to realize that written training objectives should be used to outline content, select materials, develop teaching procedures and learning experiences, and to evaluate accomplishments.

There are three levels of evaluation. The *first* level takes place before any change occurs—meaning before the training program begins. This is called pre-training evaluation. The performance level that exists before the training begins serves as a *baseline* or *benchmark* against which progress can be measured. Failure to clearly establish this baseline makes it very difficult to evaluate progress and final results.

Many trainers assume that the baseline is identical for all employees, especially when all employees are new to the job. This assumption ignores individual differences and past experiences; it can result in some trainees receiving more training than they need and others not receiving enough. Careful individual evaluation before training will establish a baseline for each trainee.

Managers often assume that they know how guests feel about employee performance. In many cases, no guest satisfaction surveys are conducted before the training begins. Without assessing guest feelings before training, it is impossible to *objectively* conclude that the training resulted in higher levels of guest satisfaction. The trainer can more accurately judge training effectiveness by evaluating guest feelings before training. Sessions can then be conducted and guest reactions assessed a second time.

If properly conducted, objective pre-training evaluation may reveal that the knowledge, skills, and attitudes of employees are better than had been previously determined by subjective methods. The evaluation may indicate that performance problems are being caused by something other than the lack of training. Such a discovery may suggest that training would not be a wise investment, and may lead managers to remove the real barriers.

The second level of evaluation should occur during the training program. Its purpose is to assess how trainees are progressing toward the specified objectives. This level is often viewed as a *progress report*. In hospitality training programs, there is often insufficient time to formally conduct this level of evaluation. Training programs for food service and lodging employees are often completed in one day. If these training programs are viewed as part of a larger training plan, they will contribute to long-term as well as immediate objectives. When evaluating long-term objectives, progress reports help monitor the program's development. The report should evaluate the effectiveness of the teaching methods and indicate where adjustments and improvements can be made. The report should indicate which steps have been accomplished and which remain. It may also suggest additional steps.

The third level of evaluation occurs at the end of the training session or program to determine whether the stated objectives were met. This evaluation must relate to the baseline determined during pre-training evaluation. Are the improvements in employee performance as good as the objectives specified? If not, it may mean that the goals were too high. More likely, it suggests that improvements are needed in the teaching and learning methods. Weaknesses can be identified and corrected before the program is repeated. Problems with the initial training can be corrected by follow-up training and coaching.

Methods of Collecting Information

Collecting information before, during, and after a training program is necessary in order to determine whether and to what extent the objectives are met. Is the job performance of the trainees improving and are guests pleased with the results? After all, the ultimate motive for investing money in the training program is to increase the operation's profitability.

It is important to select a method that is valid and reliable. A method is reliable when it consistently provides valid information; information is valid when it represents what the training was designed to affect. Information must be accurate, documented, and objective in order to provide an effective assessment. Methods of collecting evaluation information include questionnaires, interviews, case studies, planned observations, studies of available records, and tests. The following discussion points out advantages and limitations of each method.

Questionnaires. These are lists of questions that management, guests, or employees answer in written form. Guest questionnaires may be mailed or distributed within the operation. When questionnaires are mailed to guests, they are often discarded when received; returns may be too low to be useful. Techniques can be used to increase returns such as offering complimentary drinks or future discounts on food and lodging to respondents. To encourage high returns, questionnaires should be treated confidentially and no names should be used. Follow-up reminders can also increase returns.

Questionnaires are easy, quick, and relatively inexpensive, especially when compared to personal interviews. Questionnaires can be distributed over a wide geographic area and can include people who might otherwise be inaccessible. Questionnaires are also an extremely good way to reach both former and potential guests.

People who respond to questionnaires may be more honest than if they were being interviewed in person. The questionnaire provides an anonymous opportunity for guests to speak freely about employee performance or other conditions.

Questionnaires should be brief and require short answers that can be easily analyzed. Evaluators should recognize that respondents may not represent the total group; a high response rate is very important in order for questionnaires to be reliable. The entire process of securing a representative group of completed forms can be very time-consuming. Nevertheless, questionnaires are an important way to evaluate guest perceptions of employee performance before, during, and after training.

Interviews. Interviews can be based on interview schedules—a list of written questions which help ensure the objectivity of face-to-face interviews. Each person interviewed should be asked the same questions from this schedule and the interviewer should record the answers. This method is widely used by hospitality marketing professionals. For example, interviews are frequently conducted when guests leave an operation to determine what they liked or disliked about their visit. The basic process of developing an interview schedule is the same when conducting pre- or post-training evaluation interviews.

Interviews provide an opportunity to observe the physical reactions of the person being questioned. When a person hesitates to answer, the interviewer can follow up with a second question to encourage a response. However, interviewers must be trained to avoid influencing the answers that the respondent gives.

Few people will refuse to participate in a short interview if it is handled courteously. When a person does not understand a question, the interviewer can explain the meaning and thereby avoid what may be a problem with questionnaires. Interviews often cost more than questionnaires since they take more time and more training to undertake. However, the follow-up process to secure high returns of mailed questionnaires may cost just as much. Questionnaires are less expensive than interviews when they are distributed to guests who return them before leaving the premises.

Case Studies. Case studies can be used as a teaching and learning method (see Chapter 6) and also as a training evaluation method. A case study can provide a report on the development of the training program. It may begin with a description of the situation that existed when the need for training was first recognized. An objective description of the situation should be documented before training begins. As the training is planned and implemented, the case study should be prepared as a "diary" of events. When the training program ends, a review of the case might reveal whether the training has met the specified objectives.

Case studies bring realism to problems and their solutions. A case documents problems and the steps that are taken to solve the problem. Case studies often identify human factors that affect the problem and its resolution. Such factors are often overlooked by other evaluation methods.

Case studies can document the decision-making process throughout the training program. They show the importance of timing, indicate problems as they develop, and tell how these problems were solved. They also provide an opportunity to study a process in detail in order to discover how it can be improved. Cases can be analyzed to consider how the training program is progressing toward the objectives.

The limitations of case studies rest in the bias and subjectivity of the person who documents or writes the case. The writer may tend to emphasize the unique, rather than the general, situation. He/she may focus too much attention on some elements and overlook others. Case studies are time-consuming to write and require practice in observing, recording, and writing. However, once completed, they can provide an important record of the way an organization changes.

Planned Observation Procedures. Each day, managers informally observe the work of employees. To formalize this evaluation method, managers can use a system that records employee performance based on observation. Results of the observation can be compared to the performance objectives that were established for the training program.

Consider the planned observation program devised by one hospitality organization in the following Case in Point.

A Case in Point: Quality Control

A major airline catering and airport restaurant company created a "quality control" or planned observation program for each category of employees. For each employee category, an observation record was developed which identified the key behaviors, the standards for acceptable performance, and spaces for recording repetitive observations throughout the course of a month. Some employee categories required daily observations and others were observed every two days. The observations were made by a member of management.

As observations were made, the performance of each behavior was either rated "standard" (indicated with a check mark) or "below standard" (indicated with an X mark). At the end of the month, the number of standard ratings was counted and divided by the total number of ratings for the month to yield a percentage performance rating. The overall minimum percentage requirement for each employee category was set at the beginning of the program. Any employee or employee category scoring below the minimum acceptable standard was further evaluated to determine the causes for the substandard performance. If appropriate, training would be scheduled.

In order to plan a formal observation, the manager must know how employees are supposed to perform their jobs. Such understanding helps the manager know what to look for and when to recognize that training has or has not been successful. Planned observations should involve a checklist of employee duties along with the performance standards for each job task. Job breakdowns can be used to develop these checklists. This information should be available to the employees and the observer so that there is a mutual understanding of what is expected. Casual observations made without checklists or job analysis information are ineffective since they lack objectivity, and have no specific basis for communicating expectations.

The observer should be skilled in the duties or job behaviors which he/she evaluates. It is sometimes difficult to separate observation results from the observer's interpretation of what he/she saw. It is also difficult to analyze observations. If the checklist has a clear scoring procedure, the derived scores can serve to quantify the observations. These scores can give an indication of overall performance as well as identify areas of deficiency.

The major advantage of planned observation is that it helps with ongoing management. Employees may disagree with the day-to-day routine observations made by their manager. For example, they may feel that the manager does not pay enough attention to overall performance and only sees the occasional minor problems. The planned approach ensures that all important steps in the performance of the job are known, reviewed, and evaluated.

Study of Available Records. Much of the sales and cost information needed for this evaluation method is available from records used for control and accounting purposes. If it is compiled routinely by the administrative and accounting office staffs, this approach can be less time-consuming than other evaluation methods. Also, this may be the most reliable way to evaluate training since financial information must be extremely accurate. Records of past operating results enable managers to study performance over several years. This can provide a clearly defined baseline of performance before training. This baseline can be used to measure the effect improved performance has on sales and costs.

One problem with using past financial records as a basis for evaluating training is that the sales and costs figures may not reflect the efforts of the present staff. The approach can, however, be useful if managers do not reach back too far for baseline data or if employee turnover is relatively low. The method can also be useful if current operating procedures are similar to those used during the baseline period, and if there is little observable difference in the general type of employee being selected. A study of available records can be used in conjunction with other evaluation methods.

Tests. The large number of college and high school students working part-time in the hospitality industry supports the use of tests as a natural form of evaluation which places equal emphasis on job knowledge and performance. Knowledge tests are helpful evaluation tools when they assess knowledge that is essential to meeting established performance objectives. Knowledge can be tested about such items as the menu, beverage ingredients, wine selections, room rates, guest services, approved procedures, and policies.

It is also possible to use skills tests. With this plan, an employee who completes training can be asked to perform the job task which was taught while being observed. Racking dishes to be washed, carrying a service tray, preparing a white sauce, registering a guest, mixing a cocktail, preparing a daily cashier's report, and making a bed in the guestroom are examples of simple skills tests. Deciding which type of test to administer depends to some extent on training objectives. As one authority observes:

> The two most frequently used techniques for measuring knowledge and skills are paper-and-pencil and performance tests. Paper-and-pencil tests are convenient for measuring knowledge, while performance tests are most often utilized for measuring skills (although it may be possible to use the latter for measuring both knowledge and skills). The development or selection of either type of test takes us immediately back to the training objectives and the early planning for the program. That is, the material included in the tests should be based upon the specific knowledge and/or skills that the program is designed to develop.[3]

Tests may take several forms. Questions may be multiple-choice, true-false, fill-in-the-blank, discussion, mathematical problems, or performance-based depending on the nature of the content or skill being evaluated. Multiple-choice is the most popular format for written tests since it can be used to determine mastery of many different subjects. The multiple-choice format also allows trainers to measure a person's ability to digest or to think through a complex process or procedure. A multiple-choice item consists of two parts: *the stem*—which consists of a question or a statement to be completed—and the *distractors*—which consist of the possible responses.[4]

To be effective, each distractor must be plausible and match the grammatical structure of the stem. Nothing is gained when the response choices are totally unrelated to the subject and obviously not correct. All distractors should appear correct to a person who has not mastered the training. This way, guessing becomes a very risky matter. For example, if the stem calls for the trainee to give the correct food cost percentage from a food and beverage income statement, the trainer should consider the most common errors that are made in calculating food cost. Food cost should be calculated based on each incorrect calculation method to provide wrong distractors. These choices will seem right to the trainees who are using incorrect formulas for the calculation. Of course, the correct answer, arrived at by using the correct formula, must be one of the available responses.

The use of a skills test is similar to the planned observation procedures discussed earlier. As part of an ongoing training program, skills tests can quickly indicate whether training was effective or if it needs to be repeated. A simple skills test can be used during a training session to indicate when a demonstration was effective, when a film or other audiovisual aid has "made its point," or when role playing has been successful. Skills testing will also reveal non-training barriers to employee performance which will need to be removed or overcome.

Knowledge tests alone will not determine whether employees can perform their jobs. However, knowledge tests coupled with skills tests and planned observations can assess total trainee performance. Copies of completed test results and scored checklists from planned observations can be retained in employee files as a record of training results. They can also be used when conducting performance appraisals or when considering employees for promotion or dismissal.

Evaluation Tools in Action

Different evaluation tools can be used to measure trainee performance. The devices should help tell what trainees know, feel, and can do as the result of training.

When selecting an evaluation tool, the training objective must be known and the information needed to determine progress toward achieving the objective must be available. Examples of ways to develop evaluation procedures are discussed in the following sections. They focus upon the type of information needed to assess whether a training objective has been met.

Evaluation of Knowledge

Trainers want to know whether a trainee has gained knowledge as a result of training. As discussed earlier, knowledge questions are usually asked through simple paper-and-pencil type tests (although questions may also be asked through interviews). By asking questions to test knowledge, a trainer can determine whether the trainees have learned the factual information presented in training.

A knowledge test may be given to trainees in a classroom setting both before and after a specified amount of training. With this plan, the knowledge of trainees before and after training can be determined. The difference represents the amount of knowledge acquired as a result of the training.

Trainers should realize that even if an employee *knows* something, he/she may not be able to apply those facts on the job. If the training objective is to develop understanding and application of knowledge, it becomes necessary to ask questions that determine whether the trainee can apply the knowledge. The differences between knowledge of facts (stressing *what*), understanding (stressing *why*), and application (stressing *how*) can be demonstrated by some sample questions:

A "knowledge only" question: (emphasis is on whether the trainee knows simple facts)

Bordeaux is one of the most famous wine regions of France. Bordeaux wines are: (check one only)

( ) a.   always red
( ) b.   always white
( ) c.   red or white
( ) d.   sometimes pink

An "understanding" question: (emphasis is on more complex information that requires some understanding of facts)

Bordeaux is one of the most famous wine regions of France. If you were going to select a quality Bordeaux wine, what is the first information you would look for? (check one only)

( ) a.   the shape of the bottle
( ) b.   the name of the shipper
( ) c.   the size of the chateau
( ) d.   the appellation contrôlée

An "application" question: (emphasis is on understanding facts and applying them to solve problems)

Bordeaux is one of the most famous wine regions of France. A guest wishes to order a bottle of Bordeaux wine costing under $20.00. Which one would you suggest? (check one only)

( ) a.   1967 Chateau Lafite Rothschild
( ) b.   1971 Beaune-Bressandes
( ) c.   1974 Chateau Larose-Trintaudon
( ) d.   1975 Chateau Margaux

When knowledge tests are designed, trainers should consider use of each type of question. Trainees must score well on "application of knowledge" questions if their job performance is to be improved.

Here are other examples of knowledge, understanding, and application questions that can be used in a training session:

A "knowledge only" question:

There are a number of room styles in our hotel. A "double-double" room has the following feature(s): (check one only)

( ) a.   a king-size bed
( ) b.   two twin beds
( ) c.   two double beds
( ) d.   a connecting room

An "understanding" question:

There are a number of room styles in our hotel. A "double-double" room has a higher rate than a "twin" for the following reason: (check one only)

( ) a. it is actually a small suite
( ) b. it can accommodate four persons
( ) c. it is made up of two connecting rooms
( ) d. it is more popular than a "twin"

An "application" question:

There are a number of room styles in our hotel. A man and wife and two small sons request one room for their family. You should assign them the following: (check one only)

( ) a. a "king" plus two roll-aways
( ) b. a "twin" plus two roll-aways
( ) c. a "double-double"
( ) d. a "small suite"

Knowledge questions do not have to be multiple-choice. True-false questions can also be asked to assess the trainees' knowledge, understanding, and application abilities. For example:

A "knowledge only" question:

T   F   (circle one)   A béchamel sauce is prepared from milk and/or cream and white roux.

An "understanding" question:

T   F   (circle one)   A béchamel sauce is used in the preparation of a mustard sauce.

An "application" question:

T   F   (circle one)   A guest who specifies he is on a total fat-free diet can be served poached chicken with béchamel sauce.

Fill-in-the-blank or completion of statement-type questions can also be used to determine trainee abilities.

A "knowledge only" question:

When a guest reserves a room, guarantees the room for late arrival, then fails to cancel but does not show up, the situation is known as a

_____.

An "understanding" question:

When a guest reserves a room and desires to check in after 6:00 p.m., it is necessary to "guarantee" the room for a late arrival because _____

_____.

An "application" question:

When a guest reserves a room and guarantees it for a late arrival after 6:00 p.m., but then fails to claim or cancel the reservation, the room payment should be processed against the individual's credit card account by _____

_____

_____

Open-ended questions that require the trainee to list or discuss a topic can also be used to assess the level of learning.

A "knowledge only" question:

List the ten steps in the chain of service for the Sunrise Dining Room.

An "understanding" question:

Explain why it is important to serve all beverages from the right when possible.

An "application" question:

A guest requests that the salad course be served following the entree course. This is different from the normal service pattern. How should you handle this situation?

Evaluation of Skills

There are two reasons to measure skills: (1) to learn if the trainees have acquired a particular skill taught during the training, and (2) to learn which skills have been mastered to the required performance level.

Job lists and job breakdowns may be used as the index for observing and evaluating skill performance. Individual training records in the form of checklists (See Chapter 9) can also be used as a natural follow-up to job lists and job breakdowns. In addition to these standard tools, other types of separate score cards can be developed. Three sample score cards are shown in Exhibits 12.2, 12.3, and 12.4.

Evaluation of Attitudes

Managers should be concerned about the attitudes and beliefs of their employees and guests. Attitudes affect employee performance. Guests' attitudes affect repeat business. Training should be designed to influence positive employee attitudes. As guests observe employees performing their jobs effectively, they judge the attitudes exhibited; this may influence their own attitudes toward the total operation.

Tools for evaluating attitudes can take several forms. The most frequently used techniques for measuring attitudes and attitude change are the paper-and-pencil variety. These include rating scales, information quizzes, and questionnaires. In addition, interviews and behavioral observations are used.[5] Exhibits 12.5 and 12.6 show sample questionnaires which can be used with both trainees and guests. In these examples, the employee and guest questions correspond to the same concerns. This is not necessary for all attitude evaluations. Exhibits 12.7 and 12.8 show other types of questionnaires that can be developed to assess attitudes.

If one statement in a questionnaire consistently generates "dis-

Exhibit 12.2 Sample Score Card for Serving Skills

Skills Score Card			**Skill Area:** Food Service Skills	

Directions: Rate the employee's performance on each job task either 1, 2, or 3, depending on whether the level of performance meets the description in the left column (1), the right column (3), or falls between the two (2). Add scores at the bottom of the page.

Task	1	2	3	Score
How to seat guests	Greeting is pleasant; leads guest to table; assists women with chairs; welcomes guests; introduces server.		No greeting; directs guests to table; places menus; walks away with no comment.	
How to explain the food on the menu	Starts with appetizers and soups; describes preparation procedures and key ingredients; smiles and uses suggestive selling techniques; invites questions; gives guests time to decide.		Offers to help if guest needs assistance; waits to be asked for information; gives brief answers and does not attempt to increase the guest's interest in items available.	
How to take the food order	Starts with women; stands erect; practices suggestive selling techniques; communicates with guests in a pleasant manner; asks for special requests; repeats details.		Rushes the guest; does not attempt suggestive selling; slumps over table; indifferent to guest's needs or desires; fails to pay attention to special requests; unfriendly bordering on discourteous.	

Name of Rater: _____

Name of Employee Evaluated:_____

Date: _____   **Total Score:** _____

agreeable" reactions, this presents management with evidence that a problem exists. Training may be needed, or, if training was already conducted, the evaluation suggests that it was ineffective. Of course, each identified problem should be investigated and the appropriate corrective action initiated.

Evaluation of Employee Confidence

An employee can be competent and still fail to perform due to a lack of self-confidence. Competence comes from mastery of knowledge, skills, and the attitudes required by the job duties. Confidence or self-assurance is the element of courage that is required to face the guest and perform the rehearsed roles. Employees may be master performers in the classroom but experience stage fright that renders them ineffective when dealing with guests. Supervision that is too close or demanding can cause an employee to lose confidence in his/her abilities. A periodic assessment of confidence levels is a valuable way to determine whether lack of confidence is causing problems in job performance.

The following Case in Point illustrates the training approach and policies taken by one restaurant to instill self-confidence.

A Case in Point: Confident Servers

In conjunction with the opening of a fine dining restaurant, the servers were all given extensive training on wines. Training covered knowledge of American, European, German, and Italian wines, as well as service procedures for all types. When the restaurant opened, the wine list was more extensive and of higher quality than any other restaurant within the region. From the opening night, wine sales soared. In fact, the restaurant achieved wine sales that far surpassed any of the competitive restaurants in the market area, both in terms of quantity and quality of wines selected by the guests. Servers found that they were able to easily influence the selection of premium wines and that guests were pleased by the way the selections complemented their food choices.

At the end of the first two weeks of operations, the servers were evaluated on their confidence levels within each area of their service knowledge and skills. Surprisingly, the lowest confidence ratings were in the area of wine knowledge and skills. The staff was then interviewed to determine why these ratings were low since their performance indicated a high degree of competence.

The interviews revealed that the extensive wine training had made them aware of the vast amount of knowledge that could be mastered about wines. Servers were nervous that a guest might know more about a particular wine than they had learned in the training program. Furthermore, they learned that wine knowledge is not always based on facts—that emotions play a large part in peoples' wine preferences. Servers feared being embarrassed by suggesting a wine and then being challenged by a guest who did not think their suggestion was the best wine for their food choices and tastes.

The response to the situation was two-fold. The restaurant owners instituted a continuous wine training program to further increase the knowledge and skills of the staff. Second, the owners set up a small library of authoritative wine reference books within the restaurant. This library was for both the staff and guests in researching the tough questions which exceeded the mastery level of the staff or the knowledge of the guests. These reference materials became quite popular with regular guests who would research an unfamiliar wine on the list before making a dinner selection. For regular guests, the servers would often go to the table with the wine list and a reference book, with the pages already marked for the wines that they were going to suggest. Needless to say, gratuities were often very high for servers who took advantage of their training and the support system provided by the owners for them to sell and serve wines with total confidence.

Exhibit 12.3 Sample Score Card for Cooking Skills

Score Card   **Task Area:** Cooking Skills

Directions: The skills of each employee are to be rated twice, once before beginning the training program and a second time after the training has been completed.

Make your best judgment of the employee's skill in each task using the following key:
  (1) **practically no skill**—does not know how
  (2) **little skill**—needs much help and practice
  (3) **fair skill**—but still needs some help and practice
  (4) **good skill**—needs very little help and practice
  (5) **excellent skill**—does not need any help or practice

Circle the number which shows your judgment of the employee's skills.

Task		Score				
How to sauté	Beginning	1	2	3	4	5
	End	1	2	3	4	5
How to braise	Beginning	1	2	3	4	5
	End	1	2	3	4	5
How to broil	Beginning	1	2	3	4	5
	End	1	2	3	4	5
How to deep fat fry	Beginning	1	2	3	4	5
	End	1	2	3	4	5
How to steam	Beginning	1	2	3	4	5
	End	1	2	3	4	5
How to simmer	Beginning	1	2	3	4	5
	End	1	2	3	4	5
How to roast	Beginning	1	2	3	4	5
	End	1	2	3	4	5

Name of Rater: _____

Name of Employee Evaluated: _____

Date: _____

Self-assurance is often considered too intangible to measure. However, it is sometimes possible to determine an employee's confidence level through observation or interview. Along with observation and interviews, one of the best ways to assess confidence is to have the employees complete a confidence rating questionnaire. The sample confidence rating interview and questionnaire forms shown in Exhibits 12.9 and 12.10 can be adapted for use in many hospitality skill areas.

Exhibit 12.4   Sample Score Card for Housekeeping Skills

Score Card   **Task Area:** Hotel Housekeeping Skills

Directions: Observe the performance of each employee and rate his/her training needs. As you observe the skills of the employee, ask yourself "how much training does this employee need to bring the performance level up to standard?" Check one category for each task.

Task	Rating Category Amount of Training Needed				
	1 Very Much	2 Much	3 Consid- erable	4 Some	5 Little Or None
How to make beds	_____	_____	_____	_____	_____
How to dust and polish furniture	_____	_____	_____	_____	_____
How to clean mirrors	_____	_____	_____	_____	_____
How to clean windows	_____	_____	_____	_____	_____
How to vacuum	_____	_____	_____	_____	_____
How to restock guestroom supplies	_____	_____	_____	_____	_____
How to clean the toilet	_____	_____	_____	_____	_____
How to clean the bathtub	_____	_____	_____	_____	_____
How to clean tile floors and walls	_____	_____	_____	_____	_____
How to restock bathroom supplies	_____	_____	_____	_____	_____
How to "final check" room	_____	_____	_____	_____	_____

Name of Rater: _____

Name of Employee Evaluated:_____

Date: _____

Evaluation Tool Factors

There are five factors to consider when developing an effective report form, questionnaire, interview schedule, knowledge test, skill score card, or confidence rating form. These factors are validity, reliability, objectivity, practicality, and simplicity.

Validity. Validity determines whether or not a test measures what it claims to measure.[6] A valid evaluation tool will provide evidence of progress toward meeting the training objectives.

Behavior validity refers to the need to evaluate the behavior required by the training objectives. The measurement of skills, for example, requires different evaluation procedures from those required for measuring knowledge; knowledge is a different type of behavior from demonstration of skills.

Subject matter validity refers to the content of training as required by the training objective. It is obvious that questions about dining room service would be inappropriate if a manager is testing the front office staff on selling rooms. The evaluation tool must consider the subject

Exhibit 12.5 Sample Multiple-Choice Attitude Questions for Employees

---

Multiple Choice Attitude Questions
(Employees)

1. How do you feel about the performance level of our service staff? (check one)

   ( ) a. We do a great job.
   ( ) b. We do a better than average job.
   ( ) c. We do an average job.
   ( ) d. We do a rather poor job.

2. How do you feel about your ability to explain the food items on our menu? (check one)

   ( ) a. I can explain every item.
   ( ) b. I can explain at least ¾ of the items.
   ( ) c. I can explain about ½ of the items.
   ( ) d. I can explain not more than ¼ of the items.

3. How do you feel about the level of your performance compared with other servers? (check one)

   ( ) a. I perform better than anyone else.
   ( ) b. I perform better than most of the others.
   ( ) c. I perform about average.
   ( ) d. I perform at a level lower than most of the others.

Exhibit 12.6 Sample Multiple-Choice Attitude Questions for Guests

---

Multiple Choice Attitude Questions
(Guests)

1. How do you feel about the level of service in our dining room? (check one)

   ( ) a. Much better than comparably priced restaurants.
   ( ) b. Somewhat better than comparably priced restaurants.
   ( ) c. Somewhat below comparably priced restaurants.
   ( ) d. Much lower than comparably priced restaurants.

2. How do you feel about your server's ability to describe food items on our menu? (check one)

   ( ) a. He/she could describe all of them.
   ( ) b. He/she could describe at least ¾ of them.
   ( ) c. He/she could describe about ½ of them.
   ( ) d. He/she could describe not more than ¼ of them.

3. How do you feel about your server's performance as compared to other servers in our restaurant? (check one)

   ( ) a. He/she is the best server in the restaurant.
   ( ) b. He/she is better than most of the other servers.
   ( ) c. He/she is about average.
   ( ) d. He/she performs at a level lower than most of the other servers.

Exhibit 12.7 Sample Employee Questionnaire for Attitude Assessment

Employee Questionnaire: Attitude Assessment

Instructions: Read each of the statements and check whether you agree, disagree, have no opinion, or are undecided.

Statement	Agree	Disagree	No Opinion/ Undecided
1. Red wines should be served at room temperature and white wines should be chilled.	_____	_____	_____
2. French wines are usually better than American wines because they are imported.	_____	_____	_____
3. Dry wines are higher in quality than sweet wines and should be sold whenever possible.	_____	_____	_____
4. Guests who order expensive wines are usually snobs and are showing off.	_____	_____	_____
5. Guests who order red wines with fish or chicken should be told that it is wrong.	_____	_____	_____
6. Guests prefer that wine be opened away from the table.	_____	_____	_____

matter of the training and appropriate situations in which the behavior would normally be expressed.

Reliability. Reliability is the degree to which (1) the sample being evaluated represents the entire population about which inferences will be made, or (2) the subject matter being evaluated represents the total subject matter covered by the training. The sample may be a group of potential or former guests, a 30% sample of the housekeeping staff, observation of behavior over a certain period, etc. The degree to which these samples are a fair representation of the total situation is the measure of reliability. Simply stated, reliability determines the degree to which a test measures what it claims to measure (validity) in a *consistent* manner.[7]

Objectivity. Objectivity means having a concrete, observable, and tangible basis for making a judgment or interpretation. It is the opposite of subjectivity, opinions, or guesses. An objective evaluation tool is constructed so that its results are minimally influenced by the people who administer or interpret the evaluation. If equally capable people ask the same set of questions, interpret the answers, and draw closely similar conclusions, the evaluation is considered to be objective. The use of numbers helps to make interpretations more objective. For example, the phrase "100 people" is more objective than the phrase "many people."

Practicality. An evaluation tool must be practical. It is necessary to consider time, cost, and convenience. Will the process take more time

Exhibit 12.8   Sample Guest Questionnaire for Attitude Assessment

---

Guest Questionnaire: Attitude Assessment

Instructions: Please tell us whether you agree, disagree, have no opinion, or are undecided about the following statements:

Statement	Agree	Disagree	No Opinion/ Undecided
1. The receptionist who registered me was friendly and professional.	————	————	————
2. The room assigned to me was correct according to my request.	————	————	————
3. The bellperson informed me of hotel services on the way to my room.	————	————	————
4. My room was clean and completely furnished with towels, soap, etc.	————	————	————
5. The hotel telephone operator was courteous in handling my wake-up call.	————	————	————
6. The housekeeping staff cleaned and supplied my room without disturbing me.	————	————	————
7. Room service was courteous, and my order was delivered promptly.	————	————	————
8. The front desk staff was pleasant and efficient when I checked out.	————	————	————
9. The hotel staff thanked me for my stay and invited me to return.	————	————	————
10. I had a very satisfactory stay in the hotel and will return again.	————	————	————

Comments on needed improvements:

_____

_____

_____

---

than it is worth? Will it cost more than the operation can afford? The cost of any evaluation must be balanced against all other demands made upon the operation such as the time schedule, the details required by the evaluation tool, the time involved in summarizing the information, the cooperation required of all people involved, and the probable value of the results.

Simplicity. Is the evaluation tool simple, easy to understand, easy to answer, easy to administer, easy to analyze, and easy to summarize? As the process is made less difficult it becomes more practical, and the time lapse between collecting the information and evaluating the results is minimized. Simplicity is not the same as brevity. The forms do not have to be short to be simple. They need to be long enough to reliably sample the knowledge, skills, and attitudes developed by the training effort.

Exhibit 12.9   Sample Confidence Rating Interview

Confidence Rating Questionnaire

Name of Interviewer: _____

Name of Employee: _____

Date: _____

Have you ever prepared a flambé dessert at tableside? (check one)

( ) a. Yes
( ) b. No

Do you think you can prepare a flambé dessert at tableside? (check one)

( ) c. No, I don't think I can.
( ) d. Yes, I think I can, but am not sure.
( ) e. Yes, I feel sure I can.

Have you ever decanted a bottle of fine wine? (check one)

( ) a. Yes
( ) b. No

Do you think you can decant a bottle of fine wine? (check one)

( ) c. No, I don't think I can.
( ) d. Yes, I think I can, but am not sure.
( ) e. Yes, I feel sure I can.

Exhibit 12.10   Sample Confidence Rating Questionnaire

Confidence Rating Questionnaire

Duties: Food Server—General Skills (Randomly Arranged)

Employee's Name: _____

Instructions: Rate how well you feel you could perform each of the following duties as compared to our performance standards if you were called upon to do so without further training. Be honest with yourself. You will not be penalized for lack of confidence. This information will be used to determine the emphasis of future training activities.

Task	Very Confident	Somewhat Confident	Limited Confidence	No Confidence
Make coffee in the large urn.	1	2	3	4
Set tables for dinner in the Blue Room.	1	2	3	4
Open and serve still wines (red and white).	1	2	3	4
Serve beverages (water, coffee, hot tea).	1	2	3	4
Explain the food selections on the menu.	1	2	3	4
Sell and serve after-dinner drinks.	1	2	3	4
Bring clean flatware to a guest's table.	1	2	3	4
Bone fish entrees such as sautéed dover sole.	1	2	3	4
Carry a large tray loaded with dishes.	1	2	3	4

Analysis and Interpretation of Evaluation Data

Analysis is the process of looking at information in a way that yields answers to questions. Analysis involves taking facts, processing them in some manner, and obtaining answers to questions.

Interpretation is the process of searching out the meanings of the answers which are obtained. This process occurs when managers ask "so what?" questions after analyzing the evaluation information. Interpretation leads to the explanation of what happened and "what it all means."

Statistical analysis can be quite involved. However, hospitality managers can limit training evaluation and analysis to some simple mathematical techniques that will serve their purposes in most cases. These simple techniques include numerical counts, percentages, and averages.

Numerical Counts

For many evaluation situations, it may be necessary to know *how many*. For example, how many of the servers were able to increase the sale of desserts after the training? How many labor hours were saved by the improved work methods? How many of the employees who were trained increased their level of confidence in serving wine?

Counts are the first step in any analysis. Sometimes the counts are all that is needed; at other times the counts serve as the starting point for other calculations.

Percentages

Percentages are probably the next most frequently used evaluation statistic after counts. They are a good aid in making relationships and comparisons meaningful. It is difficult to compare "67 out of 179" with "30 out of 70." On the other hand, "37%" can easily be compared with "43%" (67 out of 179 = 37%; 30 out of 70 = 43%). Percentages are easily understood. This is particularly helpful when large numbers are involved.

Averages

The average is an arithmetic mean. The advantages of using an average are: (1) it is most likely to be understood, and (2) it is easy to compute. For example, consider the following:

Dishwasher	Number of Dishes Washed Per Half Hour
Sue	88
Bill	110
Joe	90

The average number of dishes washed per half hour period by three dishwashers is 96 (90 + 110 + 88 dishes divided by three dishwashers = 96).

If, for example, this statistic was known, dishwashers with less than an average productivity rate might be trained first. Conversely, the average dishwashing rate after training could be compared with the average rate before training. A measure of training success in attaining the objective "increase the productivity rate by 25 percent" could be easily developed. If the after-training productivity rate is at least 25 percent greater than the before-training rate, the training is judged successful. If the productivity rate increases by less than 25 percent, the training is only partially successful.

Reporting Evaluation Results

In order for the results of evaluation to be readily used, they must be organized and made available in an understandable and appropriate way. In many cases, a complete, written report is not required. If the results of an evaluation are to be used primarily by the manager who performed the evaluation, there may be no need for a formal report other than some summaries of test scores, attitude ratings, or observation scores.

When the results of training are to be reported to a larger group or to a higher level of the organization, a written report may be required. Evaluation is done to answer questions about the effectiveness of the training program in achieving objectives. The written report should explain what the program attempted to accomplish, how it was carried out, how the program was evaluated, a summary of the findings (to what extent the training was successful), and implications for future management decisions. It is important to report the training results in terms of behavioral changes, rather than in terms of numbers of attendees, hours of instruction, and other non-performance-related criteria.

The overall results of training evaluations should be reviewed with the employees who were involved. The feedback of objective information will help the employees evaluate their own performance in reference to the departmental results. Feedback has the tendency to further improve performance by giving employees an incentive for doing better. When employees know that their performance matters, they will work to perform at higher levels.

Notes

1. For a more in-depth study of evaluation, see Tim L. Wentling and Tom E. Lawson, *Evaluating Occupational Education and Training Programs* (Boston: Allyn and Bacon, 1975).

2. Donald L. Kirkpatrick, *Supervisory Training and Development* (Reading, Mass.: Addison-Wesley, 1971), pp. 88–102.

3. Robert S. Dvorin, "Evaluation of Training," in *Handbook of Human Resource Administration*, 2nd ed., edited by Joseph J. Famularo (New York: McGraw-Hill, 1986), p. 26-6.

4. Jeffrey Z. Cantor, "Developing Multiple-Choice Test Items," *Training and Development Journal*, Vol. 41, No. 5, May 1987, p. 85.

5. Dvorin, p. 26-9.

6. Cantor, p. 88.

7. Cantor, p. 88.

Part IV

Communication and Motivation

13 Communication in Training and Coaching

In order to train and coach, managers must be good communicators. They must be able to "get the message across" and generate trainee feedback. There are many potential barriers to effective communication. These barriers can be overcome if managers understand the basic factors that affect the communication process.

Simply stated, communication is the process of transferring information from one person to another. Communication is effective when there is a successful transfer of information from a sender to a receiver. The transfer is successful only when the receiver understands what the sender is communicating.

Four Basic Types of Communication

The primary purpose of training is to change behavior in a way which helps the operation better attain its goals. A trainer should be able to communicate effectively so that training goals—which relate to business goals—can be met. If communication is not effective, learning will be hindered; training will not be worthwhile.

The trainer can use many forms of communication. The four types discussed in this chapter are speaking, writing, acting, and listening. Trainers need to recognize that effective communication goes far beyond "telling trainees what they are supposed to do." Managers who train must be good speakers, writers, actors, and listeners.

Speaking

Oral communication is critical in training. Effective oral communication takes place when the message is (1) heard, (2) understood, and (3) acted upon.

When planning to speak, the trainer should address the issue, deal with the facts as accurately and fairly as possible, and focus upon the most efficient way to state the central idea. These principles apply whether the trainer is speaking to one or several trainees. Words are used to transmit ideas. It is not easy to develop the ability to say what is meant with a few words—but it must be done. When five words can be used to transmit a thought, the addition of five more may obscure the idea rather than clarify it. There is a tendency for individuals who think they speak fairly well to speak too much.

Oral training presentations should include the following elements:[1]

1. An opening statement that captures the attention of the trainees and causes them to want to hear more

2. Sincerity

3. Enthusiasm

4. Persuasiveness

5. Eye contact so that every trainee feels that the trainer is communicating with him/her directly

6. Gestures that reinforce the communication, naturally and smoothly

7. Absence of nervousness as indicated by how much the trainer seems to be enjoying making the presentation

8. Voice control that results in a pleasant pace and comfortable volume

9. A stimulating closing statement, equal in strength to the opening statement

Most people find speaking before a group more difficult than talking to one person. The manager who is preparing to train needs to practice clear and organized speaking. Speaking before groups also requires the ability to assess whether the audience is listening, understanding, and likely to apply what they are hearing.

Guidelines for Speaking. Observing the following guidelines should help managers improve their speaking habits in both one-on-one and group training situations:

1. Know what you want to say before you begin to talk. You can't expect another person to understand what you're saying if you don't know your own message. This is especially important in communicating expected performance standards. You must first know, and then communicate, what you want the trainees to do as a result of training; otherwise, they may have only a vague idea of what is expected.

2. Speak simply and precisely. Practice good grammar and pronunciation. While so-called "street language" may be appropriate in some social settings, trainees will regard such communication as immature and inappropriate for trainers. Slang and jargon can interfere with understanding, retention, and learning.

3. Present the facts as accurately and fairly as possible. Avoid exaggerations and unfounded generalizations. Trainees respond well to reasonable facts. When the message lacks reason and

logic, the speaker is ineffective and the message will not achieve the desired results.

4. Communicate feelings as well as information. The *way* something is said can communicate as much as, if not more than, what is said. Trainee attitudes are developed by the feeling that accompanies a spoken message. Guest service training, for example, should not only stress methods and skills but should also transmit a feeling about service (caring about guests' needs and wishes).

5. Whenever possible, look at the person to whom you are speaking. The expressions on the receiver's face can often indicate whether a message was understood. This is one reason that telephone communication can lead to more misunderstandings than face-to-face communication—even when the same words are spoken in both instances. A more detailed discussion of non-verbal communication will be presented later.

6. Ask the trainees if they understand what was said. Don't assume that communication is over when you stop speaking. *Listen* and *hear* how the trainees restate what was heard. If they are confused or uncertain, the message should be restated—possibly in another way or with different examples.

Writing   Writing, just like speaking, is a major form of training communication. The ability to write is an important management skill. As a trainer, the manager must write various training materials to be read by both trainees and other trainers. In preparing written training materials and other communications, the manager must remember the educational backgrounds and reading abilities of the people who will use the materials.

Job breakdowns provide the basic outlines for writing training materials. They list what is to be done, how to do it, and why. These concerns are the basic message of most training materials. Trainers who go too far beyond this basic outline often write more than is necessary. This can result in confusion, boredom, and wasted time.

Guidelines for Writing. When using job breakdowns to prepare training materials, much of the writing is in outline form and will not require a high level of composition skills. It is still important to apply some basic writing principles so that the materials will be usable and effective training aids. Note that many of the following guidelines are similar to those for speaking.

1. Use short, easy to understand words and phrases. Remember the reader's background. There are many words that trainers might use which have little or no meaning to trainees. If such words are used without being defined, they act as a block to learning when the trainee encounters them.[2] A writer should avoid the use of difficult words; trainees will reject training materials they do not understand. The hospitality industry hires many people for whom English is a second language. It is

frequently advisable to have training materials translated for their use into their native language.

2. Be precise. Words that have abstract or double meanings are confusing. Words that have widely accepted meaning and use are most effective in training communications.

3. Spell correctly. Misspelled words can lead to confusion and total misunderstanding. While proper spelling does not ensure understanding, it helps. It is a good habit to have all training materials checked by at least two people for correct spelling and readability.

4. Write in short, easy sentences. Say what is necessary to cover the subject and then stop. Unless the meaning of the message can be clarified by more writing, the extra words will often confuse the message.

5. Arrange sentences in logical order. The job breakdowns can serve as a model of the proper sequence. List the objectives, the points to be covered under each objective, and then expand upon each point as necessary.

6. Use good grammar. This should not be difficult if sentences are kept short and to the point. Using the right words and punctuating sentences correctly help the reader understand what is being said.

7. Be informal, but not too informal. Formal, businesslike writing can be a turnoff to trainees. Trainees are interested in learning their jobs with the least amount of effort in the shortest possible time. Write with that objective in mind.

8. Say what you mean. It is not the reader's responsibility to interpret what has been written. Rather, it is the reader's responsibility to read and understand the message without having to analyze it. Read what you've written several times to ensure that the information explicitly communicates *what* is to be done, *how* it should be done, and *why* it should be done that way. If training materials are based on that simple outline, they will usually present an understandable message.

9. Effectively use spaced repetition. Restate the key points in different ways at different points in the training documents. Variety in phrasing the same points will aid memory and understanding, while mere repetitions of the same statements will create boredom and block retention. This same principle applies to oral communication. The written outline for oral training sessions should indicate where these repetitions should occur for the best effect.

10. Proof final drafts carefully. The work required for good writing certainly justifies the time required for careful proofing. The most effective way to proof is for two people to do it together, with one reading the original or next-to-the-last draft, and the

other following in the final draft. All errors should be neatly corrected before the materials are printed or distributed.

Some excellent books are available for improving writing style.³ Most managers realize that there is room for improvement in their writing skills. Practice is the best way to overcome deficiencies. Books on writing style can help identify common writing mistakes.

Acting   Body positions, facial expressions, gestures, and movements are examples of non-verbal communication which everyone uses to communicate ideas. Sometimes this may be done overtly and sometimes with such subtlety that only the sharp observer will detect the disguised meaning.

A trainer must know about the body signals that he/she sends out to the trainees as well as those which the trainees send back. A trainer may plan the use of a particular hand gesture or body stance to emphasize a point in the training session. The ability to communicate more effectively by non-verbal methods can be learned.

Experienced trainers, like experienced actors or entertainers on the theater stage, can develop the ability to "read" an audience. The trainers can take what they see and make certain judgments about how the audience is reacting to what is occurring "on stage." The art and skill of interpreting "body language" has become popular in recent years.

Non-verbal behaviors play an important role in the communication process; the communicator may not even be aware of the non-verbal cues which he/she is sending in the message.⁴ Managers should be aware of non-verbal communications that come from their employees and be able to interpret how these communications relate to their job performance. Feelings are often communicated through non-verbal gestures and facial expressions. Body stance and the way an employee walks can communicate interest, disinterest, excitement, tiredness, or energy level if these actions are "read" with some degree of accuracy.

Role playing (discussed in Chapter 6) is a training technique that uses acting in a formal sense and normally includes verbal communications. Pantomimes—role plays in which actors do not talk but communicate only non-verbally—are effective in interpersonal skills training for employees with a high degree of guest contact. In pantomime training, trainees are forced to concentrate on what their bodies are saying. Trainees will discover that non-verbal communication becomes easier when they smile and communicate helpfulness to the guests. Frowning tends to shut off communication. After the session, trainees often recognize that if they would smile and help more, guests would be better satisfied with the service they receive. Trainees may also recognize that the most eloquently expressed words are dull if the speaker is not projecting emotions into the message.

Guidelines for Using Non-Verbal Communication. Like any other form of communication, non-verbal communication techniques can be learned. The trainer needs to learn how to effectively use non-verbal communication to help him/her get the point across. Likewise, the trainer should develop skill in interpreting the non-verbal communication of the trainees to be certain that the training message was understood and can be applied. Trainers should observe the following guidelines:

1. Accept the fact that body positions, facial expressions, gestures, etc., can communicate. The position of the speaker's body, hand gestures, and other non-verbal actions can communicate a message that is quite different from what is actually being said.

2. Learn to read "body language." The trainer should practice interpreting non-verbal messages. A good way to test the ability to read a person's non-verbal messages is by asking about them. The trainer may say something like, "I hear you saying that you understand what I just explained, but you seem nervous. Does your nervousness mean that you are still not completely sure about the procedure?"

3. Use acting (role playing) as a technique for training whenever appropriate to the objective. The trainer is *on stage* and is expected to perform in a rehearsed manner. This requires practice, rehearsals, and the desire to be a "star" in the training arena.

4. Practice improving gestures in front of a mirror. Many of the great communicators of the world learned how to command the attention of an audience by practicing in front of a mirror. Today's speakers often accomplish the same thing by recording their practice presentations using a closed circuit video camera, recorder, and monitor and then viewing the tape to see how their words and gestures can be improved.

5. Recognize signs of trainee boredom. Not everyone can wake up an audience by telling a good joke. Every trainer, however, must be prepared to be creative when it is necessary to recapture trainee attention. Consider how one trainer secured the drifting attention of his audience in the following Case in Point.

A Case in Point: Creating Attention

In a meeting of about 40 training professionals, a speaker who had a rather routine subject was scheduled to address the group following a large lunch. The group was nodding off and he recognized it. Suddenly, without ever breaking the pace of his presentation, he climbed up on the table at the front of the room and completed the second half of his speech standing on the table. Everyone in the audience woke up and remained alert, wondering what he would do next.

Listening   One of the key ways to detect training needs is to listen to employees. Employees will talk about those parts of their jobs that are causing them trouble—and may even say outright that they want to do the job better. At other times, employees may not be as direct. Managers may have to listen for intent rather than for what is actually being said. Listening is a skill which can be developed through practice. There are a number of techniques for improving listening which can be valuable to any manager who is preparing to be a trainer.[5]

During training sessions, managers should also listen carefully to make sure employees understand the hows and whys of the job's standard procedures. In the one-on-one training method discussed in Chapter 5, it was stressed that trainees should repeat the demonstration given by the trainer and explain the key points. The trainer must watch to see that no essential steps are *omitted* and listen to ensure that no key points are missed. Chapter 6 stressed the importance of involving the trainees in discussions, role plays, and other group training methods. As the trainees participate in these activities, the trainer should be listening—again to ensure understanding.

Listening Barriers. Listening is often ineffective because the speaker and the listener are simply not paying attention to what is being said. For one reason or another, one or both parties are bored with the communication. This frequently occurs when employees are involved in training they do not need, or where the need has not been adequately communicated. If the subject bores the trainees, other interests or problems will mentally interfere with or block out the message.

A trainer should be sensitive to signs of *boredom*. When trainees do not look at the trainer when he/she is speaking, boredom may be the cause. The best way to avoid or overcome boredom is through trainee participation. Active, rather than passive, learning presents less opportunity for boredom and results in more effective training.

Another listening barrier is a *closed mind*. This can affect a trainer as well as a trainee. Too often listeners decide beforehand what they think someone is going to say; this becomes all that is heard—regardless of the message. Some listeners simply shut off the thinking process as soon as they hear a word or a phrase that triggers a conditioned response. For example, a sanitation-conscious manager may be known as a cleaning fanatic. In his/her training sessions, every time the importance of sanitation is mentioned, the employees react by thinking "here we go again on the cleaning binge." Hence, they close their minds to everything else that is covered.

Other listeners hear only half of what is being said because they are *thinking ahead to their response* before the entire thought has been completed. When people complain that a trainer or manager never lets them finish what they are saying, never answers their questions, never shows any interest in their problems, or never pays attention to what is said, it's a good indication that these people are not hearing a great deal of what is being said.

The good listener must realize that words are used almost as often to *conceal* as to *reveal*. Failure to hear the implications of what is being said—and what was not said—can lead to misconceptions about the intent of the message. It is not enough to hear words alone. A good listener will interpret the thoughts and meanings of the words in the context of the situation, will listen for revealing silences, and will be alert to gestures and facial expressions added to the spoken words. To fully understand the message, it is important to listen not only to the words, but to the emotions behind the words.

Guidelines for Listening. Developing good listening skills is as important as developing any other training and coaching skill. Some suggestions for improving listening skills are presented here.

1. Listen with emotion and enthusiasm. It is important to be interested in and enthusiastic about the training. This includes being interested in what the trainees say. Enthusiasm is communicated by looking at the trainees, smiling pleasantly and approvingly at them, and responding to what they say. It is usually obvious when someone is listening to what is being said and is genuinely interested. Trainers cannot expect trainees to be enthusiastic when they show no interest in the trainees' feelings.

2. Know about listening speed. The average listener can register the message at a rate that is almost twice as fast as the average person speaks. This is the main reason listeners are easily bored by speakers—especially speakers who speak slowly. Trainers who know this should listen for the spoken message during half of the time and listen for the *intent* of the message the remainder of the time.

3. Listen for the speaker's (trainee's) viewpoint. Trainees who respond to training make points that they consider to be equally important. The effective trainer listens and pays close attention to these responses. Sometimes a trainee will take issue with or differ in opinion about what has been presented. The trainer should listen to what the trainee says from the trainee's viewpoint. For example, if the trainer is teaching from a written job breakdown, the job procedure may have changed since the job analysis was conducted. Also, the trainee may be pointing out that the procedure being taught will not work and/or is an unfair expectation.

4. Listen before acting. Trainers should know more about the task being taught than the trainees. Sometimes, however, trainers act as if they know everything. When trainees ask questions, some trainers may think they know what is being asked and begin answering before the trainee finishes asking the question. The same mistake can be made when trainees are speaking and the trainer thinks he/she knows what is being said, interrupts, and begins speaking before the trainee is finished. Such a rude manner will cause trainees to stop asking questions and making comments. An effective trainer listens patiently and gets all the facts before responding.

5. Listen for the message. An important part of listening is making sure there is agreement over what is being said. The trainer should listen carefully and try to understand what the trainee is saying. The trainer may need to repeat what he/she heard to check for clarity. Partial listening may cause a lack of understanding and a totally inappropriate response. Every trainer should remember that the trainee may have difficulty finding

Exhibit 13.1 Active Listening Check Sheet

Active Listening Check Sheet

Instructions: Observe the person being rated. Each time he/she exhibits an active listening behavior, make a small check mark in the appropriate "yes" column. If you feel that the behavior should have been exhibited but was not—or that the behavior was exhibited ineffectively—indicate by making a small check mark in the "no" column. If you are not sure whether a behavior contributed to the active listening process, indicate by placing a small check mark in the "not sure" column. You may mark behaviors more than once (each time observed) to show the frequency of use of each element during the observation process.

Elements of Behavior	Yes	No	Not Sure
1. Used body language to communicate interest (such as leaning forward).			
2. Used body language to show understanding (such as head nodding).			
3. Used encouraging words/phrases (such as "I see," "Uh-huh," "Yes," etc.) to encourage free flow of communication.			
4. Maintained eye contact most of the time.			
5. Used open-ended questions to encourage the other person to expand fully on his/her feelings.			
6. Listened quietly, refraining from interrupting, taking over, etc.			
7. Used the restatement technique to encourage communication.			
8. Sought clarification when statements were not totally clear.			
9. Summarized at various points in the conversation.			

---

the right words to express concerns or ask questions in areas of training that are new and unfamiliar.

6. Combat a wandering mind. Managers are busy people. When they are involved in training, they are taking time away from their other responsibilities. It is easy for them to allow their minds to wander to other areas of the operation that may need attention. If this occurs while a trainee is talking, the message will not be heard. To prevent this, the trainer should make it a practice to look the trainee in the eye and concentrate on listening for the message and its intent.

7. Keep an unprejudiced viewpoint. Prejudice is a general barrier to communication. Simply stated, it is a prejudgment based on ideas and information taken out of context from a specific situation and applied to a general situation. Avoid prejudging any employee.

The development of active listening skills requires practice in those behaviors that accompany the active listening process. Exhibit 13.1 presents a chart for scoring a trainer on listening skills. When learning to train, managers might use this form to assess the listening skills of their trainers. As these same managers become trainers, they can use the form for self-evaluation. This would be best accomplished by having a colleague sit in on training sessions, observe the communication process, and fill out the form as feedback for the trainer. The person completing the form should check each behavior whenever it occurs so that the trainer will know the frequency of each listening skill.

Obstacles to Effective Communication

Many factors can interfere with the communication process. When training, barriers to communication may become barriers to learning. Therefore, every effort should be made to avoid, prevent, or overcome such obstacles. A review of some of the more common obstacles is presented here.

Language Barriers

The international scope of the hospitality industry attracts many employees whose first language is something other than English. Many hospitality managers throughout the world are fluent in English, but many non-management employees are not. Special training problems can arise when a manager is not fluent in the languages spoken by the staff. Translators may be used but they slow down the training process and remove much of the control of the learning process from the manager. It may be necessary to print training materials in a bilingual format to convey the expectations, procedures, and standards. The special obstacles surrounding language barriers require special efforts by the manager to accomplish the training task. Consider, for example, the steps undertaken by a hospitality operation in the following Case in Point.

A Case in Point: Korean Cabin Stewards

A new luxury cruise ship hired much of its crew through employment agencies in various countries. Employment specifications provided to each agency included a requirement that all cabin stewards be skilled in spoken and written English. Despite this, 16 cabin stewards with limited language abilities were hired through a Korean agent. These employees had such a narrow command of English that the chief steward was unable to conduct the pre-opening training sessions he had planned.

The training had been designed by an on-board training consultant. The consultant was informed of the problem and asked to assist the chief steward in overcoming the language barrier. First, a meeting was scheduled with the chief steward and the 16 Koreans. Soft drinks were served to ease the tension; most of the cabin stewards were afraid that they were going to be sent back home. The consultant began talking informally to the group, not sure whether any of the Koreans understood what he was saying. He smiled warmly as he spoke and tried to convey a feeling of genuine concern for the welfare of the frustrated Koreans.

Fortunately, the consultant had traveled in Korea on several occasions. He began to talk about his impressions of some of the finer hotels in Seoul as well as some of the country's historic landmarks. As he mentioned these places, he could see in the non-verbal reactions of the group that some of his message was getting through. Suddenly, one of the Koreans politely interrupted him, and stated in fluent English, "My home is Seoul." The consultant asked, "Do you have family there?" The Korean steward responded, "Yes, I have a wife and two children." The consultant inquired further about each family member. In a few moments, a second Korean joined in and began to talk about his family and the hotels in which he had worked. The remainder of the group began to smile and show even more non-verbal signs of interest in what was being discussed.

As it turned out, all the Koreans spoke *some* English, but only the two who entered the conversation were reasonably fluent. The consultant explained to these two the need to communicate for training, and emphasized how much work the chief steward had done in preparing to be their teacher. The two stewards who spoke good English suggested dividing the Koreans into two groups of eight for training. The English-speaking stewards would then serve as translators for the other trainees. This recommendation was followed and the training was completed.

The consultant remained on board for seven days following this incident. There was considerable improvement in the English language skills of all the Koreans during this relatively short period. It appeared that the Koreans had received some training in English, but because they had not had the opportunity to use their skills, they had not developed confidence in their abilities.

Physical Obstacles

Most hospitality training sessions occur on the premises of an operating lodging or food service facility. The noise caused by refrigeration compressors, mixers and grinders, fans, exhaust equipment, background music, computer printers, telephones, etc., can interfere with a trainee's hearing. Whenever possible, training which must occur in these noisy areas should be scheduled during quiet periods. When not possible, it is important to limit training to one-on-one situations or very small groups.

Discomfort associated with the job being taught or the makeshift classroom which must be used is another physical obstacle. In food service, the ability to take inventory of the foodstuffs in the walk-in freezer must be mastered. It may be difficult to hold the attention of trainees for very long at freezing temperatures. Many of the principles should be covered before entering or after leaving the freezer; conversation in the freezer should be kept short and strictly to the point.

When groups are trained in a restaurant dining room or lounge, lighting is often inadequate. Dim lighting may be ideal for romantic dining or drinking, but it is not conducive to effective training. Whenever possible, training should be conducted in brightly lit areas to enhance communications.

Trainee fatigue can also create a communication barrier. This can result when trainees work a full shift before training or when a training session lasts too long. It may also happen when second or third shift personnel are required to come in during the day shift for the training sessions. People who work nights become accustomed to sleeping during the day, so it is hard for them to stay awake for training sessions under these conditions. To resolve these problems, the trainer should use a variety of training methods (especially after lunch or dinner) to adjust the pace. He/she should also schedule a variety of training times to meet the needs of each individual. Small group or other participative learning activities which involve employees are especially helpful. Breaks should be frequent—and can be short. Any outside distractions, such as telephone calls or similar interruptions, should be minimized.

Sociological Differences

Entry-level non-management employees sometimes have limited formal educational backgrounds. A barrier to communication exists when the trainer speaks at a level which the trainees do not understand. When the language of the trainer is too complicated or is filled with large words, the trainees may "tune out." Trainees can also block out training when the trainer fails to recognize their cultural heritage or differences. It is important to know as much as possible about trainees and to respect their backgrounds.

A tense atmosphere may exist when trainees feel threatened by the trainer or by the presence of upper level management or corporate personnel at the session. This problem may be overcome if attendees are assured at the beginning of the session that they are free to challenge any question and to contribute their comments and ideas. Other suggestions to reduce tenseness are: (a) allow time for discussion, (b) avoid having superiors and subordinates at the same session, and (c) let the trainees know what is expected of them during the training session.

Intervention

Trainees themselves can create obstacles to communication. They may interrupt the trainer as explanations are being given, or they may speak to points not being addressed by the trainer. These and similar types of interventions make concentration very difficult for the trainer. In this situation, a trainer may be tempted to digress from the main topic and discuss topics not originally planned.

Trainers can adopt techniques to prevent unproductive interventions. For a start, trainers can establish some ground rules at the beginning of the training session. Speaking privately with "problem" trainees during a break may also be helpful. These types of problems are more likely to occur when trainees do not clearly understand the training objectives. A trainee who is uncertain about the intent of the training may interrupt because he/she feels that the trainer is not "training."

Some trainees become excited in a training session and may be overzealous to participate and be heard. These trainees are very important because they remind the trainer that adult *learners need to participate*. If the training objectives are made quite clear, and if the trainees are encouraged to participate in *ways that relate directly to the objectives*, such enthusiasm can become an aid to the trainer.

Resistance to Change   Often the greatest single barrier to communication is resistance to change. Some people resist and resent change; when confronted with it they will resist as long as possible. To overcome this barrier, the trainer must sell the positive benefits of the training to the resistant trainees. He/she must describe how trainees will personally benefit through better working conditions, easier work, better pay, more opportunities for self-satisfaction, or whatever meets their personal needs.

Nothing is necessarily wrong with the training, the trainer, or the trainee when a trainee rejects the training. Resistance to change is a learned behavior that is developed over many years of conditioning. This resistance can be overcome through patience and reason in dealing with the trainee.

Personal Distractions   Employees come to work, spend eight hours on the job, and then leave. It is not possible for them to block out their personal problems, family concerns, and outside interests during the time they are at work or in a training session. Most of the time these outside concerns, feelings, and worries will not interfere with work. There are times, however, when personal distractions can make it impossible for an employee to concentrate. These personal distractions affect an employee's training by acting as barriers to the communication between the trainer and the trainee.

An insensitive, thoughtless trainer may attempt to order or direct the employee to keep his/her mind on the job and on the training. Such an approach often creates further disinterest in learning. A sensitive trainer who is interested in human development and is determined to increase productivity will take time to counsel the employee or recommend that he/she seek professional counseling. Until these outside distractions are resolved, it will be difficult for effective learning to occur.

Talking Before Thinking   Everyone is guilty at one time or another of "putting one's mouth into gear before engaging one's mind." As a result, things are said that do not make good sense or that should have been left unsaid. Planning is the best way to prevent this from occurring in a training session. A well-planned training session includes a mental rehearsal of (a) what will be said, (b) how it will be said, and (c) a review of the lesson plan, job breakdowns, and any other written materials or training aids to help the speaker keep his/her mind on the subject.

Jumping to Conclusions   Another barrier to effective communication occurs when assumptions are made on the basis of inadequate facts. This situation is generally referred to as "jumping to conclusions." For example, if a trainer sees a trainee perform a procedure incorrectly during a training session, he/she might assume that the trainee totally misunderstood the procedure. The trainer may then ask the trainee to stop, go back to the beginning, and explain and demonstrate the entire process again. It would be better to ask the trainee whether he/she understood the procedure or why the procedure was being performed incorrectly. The trainee may have had a good reason for changing the procedure. For example, he/she may have performed the procedure correctly a number of times but wanted to do it differently one time to be sure that the method being taught was actually better.

Wishful Hearing

Managers want their employees to succeed. They also want training to be done quickly, since it is expensive and competes with other responsibilities for the limited amount of available time.

As trainers, managers are often guilty of explaining a procedure and asking such questions as "You understand this completely, don't you?" The employee may then answer "Yes, I understand," because to answer otherwise makes the employee feel like a slow learner. The trainer has heard what he/she wanted to hear but not what needed to be heard in order to accurately judge the employee's level of understanding.

Being Secretive

Many managers maintain a degree of aloofness in dealing with employees, keeping certain information confidential. An example of confidential information is that related to profit and costs. By failing to recognize that employees who are better informed about costs can help reduce those costs, managers convey a degree of distrust and superiority toward employees. If employees perceive this as "second-class" treatment, it becomes a definite barrier to communication and to relations between managers and employees.

Prejudice

Prejudice refers to an attitude created by a group which causes an individual to prejudge another individual, group, thing, or situation. Most persons are familiar with prejudices related to skin color, race, religion, creed, national origin, sex, or social status.

There are many manifestations of prejudice. Prejudice can be expressed in such behaviors as name-calling, scapegoating, ridiculing, downgrading, excluding, rejecting, discriminating, antagonizing, being hostile, and showing violence toward a group. The way to overcome prejudices that block communication is to look at the facts which clear up misconceptions that people have about other people.

These facts can be addressed openly in groups, using team-building or problem-solving techniques. These groups should include people who hold the prejudices as well as the people who have been prejudged. The first few sessions might be very strained. The tension may remain until all participants realize that the situation is designed to overcome communication barriers and to enhance personal growth and development.

If managers harbor prejudices against employees, the prejudices will interfere with communication and reduce their ability to train and coach. People can also be prejudiced *for* certain groups or things. Managers may be prejudiced in favor of a management career and may view non-management personnel as unambitious or lazy. Such beliefs will block communication and learning. Not all employees desire to be managers or should become managers. They can find satisfaction in their positions if they are treated with dignity and respect.

Unorganized Materials

When the trainer's material is not well organized, a communication barrier is established. Trainees will not listen or will become frustrated if they don't understand. Trainers should organize their presentation so that complex ideas are separated into simple components. The job breakdowns will help the trainer do this.

Good organization will help communication and can be accomplished by (a) providing an overview of what the trainees will learn, (b) providing necessary detail, (c) allowing time for practice or other necessary activities, and (d) providing the trainees with a summary of what was taught.

Notes

1. Clark Lambert, *The Complete Book of Supervisory Training* (New York: Wiley, 1984), p. 274.
2. L. Ron Hubbard, *Basic Study Manual* (Los Angeles: Applied Scholastics, Inc., 1975), p. 8.
3. For example: William Strunk, Jr. and E. B. White, *The Elements of Style*, 3rd ed. (New York: Macmillan, 1979), and William Zinsser, *On Writing Well*, 2nd ed. (New York: Harper & Row, 1980).
4. Jerome J. Vallen and James R. Abbey, *The Art and Science of Hospitality Management* (East Lansing, Mich.: The Educational Institute of the American Hotel & Motel Association, 1987), pp. 160–161.
5. Lyman K. Steil, Larry K. Barker, and Kittie W. Watson, *Effective Listening: Key to Your Success* (Reading, Mass.: Addison-Wesley, 1983).

14 Attitudes and Motivation

Having a trained and motivated staff is a primary management goal. When trainees put into action what they have learned, managers feel proud because they see a motivated work group that displays good attitudes toward the job. They view the training as successful. When trainees fail to do what they have been trained to do, managers not only believe that training has failed but also that the trainees are unmotivated and have bad attitudes.

The level of staff motivation and the effectiveness of training are related. Trainers must be aware of the importance of attitudes and motivation to learning and performance. They must know what can be done to influence behavior, what causes good or bad attitudes, and what factors motivate employees to perform their jobs. Understanding motivation is important in the design and implementation of training for two reasons. First, managers themselves need to be personally motivated to support training efforts. Second, managers must be able to direct the motivation of the trainees toward the successful achievement of training goals.[1]

Attitudes and Training

An **attitude** is the predisposition or tendency of a person to react in a preset way toward an object, situation, person, or value. Attitudes are usually accompanied by feelings and emotions. For example, an employee's reaction to an irate guest may be influenced by the environment and his/her past experiences with other guests.

Attitudes are formed in different ways in different people. While there is some evidence of factors which affect attitude development, there are no hard and fast rules. The study of attitudes and how they are formed and influenced is a complex subject. Trainers and other managers must have a basic grasp of how attitudes can be influenced. A good manager can create and maintain positive attitudes in his/her staff and use the positive effects of these attitudes to meet required performance standards. A manager has to try different approaches to leading people in order to find the most effective formula for each individual.

An individual's personality and attitudes begin to develop early in life and are influenced by hereditary and environmental factors. By the time an individual reaches the age of employment, his/her attitudes are probably quite set. Managers and supervisors are, in effect, faced with the task of leading people who "are what they are." It becomes very difficult to modify employees' attitudes even though changes might improve job performance and training effectiveness.

Norms and Behaviors

Norms can be defined as shared group expectations. They represent expected behaviors. For example, managers expect certain behaviors from employees. As employees become aware of these expectations and as they accept the expectations as reasonable for the group, the expectations become norms against which future behavior in that group is judged. In the following Case in Point, consider how the employees respond to the norms established by one hospitality operation.

A Case in Point: Employees Like Rules

In a new hotel company, it was decided to develop a detailed list of employee rules of conduct before the first property was opened. These rules of conduct were divided into major offenses which would result in immediate suspension pending investigation. Termination of employment could also result if the investigation provided clear evidence that the rule was broken without any justifiable cause. The second category consisted of offenses that were less severe in nature. If an employee broke a rule in this second category, he/she would receive a written warning, and could be suspended or terminated if the violation were repeated. The total list contained nine major rules of conduct and twenty-four less severe rules, for a total of thirty-three very specific conduct rules.

One year after each of the first two hotels were opened, attitude surveys were completed by all of the employees in each property. The employees' level of satisfaction and dissatisfaction was assessed as it related to twenty-three aspects of their jobs and working conditions, including the rules of conduct. Factors such as pay, the bonus program, training opportunities, and insurance programs were also covered by the surveys. The surveys revealed that the highest level of employee satisfaction in each hotel was with the list of employee conduct rules.

Employees like knowing exactly what is expected of them in terms of their behavior. In general terms, behavior is classified as good or bad based upon the extent to which it approximates the expected behavior. Good behavior is that which is consistent with the norms of the group or society, and is sometimes referred to as **normative behavior.**

Behavior that is in opposition to or differs significantly from the norms of the group or society is sometimes labeled as *abnormal*—or *deviant—behavior*. In its simplest form, it constitutes *non-normative behavior* and is actually nothing more than behavior that differs from that which is generally accepted. Non-normative behavior is generally regarded as "bad behavior." In this sense, bad behavior is behavior that differs from the norm. This type of unacceptable behavior is often credited to a bad attitude.

The Impact of Expectations

A norm has been defined as a group-shared expectation. A set of expected behaviors can be associated either with a certain situation or with a given position in the social structure. For example, all employees are expected to report for work on time. Certain employees are expected to report in uniform while others are expected to change into their uniforms after they arrive at work. Still others are allowed to work in their own clothing. The key to understanding norms is understanding **the impact of expectations.** The expectations that a manager has for an employee, or that a trainer has for a trainee, can override personality and deep-seated attitudes to cause the employee or trainee to perform according to normative behavior standards.

Managers and trainers who fail to grasp the significance of the preceding statement will have little success in modifying the effects of attitudes on employee behavior. Conversely, those who do understand its meaning will begin to see how to modify attitudes brought to the job. The statement provides much of the basis for effective management, training, coaching, supervision, and leadership. Said another way, employees (or trainees) tend to behave as they perceive they are expected to behave by those individuals they consider important. As one researcher states:

> One person's expectations of another person's behavior strongly affects what that other person does. When we hold expectations regarding someone else, our expectations can subtly, but powerfully, serve as an interpersonal self-fulfilling prophecy. This fact can be observed and has been documented in a variety of settings. It is possible, moreover, for managers to create high performance expectations and get better results from those whom they supervise.[2]

When expected performance standards are established and become norms, they will be identified with a situation, no matter who the employees may be at a given time. For example, housekeeping room attendants (and all other employees) in hotels are expected not to steal guest property. This norm is shared by guests, the hotel management team, and the staff of the housekeeping department. Therefore, most guests feel confident to leave their property in the hotel room while they are out. For the same reason, hotel managers feel confident in providing room attendants with pass keys to enter guestrooms without direct supervision. The norm—do not steal from the guestroom—dictates the behavior of the guest, the management, and the room attendants in the situation. An isolated violation does not change the norm. Rather, it is treated as a deviation from the norm (non-normative behavior). In this case, the room attendant would be removed from the situation and the norm (expected behavior) would continue to apply.

Of course, not everyone in any situation abides by all the norms all the time, and no norm is always followed. If everyone always did the "right" thing at the "right" time and place, there would be no need for rules or laws, or negative consequences for non-normative behavior. Not all norms—or even most of them—are written down or formalized as laws or regulations. Managers share many informal understandings with employees. There may be no written rule that says an employee should say "excuse me" when he/she bumps a guest, or that an employee should offer to pick up an object dropped by a guest, or that employees should say "thank you" when complimented by a guest. Yet, most people have learned these expectations; they become part of the normative behavior that applies in any situation. Most employees conform to them most of the time.

Perception

A **perception** is an understanding that is generated through one or more of the senses, usually seeing or hearing. For example, when a manager explains job expectations to an employee, the extent to which the employee understands the expectations becomes his/her perception of what the job involves. A critical part of understanding normative behavior involves the individual employee's perception of the expected behavior. When an employee is corrected for deviation from a norm and responds, "I know you said that, but I thought you meant . . .," then the employee's perception of the expected behavior differed from that of the manager. In this situation the employee may argue "I heard you but I didn't understand." If the employee did actually perceive a different expected behavior, his/her perception would have affected the subsequent performance.

Three principles relate expected behavior to managing and specifically to training and coaching:

1. The manager's expectations must be communicated to employees and accepted and shared by them if the expectations are to become the basis for judging normative behavior.

2. The employees' perceptions of the manager's expected behavior dictate how well the expectations will be met.

3. Training and coaching are management activities designed to communicate expected behavior patterns and clarify perceptions. When this is done, normative behavior for every area of job performance will become the basis for evaluating individuals as they perform their jobs.

While lodging and food service managers should understand that an employee's personality and attitudes are largely shaped before the individual enters the work force, they should also know that there are some techniques which can be used to modify behavior. With proper knowledge of these techniques, managers can modify, provide direction for, and otherwise influence employee attitudes and the related behaviors.

Sanctions

Sanctions are the rewards and punishments that may be used to bring about or enforce the expected normative behavior in a situation.

For example, managers may praise (positive sanction) or threaten (negative sanction) employees. Rewards are made when employees perform according to expectations; punishment may occur when expected behavior patterns are not met. Rewards and punishments range from the use of physical force (generally not acceptable) to symbolic means such as flattery (a symbolic reward) or shunning (a symbolic punishment).

Dismissal from a job is a form of punishment that may be both symbolic and physical. For example, a situation involving a room attendant who steals a guest's garment might be handled differently in different areas of the world. In some countries, the guilty employee might be legally sentenced to severe physical punishment. If prosecuted in the United States, the employee might receive a sentence ranging from probation to a prison term of a few years (depending on past record and the leniency of the court). Most operations would not prosecute the employee—especially if the guest's property could be returned unharmed; the punishment would be limited to dismissal from employment. In some properties, it is even possible that the employee would not be dismissed, but would only be asked to return the garment with an apology to the guest.

Rewards and punishments vary in degree from situation to situation. They are used to force or persuade an individual or group to conform to the expectations. Sanctions influence people to accept the group norms, and to exhibit normative behavior.

Sanctions and Power
The application of sanctions to gain compliance with expected behavior implies the use of power. Power may be applied to positive or negative sanctions. Managers have formal power and are expected to apply rewards or punishments in an effort to influence the employees' behavior. Managers represent formal leadership and have the power to enforce their perceptions of expected behavior. The use of this power will vary greatly in form and intensity since situations differ, as do the managers themselves. A simple description of management power is built into the widely used definition of management: "the ability to get work done through other people." Consider how the "power of suggestion" works to effect change in one employee in the following Case in Point.

A Case in Point: Laundry Lethargy

Through her office doorway, the executive housekeeper in a 350-room hotel could observe the staff working in the laundry. She noticed that one of the laundry attendants, Arthur, was removing terry cloth items from the dryer, and placing the clean laundry items in a laundry cart. Arthur was removing towels slowly one at a time, using only one hand while the other hand rested on the laundry cart. The executive housekeeper went into the laundry and explained to Arthur that he could do the job much faster by using both hands, and by removing the towels directly to the folding table so they could be sorted, folded, and smoothed while they were still warm. Arthur politely thanked the executive housekeeper for the suggestion. He then simply stated that he had always done the job this way at the hotel across the street before he had come to work at this hotel six weeks ago. He further stated that he was sure he could not get the hang of doing the job in a different way.

The executive housekeeper considered ordering Arthur to perform the work in the manner she had described. But, she caught herself and walked away. She went into the storeroom and began straightening up some containers of guestroom supplies. As she worked, she felt frustrated but continued to think about the situation. She had hired Arthur when the department was extremely understaffed. Because of his extensive experience in laundry operations, she had abbreviated his orientation and skipped his training. She had merely put him to work. Until today, she had made no attempt to clarify her expectations or standards.

The executive housekeeper was determined to immediately correct her short-sightedness. She returned to the laundry, planning to apologize to Arthur for neglecting his training and tell him she planned to put him through the usual training for new hires. But when she entered the laundry, she found Arthur folding the warm linens on the folding table, using both hands—just like she had suggested. In spite of his verbal resistance, he had responded to the expectations expressed by his new employer.

There is an old saying that "you can catch more flies with honey than with vinegar." The manager's requirements of expected behavior must be achieved, but power must take an approach that makes effective use of positive human relations skills. Effective managerial use of power is demonstrated in persuasive and influential forms of leadership; physical force, dictatorial demands, and threats are inappropriate uses of management power.

Purposes of Sanctions

The basic purposes for using rewards and punishments are to bring about conformity, uniformity, and continuity of the work group. Managers want employees to do what they have been taught to do, over and over again, with consistency of speed, accuracy, quality, and hospitality. Sanctions help ensure that staff members will exhibit normative behavior patterns in their work. Predictable employee performance is essential to meeting goals and achieving productivity. The control and regulation of behavior through the use of rewards and punishments can actually make it possible to predict behavior. Both management and employees must know what the employees should do in their jobs (expected performance) and what the consequences will be if they fail to perform as expected.

Types of Sanctions

There are a number of rewards and punishments managers can use to achieve operational objectives. Most social interactions take the form of words and gestures rather than physical contact. Managers might pat an employee on the back, shake an employee's hand, or even hug an employee; however, the range of interaction possible through talking, writing, and using body gestures is much wider. A word can encourage or threaten because most of us are conditioned to relate words to actions. Consider a word like *stop.* It is clearly understood and quickly brings about the desired results.

Some spoken or written communications may be directed toward stopping ongoing or anticipated behavior. Others may encourage an employee to do more or to strive for better quality. Pleasant and positive examples of communication which can influence behavior include praise, flattery, persuasion, slogans, propaganda, and tangible objects.

Negative spoken and written communications can also be used to influence and control behavior. Consider, for example, gossip, satire, name-calling, commands, or threats. A brief discussion of these positive and negative communication tools will clarify their use.

Positive Sanctions

Praise and Flattery. Praise can be very effective when it is given by a manager to an employee. It often causes that employee to respect and try to please the manager. Flattery is undue, exaggerated, and somewhat false praise. It is frequently used when dealing with a person whose job status is superior to the person's doing the flattering. Flattery appeals directly to one's ego and can be effective in situations where prestige plays a part in control. In food service, for example, managers often flatter the chef to entice him/her to produce another artistic "pièce de résistance."

Persuasion. Persuasion is a form of suggestion. Managers may try to explain the "why" of training. When they do this they are using sales skills. Managers must explain, justify, and define the benefits or positive consequences of "doing it the right way" to employees.

Slogans. Slogans help define situations and can be used to direct behavior along desired lines. They are guideposts that can lead a group toward its objectives. Hospitality operations may develop slogans such as "We're the best," or "We really try," in order to communicate their intentions and expectations to employees and guests.

Propaganda. Propaganda, like indoctrination and advertising, conditions employees to act along lines which they like (or imagine that they like). Individuals may then want to do the things suggested for them. Managers may, for example, suggest to employees that "We can be the best in town!" Employees may then strive to meet that challenge. Advertising may support the campaign. New employees will be indoctrinated to the theme and the challenge. Some hospitality operations regularly develop campaigns designed to influence employee and guest attitudes through positive and harmless propaganda, indoctrination, and advertising.

Tangible Objects. Tangible objects can be used to reward behavior. Tangible rewards can be unexpected benefits such as a day off with pay, or a monetary bonus for doing an exceptional job. Badges are external symbols that can accompany a slogan campaign. Badges may also recognize a particular employee for outstanding performance.

Medals are usually more permanent than badges and may be used to reward good performance. When an employee wears a badge or medal that recognizes individual performance, it has a valuable control effect on the recipient and, more subtly, on all other employees who come in contact with the recipient. Other tangible symbols are uniforms and organizational insignia. The employee tends to live up to the behavior that is expected of him/her while the uniform is being worn.

Negative Sanctions

Gossip. Gossip (often unfounded rumor) may be harmless but it is sometimes used to control an individual. Nobody is perfect, but gossip has a way of accentuating petty matters until they become the focus of attention. Gossip leads to myths and helps formulate a group's opinions about the target of the gossip. Gossip by managers about an employee is unprofessional and should not be used as a means to control behavior. Gossip among employees about a fellow worker should be discouraged. Gossip disrupts morale, and has a negative effect on the motivation of the person who is the target of the gossip.

Satire. Satire is a sarcastic combination of humor and critical logic. It is most commonly seen in a work environment when employees or managers mimic the non-normative work habits of an employee who is having performance difficulties. It is a method of exposing the weaknesses of the employee in a way which makes him/her feel uncomfortable. Satire is generally unpleasant and is a form of laughing at others. The person who is being laughed at is set apart from the group psychologically and generally feels inferior to the rest of the group. The target of the satire can lose his/her sense of belonging. The employee may feel lonely, unattached, and insecure while at work. Such an employee may no longer feel a need to participate in meeting the group goals even though he/she is still physically part of the group. This type of punishment may achieve an immediate goal of drawing attention to an employee's non-normative performance. However, it is likely to lead to more serious problems if carried too far and is not recommended as a means of influencing desired behaviors.

Name-Calling. People often give each other nicknames or labels to emphasize certain characteristics or to draw attention to the way an individual performs in particular situations. Negative name-calling makes the target feel inferior or different. For example, a manager or work group may label a slow employee "pokey" or "goof-off" in an effort to draw attention to the individual's slowness. They think that such labeling will result in the targeted employee working harder and faster to overcome the label. Such name-calling can cause the group's expectations for the staff member to be lower than for other group members. Since employees perform according to how they feel the group expects them to, name-calling may have the effect of increasing the problem rather than decreasing it. Name-calling is unprofessional, and is inappropriate in a work environment where dignity is respected and protected. Even attempts at positive name-calling or labeling such as "superstar" or "whiz kid" is potentially destructive since it creates unhealthy competition within the group, sets unrealistic expectations, and communicates favoritism.

Commands. Commands are a direct form of ordering or forbidding an action. They are generally a very effective way to control actions through words. The command may be a positive order to do something or a negative statement forbidding an action. Commands represent direct power. They display more authority than satire or name-calling. In a business environment, managers have the authority to give commands. Employees will usually respond favorably to clear, fair commands. Unfair commands will be met with open resistance since most employees will regard them as violations of their dignity and rights.

Threats. Threats are severe punishments. For threats to be effective, they must be backed by the appearance of "power to take action." If a threat does not result in a change of behavior, the employee must be punished as threatened. Threats are distinctive carriers of emotions and have great potential power. Threats put two alternatives before the employee. The employee must do as told or accept the negative consequences.

Managers are often tempted to combine commands and threats in order to display their power. They may even command employees to exhibit a particular attitude and then threaten to punish the employee if they do not see evidence of the prescribed attitude. This unprofessional approach is based on a total lack of understanding of attitudes and their relationship to feelings and emotions.

Use of Sanctions

If expected behavior is clear to both managers and employees, rewards will have the effect of bringing out the best in employees. Employees will generally do their jobs well and enjoy doing them. They will display good attitudes about the work when they find that desirable and valuable rewards accompany the correct performance.

If punishments are applied, the work may still be done. Employees may meet the expectations but will generally dislike their jobs. In turn, they are likely to display negative behaviors and attitudes. Employees come to a job with their own set of attitudes developed by their experiences, environment, and heredity. Managers need to establish patterns of normative behavior and put rewards or punishments in place that bring out the best in employees. Rarely can managers develop a brand new attitude. However, an attitude can be affected by the work environment. A positive work environment brings out positive attitudes; negative influences promote negative attitudes and encourage behavior which is unacceptable or deviates from the norm. Consider how a careful manager preserves the attitude and motivation of an employee in the following Case in Point.

A Case in Point: Lovable Ms. Lundy

Ms. Lundy was the executive housekeeper's administrative assistant. She got along well with the employees in the housekeeping department. Actually, employees seemed to idolize Ms. Lundy because if a job needed doing, and she was in the area, she would quickly undertake it herself—even to the point of making beds, mopping floors, and in some instances, restocking linen closets on the hotel's four floors.

However, Ms. Lundy had been having difficulty getting her administrative responsibilities completed on time and had not been following through on the individual training plans of new employees. Furthermore, there had been several guest comments in the past few weeks about cleaning deficiencies in their rooms. Ms. Lundy was also responsible for overseeing the three housekeeping supervisors who inspected all cleaned guestrooms.

The executive housekeeper was concerned about how to increase Ms. Lundy's effectiveness—without destroying her positive attitude, her relationship with the employees, and her motivation. He decided to start with the written job performance standards for Ms. Lundy's position.

Ms. Lundy had held her position nearly eight years. Her human resources file contained a training checklist which showed that she had been trained in all her job duties when she was first hired—but that the executive housekeeper had changed numerous times over that same period. In fact, the current executive housekeeper had only been in his position for three months.

The job performance standards clearly stated what Ms. Lundy was expected to do in her administrative assignments and the criteria for evaluating performance. The executive housekeeper met with Ms. Lundy and began by asking her if she had ever seen the list of job performance standards. As Ms. Lundy read over the list, she looked embarrassed. "I guess I haven't been doing my job," she said, "if this is what you expect me to be doing." Then she went on. "I remember we covered all this many years ago in training, but there sure hasn't been much said about it since. Of course, I do most of these things, but I was not aware of how important they were to my job. I was only trying to help and keep the rest of the housekeeping staff happy with their jobs. But I guess I could have lost my job for not doing what I was supposed to do. I'll sure try to do better. Do you suppose I could have a copy of this list? I'd like to study it some more and keep it on my desk as a checklist to keep me straight until I'm satisfied that I have my job under control."

The executive housekeeper reassured Ms. Lundy that her job was not in jeopardy, and gave her a copy of the standards. Ms. Lundy returned to her desk, carefully reading and rereading the list. The very thought that she could have lost her job by doing good while leaving more important matters undone had given her quite a jolt. She began immediately to put her job back on track.

Motivation and Motivational Factors

What is the most powerful way to motivate employees? What is it that makes an employee exert extra effort and strive for excellence in performance? What makes an employee want to become an award-winning chef? What keeps a dishwasher or room attendant smiling for years as he/she washes the same dishes or cleans the same rooms over and over? These are the kinds of questions that every hospitality manager must consider. The more effective the manager is in motivating the staff, the more successful the manager will be.

Motivation can be defined as an individual's desire to do something based upon a perceived or actual need.[3] Motivation is the result of a need to receive some satisfaction or gratification. Once the gratification is experienced, the level of motivation remains "in neutral" until the need is felt again.

The most powerful motivator of all is very difficult to understand since it is neither visible nor exactly alike in any two employees. This powerful motivator is the *value* and *worth* that an employee feels as the result of personal accomplishments and efforts. There are many ways that managers can help employees see the importance of what they are doing. That assistance begins with good employee training and an understanding of the following motivational factors.[4]

"Know-How"   Employees need to know how to properly perform the job they are hired to do. They cannot be expected to do this with enthusiasm when they have never been trained to do the job correctly. Without training, the employee is left to experiment and to survive by trial and error; in doing so, the employee will make a lot of mistakes. The mistakes provide negative feedback to the employee about his/her own worth. They also help to develop negative attitudes about the job, the employer, and guests. Employees who experience these negative, frustrated feelings often leave the job and seek employment in a more satisfying environment. Turnover is extremely high in the hospitality industry; one major cause for high turnover is failure to train employees.

Training for Promotion. Knowing the job goes beyond an understanding of basic job requirements. Employees are more highly motivated when they are able to train for promotion. This involves learning the skills of a higher level job while filling a lower position. This system only works if the employee knows that he/she will be given fair consideration for promotion when a position at the higher level becomes vacant.

Cross-Training. Cross-training creates another type of "know-how" which motivates employees. Many employees become bored performing the same tasks over and over. Through cross-training, employees develop a fuller understanding of the demands placed upon co-workers, and can rotate to different jobs to avoid boredom. Of course, if the rotation involves positions with different wage scales, the employee should be paid according to the work performed at each station. Since it would be an administrative problem to change wage rates as employees rotate, a better system might be to average the various wage rates and establish a new rate for a "rotating employee" or a "cross-utilized employee." This approach can cause problems if managers use an employee to perform more jobs on upper wage scales than on lower wage scales; it then becomes an unfair way of underpaying an employee.

Involvement   Involved employees are motivated employees. This means that decisions should be made through group processes when possible. Employees need to feel that they belong to a group. A job has to be more than "a place to work." It has to afford opportunity for the individual to contribute to the goals of the organization while feeling like an important part of the team. The creative manager will find many opportunities for involving employees. For example, employees can provide assistance in preparing job lists, job breakdowns, and job performance standards. Chapter 15 provides further information about involving employees in team-building activities.

Achievement   Employees need to succeed. Trainers must assess the individual potential of each employee and then train and coach that employee to be a success. The successes of every employee should be recognized both through group and special individual recognition. While every success cannot be noted, the overall endeavors of each employee should not go unnoticed. Training and coaching are conducted for the purpose of increasing and improving individual and group performance. Failure to recognize the improved performance that results from those efforts communicates a lack of sincerity by managers and a general disregard for the employees' achievements.

Achievement is also rewarded by promotion or wage increases. Employees keep score of their achievements by the various ways that they feel recognized. Intangible recognition—such as praise and compliments from managers, fellow employees, and guests—goes a long way in filling a score card. However, tangible recognition—such as a raise, a bonus, or a promotion—is also important in developing positive feelings of personal worth. There must be a balance between both types of recognition in order to adequately reinforce good performance and achievement.

Meaningful Work   Motivation is not something that a manager does so that employees will "come to work motivated." Motivation must be viewed as an outgrowth of meaningful work. For work to have meaning it must be designed to challenge the employee. Then the employee must be trained to master the challenge. The worker without job skills and knowledge is not able to meet the normative behavior patterns which are outlined for him/her. The results will be unacceptable behavior, a poor attitude, and high turnover.

Managers may not know how to make some jobs meaningful. Jobs that managers generally perceive as falling into this category include dishwashing, cleaning rooms, and janitorial functions. In failing to realize that such jobs can be meaningful, managers may communicate through their words and actions that they do not expect much from employees in these positions. In turn, employees may start to view themselves as "second-class citizens." They begin to believe that their work is meaningless, and that they are worthless to the operation.

Every job that accomplishes goals is important. Managers can overcome biases against certain jobs by taking several steps:

- Analyze every job. Write down what a person must do in order to perform the job effectively. Ask employees who perform the jobs for their ideas about what is important as the jobs are done. Set performance standards for the jobs that establish quality and quantity factors which help in evaluating job performance. This process will point out the scope, meaning, and complexity of each job.

- Get to know the employees who perform the jobs. Visit with them at work and take an interest in them. Try to understand their goals. Managers may be surprised to learn that most of the employees they supervise do not aspire to be managers. Most employees are realistic, practical people and recognize that aspiring to be a manager would be unrealistic. If employees enjoy the work they do—in part because managers help them to—they will feel that their contributions are important and will strive to do a good job.

- Train and retrain. Take time to develop a high level of competence in each employee. Through training, the employees will become fully aware that their jobs are important and that there are performance standards which managers expect to be met.

Responsibility   A manager should look for ways to design jobs that make employees responsible for results. For example, front desk employees can be responsible for the average room rate for their shift; food service personnel can be responsible for the quality and timeliness of food which is produced. Results of these efforts can be defined with employee involvement; feedback can be provided by managers (through various operating reports) and by guests (through comment cards or other techniques used to assess guest reaction to the products/services provided by the operation).

Feedback   Feedback is a process whereby employees are informed as to how well they perform. There are four types of feedback:

1. Positive feedback recognizes a job well done. Positive feedback maintains and enhances future performance.

2. Re-directive feedback recognizes incorrect performance and reviews the original expected behavior, what went wrong, and how the employee can improve.

3. Negative feedback critically recognizes incorrect performance. Negative feedback will not improve performance and generally serves to "de-motivate" an employee.

4. Zero feedback is the lack of feedback; performance will generally decline when no feedback is provided.

Financial Incentives   The relationship between money and motivation is frequently misunderstood. It is difficult to reach a consensus about whether or how money motivates employees. Obviously, the discussion will not be settled here, but it is important to consider some of the issues that equate money with motivation.

If money does serve as a motivator, it is certainly only one of many factors that can contribute to efficiency and effectiveness. When salaries and wages are seen as the only incentives for increased employee output, other factors such as involvement, achievement, recognition, and meaningful work are overlooked or ignored.

Part of the problem of relating the lack of motivation to inadequate pay lies in establishing a formula for compensation. For example, if the employer doubles the pay of an employee, should the employee be expected to double performance and work output? If work output increases because of a pay increase, and then drops back to the performance level prior to the raise, should the pay level be adjusted back to the former level as well? Should all work be compensated on a commission basis where employees are only paid for their output or results? Or, should all employees receive a fixed base or subsistence income and then be paid bonuses or incentives for "above-standard" performance? It is extremely difficult to tie performance directly to pay in any industry; the problem is compounded in a service industry where such intangibles as "guest relations" are emphasized as an essential element of employee performance.

Tips or Gratuities. Tips or gratuities deserve special discussion because they are a large part of the income of many employees in the hospitality industry. A newly hired employee working in a tipped job classification is generally excited by the gratuities. The desire to earn large tips initially serves as an incentive to perform at high levels. This may be viewed as a motivating effect. Most tipped employees are paid a base wage that is less than minimum wage because their employer is permitted to use a "tip credit" which reduces the minimum wage requirements.

After the initial excitement of viewing tips as a bonus for good work, tipped employees may begin to establish a mental quota for tips which, when added to their guaranteed hourly wages, becomes the income they expect. They begin to regard tips as commissions, rather than as rewards. Guests are expected to tip at the "approved commission rate," and guests who tip below this rate are viewed in a negative light. Tipped employees should be warned against developing demanding attitudes toward guests. For example, if a guest fails to tip to the expected level, the employee should not, in any way, show resentment toward the guest.

It may be true that tips raise the performance level of employees in some operations, but it certainly is not true in all instances. Recognition and coaching by the manager should be as important as the monetary incentive provided by the tipping system.

Developing a Motivated Staff

Every manager is expected to develop a motivated staff. A manager must be able to lead the staff into willing action. Every employee is motivated from a different set of factors; some are external, but most are internal (within the individual). A manager must be able to stimulate employees' internal motivational factors—and apply appropriate external influence—to get employees to comply with group norms. This process is known as leadership.

Leadership and Motivation

Leadership is a necessary function of management. The individual who understands principles of leadership will find the job of managing much easier. Leadership should not be confused with "driving" employees to get the job done through use of force, fear, or coercive techniques. The manager who attempts to direct employees by instilling fear does not understand motivation. That leader only understands "movement."

Managers who apply external force to make employees "get the job done" fail to recognize that such external force will always need to be applied in order to keep the employees working. Motivation, by contrast, depends upon the employee's own desire to achieve and to be recognized. An effective manager is not a "slave driver," but a professional whose behavior influences the internal motivation of others toward compatible personal and organizational goals.

Managers cannot create positive attitudes by demanding them. Attitudes are influenced by norms. As employees accept these shared group expectations and perform in a way which is judged acceptable, they are recognized as having **good attitudes.** This same principle applies as motivational techniques are considered.

A good attitude about work can lead the employee to willing action. The employee performs and achieves because he/she is challenged by meaningful duties and by the realization that his/her work contributes to both personal and organizational goals.

The Work Environment

Managers often fail to recognize that motivation comes from within the employee. It is not something that a manager or trainer *does to* an employee. At best, the manager's capabilities are limited to affecting the environment within which the employee must work. Employees are motivated when they want to do their jobs well because of the personal satisfaction that comes from the work.

Managers also may fail to recognize that a primary factor that can "de-motivate" an employee—regardless of the position—is the job itself. Employees may see their job as routine, dull, unimaginative, or—even worse—demeaning, embarrassing, or punishing. If this is the case, something must be done to change the job or the employee's perception of the job. No outside force or even gentle, sensitive persuasion will attain the desired motivation level. Behavior may be acceptable and the job may be done temporarily. However, unless the manager and the employee resolve problems and find a way to redesign the job or reassign the employee, the outlook for a highly motivated employee is poor and the possibility that he/she will seek employment elsewhere is high.

If employees are not motivated to do their jobs according to established performance standards, who is to blame? Is it reasonable to place the burden of guilt on the employees by accusing them of being lazy, slow, or disinterested? When managers fully understand motivation, they realize that the real blame must fall upon themselves for their failure to create a positive work environment which stimulates the natural motivation within each employees.

Notes

1. Rosilind L. Rogoff, *The Training Wheel: A Simple Model for Instructional Design* (New York: Wiley, 1987), pp. 45–46.
2. Norman C. Hill, *How to Increase Employee Competence* (New York: McGraw-Hill, 1984), p. 56.
3. Clark Lambert, *The Complete Book of Supervisory Training* (New York: Wiley, 1984), p. 43.
4. This approach is adapted from work done by Frederick Herzberg in his "Maintenance-Motivation Studies." See *The Motivation to Work* (New York: Wiley, 1959) and *Work and the Nature of Man* (Cleveland: World Publishing Co., 1966).

15 Building a Team

Groups, both formal and informal, exist within all hospitality operations. With competent management, groups can be built into teams that perform effectively and efficiently. A well-organized team can accomplish much more than several employees working alone or in an uncoordinated group. Managers must know how to effectively develop and work with groups when supervising and training employees. The same basic principles apply whether working with groups on the job or in special training sessions.

The need to work with groups and build teams is directly related to an operation's training effort. As discussed in Chapter 6, group training methods are very useful in facilitating learning. When staff members function as a team, they usually need less training. Employees working together as a team normally attain goals and meet performance standards more successfully than those working independently.

A planned and organized team-building effort can draw upon group training activities to teach the staff group problem-solving and decision-making skills. Training sessions that seek group resolutions to performance problems also foster team spirit. Such efforts can help modify an existing informal group or develop a new formal group which better serves organizational goals.

A Close Look at Groups

A **group** can be defined as two or more people who participate in an activity. People become a group when they begin to *interact around* common goals. In contrast, a **team** is a group of people with similar training and interests who *work together toward* a common goal. The members of a team usually have specialized skills, all of which are interrelated and necessary to the attainment of the goal.

A group can form, without planning, whenever a need arises to interact around common goals. An effective team, however, is a planned group. Its members are usually selected for their potential contribution toward achieving the goals. Managers need to know how to convert groups into teams in order to achieve the greatest return on the human resources investment and to increase employee job satisfaction.

In a group, the degree of responsibility that each member has to other members can vary a great deal. On a team, the responsibility of each team member to every other team member is very important and is often defined in written form. Individual team members accept additional responsibilities and are directly committed to the goals shared by all team members.

The personality of a group is influenced by its goals and individual members. Some groups may be very serious and interact on a strictly-business basis. Other groups may get together only to have fun and participate in recreational activities. Thus a work group can be expected to develop its own personality, based on the nature of its goals, the work involved, and the overall environment.

The common element in any group is interaction. The more interaction there is, the stronger the group ties will become. When interaction stops, the group ceases to exist. A membership list of people who never meet does not represent a group.

Formal Groups

A formal group has a membership structure. That is, there are entry requirements such as age, educational level, specialized skills, or political affiliation. A formal group may have elected or appointed officers who lead the group according to predetermined duties and responsibilities. Formal groups usually have specific meeting times and activities.

Informal Groups

An informal group is usually not very structured; members join because they wish to interact with other members of the group, and new members are welcomed without meeting formal entrance requirements. Gatherings of informal groups tend to be more spontaneous. Members meet at the suggestion of one or more individuals rather than at a scheduled time. The activities of informal groups may vary considerably from meeting to meeting. There may be no formal structure for evaluating whether the group is accomplishing anything tangible beyond the social interaction of the participants; this interaction may indeed be an informal group's only goal.

Work Groups

A work group might be referred to as a semi-formal group. Entrance requirements are controlled largely by management. Work groups have formal leaders, such as supervisors and managers. Group members must adhere to rules or these leaders can remove them from the group. The formal aspects of work group structure are largely controlled by the formal leaders.

An informal structure also exists within work groups. Employees form friendships and interact to support these informal ties. Friendships are carried on at the workplace and often extend to outside social activities. Informal groups can contribute either positively or negatively to the formal work group goals. Managers must learn how to influence these informal groups so that they have a positive effect on formal work groups.

Cliques. One potentially harmful subgroup within a work group is a **clique.** A clique consists of two or more members of a formal group who have established their own set of goals which they view as more important than the goals of the formal group. The managers who direct work activities and training efforts should discourage the formation of cliques; this can be done most effectively by building teams. A team differs from a clique in that its goals harmonize with the overall goals of the formal work group. A team cooperates with, rather than opposes, the formal group as it works to attain goals.

Groups Within Hospitality Operations

Several types of formal work groups usually exist in hospitality operations. Managers must know how to deal with each of them.

Departments as Groups

Most hospitality operations are divided into departments; some large operations have divisions and departments. A restaurant may have such departments as food production, beverage, service, and cost control. A large hotel might have rooms, food and beverage, sales and marketing, engineering and maintenance, accounting, human resources, and security divisions; some of the major divisions, such as rooms, may have several departments.

Groups within Departments

A division or department within a restaurant or hotel can be further subdivided. For example, the production department of a restaurant may include subgroups for hot food preparation, cold food preparation, stewarding, and purchasing. A hotel's rooms division may include such departments as front office, guest reception, cashiering, telephone, uniformed service, and reservations.

Within each department or departmental subgroup, there are also shifts of employees who work together daily. Most often, these group members do not know employees from other departmental shifts or subgroups. Within each shift, work is further divided according to stations or areas of the building. Employees identify themselves with each of these groups. As the groups become smaller, interactions become more personal and lead to stronger group allegiances.

Skill or Craft Groups

Certain types of employees may form groups because they share common skills. For example, bartenders in a large hotel may work in different areas at different times and rarely interact with one another at work. However, when these bartenders judge that a particular work rule is unreasonable or unfair to them, they will quickly unite and function as a group to overcome the infringement of their "rights." Individuals who do not normally work in close contact with one another may unite readily when they feel that a group position is stronger and more effective than an individual effort.

Special Interest Groups

Groups may also form at work around similar individual interests. This can occur without any formal "boundaries" created by departments, subdepartments, shifts, or stations. Groups may form which are based on such shared factors as age, training, work or off-duty interests, job tasks, responsibilities, status, pay level, or language. Difficulties in interaction between two or more of these groups are commonplace in many hospitality operations.

For example, stewards and chefs, members of the food and beverage department, may have problems interacting with each other because of the differences in their interests and backgrounds. Chefs often perceive themselves as highly skilled technicians and artists, while they may view stewards (who oversee dishwashers and utility workers) as unskilled employees. On the other hand, stewards may perceive themselves as proud people who have had a lot of "bad breaks" and who are trying to better themselves in spite of resistance from chefs; they may view chefs as "prima donnas" who overrate themselves. When such feelings exist, and they naturally do in many organizations, team-building is a challenging process. This is especially true when the teams (such as chefs and stewards) must work together closely.

Opposition and Cooperation in Groups

Opposition and cooperation occur whenever people group together. **Opposition** may be defined as a struggle *against* another person or group for a goal; **cooperation** may be defined as working together *with* another person or group for a goal. The desire or need to achieve a goal is basic to both opposition and cooperation. The reasons employees quarrel or cooperate are largely determined by what they have learned. They can be conditioned to work as a group to achieve goals of opposition or goals of cooperation. In the workplace, opposition is a combination of competition and conflict.

Causes of Competition and Conflict

The source of competition and conflict is often the frustration that occurs when attainment of a goal is blocked. If an individual is unable to attain a goal, he/she may attempt to avoid, offset, overcome, or get around the interference. For example, employees who do not get what they want may make emotional pleas to managers to change a decision. If this fails, the employees may attempt to find other ways to achieve their personal goals—sometimes with the help of others. If the employees are still unable to find a way to achieve personal goals, they may substitute new goals. Of course, employees may give up the effort to reach the original goals or to secure substitutes. A danger to managers occurs when employees create a clique of sympathizers who begin to work at odds with the goals of the operation.

One common cause of conflict is the lack of planned opportunities for different groups or members of the same group to effectively communicate. Employees may not be provided with sufficient opportunity to discuss conflicts which may be confronting their work groups. For example, there may be some conflict between day and night shift employees since they have no opportunity to discuss one another's problems. They are unable to gain an understanding of why certain tasks are handled one way during the day shift and another way on the night shift.

Conflicts also may exist between tipped employees and non-tipped employees. When business is slow, tipped employees may feel they are being treated unfairly because they are paid less than non-tipped wage earners. On the other hand, non-tipped employees often feel underpaid when business is good and tipped employees make more money than they do. In this situation, non-tipped employees may suggest that tips should be shared. The tipping customs of the hospitality industry can be a source of constant conflict if managers allow them to become a basis for competition.

Employees must know what is expected of them, both as individuals and as members of a group. Conflict often arises when basic expectations are not clear. Managers are directly responsible for clarifying expectations, defining and restating group goals, and providing feedback when goals are not being attained.

Dangers of Competition and Conflict

While competition may encourage employees to achieve short-range and immediate goals, the long-term effects of conflict are lower morale and decreased productivity. Conflict in groups is often regarded as a natural state; this view suggests that conflict must be "coped with" rather than overcome. This has led many managers to develop plans that stimulate competition which can encourage—rather than discourage—conflict. Conflict rarely, if ever, leads to a smooth and efficient operation in which goals can be systematically attained. It usually leads to inferior performance. Individuals engaged in a conflict are working toward winning the conflict. The goals of the hospitality operation take a secondary place or are ignored.

Employees who are engaged in conflict may exhibit several forms of non-productive behavior. The most obvious of these behaviors is arguing with other employees or with managers. Even though the managers may not be directly involved, employees who are feeling the frustration of conflict will often create problems for them. Such employees may also attempt to influence the managers to "take sides." In highly emotional conflicts, employees may demand the managers' support and even threaten to resign if they do not receive it. This places managers in the middle of employee conflicts. Again, some team-building skills are essential to resolving these conflicts, which otherwise can create significant obstacles to meeting organizational goals.

Other problems involving conflict show up in inferior job performance. Guests suffer when employees work against one another. Some employees may "sabotage" the work of other employees. They may blame one another for problems that are their own or no one's fault. Employees may spread unfounded rumors about other employees, may be late for work, or call in sick if they think these tactics will help them win a conflict.

Employees who are engaged in feuding are wasting their energy on non-productive activities. They are neither effective nor efficient. Managers need to direct that energy toward productive operational goals. All too often, managers use one of the following approaches in dealing with conflict: (1) they ignore the conflict and hope it will "work itself out" over time (it seldom does); (2) they order the conflict to cease, or else (threats and commands seldom relieve conflict—this approach is more likely to draw management into the conflict); or (3) they fire the person or persons who they believe caused the conflict (this may lead to temporary resolution only).

Training and coaching can redirect non-productive opposition toward desirable goals. For example, trainees' efforts should be focused upon procedures that will help ensure that performance standards are met. This training can then be used to change opposition to cooperation. This transfer—leading to a meshing of personal, group, and organizational goals—is the basic purpose of team building.

Cooperation: Working Together

Cooperation is a desirable feature of most human interaction. Cooperation is interaction that provides mutual help or an alliance of people or groups who seek some common goal or reward. It imposes various restraints on the participants. An individual who is working cooperatively with other individuals cannot have his/her way entirely. If self-assertive feelings become too strong, cooperation will be replaced by struggle or opposition. Cooperation implies the need to sometimes restrain self-centered drives. This does not always require the individual to give up personal freedoms or rights—only to set aside personal goals in the interests of the total group effort.

For example, in a cooperative environment, an employee who is part of a housekeeping team cannot arbitrarily assume the role of "chief." There are other less exciting and less visible roles that must be filled for the total team effort to be successful. Cooperation is possible when individuals see that they have a common interest with other members of the group and have, at the same time, sufficient self-control to seek this interest through united action. When a team works cooperatively toward group goals through combined efforts, they avoid conflict.

Team-Building Strategies

Within every large group there generally exist smaller, less carefully structured subgroups. The primary goals of the subgroup are different from the primary goals of the larger group. However, not all subgroups are counterproductive. In fact, the goals of the subgroup may be consistent with those of the larger group. For example, a department may decide to plan a family party on an upcoming weekend. The group may appoint a committee of three people and give them the authority to plan the outing for the benefit of the larger group. Thus the committee's goals are completely consistent with the goals of the larger group—unless it selfishly plans an activity without considering the interests of the larger group. When such a divisive approach is taken, the committee—or subgroup—has become a clique.

Working with Cliques

Cliques are often counterproductive to the goals of the larger group. Since cliques frequently exist, managers must be able to:

- Recognize cliques

- Identify members of the cliques

- Determine the common purpose for which the cliques exist

- Know how to work with the cliques to accomplish operating goals

Managers must begin by recognizing that cliques exist and by reacting toward them as if they were legitimate groups. By doing so, managers can work with clique members to get them involved on a group project or activity that will benefit everyone. Managers can appoint the members of a clique to a committee or task force to work toward solving a problem. The committee can then focus on resolving a problem rather than on other concerns which might negatively affect the operation. Such activities can serve as a learning experience and show employees that the goals of the organization can be a source of job satisfaction.

Group Goal Setting

Goals established exclusively by managers may never be fully accepted by a group of employees. If, for example, the group tends to be "anti-management," the goals are sure to be rejected. It is generally better for managers to encourage employees to help set goals. Along with the responsibility for goal setting comes the responsibility for assessing whether—and to what extent—goals are achieved. When employees participate in goal setting, they should be expected to assess the effectiveness of the group or team in attaining the goals.

Goal-setting sessions can be a meaningful way to develop positive attitudes. Group members often think that managers are unfair because they set goals and impose them on the group from above. However, goals set by group members are often as demanding as those established by managers—if not more so. Groups will work hard to attain goals they have helped to develop. If the group was formerly a clique, the first step has been taken in transforming a group with different goals into a force that shares compatible goals with the organization.

Participation in Decision-Making

When managers allow employees to help set group goals, they have begun to practice effective participative management. Team building requires employee participation in goal setting, evaluating, and other decision-making activities. Many managers give "lip service" to participative management while allowing employees to make only simple or low-risk decisions. In using this approach, managers convey that they do not trust employees to make important decisions.

Managers may feel that employees do not want to be bothered with decision-making—that employees view decision-making as a management responsibility. Managers may consider it unfair to burden employees with duties that are clearly not part of their job. Actually, some managers regard decision-making as a "right" of management. These managers believe that employees should prepare themselves for management positions if they want to become decision-makers.

Good management is a sharing process. Responsibility is shared by all individuals who have to do the work. Responsibility carries both *expectations* and *consequences*. Whenever managers share responsibility, they must be certain that everyone involved agrees about what is expected and that everyone accepts a share of the responsibility for the group decision.

Employee Development

Training and coaching involve more than teaching skills and correcting inferior performance. Training and coaching are two of the basic approaches used to *develop* employees. Development deals with the whole individual in the setting or environment in which the work is performed. Team building is a training technique that contributes to this development while fostering an organizational "culture."[1]

As used here, the term *culture* refers to ideas, attitudes, values, norms, and habits which are shared among members of a group and that identify and distinguish that group from others. The entire staff of a hospitality operation may have a culture which sets it apart from the staffs of neighboring hotels; a subgroup within the operation may also have a different culture than the operation as a whole. It is desirable for there to be considerable compatibility between the cultures of subgroups and the culture of the larger organization.

All employees belong to groups. Much of their work is accomplished through group efforts. Every employee needs to be a member of a group and to feel like he/she belongs. When group involvement leads to meaningful accomplishments, members experience feelings of affiliation that meet basic individual needs. For an affiliation to have lasting value, it must provide a person with the opportunity to grow, develop, and feel a sense of accomplishment as a direct result of belonging to the group. To facilitate development, managers can influence employees to become active in work groups that set challenging and productive goals, allow participation in making decisions about how to meet these goals, collectively assess the results of their efforts to meet the goals, and face the consequences of their efforts. The following Case in Point describes how one hotel company applied such a team-building effort with good results.

A Case in Point: Developing Culture

During the opening of a new hotel, the entire staff was divided into teams of ten employees each and charged with the development of a constructive culture for the new operation. Each team consisted of personnel from different departments. The team leaders were management personnel. However, no employee was assigned to a team led by his/her supervisor or department head.

The first objective of the teams was to help staff members get to know each other without the usual barriers of departmental lines. Second, the teams were to work toward developing friendships that extended beyond the casual acquaintances typically developed in a work situation. Third, the teams were challenged to identify areas of the hotel operation that needed improvement. They were asked to develop plans for improving those functions themselves, or to make recommendations to the management team.

The management personnel who acted as team leaders were given no formal management responsibility within their teams except to act as team facilitators. Otherwise, they were to participate as team members. Their position on the team carried no more weight than any other team member. One goal of each team was to get to know the management member of the team as a person—not someone set apart from the rest of the staff.

Team meetings could be held at work for one hour each week, with full pay. Additionally, teams could agree to meet away from work for social and recreational activities on their own time and at their own expense. The team effort was to continue for the first 90 days of the new hotel's operation. At the end of that period, the effort would be evaluated and revised as necessary to pursue new goals.

During the first team meeting, team members were given a detailed biographical questionnaire, which they were asked to complete before the second meeting. Team members were told to complete only those portions with which they felt comfortable. Any question considered too personal or private could be skipped. Questionnaires were to remain available so that an individual could go back and add information after he/she became more comfortable with the group.

The information obtained through the biographical questionnaires was to go beyond the superficial information acquired through a job application. Its intent was to identify "common interests" within each team. The questionnaire asked the team members to trace their personal history from childhood, including everywhere they ever lived, went to school, and worked. It also asked for detailed family demographic information. Again, no one was required to supply information that they considered an invasion of privacy.

The biographical histories revealed interesting insights. One quiet employee disclosed that he was a champion bowler in one of the city leagues. As a result, his team planned an outing to attend one of his tournaments. One very young-looking woman turned out to be a proud grandmother with four grandchildren, much to everyone's surprise. The questionnaires also revealed that many people on staff had children. This resulted in all teams combining and holding an all-afternoon family picnic to help everyone on the staff get acquainted.

Several teams addressed the need for follow-up training after the opening. Others addressed needed changes in employee break facilities, lockers, and restrooms. Others discussed ways to improve guest relations. Some teams held social events and invited another team to be their guests. Overall, the top management of the hotel company was rather amazed at the positive results of the team program. The program became a regular part of all new hotel openings, as well as an ongoing activity beyond the 90-day start-up period.

In this Case in Point, some of the groups wanted to continue their team efforts, some wanted to regroup, and some wanted to end the entire activity at the end of the 90-day period. The feelings of each group member were closely related to the group's effectiveness in bonding around meaningful goals and activities. The facilitators greatly influenced the success of each group. Generally, the groups that enjoyed the most success were headed by managers who did not feel threatened by having to give up their supervisory roles.

A team approach to human resources development requires the commitment of management, budget allocations to cover the time costs, and the belief that employees are responsible people who will work together toward constructive goals if given the opportunity. The team activity described in the Case in Point was not without some snags and weak spots. However, the benefits far outweighed the drawbacks. The overall result was a higher level of morale than would have been achieved during the same time frame without the team activities.

Work should be fun. It is much more enjoyable when employees become friends and care about each other's personal lives and activities. The attitude that there should be no relationship between home and work is unreasonable and out of date. The effective use of teams will build constructive bridges between the personal activities and the professional performance of the staff.

Team Leadership

Good leadership is necessary in order for a group to function as a team. Even though managers serve as formal leaders, the success of the team often rests with informal leaders. Simply defined, a **leader** is a person who has followers. More specifically, a leader influences others to act in ways that will achieve goals which he/she considers important. Employees often follow the leadership of other employees whom they trust, respect, or fear. This form of leadership is informal, since these leaders are not elected or appointed and have not been given any formal authority to lead. They are leaders only because they are able to get other people to follow them.

Working with Informal Leaders

Managers can improve their team-building efforts by working through or with informal group leaders. If informal leaders can be influenced to support the manager's goals, the informal group can be steered toward improved productivity and the attainment of other group-developed goals which mesh with those of the organization.

One reason individuals like to be informal leaders is that they receive recognition from the group. When working with informal leaders, managers must be careful not to formalize such leadership positions. Managers may see these individuals striving for recognition and decide to promote them to formal management positions. This action is often unnecessary and goes beyond the recognition discussed here. When informal leadership is formalized, employees often will decide that they need new informal leaders who are not directly aligned with management.

Informal leaders are effective because they have the total freedom to lead according to their own style. When that leadership becomes formalized, the expectations of them as leaders also change. They often begin to lead like formal members of the management team.

Meetings: Part of the Team-Building Effort

Since interaction between people is essential to group activity, meetings are an important part of any team-building effort. There are two main categories of team-building meetings: *informational* and *problem-solving*.

Informational Meetings

The primary focus of an informational meeting is to present communications from the leader to attendees. While the members of the group may ask questions or briefly contribute further information, the meeting is largely planned and controlled by the leader.

Staff Meetings. Regularly scheduled staff meetings are a good example of informational meetings. Staff meetings are primarily used to keep the staff informed. These meetings should have planned topics. Most of the communication will probably be in the form of information given and questions answered by a manager. Staff meetings are usually held at a specified time and are frequently kept short. Such meetings are important for the smooth functioning of an operation. The larger the operation, the more important it becomes to have these regular, formal meetings.

Training Sessions. Training sessions are another type of informational meeting. The content is largely determined by the trainer, and the training goals have usually been established before the session begins. Each session is designed to pass along information to trainees that is consistent with the learning objectives. In effective training sessions, the trainees will be encouraged to ask questions and to actively participate. This type of participation does not change the primary goal of the meeting: dispensing information that will result in improved job performance.

Other Informational Meetings. Managers may call meetings at any time to announce last-minute changes in operational procedures, review sales promotions, or discuss any item of importance that cannot wait until the next regular staff meeting. Timely communications are important. Employees must be kept informed if they are to be held accountable for their performance. A short "huddle" meeting to cover such information is usually better than sending it out through the grapevine. The latter often results in confused and inaccurate information.

Problem-Solving Meetings

Problem-solving meetings are used to resolve existing or anticipated problems. They can be arranged at any time and may even be part of a regularly scheduled staff meeting or training session. When they are part of a staff meeting or training session, however, it should be clear that the problem-solving activity goes beyond the receipt of information. For problem-solving to be effective, the meeting must shift to a different format. Problem-solving meetings—or problem-solving activities during informational meetings—must be designed to provide group involvement in seeking solutions.

Existing Problems. The problem-solving group for an existing problem may be the entire staff of a department or a smaller group selected from within the department. Individuals from outside the department may also be asked to participate if they have special knowledge, skills, or interests in the problem area. There is usually no predetermined schedule for a problem-solving group.

The session may begin by discussing the problem and defining it more clearly. Goals relating to the solution of the problem are then established. The goals should describe or state the desired results of the solution. The group can then begin to brainstorm alternative approaches to solving the problem.

In a team-building effort, every member of the group should be encouraged to participate and should be drawn into the problem-solving process. Informal leaders in these groups should be allowed to give direction; however, they should not be allowed to dominate the process to the extent that their ideas are the only ones considered. An effective team involves a united effort by all members.

Anticipated Problems. For problem-solving meetings that focus on anticipated problems, the process of group involvement is the same as that used for existing problems. However, rather than devising a solution, the group develops a plan of action to avoid the problems. To do this, the group must describe the form the problems can be expected to take and how to recognize them before they actually occur. A group approach encourages everyone to work toward avoiding the problems. Without this approach, managers have access to fewer ideas about solving anticipated problems and often become "fire-fighters" responding to fires or crises that could have been anticipated, planned for, or avoided.

Team Member Roles. A problem-solving group must define the roles of each group member. If the group takes the form of a **committee,** the members will usually elect a **chairperson** who will be responsible for coordinating meeting times and places, and for ensuring that everyone is informed about these arrangements. Even though a chairperson is elected, the role should be viewed by management as that of an informal leader. This is very important to the group's continued acceptance of and support for the chairperson.

The chairperson in a problem-solving meeting should not actually conduct the meeting. The group is usually less formal, and all members generally have equal authority and responsibility. If someone must provide leadership in the group's work sessions, it is better to rotate this responsibility among the group members. A committee may also elect a recorder, who will take notes on the meeting and supply participants with copies of the notes. In other cases, the recorder function may be rotated within the group or handled by a volunteer at each meeting.

Team Direction. Problem-solving groups can be very flexible; they can operate in the manner which best suits the group members. When they are unable to make progress, they may need someone who can help them move toward a resolution without dictating the direction of the movement. This individual may be a manager who is functioning as a group **facilitator.** The facilitator helps the group get moving again, and then steps back to let members proceed on their own steam. When group members are unable to find a solution because of inadequate knowledge or ability, "subject-matter experts" may be called in to ensure that all possible alternatives have been identified and considered.

The Role of the Group Facilitator

A group facilitator's primary responsibility is to encourage participative learning and mutual problem-solving within the group. A manager or trainer can use certain leadership skills to bring about a high level of individual member involvement. However, the role of a facilitator is not the same as that of a teacher or instructor.

A group facilitator may be someone who is not a regular member of the group but who is brought in and charged with the responsibility of carrying out the facilitator role. Even when no specific individual is designated to be the group facilitator, someone within the group must perform certain facilitator-type duties. The various facilitator roles may be taken on informally by various group members at different times.

The facilitator creates an atmosphere that encourages creative expression rather than submissiveness, dependence, or repression. Such an atmosphere fosters freedom of dissent and the feeling that one does not have to be afraid of being wrong. Members of a team need to be able to say what they feel—not just what they think they ought to say. They must be encouraged to express ideas and attitudes without fear of criticism and isolation. They should not be expected to rely solely on "tried and true" methods of problem-solving, which frequently do not work. Creativity should bring out new ideas, new approaches, new solutions, and new ways of looking at old situations.

A facilitator avoids giving instructions to the group. The aim of facilitation is to solicit opinions rather than to teach theories and techniques. The facilitator should avoid using authority or status to coerce the group or overrule opinions. Rather, a facilitator should:

- Support the group as it presents opinions and ideas
- Explore the reasoning behind the positions taken
- Share in the give and take of searching for workable alternatives
- Build relationships that develop a team which pulls together

The facilitator summarizes discussions and probes for clarification of issues. He or she directs discussions toward complete analysis of problems and heads off personality conflicts.

The facilitator must be neutral and objective—not aloof or detached. The role entails respecting all statements, even when they seem incorrect or irrelevant, without being a critic or a censor. The facilitator avoids any action that would place the group on the defensive and thus inhibit discussion. The group is encouraged to disagree, since disagreement stimulates discussion in the pursuit of the best solution. An experienced facilitator can channel conflict into creative discussion and resolution of the problem at hand.

The group facilitator must be constantly aware of what is occurring in the meeting. Over time, the manner in which the facilitator serves the group becomes an intuitive act based upon the needs and goals of the group.

Conducting the Team Meeting

Managers and trainers must know how to conduct team meetings. The manager or trainer may assume the role of a coordinator or conductor, directing activities based on a set agenda, or he/she may be a facilitator. Though they overlap, there are various team meeting formats; the three most common are the *directed meeting*, the *participative meeting*, and the *brainstorming meeting*.

Directed Meetings

The primary purpose of a directed meeting is to give information to the team. Directed meetings are sometimes referred to as briefings and can be part of a staff or training meeting. For a team effort to be effective, the members of the team must be informed as to who will be on the team, who will facilitate the team effort, and how the team will be held accountable for its activities. These matters can be covered in a well-planned directed meeting before the team effort begins, or whenever it is necessary to provide additional information to the people involved.

A directed meeting is largely a one-way communication, with time allowed for questions and answers. There should be a clear statement of the purpose and the desired outcome to ensure the meeting's efficiency and effectiveness. The meeting should have a written agenda detailing objectives to be attained through the meeting, and a time frame for completing the meeting.

The leader of the directed meeting should be well prepared and know what he/she plans to say about each agenda item. The location and meeting room setup should be in order so that the meeting can be conducted in a positive manner. Sloppily conducted meetings set a tone that can carry over into the less formal meetings, and can hinder the effectiveness of the team approach.

The directed meeting should fit within the series of meetings which constitute the team activity. At the beginning of the meeting, the leader should clarify the purpose and focus on how the results will contribute to the overall team goals. Throughout the meeting, the leader should follow the agenda and steer all questions and comments back to the objectives. This does not mean that the leader should be inflexible. The group should be permitted to address agenda items out of order, so long as all agenda items are adequately covered.

The directed meeting is not the time or place for lengthy discussions or confrontations with individuals who are not completely sold on the team approach. Neither should the meeting focus on the problem's importance. As these points arise, the leader should simply state that he/she will be glad to discuss those views one-on-one after the meeting. He/she should then emphasize that it is important to cover the agenda in the allotted time. The leader should make it clear that the team effort is a group project and not his/her own personal quest.

Following each agenda item, the leader should ask questions to ensure that group members understand the information. Likewise, he/she should listen carefully to the questions raised by the team members. When questions are consistent with the objectives of the agenda, the leader should attempt to answer those questions as directly as possible. Questions that are off the subject should be positively acknowledged and set aside for one-on-one discussion or a later group meeting.

As with all good meetings, the directed meeting should always conclude with an action plan. The action plan may include future meeting times and dates. All actions discussed in the directed meeting should be planned with completion dates and assignments of responsibilities. A follow-up schedule should be the last item on the agenda and should serve to summarize the meeting.[2]

Participative Meetings

There are five key elements in an effective participative meeting: (1) the opening, (2) the warm-up, (3) the agenda, (4) the plans for future activity, and (5) the evaluation.

The Opening. The opening sets the tone for the meeting. It may include opening remarks by the person who assembled the team, a discussion of the reasons the team was assembled, and an identification of the roles which team members and the leader or facilitator will play. It is also used to present a preview of the meeting.

The Warm-Up. The warm-up can be used in a number of different ways, depending upon the kind of team involved. For a team that has worked together before, the leader may ask the members to write down what they expect to accomplish during the meeting. Each member may then be asked to share his/her thoughts with the group. The leader should write each member's main idea on a flip chart or chalkboard and display them during the remainder of the session.

For a team that is meeting together for the first time, the leader may want to spend a considerable amount of time on the warm-up. Assuming that the team consists of employees from the same department, the warm-up could take the following format:

1. Ask the members to pair up and interview one another for 10 to 15 minutes. Have members ask the following questions:

    (a) What is your background or experience?

    (b) What do you like most about your job?

    (c) What do you like least about your job?

    (d) What do you expect to happen in today's meeting?

2. Reconvene the team and ask each member to introduce his/her partner.

3. Record each member's expectations on a flip chart or chalkboard.

People often come to meetings with their own ideas of what should be covered. However, these points may not be considered at all during the meeting unless there is some way for members to feel comfortable in expressing them. The warm-up can get these "hidden agenda" items out in the open. Often, leaders will find these ideas quite appropriate for the meeting. If particular topics are raised in the warm-up that do not fit into a workable agenda, time may be allowed for some discussion. A future meeting may be planned to address the issues in more detail.

The Agenda. The agenda items represent the actual content of the meeting. It is possible to conduct a participative meeting to present information. This is best done when the meeting schedule allows time for open discussion and group input. In these meetings, the information-portion of the agenda is usually determined by the leader or by a subgroup who met earlier to plan the agenda.

In a problem-solving meeting, the schedule is set by the group. The leader should suggest that the problem be defined in as much detail as possible. This ensures that everyone is thinking of the same concerns when discussing possible solutions. Next, the group objectives should be set. Group objectives should include a clear description of the desired end result of the team effort. Objectives should also include deadlines, implementation procedures, evaluation processes, and a statement of how the team's efforts will relate to other teams within the hospitality operation. These items should be determined by the group and may also deal with establishing group rules, work methods, organization, discussion, and evaluation of alternative solutions.

As the group plans a schedule, it should allocate the amount of time that will be devoted to each item during the meeting. If the group later discovers that an inadequate amount of time has been allocated, it can discuss the problem and re-allocate the time as necessary. It is important to keep all meetings on schedule. This is difficult to do and requires a skilled leader, especially when discussion is lively.

The Plans for Future Activity. Planning future activities is one of the most important steps in the meeting process. It involves listing action steps that will be taken based on the meeting's progress. Action steps should include (but not be limited to) the following information:

- Designation of responsibilities (ideally, members volunteer for responsibilities)
- A timetable for all planned activities
- A plan for follow-through—or how the group will proceed once members leave the meeting

It may be wise to break down complicated problems into smaller workable elements in order to develop a separate list of action steps for each segment. As the group thinks through each segment of a problem, additional steps can be added throughout the meeting. Problem-solving in a participative meeting is a building-block process. As members of the team become more attuned to the nature of the problem, they will think of different approaches to solving the situation or ways of avoiding such problems.

Evaluation of the Meeting. During the evaluation process, each group member should be asked to write down thoughts about what took place during the meeting. Members should reflect on how the meeting was effective or beneficial, and how the meeting process could be improved. Then the leader can ask each individual to discuss his/her thoughts with the team. Finally, the leader may ask the team members to turn in the written evaluations. These can be summarized, given back to the participants, and used for improving future meetings.

Brainstorming Meetings

Brainstorming is a leadership technique which can be used to develop new ideas for products, guest services, methods, and processes. It is particularly suitable for solving problems and for training employees. It is also useful for determining all possible steps which must be included in a particular project; for building a strong team spirit within a department (since it encourages everyone's input); and in bringing about group decision-making.

Brainstorming works best when it involves a team of four to six employees and a group leader. The process for conducting a brainstorming meeting consists of four steps:

1. Identify the problem

2. List all ideas about the problem

3. Screen the list of ideas

4. Identify the action steps to be taken

Identify the Problem. The group should clearly identify the problem to be solved or the goal to be reached. Some examples of problems that might be approached through brainstorming are:

- How can we reduce employee turnover in the overall operation or in one department?

- How can we increase the sale of desserts, soups, wines, or other categories of products or guest services?

- How can we attract younger people, older people, or single people to the restaurant?

- How can we improve working conditions for our employees?

- How can we improve the level of training employees receive?

List All Ideas. All ideas about a particular problem should be listed. Evaluation of ideas during this step is not necessary; the leader should seek a lot of ideas without regard to their worth. Brainstorming is a process of creative thinking in which all ideas should be considered, no matter how unrealistic they may seem. The leader should encourage team members to recall their first impressions of the problem. The concept that "first impressions are the best impressions" is frequently true. At the same time, a first impression that something will not work may stifle creative thought.

The leader should allow 30 to 45 minutes for the group to list ideas. If it appears that all ideas have been exhausted and the group is beginning to drift away from the main topic, the leader should ask the members if they are ready to move on to the next step. This question may draw out additional ideas before the group proceeds.

Screen the List of Ideas. This step involves eliminating unworkable ideas from the list. It is helpful at this point to establish factors for screening the ideas. All members of the brainstorming group should be involved in selecting these factors. The factors selected should apply to the particular problem being addressed; for example:

- High, moderate, or low chance of success
- Reasonable or unreasonable cost
- High, moderate, or low acceptance by others
- High, moderate, or low overall benefit

The team leader should work with the group to delete those ideas that the group feels would be unlikely to solve the problem. In addition, the group should refine the remaining ideas by carefully evaluating them. The group should attempt to rank the ideas from most likely to least likely to solve the problem. The group should state each idea or alternative as specifically as possible. This involves reviewing all ideas and looking for ways to group or categorize them.

It is important for the leader to ensure that team members state ideas in complete sentences rather than key words or phrases. All members of the team should fully understand what is included in each idea that is retained. Finally, everyone should work together to come up with the descriptions of each alternative which is adopted for use.

Identify Action Steps. This is the final step in the brainstorming process. It involves writing down the action steps that should be taken to implement the idea. Action steps should include:

- Designation of responsibilities
- A timetable for completing planned activities
- A plan for follow-through, implementation, and evaluation

The action steps may also take the form of recommendations or proposals to higher management. If team members really want upper management to implement their ideas, it is important that they present a complete plan. The plan should include:

- A clear, unbiased statement of the problem or situation
- Workable alternatives for dealing with the situation
- An organized plan of action for implementing the alternative approaches recommended
- A plan for evaluating the results
- The role that the team will play in following through on the recommendations

The following Case in Point illustrates how the brainstorming process was used to address a problem in a newly opened hospitality operation.

A Case in Point: Easy Living

A 208-room luxury hotel had been open for three months. The 18 room attendants on staff had worked very hard during the opening stages. There had been some construction delays, which required the housekeeping staff to work harder than usual to clean up construction debris. The work continued to be difficult thereafter because of the established productivity standards. Each room attendant was expected to clean 17 rooms per day and to pass a rigid inspection after each cleaning. Through this whole process, the room attendants had been very cooperative with each other.

However, the room attendants and supervisors had noticed that the restaurant staff seemed to have a lot of free time—especially between meal periods. The restaurant service staff were often in the employee cafeteria for longer than their allotted 15-minute breaks and were often seen sitting in the restaurant with nothing to do. Several housekeeping room attendants had asked their supervisors how they could transfer to the restaurant. The executive housekeeper had spoken to the restaurant manager about the effect the situation was having on her staff's morale. The manager had brushed the matter aside by saying: "No two departments are the same. Besides, you don't get anything extra for working so hard here. I believe in taking life easy."

The executive housekeeper decided to deal directly with the growing problem before it got out of hand. She divided the eighteen room attendants into three groups of six, with one supervisor in each group. The executive housekeeper served as the facilitator for each group.

Each group met for three sessions. The first session was basically informational. The executive housekeeper outlined what was going to happen in the course of three meetings. The balance of the meeting was then devoted to establishing ground rules for the group activities and reviewing job lists, job breakdowns, and job performance standards to ensure a clear understanding of performance expectations.

One basic ground rule was that the restaurant staff would not be a topic for discussion. The executive housekeeper noted that the restaurant had its own job standards to meet and that they had little or nothing to do with the job standards of housekeeping. The groups were further informed that, if they were unhappy with the job performance standards of the department, they would have an opportunity in the second and third meetings to devise a more workable set of expectations.

The next group meeting took a participative format to explore feelings about the work situation. The meeting format gave everyone a chance to state what they perceived the main complaints to be. Every idea or complaint was recorded on a flip chart page. As the pages filled up, they were taped to the wall. This process continued until the group had exhausted the list of complaints. Then the executive housekeeper facilitated the process of narrowing down the list to seven to ten complaints for each group.

For the third meeting, the executive housekeeper started with the refined list of complaints and facilitated a brainstorming session. The executive housekeeper challenged each group to identify ways to reduce the department's workload while remaining within the budget. Again, flip chart pages were used to record comments and were displayed on the walls of the meeting room.

Many good ideas were presented. The groups were then asked to boil down their lists of suggestions to five specific ideas which could be immediately implemented. The lists of five items from each group were combined into a single list—then condensed to a grand total of nine items. These items were then presented to the general manager with the strong endorsement of the executive housekeeper.

The general manager approved the list. The workload of the department was immediately reorganized to incorporate the suggested changes. While productivity and cleaning standards remained unchanged, the complaints about the restaurant staff disappeared. The group had been allowed to analyze their situation and participate in decisions about their work. The end result was more efficiency and effectiveness—which meant accomplishing work with less effort in a more relaxed atmosphere.

The enthusiasm generated by this results-oriented style of management can be contagious. There has never been a successful team in any endeavor whose members did not feel pride when they planned their work, worked their plan, and achieved the desired results. When individuals combine their efforts as a team to accomplish a goal that they helped set, they can experience the satisfaction that comes from being able to say, "We did it!" Further, when these individuals participate in objectively evaluating the results of their efforts, they can feel very good about their accomplishments.

Notes

1. Gary L. Schulze, "Management Development," in *Handbook of Human Resource Administration,* 2nd ed., edited by Joseph J. Famularo (New York: McGraw-Hill, 1986), pp. 23-6–23-8.
2. Adapted from "Meetings That Make A Difference," *Quarter Benchmarks* (Durham, N.H.: The Center for Constructive Change, Summer, 1985), p. 1.

Part V

Coaching: An Ongoing Function

16 Coaching and Counseling

Some managers think they have no time to sit down with employees to discuss progress, performance, or problems on the job. These managers believe there are too many other "really important things" to be done. In reality, there are some crises that will need immediate attention in any operation. Regardless of the competing demands for a manager's time, an effective leader of people *must* talk with his/her employees regularly—especially when problems exist. Problems cannot be corrected without communicating with employees. The cooperation, ideas, and commitment of employees are necessary to achieving the goals of the organization.

It is very important to win the confidence of employees. Managers must be able to show employees that they are genuinely concerned about helping them become more effective on the job. This is dramatically different from situations in which managers only point out the employees' faults. If employees feel inadequate and believe that they are not being helped with their problems, the managers' work will be difficult and unrewarding, and standards of excellence will never be met.

In order to help employees, managers must understand them—how they feel and act—and allocate time to meet and talk on a personal level. Managers should set a priority to meet with each employee privately on a routine basis to find out how the employee feels he/she is doing on the job and to jointly determine areas for future development.

Most employees want to do a good job, but they need help and encouragement. They also have to know what they are doing incorrectly and how to do it correctly. An important part of a manager's job is to observe the staff closely and to coach them in ways to improve their performance.

Coaching and counseling are extensions of training and development and are an important part of effective management. *Informal* coaching and counseling occur as part of normal day-to-day supervision. *Formal* coaching and counseling sessions are usually scheduled and occur in a private place like an office or conference room. The agenda for a formal session is planned and a complete record is kept of the session.

Coaching and Counseling: Similarities and Differences

Coaching, as an extension of job training, should focus on accomplishments, job duties, and factual observations. Coaching is a process of providing positive or redirective feedback to an employee. The purpose of coaching is to individually reinforce the knowledge, skills, and job-related attitudes that have been developed through training. Coaching is intended to correct, improve, and further develop the employee's ability to execute job skills according to established performance standards.

Counseling is a process of one-on-one problem-solving during which the manager helps an employee seek solutions to his/her own problems. While coaching focuses on job execution, job-related counseling focuses on attitudes or feelings about the job and the work environment. Counseling requires skills in helping employees analyze themselves in order to help them develop insight into their own behavior, attitudes, and perceptions—all within a job-related context.

Common Concerns

In any planned coaching or counseling situation, there should be at least three concerns:

1. The specific problem which must be resolved

2. The relationship between the manager and the employee(s)

3. The overall growth and development of the employee(s)

It takes practice and experience to keep track of and address all three of these concerns during a coaching or counseling session. Planned coaching or counseling sessions should take the form and approach of an interview. (Interviewing procedures were discussed as they related to hiring employees in Chapter 3.) When used for coaching and counseling, interviewing should focus on obtaining facts, giving objective feedback, expressing consideration for feelings, and planning future actions. Such activities solve problems, build relationships, and help employees further develop their abilities.

As a general rule, interviews in coaching and counseling should be *problem-oriented*. This means that the interview should focus upon problems that an employee encounters while doing his/her job or upon problems that result from ineffective job performance. Managers should be very cautious about providing counseling for personal problems that go beyond the work situation. Management education and training is *not* designed to prepare managers for specialized counseling in non-job-related matters. Managers should maintain an up-to-date reference file of individual specialists or community organizations which provide professional counseling in specific personal areas.

Principles of Coaching and Counseling

Job-related coaching and counseling are important management activities. Employee attitudes and performance are affected by the way in which a manager gives directions or instructions, the attitude the manager displays toward employees, and the way the manager performs his/her own job. All these activities are related to coaching and counseling. Managers can be sure that if they do not care about what employees do and how they are doing it, the employees are also not likely to care. If managers accept work that does not meet established performance standards, that is what the employees are likely to produce. Coaching and counseling cannot be effective unless managers first develop a proper work environment that encourages employees to do their best.

Involvement. For coaching and counseling to be successful, the employees must become personally involved in setting goals and personally responsible for achieving results. The more active employees are in appraising problems and outlining possible courses of action, the more committed they will be to the solution.

Managers should encourage employees to participate in the coaching and counseling process. The manager's role in these sessions must go beyond telling the employee what to do or how to do it. He/she should help the employee personalize the problem and develop a plan of action. The manager should raise key questions which will help the employee find solutions. He/she should not "lead the employee by the hand" unless this is absolutely necessary (and if it is, the effectiveness of the earlier selection, orientation, training and coaching/counseling must be questioned).

Understanding. There must be mutual understanding of the topic being discussed. The only way to ensure this is to have the employee define the problem in his/her own words. The manager can restate these views to make sure he/she understands. If this is not done, the manager and the employee might finish the session with entirely different ideas about the issues and the decisions.

Listening. The manager must do more listening than talking. Even if the manager says little during the session, the interaction can yield considerable value—if the manager listens. For example, if the employee is upset, listening permits him/her to "let off steam." Likewise, the manager can also allow the employee to "try out his/her ideas on the boss" for a change.

One expert cites 12 ground rules that managers must follow for coaching to be effective. The same 12 rules apply to job-related counseling:[1]

1. Be unbiased and never play favorites.

2. Be fair in applying standards on an equal basis.

3. Be non-threatening in the coaching environment.

4. Build on trust levels that are already in place.

5. Recognize individual differences and different learning rates.

6. Support departmental and organizational goals and keep expectations out front.

7. Have a high degree of empathy to overcome anxiety or nervousness of the employee.

8. Maintain continuity between sessions to build on past progress.

9. Be consistent with standards and demands for performance.

10. Offer preparation for performance appraisal (continuous coaching should precede formal performance reviews).

11. Allow sufficient time for coaching sessions.

12. Have patience to see the job through.

Informal On-the-Job Coaching

Coaching can be both formal and informal. In an informal sense, coaching is a routine part of supervision. It is the process whereby a manager stops and talks to an employee about his/her performance, and then moves on to another employee to show the same sincere interest in the quality and quantity of work being performed. Managers should be aware of the following concepts when undertaking an informal coaching effort.

Reinforcement

When a manager wants an employee to consistently perform according to the established standards, he/she must pointedly recognize, acknowledge, praise, and otherwise commend the correct performance whenever and wherever it is displayed. This does not mean that the manager should walk around and mindlessly slap employees on the back and proclaim "good job," "well done," "great performance," or "keep up the good work." While such comments have their place—especially when they are serious and honest—positive reinforcement needs to be directed and specifically tied to the correct behaviors to be the most effective.

Informal—as well as formal—coaching should always be a directed process. The purpose of coaching is to point out which specific behaviors are up to standards and which behaviors need to be improved. Furthermore, coaching should include communicating and demonstrating correct procedures and pointing out why incorrect procedures lead to unacceptable results. In most job behaviors, there is a "right way" and a "desired result." The coaching and positive reinforcement process forms the specific behavior patterns to achieve these two equally important goals.

Restatement of Expectations

Expectations must be communicated to develop desirable behavior. Clearly stated and clearly understood expectations provide a basis for individual employee motivation and for effective supervision. Employees cannot be expected to achieve the desired standards unless they understand the specific expectations. Coaching is a process whereby the manager restates expectations upon which the employee bases individual performance goals. Notice how a manager uses such coaching techniques to resolve a performance problem in the following Case in Point.

A Case in Point: Slow Salads

The food production manager of a 160-seat restaurant with a heavy lunch volume walked through the kitchen and noticed that Susan, a cold food prep person, needed immediate help shaping rice croquettes for the lunch special. Susan's croquettes were shaped correctly, but her technique was so slow that she was falling far short of the production requirements.

The manager walked up and stood beside Susan for a moment without saying anything. He then commented, "Your results are good but you need to increase your speed. Let me show you how you can get the same good results faster. Otherwise, we won't have enough croquettes for lunch." He then demonstrated how he would shape the croquettes, moving with speed and efficiency. "Now you try it," he said. Susan followed his demonstration, smiling as she immediately saw that her speed could improve without sacrificing quality.

The manager then said, "You keep working on your speed and I'll ask Jim to come over and help you catch up. I need to check the dining room, but I'll be back in about five minutes to see how things are going."

After the lunch rush was over, the manager called Susan into his office to review the incident and to reinforce the need for speed, efficiency, and quality. The session began with Susan being placed at ease with some casual conversation. Then the manager asked her how she felt about the situation that occurred with the croquettes. Susan said she was pleased by her new-found speed and admitted being frustrated by falling behind in the production. The manager reassured her that it was his job to help her do her best and that she should feel free to ask for his assistance whenever she felt such frustrations. The manager closed the session by restating the importance of efficiency and effectiveness as goals of everyone in the operation.

The type of coaching illustrated in the Case in Point can be visualized as over-the-shoulder supervision. The manager walks up to an employee who is performing a work task and, over the employee's shoulder, specifically commends the behaviors that are excellent. The manager then tactfully restates the expectations in areas that can be further refined. There is a fine line between supervising over an employee's shoulder and "managing on the employee's back." No employee responds well to supervision that is too close or nit-picky. This type of supervision is considered demeaning and dictatorial, and employees will demand the manager "get off their backs." Positive over-the-shoulder coaching is welcomed. Employees see that the manager is interested in people—not just the procedure being performed.

Management Involvement

Coaching is characteristic of the involved, effective manager. Coaching is a natural behavior for the manager who looks for an employee doing something right so he/she can reinforce the behavior. The good manager teaches and reteaches the correct procedures. Such managers demonstrate personal mastery of skills, or recognize the mastery of experienced employees who are called upon to be role models or demonstrators.

Employees develop great loyalty and dedication to managers who are personal but professional. Involvement does not mean that all barriers between management and staff must be torn down. Employees quickly lose respect for managers who try to be too informal. Managers who are drinking and partying buddies with their staffs will find coaching and counseling difficult—if not impossible—since employees will have trouble taking them seriously.

Formal Coaching and Counseling

Formal coaching and counseling sessions are sometimes referred to as interviews. There are two main types of interviews used for coaching and counseling sessions: directive and non-directive interviews.

Directive and Non-Directive Interviews

Directive interviews are those in which the interviewer controls the direction of the interview by asking specific questions. *Non-directive interviews* are those in which the control and responsibility for the session passes on to the employee being interviewed. Usually non-directive interviews are designed to explore feelings and attitudes; directive interviews are largely information-getting and -giving in nature. Directive interviews can also be a means to explore feelings and attitudes. The benefits derived from a directive interview depend on the skill of the interviewer—how he/she communicates and how questions are asked.

Pre-Interview Evaluation

Before conducting an interview, the manager should evaluate the employee's job performance and any problems that the employee is having. This evaluation should be based on the job list, job breakdowns, and job performance standards. In addition, a score card should be used to evaluate actual employee performance against the established standards and procedures. The evaluation should cover the employee's overall effectiveness, work methods, work environment, and specific strengths and weaknesses.

Effectiveness. The evaluation process should seek answers to questions concerning the employee's job performance. How is the employee's performance now as compared with three months ago? Six months ago? A year ago? Is the employee doing the right things at the right times for the right reasons? Based on the performance of the employee and the overall performance of the group, where will this individual's performance level be at some point in the future? Is this performance trend positive or negative?

Methods. The evaluation process should also analyze the employee's understanding of established work methods. How does the employee perform the skills of his/her job? How does he/she carry out required duties? Is the employee making suggestions to improve the overall operation? Does the employee get along with other employees? Does the employee seem to understand how his/her work fits into the overall workflow of the department? Is the employee a team player or a loner?

Work Environment. Not all job performance problems are the fault of the employee. The evaluation should seek to objectively assess the work environment. Does the employee receive the help needed to do the job properly? Has he/she received basic training in all skill areas? Is the workload reasonable and fairly distributed? Is the manager working with or against the employee? Consider how a manager works with an employee in the following Case in Point to resolve a work situation which was beyond the employee's control.

A Case in Point: Full House

On a busy evening, it became apparent that a 440-room hotel was overbooked. As a result, guests were being accommodated at other hotels in the city. Suddenly, an arriving guest became irate when he was informed that the hotel was full and that he would have to stay at another hotel about ten minutes away. He began cursing the reception- ist and threatening to sue the hotel for not honoring his confirmed reservation. The receptionist began to cry, and walked away from the desk and into the reservations office. She refused to return and take any further abuse from this guest.

The front office manager was in the lobby area. She witnessed the incident first-hand. She immediately stepped behind the desk and took charge of the situation with the guest. After handling the matter and arranging accommodations for the upset guest, she closed the station and went to talk to the receptionist.

By this time, the receptionist had stopped crying. She still refused to return to the desk under the overbooked conditions. The front office manager assured the receptionist that her reaction was normal and was not a cause for disciplinary action. She added, however, that the situation needed to be discussed so that a recurrence could be pre- vented.

The manager then instructed the receptionist to punch out, go home, and to come in the next morning at 9:00 to discuss the matter. The next morning, the employee appeared on time for the meeting. The manager chose a directive tone for the session. Her objective was to instill confidence in the receptionist and to reassure her that she was not personally responsible for the guest's inconvenience. Furthermore, the manager wanted the receptionist to understand that the guest's behav- ior was inappropriate and was not a reflection of the employee's performance.

The manager expressed empathy toward the receptionist and disclosed that she, too, felt stress in similar situations. She then asked the receptionist to describe her recollection of what actually took place before the guest exploded. This helped reaffirm that the guest had become irate even though proper procedures had been followed. The receptionist was then asked whether she could identify anything that she could have done to prevent the episode (it was understood that she had no control over the overbooking situation). This helped reaffirm that the employee acted in good faith.

The manager and the receptionist then wrote down three statements that the employee could use to regain her confidence. These statements were:

1. I will regard each guest as a friendly individual who desires a hassle-free check-in; I believe I can provide accommodations that will satisfy their needs.

2. I will not lose my self-respect or self-confidence just because a guest acts in an inappropriate manner.

3. Before I lose my sense of self-control in stressful situations, I will call upon the manager or co-workers for assistance.

The receptionist left the meeting feeling better and returned to work with a positive attitude and new motivation to succeed. The manager recorded the events carefully and filed them for future reference in the employee's personnel file—just in case the guest did attempt to file a complaint or legal action. These records would demonstrate the hotel's efforts to maintain a positive guest and employee policy.

Strengths and Weaknesses. The interview should treat the employee as an individual with unique capabilities and limitations. Does the employee have strengths which should be recognized? Does the employee have weaknesses which can be changed or overcome? What are the most important skills to work toward improving immediately? The manager should use the pre-interview evaluation to determine the best way to discuss problem areas with a particular employee. Performance problems may relate to the employee's basic intelligence, past education, manual dexterity, or general comprehension. The evaluation should be a tool to gather facts on the total situation so that it can be dealt with objectively and fairly in the interview process.

Conducting Directive Interviews

Determine Objectives. The manager must first determine what will be accomplished by the interview. He/she should have a definite objective before scheduling a formal coaching or counseling session. The session will be more effective if the manager has first written out exactly what information is desired from the employee, what points will be stressed, and some typical questions which will be used to obtain information.

Know a Lot About the Employee. Managers should know their employees. Unfortunately, especially in large operations, this is often not the case. The manager should obtain as much background information about the employee as possible. Speaking to other managers who work with the employee and reviewing written records will provide background information about the strengths, weaknesses, and potential of the employee before the interview.

Set a Specific Time. The employee should be consulted and the weekly schedule reviewed in order to set an appropriate time for the interview. The interview is an extended training session; it should not interfere with the employee's work even though it is as important as the work being performed. When a suitable time has been determined, the manager should be sure that the employee knows about the session as far in advance as practical. This is not to be a disciplinary interview. There should be no surprises for the employee.

Conduct the Session Privately. The session should not be interrupted needlessly by other people or by telephone calls. It should not be conducted in busy production or public areas such as the kitchen, dining room, or employee break room. A suitable office or conference room should be used to provide an environment for serious thought and productive discussion.

Develop Attitude Awareness. The manager should be aware of his/her own attitudes toward the coaching and counseling activity, the session, and the specific employee. By thinking about these personal concerns, the manager can gain some insight into how the employee's performance may be influenced by his/her own biases or behaviors. The manager should also consider the employee's point of view. Even in the most structured and directed interview, it is desirable to have some understanding of how the employee feels about the interview process and the topics being considered.

Establish a Comfortable Atmosphere. The employee being interviewed must feel free to talk and to express ideas and feelings. This best occurs when the manager is willing to listen to the employee's point of view without becoming angry, even if the discussion raises questions concerning the manager's effectiveness. Some guidelines for establishing a comfortable atmosphere are:

1. Allow the employee to get used to the surroundings.

2. Try to help the employee feel that he/she is an equal.

3. Begin the interview by talking about something that is interesting to the employee, but not threatening.

4. Indicate understanding by responding directly to each comment the employee makes.

Allow Plenty of Time. It takes time for an employee to feel free to talk easily and openly to an interviewer, especially when the interviewer is his/her manager. Frequently the coaching or counseling interview is the first opportunity in which an employee has to associate the goals of the organization with his/her own past experiences and personal goals.

Set a Slow Beginning Pace. The manager must understand that, initially, the employee's responses to direct questions or direct statements may be somewhat hazy or confused. During the initial part of the interview, the pace must be slow so the employee has time to think about the question.

The manager should not try to force quick and clear-cut answers to beginning questions. If the manager projects a relaxed and tolerant attitude, the employee will not view the interview as threatening. The manager must adjust to the thinking and conversational abilities of the employee.

Pay Attention to the Close. Particular attention should be paid to the close of the interview. As the employee begins to feel that the session is coming to a close, his/her remarks often become more important. The last several minutes of the session can be the most productive if the manager is alert to the employee's final remarks or comments.

Recall that the purpose of the interview is to analyze employee performance or problems and to provide a factual basis for the employee's future development. The closing remarks may reveal real feelings that are related to the employee's level of performance. These may be more significant than earlier statements when the employee may have been saying what he/she thought the manager wanted to hear.

Conducting Non-Directive Interviews

It is a fairly common experience for managers to discover that employees do not always say what they mean. The primary focus of non-directive interviews is to analyze attitudes and feelings that are affecting job performance. When attitudes and feelings are involved, people frequently hold back or distort their true feelings. The non-directive interview is a basic interviewing technique which attempts to get beyond what people say on the surface to determine what they truly feel and mean.

Provide a Permissive, Receptive Atmosphere. The manager's basic approach to the non-directive interview is to provide a completely permissive and receptive atmosphere. When this is done, the employee being interviewed may say exactly what he/she feels without fear. Although it may be necessary for the manager to begin the interview by stating a problem, control of the interview should be passed to the employee. The basic idea is that whatever is bothering the employee will begin to surface when the employee feels that the manager is really ready to listen in an uncritical or non-threatening way.

Listen. The success of a non-directive interview almost completely depends upon the manager. He/she must listen with understanding and acceptance. This does not mean that the manager must agree with everything that is said. It does mean that the manager should not judge or criticize the employee. In a non-directive interview, criticism or evaluation of the employee's feelings, points of view, and comments will make the employee stop talking. If this occurs, the manager may never understand the cause of the problem or contribute to the further development of the employee.

Show Understanding. To show understanding, the manager should:

1. Nod or otherwise acknowledge what the employee says by short, affirmative, simple responses. Nods or comments such as

"yes" or "I see" are usually sufficient to communicate understanding. The manager should also look for similar affirmations from the employee to be certain that effective two-way communication is taking place.

2. Repeat the last important statement that the employee has made. For example, the employee may say, "I feel that I should have more authority to do my job." The manager's non-directive response might be, "You feel you would like more authority." This must be said without sarcasm or scorn. It must be a matter-of-fact—or even a leading—statement so that the employee will continue with the point being made. The restatement may then be followed with an appropriate probe to delve deeper into the employee's point of view, such as, "Could you give me some examples of areas where you feel that you could handle more authority?"

Developing Interviewing Skills

The ability to conduct effective directive and non-directive interviews must be learned. Interviewing, like other hospitality industry skills such as cooking, housekeeping, or scheduling, can be mastered through practice. Interviewing skills can be learned in the classroom through role plays or on the job through trial and error. Managers should practice away from the job (perhaps with friends, spouse, or children) before attempting to use the techniques in real on-the-job situations with employees. Regardless of the approach, the first few actual coaching or counseling interviews will be awkward; managers can expect to feel unsuccessful. Practice will overcome those feelings and, when it does, interviewing will become a very useful training and development tool.

Interviewing Techniques

An interview's success greatly depends upon the kinds of questions and how they are asked. Some techniques for asking good questions include:

1. Consider the ability and information possessed by the employee being interviewed. If the employee does not understand the question, he/she may feel inadequate. Questions should be understandable and sensible.

2. Phrase each question in a way that is within the employee's vocabulary range. As a brief warm-up, let the employee talk about a hobby, sports, his/her family, the weather, or some other topic to gain a good idea of vocabulary level. This is especially important when interviewing an employee whose command of the English language may be limited.

3. When it is necessary to ask questions which concern habits, attitudes, motives, personality, or feelings, ask them indirectly rather than abruptly. These questions may go beyond the employee's ability or willingness to answer. Employees often

become emotional when these types of questions are asked, and the answers given prove to be of little value.

4. In a directive interview, ask questions about the topic under discussion. Failure to stay on the topic may annoy an employee if the question does not fit the employee's understanding of the purpose of the interview. Occasionally the conversation may drift from the main topic—especially if the interview is long. Non-directive interviews permit deviation from the main topic. Recall that the control in a non-directive interview passes to the employee. When the subject is changed, this may provide a clue to a problem which the employee is reluctant to reveal.

5. Pose each question in a way which establishes a framework for the response. This should not be confused with the leading or "loaded" question. Such questions as, "What do you believe guests expect from you?" or "How do you feel about employee appraisals in this hotel?" are examples of setting the tone for the employee's response. It is not effective to begin the interview process by asking, "Do you have any problems that you would like to discuss?" This is far too general for a directive or non-directive interview if the purpose is to deal with specific performance situations.

6. Closed questions can be used to limit discussions and obtain specific data. Usually, closed questions call for a "yes," "no," "good," or "bad" response. They do not permit the employee to think through or express feeling about the subject of the question. Open questions permit the employee to think through answers—especially in areas where he/she may not have clear opinions. The decision to ask an open or closed question depends on the objective of the interview at that point. Open questions usually start with "How would you. . .?" "What do you. . .?" "Why should you. . .?" etc.

7. Avoid leading or "loaded" questions when seeking answers that involve the employee's personal feelings, opinions, and judgments. When leading questions are used, they force the employee to "color" the response by considering his/her perceptions of the manager's preferred answer. Often leading questions contain "value" words. For example: "You are not in favor of allowing minor infractions of the rules by employees, are you?" The "value" words here are "not in favor of" and "minor." These indicate that the manager may be "setting the employee up" for his/her own point of view.

8. Show support and understanding to the employee. When the manager detects that the employee feels uncertain as to whether a question was answered adequately, the manager should summarize what he/she understood the employee to say. This can be followed with a question to obtain clarification by probing further. For example: "Could you tell me some more about that, Joe?"

9. Listening is just as important as asking appropriate questions. Listening is very important in the non-directive interview. In other interviews, listening forms the basis for further questions and indicates the attentiveness of the manager to the employee's responses.

10. Use probing questions as supplements to the main question to draw out further responses. Probing questions should be characterized by an underlying attitude of acceptance (non-evaluation) and permissiveness. These questions, when asked considerately, help the employee to say what he/she may not have been able to say before. Probing questions should be related to the objective of the interview. They should not contain value words and should not challenge the validity of the employee's feelings.

11. Recognize that the attitudes expressed first by an employee are usually surface attitudes or those which the employee thinks the manager wants to hear. Basic, deep-rooted attitudes consist of emotions which are attached to a series of experiences. In successful non-directive interviews, basic attitudes are most obviously displayed by expressions of feelings. It is also possible to discover an employee's attitudes by observing the employee's behavior during directive interviews. The manager who conducts the interview should be patient and tolerant. Questions should be asked with a voice quality that indicates warmth—not harshness or intolerance.

12. Repeat the objective or purpose of the interview as often as necessary to keep the session on track. It is important to re-emphasize that coaching and counseling interviews are not disciplinary sessions, but are used to further develop the employee's potential. The employee being interviewed should always be told how the information and results of the interview will be used.

Objectives of Interviews

Within the principles of the problem-analysis approach, the objectives of a coaching and counseling interview are to:

- Develop the employee's skill in the critical analysis of his/her own situation.
- Provide the employee with an opportunity to make decisions.
- Inform the employee of the importance of and implications for his/her job.
- Inform the employee about his/her job performance.
- Help the employee understand his/her motivation, skills, and weaknesses as they relate to job performance.
- Give the employee an opportunity to develop his/her own program of self-development.

In reality, it is impossible for a manager to develop employees. He/she can only provide the proper tools, opportunities, and atmosphere for employees to develop themselves. Much of this is accomplished through training sessions, coaching and counseling sessions, and daily contacts with employees.

Employee Motivation and Behavior

A manager who knows what motivates employees will be able to help them develop to their full potential and perform their jobs according to established standards. Motivation is affected by the individuality of each employee.

Through the use of coaching and counseling techniques, a manager can help an employee define personal objectives more appropriately, clearly, and realistically. Coaching and counseling should help the employee understand personal needs which affect the objectives he/she sets with regard to work performance. A manager can also help an employee see the major obstacles which must be overcome in order for realistic objectives to be attained. The employee can be pointed in a more productive and rewarding direction, and the manager can help determine the appropriate steps that should be taken to satisfy personal needs within the work environment.

In any given situation, an employee's behavior is determined by a variety of factors. These include:

1. **Individual needs**—Each employee has needs that are unique; the employee feels that he/she knows what will satisfy those needs. Personal needs are affected by each individual's attitudes, interests, aptitudes, and skills.

2. **Individual situations**—Each employee lives with a different set of personal circumstances which he/she must deal with while trying to achieve personal and other goals.

3. **Individual perceptions**—The way an employee sees each situation may be different from reality (and from the way other people see it). These perceptions are affected by experiences, beliefs, impressions, and emotions. The perceptions that the employee has about his/her manager will govern how the employee accepts and responds to what the manager says.

In general, an employee's behavior to satisfy personal needs and goals will follow a pattern. In many cases, the employee is not even conscious that the pattern exists. The following situations or actions may occur as an employee works toward achieving a personal need or objective.

1. The employee will establish a specific personal objective—such as recognition as the outstanding employee in the department, an increase in salary, assignment to a different shift, or transfer to another job. The objective will, in *his/her opinion*, satisfy a basic need (even though the employee may not be consciously aware of the need).

2. The employee will then direct many of his/her working actions to do what *seems* appropriate to achieve the specific objective. In the process, the employee will attempt to avoid, modify, or remove whatever may stand in the way of achieving the goal.

3. If the objective is attained and the need is satisfied, the employee will set new objectives in accordance with his/her individual needs. If the objective is not attained, the employee may try other methods of meeting it and/or may try to eliminate roadblocks that stand in the way. Alternatively, the employee may blindly persist in the same behavior even though experience may show that the behavior is inadequate or inappropriate. The employee might even establish new objectives and abandon the first objective.

Coaching and Counseling Actions

Coaching and counseling aim to bring about desired changes in the actions and attitudes of employees. A manager usually has the control to bring about desired changes by taking one or more of the following courses of action.

Changing a Situation. The manager may (a) change his/her own behavior patterns or style of leadership (b) change the work group by encouraging behavior modification in the workers or by removing "problem" employees, or (c) change resources or conditions of the work situation. Any of these situational changes may bring about the desired modification of the individual employee's behavior.

Changing an Employee's Perception of a Situation. A manager can change an employee's job outlook by ensuring that the employee is accurately informed about company objectives, problems, and other matters of interest. Likewise, the manager can show the relationship between effective job performance and the attainment of the employee's own goals. The manager can also help the employee simplify his/her work. He/she can provide specific positive feedback when the employee meets—or fails to meet—established performance standards.

Changing an Individual's Skills. A manager can help an employee learn more about the job and how to respond to problems that arise in it. New skills and tools which an employee can use in dealing with situations can change the employee's self-concept and attitude.

Changing an Individual's Objectives. In an attempt to satisfy basic needs, an employee may set specific objectives that are beyond his/her capabilities. An employee might also behave in ways which defeat his/her own purposes. A manager can assist such an employee in setting short-range objectives which are within reasonable reach of the employee's capabilities. Managers should regularly review job performance standards that have been set for the group. When standards are unrealistically high, employees will be frustrated and will require constant coaching and counseling. When standards are realistic but remain unmet—even after training, coaching, counseling, and supervising—it may become necessary to replace employees who are unable to meet the standards with more capable personnel.

Special Needs That Affect Coaching and Counseling

The emphasis on coaching, counseling, and individualized training methods covered in this book should clearly indicate that managers have a definite responsibility to help meet the individual needs of employees. The hospitality industry is a "people industry." Whether by choice or directive, managers should learn to deal in a positive and personal way with all employees that they are assigned to supervise and lead.

These concerns should not be confused with what critics may refer to as "soft management." It is sound management practice to recognize the individual needs of each employee and to bring out the maximum potential of each individual.

Managers need to recognize the special problems associated with overcoming the effects of discrimination. Federal and state legislation has been passed to protect the rights of all employees. Under these laws, all employees are entitled to fair labor practices and non-discriminatory treatment.

The training methods presented in this book are basic to training and developing all employees. The trainer who follows the training process which has been outlined can be successful in training individuals and groups regardless of their race, creed, sex, national origin, or any other factor that may lead to unfair or prejudicial treatment.

Some categories of employees should be briefly discussed because of the social and legislative measures implemented on their behalf. The special needs of these groups do not necessitate a change in the training design process. However, the needs may affect decisions about who will be trained for selected jobs or which method will be used for training. From a follow-through standpoint, being aware of these special needs can improve coaching and counseling that is geared toward building pride and self-confidence.

Racial and Ethnic Minorities

Every society has a category of people whose race or culture is dominant. In some societies, all the people may be in this dominant category. Most societies have additional minority races and cultures. Managers should accept racial and cultural differences as positive in both a business and humanistic sense. A manager should never indicate that any employee is of lesser worth to the manager, to the organization, or to society because of that employee's membership in a racial or ethnic group.

All properly selected employees can learn to perform effectively when the training and coaching process has been well designed and is executed in a consistent and fair manner. The key to overcoming difficulties that may arise is the manager's ability to communicate expectations clearly and fairly to everyone. This establishes the basis for expected behavior patterns on the job. The job analysis tools developed for any training program provide the objective basis for communicating these expectations.

Within the United States, discrimination on the basis of national origin is prohibited under the guidelines of the Equal Employment Opportunity Commission.[2] Under the guidelines, "an employer has an affirmative duty to maintain a working environment free of harassment on the basis of national origin." An employer is not only liable for harassment by other employees, but may also be liable for harassment by third parties and the public at large. Also, an employer would be responsible for acts "creating an intimidating, hostile, or offensive working environment" or acts which "unreasonably interfere with an individual's work performance" or otherwise adversely affect an individual's employment opportunities.

Women

The 1964 Civil Rights Act of the United States makes discrimination because of sex a violation of the law. Women and men today hold positions that were traditionally limited to one gender. This sexual crossover in jobs should not disturb the trainer. If the jobs have been properly analyzed and the training has been planned based on the job requirements, then the sex of the trainee will not affect the results. Managers should avoid job stereotyping (assuming that certain jobs must be reserved for one sex, certain ages, etc.).

Age Factors

For the most part, people in the United States are living longer because of improvements in health care. This, in turn, has resulted in a larger pool of employees in the upper age brackets. Many companies have extended the retirement age from 65 to 70 years old. It is illegal to discriminate against applicants for jobs on the basis of age if they are between the ages of 40 and 70.[3] The overall impact of these societal changes is that there are more older workers to be trained, coached, and counseled. Through use of effective adult learning methods, employees can continue to learn throughout life.

Managers may feel that it is difficult to convince older employees that new methods are more effective. By conducting performance reviews which compare actual performance to job performance standards, the manager has an objective basis for coaching any employee—regardless of age.

There are also more young employees in the work force than ever before. Many schools offer courses in hospitality subjects through cooperative arrangements. These "co-op" programs include classroom education and training, and on-the-job work experience in lodging and food service establishments. On-the-job training programs should be planned by the hospitality operation's management in conjunction with the student employees' school to meet the needs of the student, the school, and the hospitality operation. Such programs are subject to federal, state, and local laws on employment of students and minors.

When coaching and counseling co-op student employees (and young employees in general), managers must recognize that the needs of these individuals are different from those of older workers. The student employees are exploring a career field or "testing the water." Their decision to increase their commitment to their job so that it can develop into a career is affected by their experiences at work and the attention they receive from an interested manager.

Handicapped Persons   A handicapped person is one who has a physical or mental impairment which *substantially limits* one or more of his/her *major life activities*.[4] Some handicapped conditions are obvious. Others are hidden, such as epilepsy (when seizures are under control), mental illness, diabetes, or heart conditions.

In companies within the United States covered by the Rehabilitation Act of 1973, it is illegal to discriminate against handicapped persons who are qualified to perform a job. (Companies covered by the act are those doing business with the federal government under contract for more than $2,500 and companies receiving federal financial assistance.) A person must be capable of performing a particular job with *reasonable accommodation* to the handicapping condition, if it is needed.[5]

One of the best authorities on reasonable accommodations is the handicapped person. The manager who is hiring and training handicapped people should feel free to ask what accommodations will be necessary for job performance. It is important for managers not to view handicapped individuals as "helpless." There are many capable people with handicaps who can be very productive in hospitality positions.

In coaching and counseling handicapped employees, managers should look at each individual as a unique resource. The efforts made by the manager to optimize that resource should place emphasis on the employee's *ability* rather than the employee's *disability*. In many cases, individuals without a defined handicap are much more sensitive about the handicapped person's disability than the person who has learned to live and function with the handicap.

Notes

1. Clark Lambert, *The Complete Book of Supervisory Training* (New York: Wiley, 1984), pp. 94–95.
2. 29 C.F.R. 1606.1 et seq.
3. Age Discrimination and Employment Act of 1967, Sec. 12(a).
4. The term *substantially limits* has to do with the degree of disability. A handicapped person having a hard time getting a job or getting ahead on the job because of a disability would be considered substantially limited. The term *major life activities* includes communication, ambulation, self-care, socialization, education, transportation, and, of course, employment.
5. *Reasonable accommodation* means making necessary adaptations to enable a qualified handicapped person to work. It may include (1) making facilities used by all employees accessible to handicapped people (ramps, restroom adaptations, wider aisles, etc.) and (2) making modifications in jobs, work schedules, equipment or work area as necessary (simplifying a job so a handicapped person can perform it; changing working hours, teaching sign language to a manager of a deaf employee, providing a reader for a blind person, etc.).

17 Performance Reviews

Employees at all levels within a hospitality operation want to know how they are doing regarding their job performance. Regular, formal performance reviews should be conducted to meet this basic need. Performance reviews serve other valuable purposes. A performance review is a coaching tool which provides information for both the manager and the employee. The planned use of formal performance reviews should be an important part of every manager's training, coaching, and employee development efforts.

The performance review process should be a developmental activity which actively involves both the manager and the employee. The manager and employee should examine the employee's overall performance to identify strengths and potentials, as well as weaknesses and deficiencies. Consequently, employees can determine needed changes in behavior, attitudes, skills, or job knowledge. The resulting information also equips managers with an objective basis for coaching and counseling.

Performance reviews represent an individualized follow-through of a manager's evaluation of training and development activities. The results may be used to analyze and plan future development efforts. Performance reviews may also be used to support or justify positive personnel actions such as salary increases, promotions, or transfers, or negative personnel actions such as demotions, job reassignments, or terminations. This chapter will not focus on these applications but will deal with the use of performance reviews in meeting individual training, coaching, and developmental needs.

Reviews Versus Appraisals

The term **performance appraisal** is widely used in business and industry to describe the process whereby employees are periodically evaluated by their managers. Traditionally, performance appraisals have been used to objectively assess the worth of employees in order to make wage and salary adjustments. The term **merit rating** more clearly describes that process. In recent years, performance appraisals have also been used to determine training and developmental needs and to help improve current performance. Since *appraisal* suggests establishing worth or value, the term is easily associated with pay.

This chapter will use a term that more clearly describes the relationship between evaluation and the goal of improved performance: **performance review.** This term avoids connotations of worth. To clearly separate appraisal for wage and salary purposes from reviews for improving performance, many companies conduct separate evaluations for the two purposes.

As used here, the term performance review does not ignore the concept of value; it does, however, include other aspects of equal importance. The performance review process should include the opportunity for the employee to discuss issues important to him/her, to explain his/her actions, to express feelings, to discuss aspirations, to suggest solutions, or to resolve any aspects of his/her work performance that have been identified as undesirable.

Performance reviews should evaluate employee performance rather than employee potential. The current performance review should evaluate current performance levels and serve as the basis for restating performance goals and standards. If there are obstacles to performance which are identified during the performance evaluation process—and if these obstacles can be removed—then the manager may predict improved performance.

Employee Development Through Performance Reviews

Procedures for developing hospitality employees do not include coercing them into accepting the operation's goals—nor do they include manipulating employee behavior to suit operational needs. Rather, these procedures consistently call for creating an environment in which employees can take some responsibility for developing their own potential. When this occurs, employees are treated as adults. They gain a genuine sense of satisfaction since they are using their own capabilities to achieve both personal and organizational goals. Unless the work environment provides these opportunities, **development** becomes an empty, meaningless term. An effective review of performance is an important part of the employee development process.

To be an adult learning activity, a performance review should be rooted in active two-way communication between manager and employee. It is active in nature because the review of past performance is used as a basis for planning future performance. This relationship is based upon what the employee and manager mutually agree that the employee needs to do to further improve work performance. The following Case in Point presents one option for ensuring the active exchange of ideas between managers and employees in the performance review process.

A Case in Point: Performance Reviews Lead to Goals

Making goal-setting a part of the performance review process is an effective way to ensure that the performance review process is an employee development activity. One hotel chain does this by incorporating goal-setting forms in the review packet. Following the evaluation by the employee's supervisor, a counseling session is held where the performance review results are discussed. As part of the session, the employee and supervisor identify three areas that present the most opportunity for improvement in the coming months.

In each of these three areas, the employee writes one specific goal with the assistance of the supervisor, along with criteria for evaluating improvement. For each goal, the employee agrees to specific observable and measurable indicators of progress. Finally, the employee prepares a written description of the desirable behaviors that should occur within a set time frame if progress is made. During the next performance review, the progress achieved in these three goal areas has a significant influence on the overall tone of the review process.

Benefits of Reviews

Recognition. The performance review compares what the employee is doing with what the employee is expected to do. When the review involves both the manager and the employee, the first important benefit is that it recognizes the employee. Employees need to feel that their efforts are important. They are motivated when their supervisor is concerned about their performance.

Identification of Strengths and Weaknesses. The performance review should identify the strengths and weaknesses of the employee's performance. If the employee is encountering problems that interfere with required performance levels, those problems should be identified in the performance review.

Evaluation. An employee is competent when he/she has the knowledge, understanding, skills, attitudes, opinions, and confidence which are necessary to do the job. Evaluation of competence levels should be part of every training program. In other words, after training is completed, the trainer should be able to objectively answer the question, "How effective was the training?" The performance review process can serve as a follow-up evaluation in the same areas that the training addressed. It allows the manager to assess the lasting effects of the training.

Many times employees can demonstrate mastery of the learning at the end of the training session but, a few weeks later, their performance has dropped below mastery levels. The employees appear to have forgotten what they learned. Over time, gaps may develop between the ideal performance that was demonstrated during training and the actual on-the-job performance. Such occurrences are often due to factors unrelated to training. The employee may still know the correct way to perform, but his/her performance is inhibited because of barriers which have developed. The performance review process will identify existing gaps in performance. Once these gaps are identified, the manager and the employee should discuss the situation, identify the causes for the deficiencies, and act to resolve the identified problems. It is important to re-emphasize that not all problems identified by a performance review will be training-related.

A Basis for Coaching and Counseling. Personal problems often interfere with work performance and affect job satisfaction. The performance review provides a structure for reviewing an employee's work, discussing work performance, and addressing any personal problems that the employee may wish to discuss. Without this structure, it becomes easy for managers to avoid the process of evaluating performance objectively and counseling employees on personal problems. Of course, when personal problems exceed the professional training and expertise of the manager, additional, specialized assistance should be recommended.

A Basis for Determining Pay. In this text, performance reviews are concerned with assessing and improving the results of training and coaching efforts. However, another purpose is to provide objective information that can be used to determine the appropriate pay for an employee in relation to how he/she performs on the job. The trend in business and industry is to pay the same amount of money to all people who perform the same basic job duties or have the same job classification. Raises relate as much to tenure (time in the job) and seniority (time in the organization) as they do to performance levels.

Not all employees perform at the same level of productivity even though they have the same job classification. Ideally, employees should be paid in direct relationship to their work efforts over a certain period. While pay-for-productivity is more difficult to administer than pay-by-classification or pay-based-on-tenure, it does provide a basis for treating employees with individual dignity, fairness, and true worth, while recognizing levels of acceptable performance. The pay-for-productivity approach reinforces the development of productive norms; employees will realize that normal behavior is productive behavior.

Justification of Promotions. Every manager would like to think that he/she promotes the most competent people. In situations where seniority is a matter of rule (as is often prescribed by union contracts, civil service regulations, or precedent), tenure may be considered more important than competence. One goal of managers should be to promote the most competent employees. The performance review process provides objective information about performance and competence which can be used to justify promotions. This approach can help overcome the unproductive practice of promoting people primarily because of the number of years of employment.

Needs Analysis. Every good training program should begin with a thorough needs analysis. The performance review process provides, in effect, a continuous needs analysis. The reviews will identify when and which employees need additional training or coaching. They will also indicate when and which groups of employees need to improve their performance. Performance reviews, then, help identify specific training needs. As a result, goals can be set for improving the performance of individual employees or employee groups when reviews indicate deficiencies.

Improved Management. The performance review process improves the managers within an organization. Effective managers focus on the improvement of employee performance. The performance review process encourages managers to be constantly aware of performance levels in relation to the expectations held for each employee and employee group. When identifying strengths and weaknesses of the employee, the manager must also reflect on the strengths and weaknesses of his/her own management style and practices.

Improved Employee-Management Relationships. The review process, done correctly, also improves employee-management relationships. It involves a joint effort between the manager and the employee. They become partners as the employee attempts to achieve his/her potential for productivity and job satisfaction. As the manager and the employee both learn from the process, their relationship improves. The performance review process is important in the development of competent workers and managers. It is a good way for managers and employees to periodically make necessary changes so that *actual performance* and *standards for performance* go hand-in-hand.

How and When to Conduct Performance Reviews

Ideally, performance reviews should be objective. Ultimately, most performance reviews include some subjective observations, opinions, and judgments, since performance is being judged by a manager who may have subconscious biases. Using appropriate forms to conduct the performance review can reduce this problem. The forms should indicate the criteria which will be used to evaluate performance. Guidelines must be developed regarding how and when performance will be observed for the review. The evaluation criteria and procedures should be focused on rating the employee's demonstrated performance under normal working conditions.

The manager who is responsible for the review process should not depend upon memory to recall an employee's performance. The manager should schedule time to observe the specific employee as he/she performs the job. When this is done, the manager should have the performance review forms as well as the job list, job breakdowns, job performance standards, and any other necessary information to ensure that performance is rated according to the standards and procedures taught to the employee.

The performance review process should be treated as a routine duty of managers. A manager who coaches employees on a day-to-day basis needs objective information to be effective in that role. The performance review process can help supply this information.

Performance reviews should not be conducted only occasionally—they should be conducted regularly and routinely to emphasize opportunities for improvement. Formal training sessions are held periodically. However, training should also occur daily through ongoing training, coaching, and counseling activities, and as employees are supervised. The performance review adds meaning and objectivity to this training and development process.

Basic Approaches to Performance Reviews

There are two basic approaches to conducting performance reviews in the hospitality industry. The **trait approach** attempts to identify the qualities, traits, or behaviors that are believed necessary for effective performance. The individual employee is rated against a profile of desirable traits. This approach is frequently called the **rating method.** Forms and techniques are used in an attempt to eliminate biases of the manager as he/she rates the employee. One problem with the rating method is that it usually does not focus on how well the employee performs the job. Rather, it focuses upon such traits as appearance, neatness, timeliness, friendliness, and cooperation. An employee can, of course, score high on many trait ratings and still be an ineffective performer. Used alone, the rating method is of little value in assessing training and coaching needs.

The second basic approach to performance reviews considers goals or objectives. The **objective method** focuses on performance. Beginning with the performance expectations held for an employee, the manager and the employee can plan what the employee should be able to do. This process establishes performance goals. The goals are then quantified, and a later review of an employee's performance is based on how well the employee has met the goals. Administrative actions, training plans, coaching sessions, and other activities are then planned on the basis of whether the goals were met.

The rating method used alone does not usually focus on results. The objective method tends to ignore the causes of low performance that are associated with personal traits. Used together, elements of both basic methods can analyze what the employee does or fails to do and provide clues to the reasons for the performance levels.

A performance review program that begins with performance planning and evaluates employee accomplishments in light of the plan will generally include rating some behavioral traits. The program will provide a broad basis for coaching employees to (1) achieve performance goals and (2) remove personal barriers which affect attaining objectives.

Establishing Performance Review Objectives

Before designing a performance review system, managers must decide what kind of information the system should provide and how that information will be used. It is not sufficient to merely believe that performance reviews are important in employee training and development. Managers must go beyond this belief to state specifically how the performance review process will fit into a total training and development plan and philosophy. This is especially important since the use of the information often affects the quality of the information sought by managers. For example, a manager may rate an employee one way if the objective of the performance review is to determine wage or salary increases. The manager may consider the employee differently if the information will be used to improve training and coaching efforts.

Managers should follow four basic rules when conducting performance reviews:[1]

1. Limit the performance review to the appraisal of measurable and discernible factors. Avoid generalities and personality traits.

2. Limit the performance review to the appraisal of behaviors. Focus on what the employee is and is not doing.

3. Limit the performance review to what the employee has been trained to do. Avoid the temptation to appraise potential; stick to reviewing existing skills.

4. Limit the performance review to those behaviors which can be evaluated against a known standard. Ideal behavior must be describable, observable, tangible, and reasonable.

Quality and Quantity Ratings

Managers are primarily interested in the results of an employee's efforts. In many cases these results can be quantified. For example, a pastry chef may be rated on units of production (the number of pies, cakes, tortes, rolls, and other pastry items produced during a specified period). In addition to evaluating the quantity of items produced, the rater must also judge the quality of the items produced against some standard (such as recipes) that describes the characteristics of the desired product. When possible, the measurement of performance should review the quantity as well as quality of the work performed.

Individual Differences

Managers understand that individual differences of employees affect performance on the job. For example, if an individual works as a guest receptionist or food server, he/she will be trained in procedures involving selling skills. The ability to sell is probably easier for extroverts. A person who is shy or timid may perform well in a secure training environment but may fail to effectively apply the selling skills on the job. If the manager assesses sales performance and also knows something about the employee, he/she may recognize that the problem of low sales may not be the result of lack of know-how but the result of the employee's personality. The manager might then decide to shift the employee to a non-sales position or spend time coaching and counseling the employee to overcome shyness.

An employee who comes to a job with a warm, outgoing personality has an advantage over a timid employee in guest-contact performance areas; however, the timid employee may have other strengths. For example, the timid employee may be more careful with details or may be a better judge of quality. Each employee brings his/her own individuality to the job. This should be considered when employees are selected for various positions and when performance is reviewed.

Personality and Performance

Personality is very difficult to measure. Managers must generally review attitudes that are indicative of personality rather than try to isolate and analyze the employee's personality itself. When rating an employee's efforts in terms of what is accomplished on the job, behavior and attitudes must be considered because they affect performance.

In many organizations, managers have completely stopped trying to measure personality. Instead, their performance review systems are oriented toward the results of employee performance. This trend is an outgrowth of recognizing that what employees accomplish on the job is the most important aspect of the performance review.

The Performance Review Conference

A performance review is not complete until the evaluation information is shared with the employee who has been evaluated. As stated earlier, this communication must be two-way, with the employee taking an active part in analyzing the performance data, and initiating suggestions for overcoming performance deficiencies. The tone should be active communication by both parties; the outcome should be a mutual understanding and agreement as to employee and manager actions following the review.

Preparing for the Review Session

The manager should prepare for the review session by studying the job list, job breakdowns, and job performance standards for the position being reviewed. This ensures that the manager's expectations are consistent with the standards and expectations that were communicated to the employee during training and coaching. If the documents are out of date, they must be corrected and communicated to the employee. The employee must be given time to achieve the new standards before being held accountable for revised expectations.

The manager should systematically and consciously observe the performance of the employee for several days under different job conditions before completing the review rating forms. This should take place before the day of the actual review conference so that the performance is not influenced by any nervousness. The manager should carefully study each evaluation point on the rating forms. He/she should think about the behaviors that have been observed, and try to objectively determine whether the behaviors were typical or somehow biased by extenuating circumstances.

The rating should be of *typical* performance under *average* working conditions. Good rating scales provide a basis for evaluating each area of performance based on the assigned duties of the employee, and provide a basis for making a prognosis concerning overall performance. The manager should complete this analysis before the actual review session, so that he/she can prescribe sound courses of action for the improvement and career advancement of the employee.

Selecting the Setting for the Session

A performance review conference should always be held in a private location that is free of disturbances. Interruptions by telephones, other employees, other managers, or guests should not be permitted. This is a time that the disciplined leader should hang the "do not disturb" sign on the door. An individual's self concept and future career may well be on the line. Such important matters deserve the serious undivided attention of the manager.

Honest and Open Interaction

Performance reviews are sometimes ineffective because managers and employees are not honest with each other about performance levels or performance difficulties. It is often easier for managers to talk about employees to other managers than to talk to the same employees face to face.

The review process only works when the parties involved talk to each other in an open and objective manner. The manager is responsible for controlling the objectivity of the session. It must not become a gripe session, or an opportunity for the employee to avoid personal responsibility by blaming all weaknesses on someone else or on unreasonable demands of guests. The session must never turn into a name-calling, mud-slinging, knock-down, drag-out, contest of insults. It must be constructive communication that is committed to forming a plan of action that leads to continued performance improvement.

Balancing Employee-Manager Input

The employee must communicate with more than a passive nod of the head, or a simple acknowledgment. The employee must be given the opportunity to talk about the job, and to express in his/her own words what is going well and what is not. During these times, the manager must listen without interrupting and correcting the employee. The manager must tactfully and politely ask the employee "What do you see as your responsibility in this area we are discussing now?"

A good session involves give and take communications—meaning that the manager and employee should each speak approximately half of the time. If the manager does 70 to 80% of the talking, the review session has become a lecture. In these situations, most employees will remember very little of what they hear. If the employee controls 70 to 80% of the conversation, the manager has probably lost control. Most likely, the employee will go back to the job thinking that the manager is not very aware of what is going on in the job setting. Balance is the key word to effective communications in a performance review session.

Clarifying Follow-Up

The plan of action that comes out of the review conference should be very clear to the manager and to the employee. The best way for this to occur is for the two parties to write down the specific, agreed upon action steps during the review conference. Next, the manager and employee should assign dates by which each action step can be expected to be in place so that the desired changes in performance can be observed. Both the manager and employee should then sign and date the steps. This signifies that both parties accept joint responsibility for meeting the established goals. If some of the steps require a long period of time to implement, interim progress review dates should be set and agreed to.

Living Up to Agreements

A leading reason why the achievement of action steps sometimes breaks down is that managers agree to make changes which are out of their control. Often, performance is hindered by operational problems that go beyond the specific performance of job duties by an employee. These are *systemic* or *organizational* in nature—and the typical department manager does not control the systems or the organizational structure. Changes of this magnitude require the cooperation and participation of the entire management team. Changes may even require approval or funding by the owners or management company.

When a manager agrees to remove the obstacles which hinder an employee's performance, and the employee agrees to improve the performance as soon as these obstacles are removed, the manager has probably walked into a "no win" trap. Systemic and organizational changes usually take a lot of time to bring about. Meanwhile, the employee is watching the skills of the manager with a critical eye. Unless the changes begin to happen almost immediately, the manager's credibility will begin to falter, and the other action steps which had nothing to do with the systemic or organizational changes will likely fall by the wayside. Action steps should be within the day-to-day operational control of the manager and the employee. The need for systemic and organizational changes may be discussed in the review conference. Such changes, however, must not be part of the action plan for improving the performance of the employee.

Problems with Performance Reviews

At best, the performance review process is a structured, but subjective, process. Efforts to quantify human behaviors are all limited by subjective judgment. The structure of some review instruments go further in describing the criteria for rating observed behaviors. This adds an element of objectivity, but the limitations of any rating approach must be acknowledged. The success of a review process rarely lies in the design of the rating scale. Rather, it lies in the two-way interaction of the manager and the employee concerning the relationship between actual and ideal performance. Nevertheless, it is worthwhile to discuss some of the common problems which negatively affect the performance review activity.

Incorrect Usage

There are probably critics of any approach to reviewing performance. Some of this criticism is justified, since many organizations do not administer their performance review program correctly. In some operations there are no policies or schedules for required reviews and, therefore, they are rarely, if ever, conducted. Under these circumstances, reviews may be done primarily when managers are upset with employees. They use the reviews as a form of disciplinary action or "to build a case" against employees.

Ineffective Forms

In other situations, the review process is not effective because of poorly prepared forms and other devices. Such forms focus on popularity or personality traits of the employee rather than performance results.

No Review At All

The greatest abuse of the performance review concept is to have no formal review at all but, at the same time, to make management decisions about training and coaching as if a review had been performed. Managers who are guilty of this will tell employees, "I have reviewed your performance, and it is obvious that some steps must be taken to improve it." In this approach, the manager relies on unstructured observations and generalizations to evaluate performance levels. Employees are ill-treated by this process since almost every employee does some things well while others do almost everything well.

Employees who are not evaluated individually never know exactly how well they are doing in their job. When employees do not have the opportunity to meet with their manager to discuss their performance and their feelings, they may believe that they are not very important. As this occurs, employees will become less motivated to meet the performance standards since the standards will seem less important.

Lack of Knowledge, Skills

One of the major reasons some managers do not meet their responsibility for training and coaching is that they lack the knowledge and skills to be effective trainers. The same problem exists with respect to performance reviews. In many cases, managers have received no training in how to conduct performance reviews and may have never been exposed to reviews conducted by someone else.

An operation that requires managers to periodically conduct performance reviews and yet provides no training in how to do it effectively shows that it regards the process as unimportant. Managers will give a sufficient amount of attention to conducting effective reviews when they clearly understand that the performance review process is essential in developing employee efficiency.

Complexity

Some performance review systems fail because they are too complicated. The forms may be difficult to complete or score. The manager using such materials may have difficulty interpreting the findings of the review or in using the information to plan improvements with the employee. Performance review forms do not need to be complicated to be effective. The manager should remember that the primary purpose of a performance review is to objectively assess how an employee is performing in comparison with established targets or goals. When the review indicates that performance has fallen below those targets and standards, the manager and the employee can begin planning to correct those deficiencies and improve performance levels.

Irregular, Infrequent Reviews

One possible weakness with performance reviews is that they may be conducted on an irregular or infrequent basis. The review process should be continual. Even if an annual or semi-annual formal review is conducted, there should be informal reviews on a more frequent basis to constantly develop information for feedback to the employees. The need to improve performance should be a constant concern. A performance-oriented climate within the organization and among employees is necessary if managers are to receive the maximum return from their investment in human resource development.

Fear of Offending Employees

Managers may be afraid of offending an employee if they are completely honest about their observations of the employee's performance. This is particularly true if the employee is not performing up to established standards. It is easy to compliment an employee for doing an outstanding job. It is much more difficult to tell an employee that performance is not satisfactory. When this is done, it is necessary to relate specific observations to substantiate the problem. The manager must then explain the specific steps that an employee must take to bring performance up to an acceptable level.

In a participative performance review process, the employee has the opportunity to explain his/her perception of observed problems. If the employee's defense takes the form of excuses, the entire session can get out of hand. If, for example, the employee blames the substandard performance on mismanagement or inadequate supervision, the manager who is conducting the session may suddenly feel a need to defend his/her own performance. This non-productive discussion can be avoided if the employee (a) knows what he/she is expected to do, (b) is trained until he/she can demonstrate competence, and (c) is reviewed as part of a day-to-day coaching process. In this situation, employees recognize that it is the manager's responsibility to expect good performance, to point out deficiencies in performance, and to suggest ways that unsatisfactory performance can be improved.

Employee Comparison

Managers may be tempted to compare one employee's performance with that of another. In the performance review process, this kind of comparison will lead to conflict and hinder growth and development. The only comparison that is valid in performance reviews is a comparison between the expectations held for an employee and the actual performance of that same individual. It is never a good practice to compare employees.

Telling an employee that "you do your job better than (or not as well as) another employee" is not helpful to the employee who wants to know what he/she should do to perform satisfactorily. It is more effective for the manager to say, "We agreed in the beginning that your job would include the following duties or skills, and that you would be expected to perform those duties in the prescribed manner. Now that you have been doing the job, your level of performance is below the agreed-upon standards in certain skill areas. How do you feel about your performance and how can we work together to overcome any problems that may be causing the deficiencies?" At this point, the employee has a clear opportunity to give reasons for the substandard performance and to request training, coaching, or any other assistance. The employee may feel that the performance ratings are biased or unfair. If so, the manager and employee should discuss the matter in an attempt to reach an understanding about the current level of performance and what can reasonably be done to raise performance to expected levels. This approach recognizes the individual differences of each employee. It also helps to develop the full potential of each employee.

"File-It" Approach

Some hospitality operations use a "fill-it-out and file-it" approach to performance reviews. This approach should not even be called a performance review. It is, at best, a one-sided performance documentation process; the manager may fill out the performance review forms and then file them without sharing the information or the ratings with the employee. As already noted, the employee must be actively involved in the review process for it to be of any value. This exchange and feedback session is essential to using the performance review as a training and development tool. The review provides information for coaching and counseling sessions. It is proper for the review forms to be filed for future reference as a means of tracking changes in performance levels over time. The ratings, however, should not be permanently filed until they have been discussed fully with the employee in a coaching or counseling situation.

The performance review process should be a dynamic, ongoing

process. This means that the performance review is (a) planned ahead of time, (b) conducted as a routine part of the manager's day-to-day supervisory duties, (c) discussed in a coaching and counseling session, and (d) followed up.

Lack of Follow-Up

Follow-up helps ensure that the employee is improving as a result of the feedback received in the review process. Many managers conduct a review, discuss it with the employee, and then forget about it until it is time to conduct another review. Consider, for example, that six months may pass before the next scheduled review. If, during that time, no follow-up has taken place and performance has not improved significantly, the manager may assume that the employee ignored the opportunity to improve and should therefore be reprimanded. The manager in this situation is just as guilty of non-performance as the employee. The employee did not improve job performance. However, the manager did not carry out his/her responsibility of following up with coaching, counseling, training, or other techniques to facilitate the performance improvement.

Employees should not be held accountable for performance that is unrealistic under the existing working conditions. Appropriate management follow-up is important to an effective performance review process. Sometimes, the problems experienced by an employee cannot be corrected by training and coaching. Performance deficiencies may result from the employee having inadequate equipment to do the job properly or having an inefficiently designed work station. In these instances, the manager should follow up to acquire the correct equipment or to rearrange the work station.

Concerns About Errors

No performance review process is perfect. If a manager waits for the perfect system before systematically reviewing employees, the process will never begin. Since there are human elements involved in the performance review process, the best that a manager can ever expect to accomplish is a *reasonably objective* and *fair* system for comparing expectations with actual performance. Errors will exist in judgments made by the manager, but an open discussion between the manager and the employee will resolve most of these errors. Judgments about performance must be made in every organization. Even without a formal performance review system, judgments will be made as a manager considers whether to keep or dismiss employees, give raises or promotions, or make adjustments to work schedules. A well-designed performance review system reduces the human error in these decisions; however, that error can never be eliminated completely.

Concerns About Fairness

An effective manager does everything possible to be just and fair in dealing with employees. When a performance review is conducted, the manager is faced with the problem of how to fairly deal with the information. Managers may be concerned about whether the negative aspects of the review will damage or harm the employee's self-image. This is a major concern when it is necessary to record on performance review documents that an employee's performance is below established standards. Managers may realize that once this information becomes part of an employee's permanent human resource record, it may continue to affect the employee—even when the performance problems are overcome and the employee begins to perform at very high levels.

There is a tendency for anyone who reads an individual's human resource file to become biased, even though some of the information may be out of date and no longer valid. It is one thing to discuss performance deficiencies with employees. It is another to record negative information on a permanent record when the manager knows that the information may later be read without allowing the employee an adequate self-defense. Consider the feelings of one manager regarding performance information in the following Case in Point.

A Case in Point: Damaging Data

During her first week as a new department head, Mary Mellen reviewed all of the human resource files for the department's current employees. The following note appeared in the file of Suzie Swartz, cashier:

Performance Review Note on Susie Swartz, Jan. 3, 19XX

For the past three weeks, Suzie's bank has been consistently short by amounts ranging from $4.50 to $5.00. I discussed this with her today and she insisted that the series of shortages was just coincidental and that she was trying to be more accurate. The shortages are not sufficient to take disciplinary action under our cashiering policies, but something sure looks "fishy." I plan to keep a close eye on this situation to determine if she is stealing from her bank in small amounts.

The manager who had written the note had been gone for more than a year. The note was nearly two years old. The new department head faced the following dilemma: Should she pull Suzie's cashiering reports for the past month to see if this is still a problem or should she discard the note and try to forget that she ever saw it.

Actually, the damage was done. Mary Mellen found it impossible to forget that she had read the note. The negative bias was passed along. Suzie would have to live with the doubts of the new manager regardless of her honesty.

Much of the concern surrounding performance information can be overcome by maintaining detailed information of an extremely negative nature in a separate file. This information should never become a permanent record; it should only be part of a working file to use in planning performance improvement activities. As the employee's performance improves, the "plain paper notes" can be discarded. The information that is entered in the permanent record is limited to factual information that describes the manager's observations about the employee's actual performance compared with standard performance. The permanent record of the performance review should not evaluate the employee as a person; it should only be a record of the employee's performance levels.

For the performance review process to be fair, the employee must be (a) completely clear about what he/she is expected to do, (b) trained in how to do the job, and (c) given adequate equipment and an efficient work station to carry out assigned tasks. The performance review process is an evaluation system to keep each of these elements in place. It is not fair to judge an employee's performance as below standard if the employee is working without adequate knowledge of standards, adequate skill development, or essential equipment and facilities.

Designing a Performance Review System

A manager may find a performance review system in place when he/she takes a position with a hospitality operation. On the other hand, the system may need improvement or may not exist at all. All managers should be able to design effective tools for the performance review process and a plan for executing the performance reviews.

Establish Objectives

Like anything else a manager does, the first step in planning a performance review system is to establish objectives for the review activities. What is it that the review process is intended to accomplish within the organization? Is it merely to collect information that can be stored in human resource files and used when a manager needs to justify a personnel action? Is it information collected and discussed with the employee in order to make the employee more aware of what is expected in the job, and to make the manager more aware of what coaching, counseling, and supervision efforts will help the employee? These and similar questions must be answered to establish the specific objectives for a performance review system.

If the objective of the performance review is to enhance the training and development process, the rating forms should be simple and easy to use. The types of forms discussed in Chapter 12 are adaptable for use in reviewing performance. The evaluations that make up the performance review do not have to be different from the evaluations performed during and following training. The performance review is nothing more than periodic "after-training testing" to determine whether performance levels are improving, declining, or holding steady.

Exhibits 17.1 through 17.3 show examples of performance review forms that are used in conjunction with a restaurant's training program. Note that each evaluation form has the same format, but the job-related portions of each form are tailored to the job list for the position. All three employee categories are required to know policies and procedures that affect all employees, but the skills differ for each. In the training program for this restaurant, there is a job breakdown for each duty listed in the review forms and there are other materials (menus, wine lists, plating specifications, beverage specifications, side-work assignment charts, seating charts, etc.) that supplement the job breakdowns as training aids. The performance review is conducted before training begins, immediately following training, and periodically according to an established schedule. The performance review process is used to maintain the clearly defined standards of the restaurant.

Exhibit 17.1   Sample Performance Review: Host/Hostess

HOST/HOSTESS PERFORMANCE REVIEW

HOST/HOSTESS NAME _____

DIRECTIONS: Rate the performance level of the employee.

4 — Excellent — Usually meets established standards
3 — Good — Acceptable but could improve
2 — Fair — Definite need for improvement
1 — Unacceptable — Definite need for counseling

Performance Area	Before Training	After Training	25-Day Eval.	90-Day Eval.	180-Day Eval.	270-Day Eval.	360-Day Eval.	Comments
Date	/ /	/ /	/ /	/ /	/ /	/ /	/ /	Indicate Date by Each Comment
Policies and Procedures (Knowledge)								
Use of exits and entrances								
Uniform exchange/cleaning procedures								
Sign-in and sign-out sheets								
Cafeteria hours								
Restaurant hours of operation								
Employee schedules								
Fire procedures								
Accident reports								
Absenteeism, sick calls, tardiness								
Table numbers and stations								
Pre-meal meetings								
Bulletin board information								
Performance reviews and evaluations								
Rules of conduct								
Locker issue and use								
Personal phone call rules								
Transfers and promotions								
Exit interview policy								
Paycheck procedures								
Service Concept (Knowledge)								
Upper level service standards								
Personal appearance specifications								
Restaurant safety								
Menu knowledge								
Wine knowledge								
Beverage knowledge								
Service scenario								
Reservations (Knowledge/Skills)								
Telephone etiquette								
Telephone reservations procedures								
Confirming reservations								
Walk-in reservations procedures								
Reservations control procedures								
Delivery of reservations scenario (Host/Hostess)								
Opening Procedures (Knowledge/Skills)								
Assisting Manager with opening								

Exhibit 17.1 *(continued)*

Performance Area	Date	Before Training	After Training	25-Day Eval.	90-Day Eval.	180-Day Eval.	270-Day Eval.	360-Day Eval.	Comments Indicate Date by Each Comment
Setting up Host/Hostess station		/	/	/	/	/	/	/	
Controlling restaurant environment									
Checking menus									
Seating Procedures (Knowledge/Skills)									
Anticipating guest arrivals									
Assisting guests with coats									
Controlling station flow									
Greeting and guest courtesy									
Handling guests without reservations									
Seating guests									
Introducing server									
Delivery of service scenario									
Supervision (Knowledge/Skills)									
Service bar employees									
Restaurant employees									
Handling guest complaints									
Logging guest complaints									
Service Procedures (Knowledge/Skills)									
Assisting with water service									
Assisting with wine service									
Assisting with coffee service									
Changing ashtrays									
Guest Departure Procedures (Skills)									
Assisting guests with chairs									
Assisting guests with coats									
Bidding farewell to guests									
Closing Procedures (Skills)									
Securing Host/Hostess station									
Collecting menus									
Assisting Manager with closing									
Personal Attributes									
Attitude toward work									
Appearance and uniform									
Cooperation with fellow workers									
Acceptance of directions									
Attendance									
Desire to learn in job									

RATED BY (INITIALS)

Describe specific training needs (areas with scores of 2 or below):

Exhibit 17.2 Sample Performance Review: Food Server

FOOD SERVER PERFORMANCE REVIEW

FOOD SERVER NAME _____

DIRECTIONS: Rate the performance level of the employee.

4 — Excellent — Usually meets established standards
3 — Good — Acceptable but could improve
2 — Fair — Definite need for improvement
1 — Unacceptable — Definite need for counseling

Performance Area	Date	Before Training	After Training	25-Day Eval.	90-Day Eval.	180-Day Eval.	270-Day Eval.	360-Day Eval.	Comments (Indicate Date by Each Comment)
Policies and Procedures (Knowledge)									
Use of exits and entrances									
Uniform exchange/cleaning procedures									
Sign-in and sign-out sheets									
Cafeteria hours									
Restaurant hours of operation									
Employee schedules									
Fire procedures									
Accident reports									
Absenteeism, sick calls, tardiness									
Table numbers and stations									
Pre-meal meetings									
Bulletin board information									
Performance reviews and evaluations									
Rules of conduct									
Locker issue and use									
Personal phone call rules									
Transfers and promotions									
Exit interview policy									
Paycheck procedures									
Service Concept (Knowledge)									
Upper Level service standards									
Personal appearance specifications									
Restaurant safety									
Menu knowledge									
Wine knowledge									
Beverage knowledge									
Service scenario									
Opening Sidework (Knowledge/Skills)									
Preparing flowers									
Preparing butter									
Preparing sugar bowls									
Preparing salts and peppers									
Preparing gueridons									
Folding napkins									
Preparing silverware (regular/special)									
Setting up service trays									
Stocking chilled forks/plates									
Checking Benny Wafers									
Stocking ashtrays and matches									
Setting tables									
Checking overall station appearance									
Service Procedures (Knowledge/Skills)									

Exhibit 17.2 *(continued)*

Performance Area	Date	Before Training	After Training	25-Day Eval.	90-Day Eval.	180-Day Eval.	270-Day Eval.	360-Day Eval.	Comments — Indicate Date by Each Comment
		/ /	/ /	/ /	/ /	/ /	/ /	/ /	
Greeting guests									
Taking cocktail order									
Picking up drinks									
Serving cocktails									
Presenting menus									
Taking the food order									
Presenting the seafood tray									
Suggestive selling									
Taking the wine order									
Assisting with wine selection									
Performing pre-check operation									
Ordering food									
Serving wine/champagne									
Picking up food orders									
Serving food orders									
Serving food courses									
Clearing between courses									
Preparing table for each course									
Checking tables for needs									
Changing ashtrays									
Removing soiled dishes to dishroom									
Clearing after entree course									
Crumbing the table									
Taking dessert and coffee order									
Serving dessert and coffee									
Serving hot tea and Sanka									
Selling and serving cordials									
Preparing the guest check									
Presenting the guest check									
Processing payment									
Assisting guests upon departure									
Delivery of the service scenario (Server)									
Resetting tables									
Closing Sidework (Knowledge/Skills)									
Storing flowers									
Cleaning gueridons									
Taking linens to laundry									
Storing condiments									
Breaking down breads and butters									
Breaking down coffee station									
Breaking down wine buckets									
Breaking down water pitchers									
Straightening and cleaning side stands									
Setting station for next meal (w/o silver)									
Securing all silverware									
Bussing all soiled items to dishwasher									
Vacuuming carpet									
Personal Attributes									
Attitude toward work									
Appearance and uniform									
Cooperation with fellow workers									
Acceptance of directions									
Attendance									
Desire to learn in job									

RATED BY (INITIALS)

Describe specific training needs (areas with scores of 2 or below):

Exhibit 17.3 Sample Performance Review: Busperson

BUSPERSON PERFORMANCE REVIEW

BUSPERSON NAME _____

DIRECTIONS: Rate the performance level of the employee.

4 — Excellent — Usually meets established standards
3 — Good — Acceptable but could improve
2 — Fair — Definite need for improvement
1 — Unacceptable — Definite need for counseling

Performance Area	Date	Before Training	After Training	25-Day Eval.	90-Day Eval.	180-Day Eval.	270-Day Eval.	360-Day Eval.	Comments — Indicate Date by Each Comment
Policies and Procedures (Knowledge)		/	/	/	/	/	/	/	
Use of exits and entrances									
Uniform exchange/cleaning procedures									
Sign-in and sign-out sheets									
Cafeteria hours									
Restaurant hours of operation									
Employee schedules									
Fire procedures									
Accident reports									
Absenteeism, sick calls, tardiness									
Table numbers and stations									
Pre-meal meetings									
Bulletin board information									
Performance reviews and evaluations									
Rules of conduct									
Locker issue and use									
Personal phone call rules									
Transfers and promotions									
Exit interview policy									
Paycheck procedures									
Service Concept (Knowledge)									
Upper Level service standards									
Personal appearance specifications									
Restaurant safety									
Service scenario									
Opening Sidework (Knowledge/Skills)									
Preparing flowers									
Preparing butter									
Preparing sugar bowls									
Preparing salts and peppers									
Preparing gueridons									
Folding napkins									
Preparing silverware (regular/special)									
Setting up service trays									
Stocking chilled forks/plates									
Checking Benny Wafers									
Stocking ashtrays and matches									
Setting tables									

Exhibit 17.3 *(continued)*

Performance Area	Before Training	After Training	25-Day Eval.	90-Day Eval.	180-Day Eval.	270-Day Eval.	360-Day Eval.	Comments — Indicate Date by Each Comment
Date	/ /	/ /	/ /	/ /	/ /	/ /	/ /	
Checking overall station appearance								
Service Procedures (Knowledge/Skills)								
Serving water								
Serving bread/butter								
Checking tables for needs								
Clearing tables								
Bussing to dishroom								
Crumbing the table								
Setting up coffee								
Setting up hot tea and Sanka								
Setting up wine buckets								
Taking linens to laundry								
Delivery of service scenario (Busser)								
Closing Sidework (Knowledge/Skills)								
Storing flowers								
Cleaning gueridons								
Taking linens to laundry								
Storing condiments								
Breaking down breads and butters								
Breaking down coffee station								
Breaking down wine buckets								
Breaking down water pitchers								
Straightening and cleaning side stands								
Setting station for next meal (w/o silver)								
Securing all silverware								
Bussing all soiled items to dishwasher								
Vacuuming carpet								
Personal Attributes								
Attitude toward work								
Appearance and uniform								
Cooperation with fellow workers								
Acceptance of directions								
Attendance								
Desire to learn in job								

RATED BY (INITIALS) _____

Describe specific training needs (areas with scores of 2 or below): _____

Determine Criteria for Judging Performance

The second step in designing the review system is to determine the criteria that will be used to judge performance. This is not a new process; it involves reviewing the performance standards and job breakdowns that were developed as the basis for training each employee. That information indicates what the training included (what duties must be performed, how each step should be executed in the performance of each duty, and what constitutes acceptable quality and quantity performance levels). The performance review forms can be adapted from the job analysis forms that indicate (a) what an employee who is performing at the ideal level should be doing, (b) what the employee should know, and (c) how the employee performs when acceptable attitudes are displayed. By using rating scales, actual performance can be subjectively scored on objective descriptions of behavior. A perfect score would indicate that the employee is performing at the ideal level in those areas of skills, knowledge, and attitudes that are assessed by the performance review forms.

Determine Who Will Conduct Reviews

The next procedure is to determine who will conduct the performance reviews. To be the most effective, the performance review should be conducted by the person to whom the employee feels most directly accountable. Sometimes performance reviews are viewed as a duty of upper management and are only performed by unit managers or department heads. In these cases, the primary purpose of the data is probably to justify compensation and promotion decisions. In other cases, the reviews are performed by each employee's immediate supervisor—even if he/she is an employee who functions as a shift leader and is not regarded as a manager. The person who conducts the review should be the same person who is responsible for the employee's training and coaching. Line supervisors should conduct performance reviews for and with their team of employees if the individuals are expected to excel and if the group is to function efficiently.

Determine Frequency

The next step in the design process is to determine how frequently performance reviews will be conducted. The review process should be part of the routine supervision of employees. Obviously it would be impractical for formal reviews to be conducted daily or weekly. This would not allow time for employees to work on follow-up activities necessary to improve performance. A monthly or quarterly review might be reasonable. As an absolute minimum, formal reviews should be held semi-annually. They should be done more frequently for employees who have performance problems. However, all employees need and desire periodic feedback on their performance—even when they are consistently meeting the desired standards.

Establish Employee Participation Procedures

Procedures should be established for employees to participate in their own performance review. If the employees feel that the process is unfair because performance criteria are too high, because they are not really included in the process, or because the manager rating performance is extremely biased, the effectiveness of the process will be lost.

Establish Appeal Procedures   There should be a clear procedure for an employee to appeal to the next level of management if he/she feels that the review was handled unfairly. If employees are given no opportunity to appeal an unfair review, the credibility of the entire process will be lost.

Plan for Follow-Up   The design of the review system should include procedures for follow-up training, coaching, and counseling sessions. Likewise, subsequent reviews to judge the improvement in performance that results from these efforts should be addressed. Follow-up plans should ensure that the employee is not forgotten from one scheduled review until the next. The coaching process should be ongoing to foster employee growth and development.

Develop an Employee Information Plan   The final step in the design process is to plan how the employees will be fully informed of the system. They need to know that all training and coaching activities, including the performance review process, are part of an overall style of management. Competence and productivity are the business goals of this management effort. Motivation and job satisfaction through meaningful work, fair treatment, and high levels of "know-how" are the goals of the approach. If employees understand this style of management, they will not be surprised by the standards against which their performance is rated. They will know what is expected of them, and they will accept the fact that they must perform at high levels.

Notes

1. Martin M. Broadwell, *The Practice of Supervising*, 2nd ed. (Reading, Mass.: Addison-Wesley, 1984), pp. 152–155.

Sources of Help
for the Trainer

American Culinary Federation (ACF)
P.O. Box 3466
St. Augustine, Florida 32084
(904) 824-4468

American Hotel & Motel Association (AH&MA)
1201 New York Avenue, N.W.
Washington, D.C. 20005
(202) 289-3100

American Society for Training and Development (ASTD)
1630 Duke Street
Box 1443
Alexandria, Virginia 22313
(703) 683-8100

Council of Hotel and Restaurant Trainers (CHART)
For current address contact:
The Educational Foundation of the National Restaurant Association
250 S. Wacker Drive
Chicago, Illinois 60606
(312) 715-1010
1-800-522-7578

**Council on Hotel, Restaurant, and Institutional
Education—International CHRIE, The Hospitality and
Tourism Educators**
1200 17th Street, N.W.
Washington, D.C. 20036
(202) 331-5990

The Educational Foundation of the National Restaurant Association
250 S. Wacker Drive
Chicago, Illinois 60606
(312) 715-1010
1-800-522-7578

The Educational Institute of the American Hotel & Motel Association
1407 South Harrison Road
P.O. Box 1240
East Lansing, Michigan 48826
(517) 353-5500

Foodservice Consultants Society International (FCSI)
12345 30th Avenue, N.E.
Suite A
Seattle, Washington 98125-5405
(206) 362-7780
(206) 367-3274

Hotel Sales Management Association (HSMA)
333 North Gladstone Avenue
Margate, New Jersey 08402
(609) 823-1979

or

1300 L Street, N.W.
Suite 800
Washington, D.C. 20005
(202) 789-0089

International Foodservice Manufacturers Association (IFMA)
321 North Clark Street
Suite 2900
Chicago, Illinois 60610
(312) 644-8989

National Restaurant Association (NRA)
1200 17th Street, N.W.
Suite 800
Washington, D.C. 20036-3097
(202) 331-5900
1-800-424-5156

or

250 S. Wacker Drive
Chicago, Illinois 60606
(312) 715-1010
1-800-522-7578

National Society for Performance in Instruction (NSPI)
1126 16th Street, N.W.
Suite 102
Washington, D.C. 20036
(202) 861-0777

Small Business Administration (SBA)
1441 L Street, N.W.
Washington, D.C. 20416
(202) 653-6365
1-800-368-5855

Index

The
Educational Institute
Board of Trustees

The Educational Institute of the American Hotel & Motel Association is fortunate to have both industry and academic leaders, as well as allied members, on its Board of Trustees. Individually and collectively, the following persons play leading roles in supporting the Institute and determining the direction of its programs.

Caroline A. Cooper, CHA
Department Chair
Hospitality/Tourism
Johnson & Wales University
Providence, Rhode Island

Arnold J. Hewes
Executive Vice President
Minnesota Hotel & Lodging Association
St. Paul, Minnesota

Edouard P.O. Dandrieux, CHA
Director
H.I.M., Hotel Institute Montreux
Montreux, Switzerland

Howard P. "Bud" James, CHA
Hotel Consultant
Steamboat, Colorado

Robert S. DeMone, CHA
President, Chairman & CEO
Canadian Pacific Hotels & Resorts
Toronto, Ontario
Canada

Richard M. Kelleher, CHA
President & CEO
Guest Quarters Suite Hotels
Boston, Massachusetts

Ronald A. Evans, CHA
President & CEO
Best Western International, Inc.
Phoenix, Arizona

Donald J. Landry, CHA
President
Manor Care Hotel Division
Silver Spring, Maryland

Robert C. Hazard, Jr., CHA
Chairman & CEO
Choice Hotels International, Inc.
Silver Spring, Maryland

Bryan D. Langton, CBE
Chairman & CEO
Holiday Inn Worldwide
Atlanta, Georgia

Lawrence B. Magnan, CHA
President & CEO
Select Asset Management
Mercer Island, Washington

Gene Rupnik, CHA
General Manager/Partner
Days Inn
Springfield, Illinois

Jerry R. Manion, CHA
Executive Vice President - Operations
Motel 6
Dallas, Texas

Charlotte St. Martin
Executive Vice President
Operations & Marketing
Loews Hotels
New York, New York

John A. Norlander, CHA
President
Radisson Hotel Corporation
Minneapolis, Minnesota

William J. Sheehan, CHA
Vice Chairman
Omni Hotels
Hampton, New Hampshire

Michael B. Peceri, CHA
Chairman
Marquis Hotels & Resorts
Fort Meyers, Florida

William R. Tiefel
President
Marriott Lodging Group
Washington, D.C.

Philip Pistilli, CHA
Chairman
Raphael Hotel Group
Kansas City, Missouri

Paul E. Wise, CHA
Director
Hotel, Restaurant
    & Institutional Management
University of Delaware
Newark, Delaware

The
Educational Institute Fellows

Respected experts dedicated to the advancement of hospitality education

Scott W. Anderson, CHA
President & CEO
Callaway Gardens Resort, Inc.
Pine Mountain, Georgia

W. Anthony Farris, CHA
President & CEO
Rank Hotels N.A.
Dallas, Texas

Edward W. Rabin
Executive Vice President
Hyatt Hotels Corporation
Chicago, Illinois

Michael J. Beckley, CHA
President
Commonwealth
    Hospitality. Ltd.
Etobicoke, Ontario
Canada

Creighton Holden, CHA
President, Hotel Division
Encore Marketing
    International
Columbia, South Carolina

John L. Sharpe, CHA
Executive Vice President
Four Seasons Hotels
    & Resorts
Toronto, Ontario
Canada

Stephen W. Brener, CHA
President
Brener Associates, Inc.
New York, New York

Michael W. Jalbert
Vice President
National Sales & Marketing
    Non-Commercial Accounts
Pepsi-Cola Company
Somers, New York

Melinda Bush, CHA
Executive Vice President,
    Publisher
Hotel & Travel Index
Hotel & Travel Index/
    ABC Int'l. Ed.
Secaucus, New Jersey

Allen J. Ostroff
Senior Vice President
The Prudential Realty Group
Newark, New Jersey